ARMY HISTORICAL SERIES

THE U.S. ARMY'S TRANSITION TO THE ALL-VOLUNTEER FORCE
1968–1974

by

Robert K. Griffith, Jr.

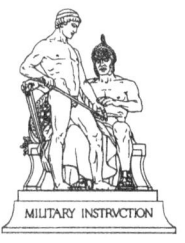

CENTER OF MILITARY HISTORY
UNITED STATES ARMY
WASHINGTON, D.C., 1997

Published by Books Express Publishing
Copyright © Books Express, 2011
ISBN 978-1-780394-34-3

Books Express publications are available from all good retail and online booksellers. For publishing proposals and direct ordering please contact us at: info@books-express.com

Army Historical Series
Jeffrey J. Clarke, General Editor

Advisory Committee
(As of October 1995)

John W. Shy
University of Michigan

Ira D. Gruber
Rice University

Maj. Gen. Joe N. Ballard
U.S. Army Training and
Doctrine Command

D. Clayton James
Virginia Military Institute

Carlo W. D'Este
New Seabury, Mass.

Brig. Gen. Fletcher M. Lamkin, Jr.
U.S. Military Academy

Darlene Fuller-Farrell
Office of the Director of Information
Systems for Command, Control,
Communications, and Computers

Brig. Gen. David H. Ohle
U.S. Army Command and
General Staff College

Joseph T. Glatthaar
University of Houston

Carol A. Reardon
Pennsylvania State University

Rose L. Greaves
University of Kansas

Col. Everett L. Roper, Jr.
U.S. Army War College

Michael J. Kurtz
National Archives and Records Administration

U.S. Army Center of Military History
Brig. Gen. John W. Mountcastle, Chief of Military History

Chief Historian
Chief, Histories Division
Editor in Chief

Jeffrey J. Clarke
Col. Clyde L. Jonas
John W. Elsberg

Foreword

More than twenty years have passed since the United States drafted young men for service in the armed forces. The all-volunteer force, the historic norm in peacetime America from the colonial era to the eve of World War II, was reestablished in the United States at midnight on 30 June 1973, when induction authority expired. But never before had this nation attempted to field a standing Army in peacetime—based on voluntary enlistments—with the worldwide responsibilities that faced this force. For years after the draft expired, manning the all-volunteer force was problematic, but since the mid-1980s the ability of the armed forces to recruit and retain both the quantity and quality of men and women needed to provide for the common defense has not been seriously questioned.

The success of the volunteer force in peace and war since its inception makes it easy for us to forget the debates that attended its origin in the aftermath of the Vietnam War. Twenty years of success also obscure the difficulties of the services' transition, especially that of the Army, from virtual dependency on the draft to a manpower system based on volunteerism. That the transition was accomplished nearly simultaneously with the withdrawal from Vietnam and the subsequent partial demobilization is all the more remarkable.

Robert Griffith takes us through those turbulent years of transition, examining both the broad context in which the end of the draft occurred and the less well known perspective which the Army's leaders brought to bear on the challenge they faced. The result provides both a glimpse into the dynamics of the reciprocal relationship between the Army and society and a case study in the successful management of fundamental organizational change. I recommend this study to those interested in the complex role of the Army in society as well as the history of the Army as an institution.

Washington, D.C.
September 1996

JOHN W. MOUNTCASTLE
Brigadier General, U.S. Army
Chief of Military History

The Author

Robert K. Griffith, Jr., is chief of strategic planning for the state of Rhode Island. Dr. Griffith, who retired from the Army in 1987 as a lieutenant colonel, served at the Center of Military History from 1982 to 1985, during which time he completed the research and first draft of this volume. Other assignments included nine years teaching history and other subjects at the United States Military Academy, the U.S. Army Command and Staff College, and the Industrial College of the Armed Forces where he was also director of research. As a combat arms officer Colonel Griffith served in armored and armored cavalry units in the United States, Germany, and Vietnam. He is a decorated combat veteran.

Dr. Griffith is also the author of *Men Wanted For the U.S. Army; America's Experience with an All-Volunteer Army Between the World Wars* (Greenwood Press, 1982), and several articles on the history of American military manpower systems. He has a B.S. from the U.S. Military Academy and an M.A. and Ph.D. in history from Brown University.

Preface

In 1968, 455,176 men and women entered the U.S. Army for the first time as enlistees. Over half that number came unwillingly as conscripts, and of the remaining 200,000 "volunteers" half again joined under pressure of the draft. In 1974, 166,798 men and women enlisted for the first time; all were true volunteers. The draft had ended. Ending its dependency on the draft was not a simple matter for the Army, but by and large the transition to the all-volunteer force was both an orderly and a successful process. The history of that transition shows the key role played by the Army staff and Army secretariat in shaping the Army as it underwent deep alterations in the very foundations of its structure. Indeed, failure either to effect a smooth transition or to produce a new Army that could be supported by the nation might have been catastrophic.

During the transition critics of the Army charged that senior Army officers privately opposed ending the draft and threw up obstacles to the transition in an effort to sabotage it. In fact, in 1968 most military men did incline toward retaining the draft. Comfortable with the status quo which assured them a dependable supply of replacements, they knew that ending the draft would be a major undertaking that presented many uncertainties. On the other hand, the Army's leadership also recognized that opposition to the popular will—which by 1968 seemed to be shifting rapidly against both the war in Vietnam and the draft—was futile and counterproductive. Furthermore, many saw in the volunteer force the opportunity to restore a concept of military professionalism which they believed had been lost during the turmoil of the Vietnam era when so many unwilling conscripts had flooded the Army's ranks. Concerned that opposition to the war and involuntary service were responsible for what they saw as rising animosity toward the military, many Army leaders also concluded that their acquiescence to elimination of the draft would help reduce dissent and restore the Army's lost prestige. Thus, while viewing the end of the draft with misgivings, those charged with developing and implementing the Army's program to achieve all-volunteer status approached the task with a determination to succeed.

The Army accomplished its transition from the draft to the all-volunteer force in three phases. Beginning in September 1968 and continuing through most of 1969, the Army conducted a rigorous in-house study of the feasibility of an all-volunteer force and the resources necessary to achieve one. The Army's study coincided with and contributed to studies done by the Department of Defense and the President's Commission on an All-Volunteer Armed Force (Gates Commission). These combined studies culminated in April 1970 when President Richard Nixon formally announced his program to phase out the draft over a two-year period ending in 1973.

The second phase of the transition overlapped the first. For the Army the "experimental phase" began with the creation of a special assistant for the Modern Volunteer Army (SAMVA) in October 1970. Under the direction of the SAMVA the Army's recruiting force underwent a transformation. The recruiting command experimented with new techniques designed to attract volunteers, including a controversial experiment with paid radio-television advertising. The SAMVA also directed the VOLAR experiments designed to gather data on making military service more attractive. This second phase of the transition concluded with the development of the Master Plan for the Modern Volunteer Army and the "Soldier-Oriented Budget" early in 1972.

In June 1972 the chief of staff abolished the SAMVA organization, ushering in the "implementation phase" of the transition to the all-volunteer force. During the final phase the Army adopted those techniques which had proved successful in attracting and retaining volunteers and turned management of the volunteer effort over to appropriate command and staff agencies. Draft calls ended in December 1972. The Army had only a six-month grace period before induction authority officially expired in June 1973. In June 1974 Secretary of the Army Howard ("Bo") Callaway reported to President Nixon that the transition was complete.

This study examines and analyses the transition to the all-volunteer force from the perspective of Headquarters, Department of the Army. In order to assure a proper context, it also examines the Army's interaction with the other major participants in the transition, including the Department of Defense, White House, and Congress. The study focuses primarily on the problems, plans, and programs associated with enlisted personnel. Topical sections on officer manpower procurement, the reserve components, medical personnel, and female soldiers in the transition are included, but not in any comprehensive fashion. Rather, the purpose of the study is to examine the management of change within the Army, a bureaucratic process that may lack the excitement of combat narrative but that in the end is an equally important process to understand and appreciate.

Many people made this book possible. Brig. Gen. James L. Collins, Chief of Military History from 1970 to 1982, first proposed an examination of the Army's role in ending the draft. Col. William A. Stofft (then director of the Combat Studies Institute at Fort Leavenworth) encouraged me to seek an appointment to the Center of Military History (CMH), as a military author, specifically to write the volume. While assigned to CMH, I benefited from the support and guidance of Col. James Dunn, chief of the Histories Division, and Morris MacGregor, chief of the General Histories Branch.

I am especially indebted to the many individuals who consented to oral history interviews, all of whom are identified in the bibliographical note. Several deserve special recognition, however. Lt. Gen. George Forsythe submitted to several interviews, frequent phone calls, and many letters with unfailing grace. Martin Anderson greatly assisted me in understanding the role of the Nixon White House in the process. John Kester gave me a clear picture of the role of the Army secretariat in the crucial early days of the transition, when the Army was rushing to meet a deadline before the course was clearly set and the goals properly established.

Mrs. Gina Dunn Wilson typed the original manuscript. The members of my review panel contributed many very useful comments and not a few corrections to both form and content. John W. Chambers, J. Garry Clifford, and Paul D. Phillips also provided many helpful comments. Although not a member of the review panel, Robert Goldich of the Congressional Research Service took a personal interest in the volume. He read several versions and never failed to offer suggestions and encouragement to see the project through to the end.

After I left CMH several people played key roles in keeping the project alive and made it their personal goal to get it published finally. As Chief of Military History, Brig. Gen. William A. Stofft made sure I kept at the revision process even after I was reassigned. His successor, Brig. Gen. Harold W. Nelson, kept in touch after I retired and started a new career. Morris MacGregor reviewed later drafts and Jeffrey Clarke subjected the final draft to a thorough review before it was edited by Susan Carroll. Diane Donovan, Joycelyn Canery, and Scott Janes took on the task of proofreading the manuscript before printing. R. Cody Phillips researched and obtained the illustrations and Beth MacKenzie designed the photo layout.

Members of my family, especially my wife Johana, deserve special thanks for literally years of patience and tolerance as I researched and wrote and reresearched and rewrote this, my second book on an all-volunteer Army. If personal dedications were permitted for official histories this one would be for Jo. To all of these people and many others not named I am deeply indebted.

The views expressed in this book are those of the author and do not reflect the official policy or position of the Departments of Army and Defense or the U.S. government. The author alone is responsible for all interpretations and conclusions in the work that follows, including any errors that may appear.

ROBERT K. GRIFFITH, JR.

Contents

Chapter		Page
I.	TO RAISE AND SUPPORT ARMIES: MILITARY MANPOWER IN THE UNITED STATES	3
	The Historical Perspective	4
	The Overseas Armies	6
	The Vietnam Era	10
II.	ABOUT FACE: THE ARMY AND THE DRAFT, 1968–1969	17
	The Butler Study	17
	The New Administration	19
	PROVIDE	21
	Hard Choices	24
III.	BY EXECUTIVE DIRECTION: THE DECISION TO END THE DRAFT, 1969–1970	29
	The Gates Commission and Project Volunteer	29
	Army Response	30
	Interim Evaluation	33
	Means and Ends	34
	Rebuttal	37
	More Counterproposals	38
	Results	42
IV.	SLICING THE PIE: THE BATTLE OF THE BUDGET, 1970	47
	The New Budget	47
	The Army Staff	50
	SAMVA	53
	The Army Budget	54
V.	THE MANPOWER LABORATORY: SAMVA AND THE MODERN VOLUNTEER ARMY PROGRAM	63
	SAMVA Planning	63
	The Modern Volunteer Army Program	67
	High-Impact Actions	69
	SAMVA and the Media	74

Chapter		Page
VI.	**VOLAR: THE VOLUNTEER ARMY FIELD EXPERIMENT, 1971**	81
	Initial Proposals	81
	VOLAR Funding	87
	Evaluation	91
VII.	**THE PERMISSIVE ARMY: EVALUATING VOLAR, 1971**	101
	Media Reaction	101
	Evaluating VOLAR	104
	Form and Substance	109
VIII.	**THE BOTTOM LINE: RECRUITING, 1969–1971**	115
	The Organization Base	115
	Army Planning	116
	Consensus and Dissent	120
	USAREC Acts	124
IX.	**TODAY'S ARMY WANTS TO JOIN YOU: MILITARY SALESMANSHIP, 1971**	135
	The Advertising Issue	140
	Interim Evaluations	146
X.	**A PILGRIM'S PROGRESS: THE TRANSITION BEGINS, 1971**	149
	Continuity and Change	149
	The Revised Master Plan	150
	The Soldier-Oriented Budget	151
	Progress and Problems	155
	Extension of the Draft	160
XI.	**THE WASHINGTON BATTLEFIELD: PUSHING THE AVF IN 1972**	165
	Reduction in Force (RIF)	165
	Kitchen Police	167
	Bonuses	170
	Changing the Guard	171
	New Battle Plans	172
	Evaluations	174
	Ending the Experiment	177

Chapter		Page
XII.	LAST YEAR OF THE DRAFT, 1972	181
	Optimistic Beginnings	181
	The Search for Quality	185
	The Women's Army Corps (WAC)	188
XIII.	KEEPING PROMISES: RECRUITING AND RETENTION, 1972	197
	The 1974 Budget	197
	Recruiting	199
	Charges of Sabotage	205
XIV.	MAKING IT WORK: THE NEW ARMY, 1973	225
	The Issue of Standards	226
	Selling the All-Volunteer Army	228
	The Issue of Race	235
XV.	SUCCESS AT LAST	239
	Cooperation and Dissent	239
	Turning the Corner	245
	Results	249
XVI.	UNFINISHED BUSINESS: THE MEDICAL PROFESSIONALS	255
	Medical Personnel	255
	Health Care	258
XVII.	UNFINISHED BUSINESS: THE RESERVE COMPONENTS	263
	Policy and Planning	263
	Resources	267
	Reserve Recruiting	271
XVIII.	THE TRANSITION IN PERSPECTIVE	281
	Overview	281
	Quantity vs. Quality	286
	Leadership	289
	The Larger Perspective	291
BIBLIOGRAPHICAL NOTE		295
INDEX		301

Tables

No.		Page
1.	PROVIDE Estimates of Additional Annual Costs of Volunteer Army..	23
2.	Mental Test Scores of Male Enlistments, FY 1972, Compared to Noncollege Population	183
3.	Mental Test Scores of Army Enlistees and Inductees, FY 1972, Compared to Reference Population	185
4.	DOD Outlays in Constant FY 1974 Dollars	204
5.	Army National Guard Non–Prior-Service Accessions	276
6.	Percent Expected Army Attrition During First 36 Months of Service by Quality and Sex	287
7.	Educational Level of Army During Last Years of the Draft	288

Illustrations

The following illustrations appear between pages 94 and 101:

President Richard M. Nixon
Congressman F. Edward Hebert
Lt. Gen. George I. Forsythe, Jr.
Brig. Gen. Robert M. Montague, Jr.
Renovated Enlisted Quarters, Camp Zama, Japan
"Trucker's Lounge," Edwards Kaserne, Frankfurt, Germany
Unit Commander Conducts "Rap Session"
Company Commander and Troops Play Pool
Trainees Enjoy Dining Outdoors

The following illustrations appear between pages 218 and 225:

Senator Sam Nunn
Secretary of Defense Melvin R. Laird Briefs the Media
Senator John C. Stennis Meets With Noncommissioned Officers
Assistant Secretary of Defense Roger T. Kelley Discusses MVA Initiatives With Soldiers
Assistant Secretary of the Army Paul D. Phillips
Drill Sergeant Instructs the Last Army Draftee
Civilian Replacements for Military KPs at Fort Polk
Secretary of the Army Howard H. Callaway at a Dining Facility
Secretary Callaway Talks With WAC Trainees

THE U.S. ARMY'S TRANSITION TO THE ALL-VOLUNTEER FORCE
1968–1974

CHAPTER I

To Raise and Support Armies
Military Manpower in the United States

The ability of the state to exact military service ranks with the power to tax. Just as the state reaches into the purses of its citizens for the money to support it, so it reaches into the homes and communities of its society for the men and women needed to defend it. Both processes find the state in intimate contact with the individual citizen. In a democracy the methods of raising both financial resources and military manpower generally reflect the norms and values of the society at large as well as the duties for which its government is responsible. Changes in a society and in the threats posed to that society can modify both its military institutions and the methods for supporting them. However, only fundamental changes in the values of a society can lead to significant changes in the way it raises its armed forces.

Although American military institutions have been heavily influenced by developments in technology, organization, and tactics outside the borders of the United States, the manner in which the nation has raised the manpower to staff its armed forces has always been heavily dependent on internal political, economic, and social factors. Such factors have historically produced a peculiarly American ethos which has been difficult to examine in any empirical fashion. Historians have often cited a stubborn individualism—whether a product of the early frontier society or an outgrowth of the highly decentralized political tradition—as a peculiar trait of those inhabiting the American continent. Accompanying that has been an aversion to any arbitrary or distant authority, a feeling that is easily triggered by the detailed rules and regulations common to military service. Paradoxically, in the United States those same historical inclinations have also produced a strong sense of volunteerism—the belief in the responsibility of the individual citizen to bear arms in the defense of the nation and, by implication, the need for compulsory military training. In this sense the bearing of arms has been seen as a "right," or obligation, rather than as a chore to be performed under duress.

Other significant U.S. traditions include an inherent distrust of standing armies—institutions that are both costly to maintain and often isolated from society at large—and a reluctance to station or employ large military forces far from the borders and shores of the Republic.

Not surprisingly, early U.S. military manpower systems relied primarily on decentralized and voluntary militia levies supplemented by regular, or standing, forces and those forcibly conscripted only when absolutely necessary. Also not surprising, the methods of raising such manpower, especially during periods of change, have involved an intense and complex interplay between the American public, Congress, and the military services, with the role of the media and local politics often being no less important than the purely military considerations of those in the executive branch charged with the nation's security. During the two hundred years of the existence of the United States, these traditions and relationships have provided the themes critical to understanding how the nation goes about raising its military manpower and the constant adjustments and compromises effected to keep that force in place. Their role in the 1970s was no less important than their role in 1776, in 1860, in 1917, or in 1941.

The Historical Perspective

Although the colonial militia was clearly a transplanted English institution, the concept proved particularly well suited to the conditions of early America where a labor-scarce economy could ill afford a standing army. In general, adequate security in frontier settlements was provided by mobilizing all available local manpower until the threat had passed. Military drafts were rare, and local laws usually allowed those impressed to hire substitutes, or simply buy out of service, a provision that continued until the end of the Civil War.[1]

The American Revolution highlighted both the strengths and weaknesses of the militia system. Militia service cemented the bonds between Americans and their fledgling army while supplying a constant source of armed and semi-trained manpower without disrupting the society or economy. Nevertheless, the exigencies of the war quickly forced the Revolution's political leaders to create a more permanent standing army, the Continental Line, based on volunteers enlisting in federal service for first one and then three years. Only such regulars could provide the professionalism and continuity that General George Washington's decision to fight a semi-conventional war of position demanded. Ultimately these measures allowed him to keep an effective, or at least partially effective, army in the field for the duration of the conflict. But there were never enough volunteers to fill the ranks of even those regular units Congress was willing to authorize, while state-organized (and controlled) militia units filled with short-term volunteers were supplemented only by conscripts. And once the war was over, Congress virtually eliminated the Regular Army and returned to a security system based on regional (state) militia forces.

Between 1784 and 1860, as the need for a standing peacetime army became apparent, Congress reestablished the Regular Army and refined the dual military system of the Republic. During this period the regulars provided a full-time constabulary force while state militia units served as both a reserve and a political counterweight to federal authority. Both depended on volunteers and both could be supplemented in emergencies either by Congress or by the concerned state legislatures through additional volunteers. When necessary, Congress increased the strength of the professional force, authorized the creation of short-term federal volunteer units, and ordered the states to furnish militia. As long as the nation remained on the rim of the civilized world, protected by its oceans and largely ignored by the major powers, this solution seemed sensible. It thus served the nation until the Civil War and lingered on until the Spanish-American conflict.[2]

The Civil War saw major changes in the nation's military manpower procurement system. Initially President Abraham Lincoln increased the size of the Regular Army and called for 85,000 three-year volunteers. Congress quickly ratified Lincoln's actions and the day after the disaster at Bull Run gave the president authority to raise 500,000 additional volunteers.[3] But despite an impressive response in volunteers and militia during 1861 (state militia personnel "volunteered" for federal service) and the later offer of significant enlistment bounties, recruiting lagged. Convinced that pure volunteerism had reached its limit, the Union tried a militia draft to be administered by the states.

The Militia Act of 1862 authorized the president to accept twelve-month volunteers, call as many as 300,000 militia for up to nine months, and, if insufficient numbers volunteered, meet the deficiency with men drafted from the militia. But almost immediately disputes arose over whether one-year volunteers counted against the militia or draft quotas. Governors asked for and received delays of the militia draft requirement. Violence against state officials charged with enrolling militia for the draft occurred in Maryland, Indiana, and Pennsylvania; full-scale riots erupted in Wisconsin. Ultimately the states furnished over 400,000 volunteers and 87,000 militia, and resort to a militia draft proved unnecessary. Nevertheless, for the first time the federal government had ordered the states to draft men for military service, and no state government not already in rebellion had challenged its authority to do so.

As the war continued, the need for military manpower rose steadily. One result was the act of 3 March 1863, "for enrolling and calling out the National Forces, and for other purposes." Known as the Enrollment Act, it broke with all precedents and authorized the first truly national draft in the United States. The act made no reference to the states or their militias. It declared all able-bodied male citizens and alien declarants liable for military service, divided the states into enrollment districts, and established federal machinery for enrolling, examining, and selecting conscripts. It was not, however, a levy en masse. Numerous exemptions kept many off the rosters altogether, and men actually drafted could hire substitutes or pay a commutation fee. Congress included the latter provision at the urging of northern manufacturers who feared conscription would strip their factories of skilled laborers. But commutation was unpopular, especially among unskilled laborers, immigrants, and agricultural workers who could afford neither the fee nor a substitute. In 1864 Congress repealed commutation, and the price of substitutes soared as high as $1,500. In an attempt to offset the rising cost of substitutes Congress authorized the enlistment of blacks, and black volunteers, charged against quotas, held down the number of whites conscripted for the remainder of the war.

The Enrollment Act stirred resentment and opposition in the North. The New York City draft riot of July 1863 was but the most dramatic example. The bounty and substitute practices bred corruption. Agents who brokered enlistments and substitutes and bounty jumpers appeared in every community to profit from the insatiable need for replacements. Legally, the Enrollment Act directly compelled relatively few men to serve. Only about 6 percent of the Union Army were true conscripts. Of the total 249,000 drafted, approximately 57,000 avoided service by paying the commutation fee, another 116,000 hired substitutes, and only 46,000 actually served. Nevertheless, how many of the nearly three million men raised by all systems—short-term volunteers, three-year volunteers, militia calls—responded out of fear of being drafted cannot be known.[4]

The Overseas Armies

Between the Civil War and United States entry into World War I, some Americans reached the conclusion that conscription would be necessary at the onset of any future major war. Nevertheless, acceptance of the principle of compulsion over volunteerism was never universal and grew gradually. Although Regular Army officers favored a larger standing army augmented by wartime conscription, the country as a whole remained wedded to the myth of the militia and the volunteer principle. In the 1870s the states had begun to organize their voluntary militia units into more cohesive "national guard" forces, and by the end of the following decade these units were receiving federal appropriations for arms and equipment.[5] In 1903, following the poor showing of volunteerism in the Spanish-American War, Congress established the National Guard as the formal reserve component of the Army, directing additionally that its organization, equipment, and training conform to regular standards. Meanwhile, another group of reformers, later referred to as the Preparedness Movement, championed compulsory universal military training as both a hedge against the mass armies of Europe and an aid to the promotion of civic virtues within the United States. Despite significant similarity among these schools of thought, a consensus seemed impossible.

The outbreak of World War I elevated the debate over military manpower to one of national proportions. President Woodrow Wilson's initial proposals called for a larger Regular Army, backed up by a federally controlled reserve corps and an expanded National Guard. They made no mention of universal training or compulsory conscription and were rapidly passed by Congress. Nevertheless, when recruiting for the regulars lagged and National Guard units mobilized during the border crisis with Mexico proved of limited value, Wilson was forced to seek other alternatives. Maj. Gen. Hugh L. Scott, the Army chief of staff in 1916, favored conscription, and Wilson acceded to the measure, albeit reluctantly, the following year upon the American entry into the war in Europe.

The conscription legislation of World War I, drafted by Maj. Gen. E. H. Crowder, judge advocate general of the Army, sought to avoid the most serious problems of the Civil War. Crowder's work took the military out of the business of enrolling and selecting citizens for service. If service was obligatory, then registration was a civic duty and did not require direct military involvement. Citizens would enroll themselves, and local boards of "friends and neighbors" would manage the selection process. The procedures, he hoped, would remove the odium of the draft from the Army and the federal government. Thus the draft could claim the spirit of local self-government and simultaneously be "a uniform national policy, nationally defined and nationally directed." Second, Crowder left the Regular Army and National Guard open to voluntary enlistment, but prohibited the worst feature of earlier volunteer systems—bounties. He also eliminated substitution and commutation, which most officers considered blatantly unethical.[6]

The result, the Selective Service Act of 18 May 1917, proved a major success. The draft supplied 2,810,296 men to the armed forces, fulfilling 67 percent of its needs. It also convinced most of the nation's leaders, civil and military alike, that such measures represented the most effective and most equitable method of satisfying future mobilization requirements.

Immediately following the war the Army staff developed a legislative initiative to establish a 500,000-man standing army and an organized federal reserve trained in peacetime on a compulsory basis. But Congress quickly objected. It balked at the proposed size of the peacetime force and understood that the country was not ready for compulsory peacetime military service. Despite a vigorous campaign by supporters of universal military training—essentially by the old Preparedness Movement—many of the proposed measures were easily defeated. However, the concept of a federal reserve was approved; the National Guard came under greater federal control regarding organization and training; and the War Department received explicit directions to conduct peacetime manpower planning on the assumption that conscription would accompany a general mobilization in a future war. The interwar U.S. Army thus consisted of a volunteer standing army (the regulars), an organized voluntary citizen reserve (the National Guard), and an organized regular reserve (the Army Reserve), all backed by the unorganized and untrained "militia"—the male population at large—which could be called as needed.

The German invasion of France and the Low Countries in the spring of 1940 created consternation in the United States. A group of eastern businessmen with strong ties to the old Preparedness Movement launched a well-financed campaign to institute peacetime conscription at once. Initially General George C. Marshall, chief of staff of the Army, questioned whether the public would tolerate the measure without a declaration of war. However, following the appointment of Henry L. Stimson as secretary of war, his concerns lessened. Stimson, a prominent member of the group supporting the draft, had accepted the post with the understanding that President Franklin D. Roosevelt favored conscription. Furthermore, Marshall's own planners had concluded in early 1940 that volunteerism alone would not sustain a rapid buildup of the Regular Army and National Guard. Armed with the foregoing information and with the understanding that the president supported peacetime conscription, Marshall dropped his opposition and publicly called for a draft.

The debate over peacetime conscription in 1940 pitted advocates of preparedness against a broad coalition of opponents who argued that a peacetime draft was unnecessary, anti-American, and militaristic. The arguments on both sides reached back to the colonial roots of the Republic. But the panic that swept through the United States following the fall of France quickly overwhelmed objections to a draft. The Selective Service Act of 1940 passed the Senate by a vote of 47 to 25 and the House by 232 to 124 on 14 September. The president signed the act on 16 September and immediately invoked its provisions.[7]

The Selective Service Act of 1940 built on the nation's past experience. A civilian agency, the Selective Service System, would administer the new draft. However, many of its key people, including the director, Lewis Hershey, came from the military. Initially inductees were to serve for one year, and, according to a provision not unlike those of colonial laws prohibiting use of militia beyond county borders, conscripts could not serve outside the Western Hemisphere or U.S. territorial holdings.

Between November 1940 and December 1941 the draft inducted nearly 922,000 men for one year of training and service in the Regular Army or National Guard. In July 1941 Congress, by the narrow margin of one vote, extended the terms of service of those guardsmen and inductees already on active duty, and after the declaration of war in December 1941 the geographical restrictions on draftees were lifted.

Voluntary enlistments did not end with the enactment of peacetime selective service. Indeed, Congress and the public expected the services to recruit actively to hold down involuntary draft calls as much as possible. Even after Pearl Harbor, draft-eligible men could volunteer for service prior to induction. The Navy, Marine Corps, and Army Air Corps profited from these draft-motivated volunteers until Secretary of War Stimson and the War Manpower Commission convinced the president that the practice was wasteful and disruptive. In December 1942 Roosevelt forbade draft-age men from volunteering altogether. Nearly two-thirds of the approximately fifteen million men who served in the armed forces during World War II entered through selective service.[8]

Convinced that postwar American security would depend on a high level of peacetime readiness, American military leaders once again proposed universal military training. General Marshall himself believed that U.S. citizens would continue to oppose a large peacetime Regular Army, but was also convinced that the long mobilization lead time enjoyed by the United States in both world wars would not repeat itself. Roosevelt's successor, Harry Truman, also embraced the concept, as did leading administration figures. Nevertheless, following the end of World War II the proposal once again quickly foundered, probably due more to America's traditional aversion to military service and the ensuing pressure for a complete demobilization than to changes in the nation's military strategy and its perceived role in the postwar world.[9] Still, the need to occupy both Germany and Japan and a postwar security strategy based on atomic deterrence not only demanded a large peacetime standing army and a large air force but also reduced the requirement for large numbers of partially trained citizens on permanent standby alert. In the area of manpower procurement the net result was the revival of peacetime selective service in 1948. Intended to expire in 1950, the draft would continue until 1972, becoming a permanent fixture in postwar American society.

The congressional debate surrounding the reimposition of the draft in 1948 centered around many of the same issues that would attend its demise several decades later. Most congressmen viewed the situation facing the nation as similar to that of 1940. Indeed, members who voted against the Selective Service Act of 1940 supported renewal in 1948. Critics of the draft argued in vain that not enough had been done to stimulate volunteerism. Why, they asked, could not the Army lower intelligence standards to wartime levels, increase pay, or offer enlistment bonuses? Senator Chan Gurney (Republican, South Dakota), who managed the bill, replied that the higher intelligence standard "represents the level of aptitude for instruction which experience shows is required for satisfactory training in the vast majority of jobs in the modern military service in peacetime." He reminded his colleagues that American servicemen already received higher rates of pay than any other nation. "Monetary inducements would have to be raised so high as to be out of all proportion to reason" to stimulate higher rates of voluntary enlistment, he maintained, and concluded that, "It is therefore necessary to invoke the obligations of citizenship, through Selective Service." [10]

Between the Korean War and the buildup for Vietnam the draft attracted little attention. The Dwight D. Eisenhower administration recognized that tensions with the Soviet Union would continue and concluded that partial mobilization for the long haul best served the nation's needs. But Eisenhower also believed that a healthy economy contributed as much to security as did a strong defense. His "New Look" in national security policy thus attempted to reduce defense expenditures and stimulate the general economy. Continuation of the draft in peacetime helped facilitate this goal. Using draftees to close the gap between the Army's manpower requirements and the supply of volunteers enabled the service to keep personnel costs low. At the same time, the administration's decision to rely on strategic nuclear forces as the centerpiece of its deterrent strategy enabled it to reduce its overall military manpower. Active duty strength declined from 3.5 to 2.5 million between 1953 and 1961, while the Army's size dropped from 1.5 million to 860,000, with the requirements for draftees falling accordingly. Some 58 percent of the men entering the Army in 1954 were inductees; by 1961 the figure had dropped to 22 percent.[11]

Meanwhile the pool of men eligible for induction grew. In order to balance the growing supply with declining demand and, at the same time, further the administration's economic and social goals, the Selective Service System increased the number of deferments. Hershey, director of Selective Service since 1940, believed the draft to be a necessary and equitable system for providing manpower to the armed forces, but he also saw a larger role for selective service. Through a liberal but judicious application of deferments, he believed, men could be "channeled" into other pursuits that also strengthened the nation. For example, men deferred for paternity or dependency reasons contributed to the American family; youths who might not have continued their education did so to obtain deferments and ultimately entered more productive career fields. In all cases, Hershey reasoned, national security prospered, and the draft was its agent. Like the graduated income tax and its attendant provisions, the draft thus served as a primary tool for social engineering at the national level. With the draft disrupting relatively few lives, opposition to its existence dwindled. When in 1956 and 1964 presidential candidates Adlai Stevenson and Barry Goldwater respectively suggested that peacetime conscription be ended, they found the issue attracted little attention.[12]

The Vietnam Era

By the mid-1960s the Selective Service System was running out of legitimate ways to defer men from induction. As the "baby boom" generation approached eligibility for military service, it appeared evident that increasing numbers of men qualified and available for induction would never be called because the military could not absorb them. As early as 1963 some members of Congress, private groups, and the manpower office of the Department of Defense began to question the resulting inequity.

In 1964 Secretary of Defense Robert S. McNamara, anticipating future questions on the continued use of selective service, directed his assistant secretary of defense for manpower to examine the issue. The subsequent Defense Manpower Study found that, given the continuation of active force levels at approximately 2.65 million and the rising pool of eligible men, only 11 percent of the services' annual intake of men need be draftees. That figure could be reduced to zero by a combination of lower standards, civilianization of many positions filled by uniformed personnel, and increased incentives such as pay. However, the study group concluded that the direct cost of civilianization and increased military pay and benefits combined with the loss of inductees with above-average intelligence and draft-motivated volunteers mitigated against ending the draft. Proponents of the draft within the Department of Defense also worried that loss of induction authority would restrict the ability of the active forces to expand rapidly in an emergency.[13]

The defense manpower study group concluded its work in mid-1965, almost simultaneous with the beginning of American military intervention in Vietnam. When President Lyndon B. Johnson decided to commit American fighting men to Vietnam, he chose not to build up the active force by calling on the reserve components. Instead, selective service inductions fueled the buildup. Draft calls more than tripled by mid-1966. Of the nearly 340,000 men inducted in the first twelve months of increased U.S. involvement in the Vietnam War, 317,500 went into the Army, 19,600 to the Marine Corps, and 2,600 to the Navy. Ironically, the peacetime draft, which a year earlier seemed an unnecessary holdover from an earlier time, was saved by the war which ultimately assured its doom.[14]

Rising inductions soon ended public apathy toward the draft. The system of deferments which had evolved to find ways not to draft people, combined with the autonomy of local selection boards, assured that as induction calls rose inequities multiplied. Subsequent studies revealed that local boards often were unrepresentative of their districts and had little contact with registrants; discrepancies in granting or changing classifications or deferments occurred between boards in and across state boundaries. At first General Hershey, who continued to preside over the system, resisted recommendations to issue instructions to the boards. When he finally did suggest that local boards reclassify student draft resisters and expedite processing of delinquent registrants and report them to the Justice Department, he created a cause celebre. Hershey's truculent defense of the status quo became part of the entire war issue as both opponents and supporters of the country's involvement in Vietnam became increasingly critical of the draft.[15]

Mounting opposition to selective service involved more than criticism of the system of deferments and the inequities it spawned. As direct American involvement in Vietnam deepened after 1965, opponents of the war and draft quickly noted that the casualty rate among draftees rose more rapidly than among volunteers. Volunteers frequently could choose their assignments, and many opted for technical specialities that involved long-term training and career commitments. Draftees were more likely to be shunted to combat assignments. Some 28 percent of Army battle deaths in Vietnam in 1965 were draftees; the figure rose to 34 percent in 1966 and 57 percent in 1967. Opponents of the draft also noted that, because of the exemption and deferment policies established for peacetime selective service, conscripts tended to come from blue-collar or lower white-collar families and that young men who did not complete high school or had no plans for college were more likely to be inducted than college-bound high school graduates. In addition, minority youths (who more likely came from blue-collar families and were not college bound) faced a higher risk of induction than white males of draft age. Armed with these data, critics of conscription escalated their opposition on the grounds that the draft discriminated against the poor and minorities and sent them to their deaths.[16]

The antidraft movement of the 1960s drew inspiration from other sources as well. A new generation of Americans, sensitized by the civil rights movement and the war on poverty and exhibiting heightened concern for the rights of individuals, questioned the fundamental premise of conscription. The state, they reasoned, did not have absolute authority to compel an individual to perform military service; certainly it should not exercise that power in an undeclared war that did not constitute a clear and present danger or require mobilization of all military eligibles. Critics of the draft sought reforms to make it more equitable;

critics of the war looked for alternatives. With induction authority under the Selective Service Act due to expire in June 1967, all parties regarded the quadrennial extension hearings as the logical forum to effect change.

President Johnson supported moderate draft reforms in 1967. Based on the report of the National Advisory Commission on Selective Service (yet another study on the draft, prepared for Johnson under the direction of Burke Marshall, a former assistant attorney general for civil rights), Johnson urged Congress to extend induction authority but end most deferments, consider a national lottery, and call the youngest eligibles first. Some Republican congressmen proposed phasing out the draft altogether. Senator Mark Hatfield of Oregon called for higher military pay and a transition to a volunteer system. In the House of Representatives, Donald Rumsfeld proposed a two-year extension of induction authority pursuant to a detailed feasibility study of the volunteer concept. But both the House and Senate rejected the opportunity to reform or consider alternatives to the draft. The Senate Armed Services Committee reported a bill that provided for a lottery draft on a trial basis but that retained most deferments; the House Armed Services Committee opposed even a trial lottery and refused even to consider authorizing funds for the study of an all-volunteer system. Final action preserved the status quo. Supporters of draft reform and advocates of broader change accused defenders of the draft of using the committee system and rules governing debate in Congress to impede the legislative process.

The failure of the reform effort led many moderates on the issue to look at more extreme alternatives. Several members of the Wednesday Group, an association of moderate and liberal House Republicans so named because it met on Wednesdays, quietly commissioned a separate study of the all-volunteer alternative. Wednesday Group staff members researched and wrote the report "How To End the Draft: The Case for an All-Volunteer Army." Five congressmen, including three members of the House Armed Services Committee (HASC), published the report in late 1967. They concluded that an All-Volunteer Army was possible and could be achieved in two to five years. Efforts like this, along with the growing unpopularity of the continuing war with its demand for more and more men, assured that the draft would be an issue in the coming presidential election.[17]

By the summer of 1968, a presidential election year, both major parties endorsed draft reform, and candidates for political office at all levels articulated positions that clearly presaged an end to the status quo. At the national level Vice President Hubert Humphrey, the Democratic candidate for president, supported a lottery draft with provisions which gave draftees credit for "domestic alternative service" such as hospital work. The Republican Party's "Youth Plank" platform pledged to study the possibility of ending the draft after Vietnam or at least reducing the number of years a man would be liable for induction. Richard Nixon, the Republican presidential candidate, went even further. He favored ending the draft altogether after Vietnam. Nixon publicly supported a smaller "professional military corps," an all-volunteer force.[18]

Shortly after he took office in January 1969, President Nixon commissioned his own study of alternatives to the draft, the fifth such effort since 1964. Thomas S. Gates, Eisenhower's third secretary of defense, chaired the President's Commission on an All-Volunteer Armed Force. Nixon directed the Gates Commission "to develop a comprehensive plan for eliminating conscription and moving toward an all volunteer armed force." At the same time the new president took steps to reform the draft along lines recommended by the Marshall Commission by asking Congress for authority to place the draft on a random lottery basis and induct according to a "youngest first" policy. Meanwhile the Department of Defense began exploring ways to reduce current reliance on draftees.

The Gates Commission reported favorably on the feasibility of an all-volunteer force in February 1970.[19] However, its work was only the most visible evidence of the deliberations that had been taking place within the various echelons of both the Johnson and Nixon administrations since 1968 regarding manpower procurement policies, deliberations that would continue for the indefinite future.[20] Eventually the discussion would come to encompass everything from the war in Southeast Asia to demographic trends in the United States and from the style of an individual solider's haircut to the prose of the Army's advertising jingles that would soon be broadcast throughout the American heartland. In the process the arena for the debate would expand from the halls of Congress and the boardrooms of the Pentagon to the Army's troop barracks, training areas, and recruiting stations, all bedrock institutions which would be forever changed. How this change occurred—how the Army accomplished the transition from a draft-dependent organization to an all-volunteer force—is the subject of the remainder of this book, with special attention paid to the vital role of the Army staff in this process.

Notes

[1] For a detailed treatment of early American manpower systems see Douglas D. Leach, *Arms for Empire: A Military History of the British Colonies in North America, 1607–1763* (New York: Macmillan, 1973); John K. Mahon, *History of the Militia and the National Guard* (New York: Macmillan, 1983); and Marcus Cunliffe, *Soldiers & Civilians: The Martial Spirit in America, 1775–1865* (Boston: Little, Brown, 1968).

[2] The best analysis of the formulation of the military policy of the new United States remains Richard Kohn, *Eagle and Sword: The Beginnings of the Military Establishment in America* (New York: The Free Press, 1975).

[3] For an excellent summary of the Civil War mobilization see Marvin A. Kreidberg and Merton G. Henry, *History of Military Mobilization in the United States Army, 1775–1945* (Washington, D.C.: Government Printing Office, 1955), pp. 83–101; and also Eugene C. T. Murdock, *One Million Men: The Civil War Draft in the North* (Kent, Ohio: Kent State University Press, 1967).

[4] Figures are from Kreidberg and Henry, *History of Military Mobilization*, p. 108.

[5] The best analysis of the National Guard as a political pressure group remains Martha Derthic, *The National Guard in Politics* (Cambridge: Harvard University Press, 1965).

[6] E. H. Crowder, *The Spirit of Selective Service* (New York: The Century Company, 1920), pp. 90, 92, 115–21; Kreidberg and Henry, *History of Military Mobilization*, pp. 243–46.

[7] See Robert K. Griffith, Jr., *Men Wanted for the U.S. Army* (Westport, Conn.: Greenwood Press, 1982), pp. 191–92.

[8] *Selective Service in Peacetime: First Report of the Director of Selective Service, 1940–41* (Washington, D.C.: Government Printing Office, 1942), pp. 235–36; *Selective Service in Wartime: Second Report of the Director of Selective Service, 1941–42* (Washington, D.C.: Government Printing Office, 1943), pp. 66–69, 122, 672–74.

[9] The best analysis of the postwar debate on universal military training is found in James M. Gerhardt, *The Draft and Public Policy: Issues in Military Manpower Procurement, 1945–1970* (Columbus: Ohio State University Press, 1971), especially pp. 3–38.

[10] U.S. Congress, Senate, *Congressional Record*, 80th Cong., 2d sess., June 3, 1948, pp. 6998–7002; Gerhardt, *The Draft and Public Policy*, pp. 104–14.

[11] Gerhardt, *The Draft and Public Policy*, pp. 192–218.

[12] Ibid., pp. 212–13, 235, 238–42, 286. For an excellent biography and analysis of Hershey see George Q. Flynn, *Lewis B. Hershey, Mr. Selective Service* (Chapel Hill: University of North Carolina Press, 1985).

[13] The report of the Defense Manpower Study was not published. Portions were released in 1966 during congressional testimony. Summarized from Gerhardt, *The Draft and Public Policy*, pp. 286–92.

[14] Figures are from Department of Defense, *Annual Report for Fiscal Year 1966* (Washington, D.C.: Government Printing Office), pp. 59–60. For an analysis of Johnson's decision not to use the reserve components in 1965, see John D. Stuckey and Joseph H. Pistorius, "Mobilization for the Vietnam War: A Political and Military Catastrophe," *Parameters* 15, no. 1 (Spring 1985): 26–38.

[15] For examples of the antidraft literature of the period see Jean Carper, *Bitter Greetings: The Scandal of the Military Draft* (New York: Grossman, 1967); George

Wilson, *Let's End the Draft Mess* (New York: David McKay, 1967); and James W. Davis and Kenneth M. Dolbear, *Little Groups of Neighbors: The Selective Service System* (Chicago: Markham, 1968). Hershey's letter to local boards is reprinted in Martin Anderson, ed., *The Military Draft* (Stanford, Calif.: Hoover Institution Press, 1982), pp. 523–25.

[16] Michael Useen, *Conscription, Protest, and Social Conflict: The Life and Death of a Draft Resistance Movement* (New York: John Wiley & Sons, 1973), pp. 82–83, 106–08.

[17] Robert T. Stafford et al., *How To End the Draft: The Case for an All-Volunteer Army* (Washington, D.C.: The National Press, 1967). The other authors were Frank Horton, Richard Schweiker, Garner Shriver, and Charles Whalen. Stafford, Schweiker, and Whalen were members of the HASC. Wednesday Group staff members Douglas Bailey and Stephen Herbits prepared the report. Herbits later served as a member of the Gates Commission.

[18] *New York Times*, 11 May and 5 Aug 1968, and 18 Nov 1967.

[19] *Report of the President's Commission on an All-Volunteer Armed Force* (Washington, D.C.: Government Printing Office, 1970).

[20] For example, Dr. Martin Anderson, a policy adviser on the White House staff, chaired a special committee to review agency reactions to the Gates Commission recommendations and provide alternative proposals to Nixon. A summary of the deliberations of the Anderson committee is found in Memo, Martin Anderson for multiple addressees, 17 Mar 70, sub: Draft Memorandum on All-Volunteer Armed Force, files of the Office of the Secretary of Defense (hereafter cited as OSD), Record Group 330, Washington National Records Center (WNRC); Interv, author with Martin Anderson, 22 Sep 83.

CHAPTER II

About Face
The Army and the Draft, 1968–1969

Conventional wisdom holds that the Army opposed ending conscription in the 1970s and had to be dragged reluctantly into the all-volunteer force era. This myth was popularized by ideological opponents of the draft and others who urged a more rapid end to inductions than Army leaders were prepared to accept.[1] But to equate caution with opposition is a great disservice. In fact, well before the Gates Commission rendered its report, the Army's leadership had concluded that an end to conscription was in the service's best interest. Psychologically at least the Army's leaders were thus prepared for the transition many months before it was officially ordered.

The Butler Study

Fully a month before candidate Richard Nixon gave his policy statement on ending the draft in October 1968, the Army began to study the issue on its own. General William C. Westmoreland, who had returned from Vietnam in June 1968 to become chief of staff of the Army, ordered the study personally in September of that year. Officially the Army already espoused a policy of relying on volunteers to meet its manpower needs and of using selective service only to make up shortages. But the highly charged political campaign of 1968 and the ongoing talk of draft reform or even an end to conscription convinced Westmoreland of the necessity for a review of the Army's personnel requirements as well as its position on the draft and the available alternatives. He thus directed the Army staff to study the effects that ending the draft and shifting to an all-volunteer force would have on the Army and to reexamine the Army's position on the subject "if such is warranted."[2]

The Personnel Studies and Research Directorate of the Office of the Deputy Chief of Staff for Personnel conducted the study on a "close-hold" basis. Lt. Col. Jack R. Butler, an action officer in the directorate with a degree in research psychology, received the task. Butler's initial report, entitled "Career Force Study," was completed in thirty days and briefed to Westmoreland in December. The prospects for the Army in an all-volunteer environment were gloomy, the report concluded, but not hopeless.[3]

Butler's group had examined four broad issues related to military manpower procurement and retention on a voluntary basis: quantity, quality, cost, and social implications. With respect to quantity, the Career Force Study verified that the Army's dependency on the draft had grown during the Vietnam War. Prior to 1965, 43 percent of all enlistees were draft motivated; by 1968 the figure had risen to 52 percent. Assuming an enlisted force of 850,000 men following the end of the Army's involvement in Vietnam, the study group concluded that without draft motivation or inductions the Army's strength "would steadily decline and stabilize in seven years at about 500,000 men." Furthermore, the strength of the reserves (including the National Guard) could be expected to decline from 633,000 to 60,000 men in seven years in a draft-free environment.[4]

Quality also would drop in an all-volunteer Army, Butler reported. The Army wanted soldiers who were high school graduates, with average or above average mental ability as measured by established standards. Nearly 70 percent of the enlisted Military Occupational Specialties (MOS) were classified "High Skill" in 1968. Based on a 1967 survey the group concluded, "without the draft and draft-induced enlistments, Mental Categories I and II [those with above average or average abilities] enlistments can be expected to drop by nearly 50 percent."

Drawing largely from the work of the 1966 Report of the Defense Manpower Study, Butler's study group calculated that higher pay and improved in-service education benefits for both the active Army and reserve components could offset most of the quantitative decline. The group recommended that the Army investigate substituting more civilians for uniformed personnel and increasing the strength of the Women's Army Corps. Substantially increased expenditures would be necessary in the areas of recruiting, public information, and advertising. The group estimated that the Army needed approximately $3 billion in additional annual expenditures for military personnel—the Army's total budget for the current fiscal year was approximately $23.6 billion—to raise and maintain a 950,000-man active Army backed up by a 700,000 man Ready Reserve on an all-volunteer basis. Butler had no particular basis for picking a force of 950,000 active and 700,000 reserve personnel except that it represented the approximate strength of the Army before Vietnam. But these cost figures included additional money for training on the assumption that a reduction in the quality of future volunteers would dictate longer periods of instruction.

Even if an all-volunteer Army could be achieved at an acceptable cost, the Career Force Study group questioned the social implications of abandoning the draft. "The draft serves as a vehicle for identifying the military with the society it seeks to defend," the group declared in its report to Westmoreland. Without it, "the citizens might tend to no longer feel responsible for the defense of this country."[5] In expressing its reservations about the social efficacy of an all-volunteer Army, the Career Force Study group echoed the sentiments of most of the Army's civilian and military leadership. Generally the Army's leaders opposed the notion of a volunteer force. In addition to the obvious practical problems associated with ending reliance on selective service after nearly thirty years, the Army's senior officers and their civilian counterparts shared strong convictions that citizenship carried an obligation to perform military service. Most believed that continuation of the draft was essential to preserving the tie between the American citizenry and its army.[6]

Despite reservations about the social drawbacks of an all-volunteer force, Butler recommended that Westmoreland "take a positive approach and support a post [Vietnam] reduction in draft calls contingent upon the Army's ability to attract by voluntary means the numbers and quality of personnel needed." Butler considered such an approach "politically and socially acceptable." The Army bore the brunt of antidraft sentiment as the major recipient of conscripts. But it was infeasible for the Army to support outright abolition of selective service since such a position would jeopardize mobilization flexibility. On the other hand, Butler pointed out, to oppose an all-volunteer force outright might further fuel antidraft opposition and "further dichotomize the issue and work against the Army's image." Furthermore, the Army lacked certainty that an all-volunteer system would not work "given the proper mix of incentives and management."[7]

The Career Force Study conducted by Colonel Butler between September and December 1968 was significant in three respects. First, it indicated a willingness on the part of the Army to consider the subject of an all-volunteer force in advance of events. Westmoreland and his colleagues hardly were keen on the idea of losing the draft, but they recognized that circumstances beyond the Army's control might lead to such a contingency and that they needed information on the subject. Second, the Career Force Study, although neither exhaustive in its research nor comprehensive in its conclusions, identified most of the key issues, problems, and potential solutions associated with moving the Army from its dependency on the draft to an all-volunteer basis. Finally, in Butler and his study group the Army had the core of an organization capable of pursuing the issue further if necessary.

The New Administration

The new year brought new leadership to Washington and with it greater urgency on the subject of the draft and its alternatives. Shortly after the Nixon administration took office, Dr. Arthur Burns, counselor to the president, compiled a list summarizing promises made during the campaign and proposing measures to fulfill those pledges. On the subject of the draft Martin Anderson wrote:

One of your strongest pledges during the campaign was the eventual abolition of the draft. It is the major issue that you can use to establish a rapport with the youth of the country.

There is, of course, substantial opposition to such a move, partly on the grounds that it may endanger national security and partly for budgetary reasons.

Thus, it is important that you work toward the objective of abolishing the draft, but that you do so in a manner that protects both the national security and the budget.

Martin Anderson, Nixon's policy adviser on the subject, recommended that the president begin draft reform by reaffirming his pledge to end conscription, increasing military entry pay to "induce a rise in enlistments and allow draft calls to be reduced," and appointing a special commission to develop a comprehensive plan for eliminating conscription. He urged Nixon to involve the Department of Defense in the effort immediately.[8]

On 29 January 1969, Nixon wrote to Secretary of Defense Melvin R. Laird of his intention to establish an all-volunteer armed force. He asked Laird to provide him with suggestions for membership on "a special Commission to develop a detailed plan of action for ending the draft."[9] Nixon's request precipitated a series of actions in the Department of Defense and Army that culminated in the creation of three studies of the draft and the all-volunteer force concept.

Laird considered Vietnam his first priority and had not given much thought to ending the draft. While a congressman from Wisconsin, he had come to favor some form of national service as an alternative to the draft, and during the recent campaign Laird unsuccessfully urged Nixon against making an explicit pledge to end conscription after Vietnam. Laird was uncomfortable with Nixon's request and passed it to Alfred B. Fitt, a holdover assistant secretary of defense for manpower and reserve affairs, for advice on an appropriate response.

Fitt replied by offering Laird a study plan his office had developed in October 1968 following a speech Nixon gave on ending the draft. Fitt and his staff assumed pay reforms designed to attract recruits and increase retention among career service personnel were key to reducing reliance on the draft. He also assumed that induction authority would be retained. Fitt worried that some economists on the Council of Economic Advisers "who were fanatic opponents of the draft" and Milton Friedman would get "the President's ear." If that happened, Fitt told Laird, they might "stack the deck against a thoughtful, careful objective study of the problem." He cautioned Laird against rushing the study and urged him "to be sure that the President gets at least some of his advice on this score from the men charged with operating the Armed Forces and recruiting their personnel."[10]

Laird agreed with Fitt's analysis and forwarded a proposal to Nixon for an in-house study with the caveat that "a comprehensive study of this type will take at least one year to complete." As a proponent of participatory management Laird knew that the details of any successful alternative to the draft required the active contributions of the people who ultimately would implement it. At the same time, Laird urged the president to begin immediately to reform the Selective Service System. He proposed ending the practice of calling the "oldest first" from the draft-liable pool, the establishment of a lottery selection system, and the appointment of a civilian director of the Selective Service System. The first two recommendations aimed at making the draft more equitable. The third was symbolic. In his memo to Laird, Alfred Fitt had advised the secretary of defense that Lewis Hershey, director of the Selective Service System, posed a major obstruction to draft reform efforts in 1966–67. Laird took the hint and suggested to Nixon that Hershey be replaced. But Hershey had powerful friends, so Laird used the indirect approach of suggesting that the selective service director ought to be a civilian. Although the Selective Service System was an independent agency, Lewis Hershey held the rank of lieutenant general in the Army, an inconsistency that detracted from the "little groups of neighbors" image of the selective service. As Laird put it, "The Armed Forces have enough of an image problem as it is without being blamed for the wrongs or apparent wrongs of Selective Service."[11]

Nixon rejected Laird's proposal for an in-house study. The president insisted it was time "to develop a detailed plan of action for ending the draft" and restated his conviction that the blueprint should be developed by an independent commission. The president told Laird to proceed with his own study, which could form the basis for a White House review of the commission's report. Laird relented, provided the White House with his nominations for the commission, and directed the Defense Department to conduct its own study, "Project Volunteer." Laird announced that Roger T. Kelley, Fitt's successor as assistant secretary of defense for manpower, would chair the Project Volunteer Committee, which would consist of the assistant secretary of defense (systems analysis), the assistant secretaries of the military departments (manpower and reserve affairs), the deputy chiefs of staff for personnel of the Army, Air Force, and Marine Corps and their Navy counterparts, and the director, J–1 (personnel), of the Joint Staff, JCS. Planning on Project Volunteer began in February 1969, even before Kelley's confirmation, but Laird delayed announcing commencement of the study until after Nixon appointed the President's Commission on an All-Volunteer Force (the Gates Commission).[12]

PROVIDE

Simultaneously the Army staff had begun its own detailed study of the problem. The chain of events that led to the creation of the Army study, known as Project Volunteer in Defense of the Nation (PROVIDE), began in January when the Army staff received a bootleg copy of Nixon's letter to Laird requesting nominations for the presidential commission. That the Army was able to begin its own study so quickly is no surprise. Colonel Butler's Career Force Study, done only two months earlier, laid the groundwork. On receipt of news that the new president intended to appoint a commission to study means to end the draft, Westmoreland immediately reviewed the Army's position on the volunteer force issue. He directed the Army staff to support any studies done on the subject, but added that "DCSPER [the Army staff's deputy chief of staff for personnel] should take the lead and study this in-depth on a close-hold basis." He did not want to publicize the fact that the Army was conducting a study of its own.[13]

Westmoreland's desire for secrecy was consistent with his cautious nature and was not unusual. The Army remained utterly dependent on the draft in early 1969. To announce that the Army staff was embarking on a study of how to end the draft would surely fuel press speculation, a problem Westmoreland wished to avoid. He harbored bitter memories of post hoc criticism by the news media of his handling of the Tet offensive in 1968, which occurred shortly after his assessment that the United States had gained the upper hand in Vietnam, and was not inclined to premature disclosures again. Furthermore, it was by no means clear how far the new administration really was willing to go on its promise to end conscription after Vietnam. The Army's strategy was thus to study the subject and be prepared to act as events developed.

Lt. Gen. A. O. Connor, the deputy chief of staff for personnel, gave the PROVIDE assignment to his Personnel Studies and Research Directorate. "Because of the far-reaching implications of this study and the importance attached to this subject," O'Connor placed "the highest priority" on the project and named Butler the study team leader. The PROVIDE study group was "to determine how the Army can meet its manpower requirements under alternative forces levels and conditions short of total war by means of an all-volunteer Army." Westmoreland also designated the PROVIDE group as the major source of input to the Defense Department's Project Volunteer study and, through Roger Kelley's office, to the president's commission.[14]

The PROVIDE study group completed its preliminary work by June 1969 and submitted an interim report. Butler's group concluded that a volunteer Army could be achieved, but for a price, and recommended that the Army support the concept of a peacetime volunteer force. Transition to such an all-volunteer Army could be accomplished in three phases: Phase I included the development and implementation of inexpensive programs to improve service attractiveness and to reduce reliance on the draft that did not require legislative or budgetary actions; Phase II included programs that were more costly and required congressional sanction but were of an immediate nature, such as increasing pay, raising the strength and budget of the Recruiting Command, building new barracks and housing, expanding the Women's Army Corps, and so forth; Phase III comprised budgetary and legislative programs of a long-range nature and actions deferred from Phases I and II that would have to be reconsidered should those phases "fail to provide the quantity and quality of personnel required." Phase III included "as a last resort" using a lottery draft for the reserve forces. Indeed, implicit in the PROVIDE scheme and running throughout all Army considerations of achieving an all-volunteer force was the retention of draft legislation and machinery as insurance to maintain sufficient volunteers.[15]

One of the fundamental revelations of the PROVIDE study was the extent to which the Army's public image had declined. Butler's group cited surveys which indicated that veterans rated the Navy and Air Force ahead of the Army as the service of preferred enlistment and that the general public and educators ranked the Army last. More troublesome was the discovery that 70 percent of Army veterans advised prospective volunteers to join services other than the Army. Given such attitudes, the study group concluded, rebuilding the Army's public image was a prerequisite to achieving an all-volunteer force.

"Among the significant areas needing improvement are pay, educational benefits, career management, job satisfaction, housing and medical benefits."[16]

The study group examined the feasibility of achieving an all-volunteer Army at four force levels (*see Table 1*) and estimated a high- and low-cost range for each level.

TABLE 1—PROVIDE ESTIMATES OF ADDITIONAL
ANNUAL COSTS OF VOLUNTEER ARMY

Force Levels		Cost (Billions)	
		Minimum	Maximum
A.	650,000 Active 250,000 Reserve	$1.1	$1.1
B.	950,000 Active 550,000 Reserve	$2.2	$8.4
C.	1,100,000 Active 675,000 Reserve	$2.4	$10.9
D.	1,500,000 Active 750,000 Reserve	$5.4	——

Source: PROVIDE, Project Volunteer in Defense of the Nation, vol. I, U.S. Department of the Army, 20 June 1969, p. 25.

NOTE: No maximum figure was given for Force Level D. At that level the study's methodology became suspect.

The annual additional cost estimate ranged from a low of $1.1 billion in current dollars for an active force of 650,000 to $10.9 billion for an active Army of 1.1 million. The Army's total budget for the current fiscal year was $23.6 billion. Butler's study group doubted that a force above 1.1 million active duty soldiers could be achieved. The minimum additional cost recommended for the force levels considered represented "a substantial increase in entry pay and adoption of a career sustaining salary concept."[17]

In mid-1969 projections of the actual number of volunteers that would be needed to maintain the strength of the Army following Vietnam remained unclear. At the height of the U.S. involvement in the war the Army had required nearly 1.6 million active duty troops to sustain nineteen and two-thirds divisions. It would not be for another two years, until June 1971, that the Army staff would conclude that thirteen active divisions were necessary to support the post-Vietnam foreign policy and national security objectives of the Nixon administration. Eventually the Army would settle on an active duty requirement of approximately 950,000, close to PROVIDE's mid-range figure, as the strength necessary to achieve the "thirteen division objective." The figure and the objective would become key measures in the debate over whether and how well the Army accomplished the transition.[18]

Butler formally briefed Westmoreland on his group's findings and recommendations in October. By that time, as was routine, all Army staff agencies had reviewed and commented on the report. Thus Westmoreland knew in advance that his principal deputies agreed with its broad findings and recommendations. Butler told the chief of staff that the Army had three options with regard to the all-volunteer force: it could oppose the concept and risk a further public and political struggle over the draft; it could wait for orders to implement an all-volunteer plan, but such a course of action would place the Army "in the position of acting wildly to keep up with events rather than controlling them"; or it could "seize the initiative" and begin actions immediately to reduce reliance on the draft along lines outlined in the PROVIDE report.[19]

Butler told Westmoreland that many of the PROVIDE transition recommendations for Phase I could be implemented immediately at little cost to the Army. He proposed the creation of a high-level task group to direct implementation of the PROVIDE recommendations. He added that Assistant Secretary of the Army for Manpower and Reserve Affairs William K. Brehm had expressed interest in pressing ahead with actions requiring funds but would not yet support legislation needed to increase recruiting and recruiting advertising for the active Army and reserve components or the civilianization of food-service chores (the elimination of "KP"—kitchen police—a major source of irritation to junior enlisted soldiers).

Hard Choices

Approximately one year elapsed between the creation of the Career Force Study group and Westmoreland's consideration of the final Project PROVIDE report. PROVIDE's purpose essentially had been to assess the feasibility of a post-Vietnam all-volunteer Army and to make recommendations concerning the steps and resources necessary to achieve one, if possible. But during the interval much occurred that indirectly linked PROVIDE to broader trends affecting the Army, and as Westmoreland listened to Butler he viewed the volunteer Army issue from a different perspective. A rising tide of alcohol and drug abuse, dissent, professional misconduct, and racial unrest had begun to undermine the foundation of the Army in the late 1960s. Indications of undiscipline had risen steadily beginning in 1968. The Army attributed the rise in undiscipline and accompanying increases in drug usage, antiwar agitation, and racial tension to changing national attitudes and social problems. To a certain extent it is true that the Army could not insulate itself from society; dissent, drug usage, and heightened racial tension in America clearly were affecting the entire defense establishment.

Initially the Army claimed these problems were imported from the larger society. But gradually it also became evident to the Army's leadership that internal programs and policies exacerbated the situation. The rapid expansion of the Army for combat in Vietnam and the decision to achieve the buildup through increased draft calls instead of a reserve mobilization fed the opposition to an already unpopular war. Since the Army received most of the conscripts, it became the focus of much of the antiwar rhetoric. Furthermore, in 1969 revelations of corruption, fraud, and mismanagement in the military club system, of illegal currency manipulations in Vietnam, and of battlefield misconduct and a subsequent coverup of the murder of Vietnamese civilians at My Lai in 1968 further undermined the self-confidence and sense of professionalism of the Army.[20]

All of these discouraging trends demanded attention, and the PROVIDE report served to clarify the urgency. The opinion surveys on the image of the Army commissioned by the PROVIDE study group in April 1969 gave clear evidence of the effects that war, dissent, and social upheaval were having on the Army. As they reviewed the findings of the PROVIDE report and reports of growing undiscipline, drug abuse, racial incidents, and malfeasance, Westmoreland and his colleagues became increasingly convinced that the professional fabric of the institution was unraveling.[21] While conduct of the war in Vietnam remained their primary concern, Westmoreland and the Army staff devoted increasing attention to rebuilding the institution and restoring public and self-confidence in the organization.

Very early on the chief of staff and his closest colleagues perceived a link between manpower procurement and the Army's social problems. If the dissent, undiscipline, and drug and alcohol abuse were indeed imports from society, they reasoned, reduced reliance on the draft and unwilling draft-motivated volunteers might offer a way for the Army to solve some of its own social problems. In a smaller post-Vietnam Army of true volunteers, professional standards could be reestablished and dissidents, malcontents, and misfits weeded out.

Vice Chief of Staff of the Army General Bruce Palmer, Jr., the number-two man in the Army and one of Westmoreland's closest confidants, had the final say before Westmoreland. He agreed with Butler's recommendations, but advised the chief to approve the PROVIDE recommendations "in principle" only. Palmer further cautioned that all specific actions emanating from the recommendations be forwarded to the chief of staff for final approval. Palmer was skeptical about the volunteer Army concept, but he was politically astute and realized that the draft was dying. His recommendation to approve the PROVIDE proposals in principle was consistent with Westmoreland's earlier caution. Such a decision would allow the study to move into an implementation planning phase without committing the Army to a definite course of action. And by requiring that all subsequent decisions be approved by the chief of staff, or Palmer in his stead, the vice chief of staff assured a greater degree of control over further developments.[22]

Westmoreland was ambivalent. Like most of his generation he considered a draft-supported Army the norm. Such an army won World War II and fought in Korea and Vietnam. Popular rejection of the draft seemed tantamount to rejection of the Army itself. Like Palmer he realized that peacetime conscription probably was doomed, but he saw in the PROVIDE recommendations a way to turn the all-volunteer force concept to the Army's advantage.

Westmoreland agreed with Palmer's recommendations but emphasized his conviction that the Army should remain firm on its position that draft legislation and machinery be retained "to insure flexibility and rapid response in the event of national emergency." This approach, which if followed would result in an end to inductions but not a formal ending of the draft, became known as the "zero-draft" goal. Many in the military, and some conservative elements in Congress, tried unsuccessfully to advance the zero-draft approach as an alternative to ending induction authority altogether. Throughout his tenure as chief of staff of the Army, and after his retirement, Westmoreland persisted in pressing this alternative, sometimes publicly, to the consternation of supporters of the all-volunteer force, and always privately. His actions in this regard contributed to the belief in the minds of staunch all-volunteer force advocates that Westmoreland not only opposed ending the draft—he did oppose ending induction authority—but that he was undermining the effort to do so.

Consistent with his inner convictions, Westmoreland in October 1969 directed that the PROVIDE recommendations be modified "so as not to commit the Army to a particular course of action at this time." Thus, for example, Westmoreland directed that the wording describing PROVIDE recommendations for Phase I of the proposed transition be changed to show emphasis on enhancing service attractiveness rather than reducing reliance on the draft. This change in emphasis represented more than an exercise in semantics. Improving service attractiveness facilitated rebuilding the image and professionalism of the Army. If it helped reduce reliance on the draft, so much the better. Westmoreland approved items in Phase I requiring funds but no legislation as unfunded requirements. This meant that staff planning, coordination, and approval could proceed with respect to stepped-up recruiting and advertising, for example, but actual implementation would be delayed until money could be reprogrammed from other accounts.

The chief of staff also went along with Butler's proposal to brief the Army commands and major schools on the PROVIDE program and the Army's position on the draft and the all-volunteer concept. Westmoreland knew that most of the Army's officers opposed ending the draft, and he recognized the need to educate them on the realities of the situation facing the institution. Butler would spend much of his time during the next year on the road giving PROVIDE briefings.

In November 1969 Study Group PROVIDE became a task group. Its new charter directed it to accomplish the planning, coordination, and phased implementation of the study group's recommendations. No completion date was given. Indeed, the President's Commission on an All-Volunteer Armed Force had not yet rendered its report.[23]

Notes

[1] See, for example, David Smith, "The Volunteer Army," *The Atlantic Monthly* 234, no. 1 (July 1974): 6–12; Bruce Bliven, Jr., "A Reporter at Large: All-Volunteer I," *The New Yorker*, 24 November 1975, pp. 55–91, and "All-Volunteer II," 1 December 1975, pp. 137–56; James Lacey, "Military Manpower: The American Experience an Enduring Debate," and Richard V. L. Cooper, "The All-Volunteer Force: Status and Prospects of the Active Forces," both in Andrew J. Goodpaster et al., *Toward a Consensus on Military Service: Report of the Atlantic Council's Working Group on Military Service* (New York: Pergamon Press, 1982), pp. 22–51 and 76–112. In an interview with the author, Dr. Martin Anderson alleged that Secretary of Defense Melvin R. Laird "ordered" Army Chief of Staff General William C. Westmoreland to cease opposition to the all-volunteer force (AVF) or risk dismissal. Stephen Herbits related a similar story to the author concerning Westmoreland's successor as chief of staff, General Creighton Abrams.

[2] U.S. Department of the Army, DA Pamphlet 600–12, *Digest of Military Personnel Policies*, March 1969, ch 3; MFR, Brig Gen William A. Knowlton, Secretary of the General Staff, 3 Sep 68, sub: Study of the Draft, in background material collected by the Center of Military History in the preparation of this volume from Record Group 319, Washington National Records Center (hereafter cited as Background Material).

[3] U.S. Department of the Army, *PROVIDE: Project Volunteer in Defense of the Nation*, vol. 2 (Washington, D.C.: Office of the Deputy Chief of Staff for Personnel, 15 September 1969), p. 1–1; Interv, author with Col (Ret) Jack R. Butler, 24 May 83.

[4] Undated transcript of briefing for Chief of Staff, Army (CofSA), Background Material, pp. 1–2.

[5] Ibid., pp. 11–12.

[6] Intervs, author with Gen (Ret) Bruce C. Palmer, Jr. (vice CofSA, 1968–72), 28 Feb 83; William K. Brehm (assistant secretary of the Army, manpower and reserve affairs, 1967–69), 13 Apr 83; Gen (Ret) Walter T. Kerwin, Jr. (DCSPER, 1969–73), 13 Apr 83; Stanley R. Resor (secretary of the Army, 1965–71), 21 Jun 83.

[7] Briefing for CofSA, Background Material.

[8] Xerox extract, memo for the president, no subject or date, item 11, All-Volunteer Armed Force, pp. 61–63, Background Material; Interv, author with Martin Anderson, 22 Sep 83.

[9] Memo, Nixon for Laird, 29 Jan 69, in Historical Records Collection, U.S. Army Center of Military History, Washington, D.C. (hereafter cited as HRC, CMH).

[10] Interv, author with Melvin Laird, 31 Mar 83; Memo, Fitt for Laird, 29 Jan 69, Office of the Secretary of Defense (OSD) file 340, Record Group 330, Washington National Records Center (WNRC).

[11] Memo, Laird for Nixon, 31 Jan 69, file 327.02 Volunteer Army, HRC, CMH; Draft Memo, Laird for Nixon, n.d., OSD file 340, RG 330, WNRC.

[12] Ltr, Nixon to Laird, n.d.; Memo, Laird for Nixon, 7 Feb 69 (in reply to preceding), both in OSD 340, RG 330, WNRC; Transcript of briefing by Vice Adm William Mack, Acting ASD (M&RA), on Project Volunteer, 18 Feb 69, HRC, CMH; Memo, Laird for Secretaries of the Military Departments, Chairman of the JCS, Asst Secys of Defense, 10 Apr 69, sub: Project Volunteer, HRC, CMH.

[13] MFR, Jack R. Butler, 3 Feb 69, sub: Draft and the All-Volunteer Army, w/3 Incl, in Background Material.

[14] The PROVIDE study group drew participants from all major elements of the Army staff. Ultimately the study team included 22 full-time and 11 part-time participants; all Army staff agencies not providing participants were required to designate points of contact. Memo, Lt Col Butler for ADCSPER/DCSPER, 18 Feb 69, sub: Study: Project Volunteer in Defense of the Nation (PROVIDE), in Background Material; Chief of Staff Memo (CSM) 69–113, 17 Mar 69, sub: Study: Project Volunteer in Defense of the Nation (PROVIDE), HRC, CMH.

[15] Study, U.S. Department of the Army, PROVIDE: Project Volunteer in Defense of the Nation, 20 Jun 69, vol. I, pp. ii–ix (hereafter cited as PROVIDE, I).

[16] PROVIDE, I, p. 8.

[17] Ibid., pp. 23–25.

[18] See William C. Westmoreland, *Report of the Chief of Staff of the United States Army, 1 July 1968 to 30 June 1972* (Washington, D.C.: Department of the Army, 1977 [hereafter cited as Westmoreland, *Report*]), pp. 3, 24–25, for the thirteen-division goal.

[19] Information Memo for ADCSPER/DCSPER, 15 Oct 69, sub: Briefing of CofSA on PROVIDE, w/2 Incl, in Background Material.

[20] Department of the Army, *Historical Summary, Fiscal Year 1973* (Washington, D.C.: U.S. Army Center of Military History, 1977), pp. 27–28, 61–62. For examples of rising undiscipline, see Westmoreland, *Report*, pp. 5–6, 48–54, 62–70.

[21] Palmer Interv; Kerwin Interv.

[22] Information Memo for ADCSPER/DCSPER, 15 Oct 69, sub: Briefing of CofSA on PROVIDE; Palmer Interv.

[23] CSM 69–473, 3 Nov 69, sub: Task Group: Project Volunteer in Defense of the Nation (PROVIDE), file 327.02, All-Volunteer Army, HRC, CMH; Butler Interv; MFR, Under Sec Army, 22 Oct 69, sub: Project Volunteer in Defense of the Nation (PROVIDE), in Background Material. The MFR is a summary of the CofSA Decision Briefing on PROVIDE, dated 17 Oct 69.

CHAPTER III

By Executive Direction
The Decision To End the Draft
1969–1970

While the Army's study group conducted its research and prepared its report for Westmoreland through the middle of 1969, the Department of Defense and the presidential commission pursued their research on the same subject. Throughout the summer and autumn of 1969 the several studies on ending the draft continued apace. On several occasions the Gates Commission staff requested the views of the Defense Department and services on specific issues. In such instances the work of the PROVIDE study group formed the basis for the Army's response. The three studies overlapped, and information and views were exchanged, although more frequently the information flowed from the Army and Defense Departments to the Gates Commission rather than the other way. Indeed, although each service provided a liaison officer to the commission staff, the presidential study group had little contact with the Defense Department or the services. This self-imposed isolation later fed the suspicions of Army and Defense manpower analysts that the Gates Commission's findings and recommendations were preordained and biased.

The Gates Commission and Project Volunteer

President Nixon announced the creation of his Commission on an All-Volunteer Armed Force on 27 March 1969 and named Thomas S. Gates, secretary of defense during the Eisenhower administration, as its chairman. Nixon directed the commission "to develop a comprehensive plan for eliminating conscription and moving toward an all-volunteer armed force." Martin Anderson advised the president on the creation of the commission and the selection of its members and acted as White House liaison. His guiding rule in setting up the commission, in addition to meeting the usual requirements for bipartisan, geographical, and minority representatives, was to avoid giving the impression that the body was stacked in favor of an all-volunteer force. Gates was known to be neutral. Generals Alfred Gruenther and Lauris Norstad, both former supreme allied commanders for Europe, assured representation of the services' interests. Milton Friedman, an outspoken opponent of the draft, and Stephen Herbits, the House Wednesday Group staffer who had helped prepare the book *How To End the Draft* in 1967, would provide the pro all-volunteer force perspective. Key members of the commission staff, on the other hand, displayed a predisposition against the draft. Dean William Meckling, the executive director, and Dr. Walter Oi, a research director, vigorously supported an all-volunteer force. Their presence on the staff, combined with the active participation of Friedman and Herbits on the commission, reinforced doubts among Defense Department personnel experts concerning the objectivity of the Gates Commission.[1]

The Department of Defense study group, known as Project Volunteer, first met on 21 April 1969. Roger T. Kelley chaired the committee; Dr. Harold Wool, Kelley's director of procurement policy, headed the committee's staff. The Army was well represented at the initial Project Volunteer meeting. William K. Brehm, General Connor, and Col. John B. Bennet, Butler's immediate superior in the Personnel Studies and Research Directorate, attended. Kelley explained that Secretary Laird expected the committee to actively involve itself in the development of a "comprehensive action program for moving toward a volunteer force." Project Volunteer would initiate studies on behalf of the services and review studies prepared by the services. The aim was twofold. Laird knew that the services ultimately would have to implement whatever program was designed. Thus, he included them in the program's development from the start. At the same time, Defense Department manpower experts, led by Dr. Wool, doubted the Gates Commission's objectivity and viewed Project Volunteer as a "check and balance" to the presidential commission. Kelley directed the services to submit by 1 July 1969 a report of actions they could take in the following twelve months to reduce reliance on the draft "within present constraints" and a second list of actions that could be taken "with constraints removed." Subsequently, he established the Program Evaluation Group to review all proposals and studies with an eye toward consolidating service input.[2]

In May the Gates Commission invited the Defense Department and each of the services to present their "views both as to the problems of moving to an all-volunteer force and the means of reaching that end." In tendering the invitation William Meckling, executive director of the presidential commission, asked the services to focus on five areas: sources and uses of manpower, pay and benefits for uniformed personnel, overall military personnel costs, the role and cost of civilian employees, and reserve force doctrine.[3]

Army Response

The Army achieved an early unity of effort in its response to those requests from the Defense Department and Gates Commission through the efforts of Assistant Secretary William K. Brehm. Brehm had come to the Army in April 1968 from the systems analysis staff of the Office of the Secretary of Defense where he had been responsible for Army and Marine Corps land forces policy since 1964. He worked closely with General Connor, his military counterpart on the Army staff, and Lt. Gen. Walter T. "Dutch" Kerwin, Jr., who succeeded Connor as deputy chief of staff for personnel in August 1969. All drew on the work of Jack Butler's PROVIDE study group. Connor's staff prepared the briefing for the Gates Commission and the requested reports for Project Volunteer; Brehm reviewed the former and finalized the latter. Connor directed the Army briefing for the Gates Commission and kept Brehm's office informed of its contents. Reflecting the Army's skepticism of the objectivity of the commission, Connor told his staff, "It could very well be that this will be the only time the services will be able to present their views to the Commission other than through the input provided the Project Volunteer DOD Committee." He designated his assistant, Maj. Gen. Walter E. Brinker, to brief the commission members who gathered at the Pentagon to hear from the services on the weekend of 28–29 June. The briefing was straightforward and informative. It did not reveal the Army's position on an all-volunteer force, the Army's preliminary ideas on how such a force could be achieved, or the projected costs of the undertaking.

Brinker concentrated on several points. In the area of procurement he explained the basis for the Army's enlistment standards, motives for enlistment, and the extent to which the draft influenced voluntary enlistments. Brinker emphasized the extent of the Army's dependency on draftees since the Vietnam buildup. Enlisted personnel requirements had increased 60 percent between 1965 and 1969, he pointed out. In 1969 the Army expected to turn over approximately one-third of its enlisted strength; 56 percent of its new soldiers would be two-year draftees. Of the remaining 44 percent of three-year volunteers, half were draft motivated. The high proportion of draftees and semi-volunteers in the ranks depressed reenlistment rates, forcing even greater reliance on selective service, Brinker noted. Policy decisions limiting tours of duty in Vietnam to one year affected career reenlistments too. Faced with the prospect of repeated assignments to the war zone every eighteen months, many experienced career soldiers dropped out of the service. Reenlistments by young sergeants with between four and six years of service fell from 47 to 11 percent between 1965 and 1968. The decline was most alarming since the people in that category represented the future of the Army's noncommissioned officer corps.

More than the war influenced the decline in retention, Brinker continued. He explained how frequent moves, family separation, lack of housing, and inadequate pay discouraged officer and enlisted retention, thereby increasing annual requirements for new personnel. Finally, he also highlighted the relationship of the reserve components to the active Army and emphasized the extent to which the reserves also had become draft dependent during recent years.

At no point in the briefing did Brinker hint at the Army's thoughts on possible solutions to the bleak situation he outlined. His purpose was to inform, not lead, the opinion of the Gates Commission. Although the Army had its own ideas on how an all-volunteer force could be achieved, it was not anxious to share them. Clearly, at that time, with Vietnam demanding such a large annual infusion of personnel, the Army needed the draft and did not want to upset the status quo by offering alternatives.[4]

Simultaneously with the briefing to the Gates Commission, Army representatives made a somewhat analogous report to Roger Kelley's Project Volunteer Committee on 12 July 1969. Its report to Kelley, however, was far more forthcoming. In it Brehm told Kelley that the Army approached the problem of reducing reliance on the draft from two directions. First, he and the other personnel specialists in the Army were trying to find ways to prevent active duty requirements from increasing. Second, Brehm said, "We are seeking ways to make active duty and reserve duty more attractive." The philosophy was simple. The Army again avoided the debate over the merits of ending the draft; it merely would seek to reduce its need for draftees. The approach was equally simple: since active duty personnel cost more than reservists, one solution was to limit or reduce active duty requirements; since recruiting and training new personnel also were expensive, more efforts had to be devoted to retaining more of those already in the service. Brehm acknowledged the obvious. "The steps suggested for dealing with these issues may appear prosaic when stated briefly," he wrote. "It is the implementation, however, that must be dramatic and innovative. We intend that it shall be so," he added, and then he went right to the heart of the matter, "but we will need budgetary and legislative assistance." Indeed, Brehm's report implied that not much could be accomplished without substantial funds and new initiatives, all of which required congressional approval and appropriations. That portion of the report that dealt with actions that "can be accomplished within existing budgetary and legislative constraints" received less attention.

On top of Brehm's list was "a large increase in the Recruiting Command's advertising budget—now." Drawing almost verbatim from the interim PROVIDE report, he declared, "The prerequisite to improvement in the enlistment and retention area is a sharp improvement in the image which the public has of the Armed Services." He proposed to increase the advertising budget from $3 to $36 million "in order to let advertising do for the Army what it has done successfully for business." Pursuing the advertising metaphor, Brehm labeled the bulk of the remaining Army proposals "product improvements." Thus, again following the logic and recommendations of the PROVIDE report, he requested funds to replace soldiers performing menial tasks with direct-hire civilians, to build or lease new family housing, to build new and rebuild existing barracks to provide soldier privacy, and to increase to more realistic levels allowances and reimbursements paid to service members required to move. Brehm noted that "Many of these deficiencies have become traditionalized and institutionalized as the result of long-term budgetary limitations," and added, "We cannot successfully advertise a product which retains... the present deficiencies."[5]

Brehm hardly mentioned pay. To the Army the subjects of increased first-term pay and an improved package of retention pay and benefits for career soldiers needed no justification. Indeed, as the studies and reports from the other services and the Gates Commission ultimately revealed, higher pay was one of the few areas of agreement among all parties concerned with ending the draft. Disagreements developed over how much pay should be increased, how it would be distributed, and the extent to which it would influence enlistments and retention.

Interim Evaluation

By the end of 1969 the study phase of the transition to an all-volunteer force had neared completion. The Army's effort, already finished and approved by Westmoreland, had a significant impact on the Defense Department study. Indeed, the Department of Defense director of procurement policy and staff director of Project Volunteer termed PROVIDE "the best of the Services studies," and later observed that it "anticipated subsequent plans and programs with unusual accuracy."[6]

Input from various Department of Defense staff sections seemed encouraging. The preliminary report from the assistant secretary of defense for systems analysis concluded that the outlook for a post-Vietnam all-volunteer force looked favorable based on the assumption that enlisted retention in an all-volunteer force would increase, thereby reducing new accession requirements. Furthermore, since the population base would grow in the 1970s, more men could be expected to volunteer. Thus, the increased cost of switching to a volunteer force might be lower than some reports, such as the Army's, suggested. Paul Wollstadt, director of the Project Volunteer Program Evaluation Group, also expressed optimism. "I believe an All-Volunteer Force is feasible at the low total force levels that have been discussed as possibilities for the future," he wrote to Roger Kelley in December. Like others, Wollstadt included better personnel management, housing, and pay and an improvement in the public attitude toward military services as necessary preconditions for success. But in a prescient warning he added, "I am concerned, however, that some of the ardent proponents of the All-Volunteer concept, particularly the key members of the Gates Commission staff, may underestimate what it will take in terms of money and effort to sustain an All-Volunteer force beyond the rapid draw-down period." He expressed special concern at the tendency of the presidential commission to "rely too heavily on increasing under-2 pay [a reference to service members with less than two years of service] as the solution to the All-Volunteer Force problem."[7]

The fact that the Defense Department and the services were conducting studies of their own troubled some members of the Presidential Commission on an All-Volunteer Armed Force. While some members welcomed the input the studies provided, others worried that the publication of parallel reports would lead to confusion. More worrisome was the concern that public differences between the Defense Department and the commission might jeopardize the prospects for achieving an all-volunteer force. Gates expressed his misgivings in July about the release of studies on ending the draft. Laird agreed not to prepare a formal Project Volunteer report and advised the services of his decision. The Army classified the final Project PROVIDE report Secret. Furthermore, in keeping with the spirit of Laird's agreement with Gates, General Westmoreland omitted references to the PROVIDE report and the Army's official position on the feasibility of an all-volunteer force in an interview with *U.S. News & World Report* in August and indefinitely postponed an address on the subject.[8] Unfortunately, this imposed silence obscured the Army's early and active role in planning for the transition to the all-volunteer force and contributed to later allegations of official Army opposition to the concept of an all-volunteer force and foot dragging on its implementation.

Despite the self-imposed secrecy that surrounded Projects PROVIDE and Volunteer, word of their existence leaked out. The *Army Times*, a weekly newspaper that catered to military personnel, obtained a copy of the PROVIDE report and published a factual summary of its recommendations. At the same time the *Army Times* began a series of editorials condemning the volunteer force concept as too expensive and, by quoting the PROVIDE report out of context, implied that the Army officially opposed the idea. The Army's leadership made no attempt to disassociate itself from the editorials. Colonel Butler made an unsuccessful attempt to identify the source of the leak of the PROVIDE report. Through the deputy chief of staff for personnel (DCSPER), he advised Westmoreland not to make a statement until publication of the Gates report: "since the entire matter is still under study by the President's Commission on an All-Volunteer Force any further comment would be premature."

The *Army Times* series on Project PROVIDE in late 1969 coincided with the circulation of a draft of the Gates Commission's findings and recommendations to the armed services. The Army's private reactions to the recommendations report convinced at least one member of the commission, Stephen Herbits, that the Army had embarked on a program to sabotage the volunteer force effort.[9]

Means and Ends

In December 1969 and January 1970 the Gates Commission staff briefed interested parties in the services and Defense Department on its draft findings and recommendations. The Army liaison to the commission discussed the report with Assistant Secretary Brehm and General Kerwin, the DCSPER, in December; William Meckling, the commission staff director, formally briefed the Army Policy Council on 7 January. It became evident immediately that the Army and the commission differed primarily over the means necessary to obtain an all-volunteer force.

The briefings by the Gates Commission staff and the copies of their draft report that circulated in the Pentagon in early January 1970 confirmed the worst fears of Defense Department and service manpower planners. According to one account the members of Roger Kelley's Project Volunteer committee considered the commission's recommendation to end the draft as early as 30 June 1971 "as impractical, if not irresponsible." Defense Department personnel and compensation specialists disagreed with both specific aspects of the commission's pay proposals and the general econometric underpinnings of the report's philosophy. According to Gus Lee, Kelley's director of manpower utilization, "Virtually everyone in the Department who had worked on the problem thought that the Commission had underestimated the difficulties of achieving a volunteer force."[10]

That the Gates Commission would recommend ending reliance on the draft was a foregone conclusion. Nixon's charter to the commission had not asked it whether the draft should be ended; rather, it directed Gates "to develop a comprehensive plan for eliminating conscription and moving toward an all-volunteer force." Nevertheless, the commission's draft recommendation, supported unanimously by the commission membership, that the draft be ended when induction authority expired in June 1971 caught many in the defense establishment by surprise.

Of almost equal concern to Defense Department manpower specialists who reviewed the Gates Commission draft findings and recommendations was the way it proposed to end conscription by that date. The commission examined the manpower requirements and budgetary implications of active duty force levels of 2.0, 2.25, 2.5, and 3.0 million service members. It concluded that young Americans of requisite quality would volunteer for armed service in sufficient quantity to maintain each assumed force level provided Congress raised entry pay approximately 50 percent for enlisted personnel and 28 percent for officers. Additional monetary inducements were necessary to attract volunteers for the military medical corps. The commission proposed to attract and retain volunteers with special skills through a combination of lateral entry, proficiency pay, and accelerated promotion programs. In order to reduce the services' requirements for new accessions annually, the commission calculated that "95,000 positions in a force of 2 million men could be staffed by civilians with no loss in effectiveness." Furthermore, since, as the commission concluded, true volunteers reenlisted at a higher rate than draftees and draft-motivated volunteers, the requirement for new personnel would decline. The commission predicted that the combination of a civilian substitution program with higher retention would reduce the annual requirement for enlisted accessions necessary to maintain a force of 2.5 million from 440,000 to 332,000 by 1979, with the Army's share dropping from 235,000 to 148,000.

The Gates Commission apparently rejected service proposals involving increased benefits such as improved housing, dental care for families, or improved in-service or post-service educational programs. While it agreed that "military life needs to be improved generally," the commission opposed increased benefits and stressed purely monetary inducements to enlistment on the grounds that a generous entry pay increase and a military salary system for career service members allowed "each individual to decide how he or she will use whatever he earns." Thus, while it insisted that "Pay is not the only, and perhaps not even the primary motivating force for joining or remaining in the military services," the commission persisted in viewing potential enlistees and reenlistees as "rational economic men" driven by the forces of a market economy. Indeed, the commission believed that only $20 million of a total $2.7 billion necessary to implement an all-volunteer force beginning in July 1971 would be required for non-pay items such as recruiting, and it believed that the transition should begin at once.

The Gates Commission also proposed an economic solution to the problem of manning the reserve components in an all-volunteer environment. The commission assumed that the strengths of the various elements of the reserves would decline in a draft-free situation, but it argued that the services maintained unnecessarily high strength requirements for their Ready Reserves and could sustain some decline without loss of effectiveness. Pay increases for the active forces automatically applied to the reserves. The commission believed that higher reserve pay would attract enough volunteers to meet the reserve needs. The commission conceded that the quality of the reserves, as measured by educational levels, might drop following the end of the draft, but dismissed the probability as irrelevant since "the reserves do not require such an educationally rich force" as they acquired during the period of high draft pressure. Data on which to base reserve component requirements and volunteer projections were seriously lacking, the commission admitted, and its estimates might prove optimistic. But the commission chose to be optimistic. "Given the uncertainties which surround projections of reserve enlistments and losses ... further steps should await the results of experience with higher pay during the next few years." [11]

The Army in particular took exception to the draft Gates report. Task Group PROVIDE received a copy of the draft report in advance of the commission staff's briefing to the Army Policy Council on 7 January. Butler and his people found what they considered to be numerous logical and methodological errors in the commission's estimates of the Army's manpower needs, its ability to meet them, and the costs necessary to overcome personnel deficits. In particular, the Army's personnel specialists concluded that the commission underestimated by 76,000 the number of new volunteers needed in the first year following the end of the draft and overestimated by 27,000 to 37,000 the number of youths that could be expected to volunteer in the absence of a draft. Thus, whereas the Gates Commission staff saw a need to provide incentives for 41,000 additional volunteers, the Army looked at a deficit of between 174,000 and 184,000. According to Army analysts the commission staff compounded the above errors by overestimating the ability of an across-the-board increase in entry pay to make up the difference. The Gates Commission staff calculated that a 10 percent increase in pay would yield a 12.5 percent rise in enlistments (a ratio known as the "elasticity of supply" factor). The Army questioned the commission's supply elasticity factor on two points. First, the commission applied the factor to aggregate service needs but did not take into account hard-to-fill combat-related positions. Thus, to raise pay according to the commission's formula ran the risk of leaving critical vacancies unfilled. On the other hand, if entry pay were raised to a point necessary to attract volunteers to all military jobs the services would, in effect, be paying too much to fill noncombat vacancies.

Rebuttal

The PROVIDE task group and other elements of the Army staff concerned with the issue worked closely with Assistant Secretary Brehm and his staff to prepare a rebuttal to the commission staff's draft report. On 9 January Secretary of the Army Stanley R. Resor and Brehm met with Gates and the commission, and Resor delivered the Army's views in person. Resor reviewed the Army's concerns for the commission members. On the subject of supply elasticity he reminded the commission that "historically, many more draftees than enlistees go into the combat positions—particularly infantry—because the enlistees tend to select jobs that will give them a technical skill and keep them out of direct combat." The secretary suggested that it might be necessary to stratify service requirements into combat and noncombat positions with different elasticities. He urged further analysis and cautioned "when we cannot predict the consequences with reasonable certainty, we must act conservatively and take no irreversible steps."

The secretary of the Army also questioned the commission's assumption that increasing pay was the most efficient and least costly method of acquiring an all-volunteer force. He cited a Census Bureau study that revealed that less than 9 percent of young people considered pay as the key factor in job selection and added that Army surveys showed "that more volunteers could be attracted if funds were used to provide increased educational and training benefits." Resor also expressed the fear that exclusive reliance on pay would "attract the man on the economic margin" with the attendant danger of "recruiting the person whose prospects in civilian life are relatively meager." The consequences of that happening were intolerable, he warned. "We cannot have a force in which all are of a level just sufficient to meet the enlistment standard."

Resor also worried about the reserve components. The Army's analysis of reserve requirements and prospects in an all-volunteer environment was as skimpy as the commission's, Resor told the gathering. "How will we fill the reserve components if the draft is gone?" he asked rhetorically. "I have yet to hear a clear answer to this question." He predicted a decline in Army National Guard enlistments of up to 60 percent in the absence of draft pressure. Furthermore, the individual reserve, which provided fillers for active and reserve units upon mobilization and casualty replacements in the early stages of a conflict, might dry up altogether. Loss of an effective individual reserve pool would require cannibalization of units to provide replacements in a mobilization.

Finally, Resor urged the commission to consider some intangible consequences of creating an all-volunteer force. "An all-volunteer force is not beyond our technological capabilities or the gross national product," he said. "But will we get the kind of force we need for the price we are willing to pay?" Given the budget realities of the day, Resor reminded his audience, an all-volunteer force would have to compete for funds. "The draft may be a factor causing unrest in the country," he acknowledged, but if an all-volunteer force displaced funds "designed to correct the social ills and domestic problems of the Nation [it could be] responsible for uneasiness in all groups, young and old." If, as was a more likely alternative, a costly all-volunteer force had to compete for funds within a limited defense budget the result might lead to reductions in general-purpose forces and, perforce, greater reliance on strategic deterrent weapons. That prospect he considered highly dangerous.

The commission was unmoved by Resor's effort. Later, he recalled that the Gates Commission "was like a lot of Presidential commissions." The outcome, he believed, was preordained. At the 9 January meeting, Resor remembered, Milton Friedman and William Meckling, the commission staff director, dominated the discussion in defense of the draft report. Martin Anderson, who attended the meeting in his capacity as White House liaison, was surprised by the vigor of Resor's critique of the commission's draft. He termed Resor's remarks "provocative." The outcome of the meeting further convinced commission member Stephen Herbits that the Army steadfastly opposed the very idea of an all-volunteer armed force.

The next day Resor sent Gates a summary of his remarks "in the hope that they may be useful to you and the Commission staff as you complete work." Evidently they were not. The final report of the commission, presented to the president and released to the public on 21 February 1970, contained virtually no changes.[12]

More Counterproposals

The circulation of the draft Gates Commission report coincided with the completion of the Project Volunteer Program Evaluation Group report, which Kelley intended to serve as the basis for creating a united position between the services and the Defense Department on the volunteer force issue. President Nixon had promised Secretary Laird the opportunity to review the findings and recommendations of the commission's report, and Kelley intended to be well armed for the moment. The Program Evaluation Group report, prepared by Paul Wollstadt, deputy assistant secretary of defense for manpower research and utilization, reached Roger Kelley on 14 January 1970. The findings and recommendations, which clearly reflected the influence of the Army's Project PROVIDE study, differed significantly from those of the Gates Commission. Like the commission report, Wollstadt's study recommended major improvements in military pay. However, the Wollstadt report did not propose to use a massive pay raise to attract volunteers to the services. Instead, the Program Evaluation Group recommended a mix of across-the-board pay raises for both first-term and career service members, enlistment bonuses to attract volunteers with special skills or for hard-to-fill combat assignments, and differential pay to help retain people in key positions. Of greater significance, however, was the fact that Wollstadt's group viewed necessary improvements in pay only as "an essential first step." Wollstadt also recommended substantial educational and training benefits including precommissioning scholarship programs for officer-cadets, on- and off-duty in-service education and training, and counseling and job-referral assistance for personnel about to reenter the civil sector. Furthermore, he proposed a major increase in and improvement of housing for military personnel and their families to include constructing more housing, extending family housing benefits to all married military personnel including noncareer service members, providing greater privacy for bachelor enlisted personnel, and giving unmarried service members greater freedom to live off base.

Wollstadt also addressed the utilization and management of military personnel, recruitment, and special reserve component and medical personnel issues. Wollstadt borrowed directly from the PROVIDE report for his recommendations on the elimination of the practice of assigning enlisted service members to menial, extra-duty jobs such as KP and proposals on the subject of paid recruitment advertising on radio and television.

The Project Volunteer Program Evaluation Group concluded "an All-Volunteer Force is feasible... if we provide sufficient incentives including, but not limited to, better pay." Wollstadt attached no price tag to his recommendations, but cautioned Kelley that "we must guard against underestimating what it will take in money and effort." In a major break with the thrust of the Gates Commission report, he also recommended that induction authority be retained beyond 1971 as a hedge against the "inherent uncertainties as to both future military manpower requirements and supply conditions."[13]

Kelley forwarded the report to all the services and used the occasion to reconvene the Project Volunteer committee. The Wollstadt report, he said, would form the agenda of the committee's discussions, which were aimed at preparing a Defense Department position on the Gates Commission report.[14]

The Project Volunteer committee met on successive Saturdays beginning 31 January 1970 and hammered out its position on the Gates report and an all-volunteer force. On 17 February the committee reached agreement on a tentative position. The essence of the agreement was that Defense agreed with the Gates Commission that the long-term defense needs of the nation would be better served by an all-volunteer force but disagreed with the Gates Commission's estimate of requirements and its proposed programs and timetable. As an alternative the Department of Defense would offer the president its own action program for ending reliance on the draft. That program, to be prepared in detail by the Project Volunteer committee, would include a substantial budget increase to support initiatives for improving service attractiveness and phased implementation of an all-volunteer force. Above all, the Project Volunteer committee insisted, "the draft should not be abolished in July 1971 but should be renewed for one, two or three years or as long as our [Southeast Asia] commitments remain large."[15]

The Department of Defense worked out the details of its position simultaneously with the White House review of the Gates Commission recommendations. Richard Nixon formally received the Report of the Presidential Commission on an All-Volunteer Armed Force on 21 February 1970. Nixon announced that Martin Anderson would chair a special White House committee to review the Gates Commission proposal and recommend a course of action. William K. Brehm would represent the Army on Anderson's White House review group. Throughout the deliberations with the White House staff, members of the National Security Council, and representatives from the Council of Economic Advisers and Office of Management and Budget, Brehm worked with Kelley to advance the Department of Defense perspective, which embodied the Army's position on the volunteer force. Brehm and Resor had argued their views before the Gates Commission on 9 January in their unsuccessful effort to urge modifications to the report's timetable and its estimates of personnel and cost requirements. Brehm restated these views to the Anderson group in February and March as part of the Defense proposal, which the Project Volunteer committee finalized even as the deliberations of the Anderson group proceeded.

Secretary of Defense Laird formally presented the Defense Department alternative to the president on 11 March 1970, while Kelley advanced it within the context of the Anderson review committee. Laird reiterated Defense Department support for the Gates Commission's conclusion that the draft should be ended but emphasized his contention that achievement of that goal depended on assurance that the uniformed services could in fact "attract and retain an Armed Force of the required size and quality through voluntary means." He urged deliberate caution and warned Nixon against taking "irreversible steps to eliminate the draft" that would result in "reducing forces below National Security Council recommendations."

The secretary of defense suggested a phased program aimed at "reducing draft calls to zero rather than achieving the All Volunteer Force, even though the objective of each is identical." Achievement of a "zero draft" would appeal to those who opposed conscription without antagonizing elements of society who objected to pure military volunteerism. The proposal thus retained many of the features of the twofold approach he had offered Nixon in January 1969: reform the draft while phasing in the all-volunteer force. Laird told Nixon that success of the Vietnamization program, the plan to transfer conduct of the war from American to Vietnamese forces, would probably reduce the need for inductions to around 5,000 a month by mid-1972, which, combined with initiatives to make voluntary service more attractive, would make it possible to place the draft in standby status. Retention of induction authority beyond that date would simply be insurance.

To advance the goal of achieving an all-volunteer force, Laird recommended a 20 percent pay increase for enlisted service members with under two years of service beginning 1 January 1971. He restated his disagreement with the findings of the Gates Commission regarding the ability of pay raises alone to achieve the all-volunteer objective. Instead, he requested funds to expand the recruiting programs of each service; to increase on-base military housing and allowances for service personnel living off base; to improve the attractiveness of service life for prospective volunteers and career personnel through expansion of educational and training opportunities; and to eliminate service irritants such as KP and other additional duties. Other recommendations included extension to junior enlisted members of family-related benefits such as housing, health care, and travel for spouses and children and creation of job transition programs for personnel reentering civilian life. The cost of these recommendations would add $2 billion to the Defense Department's budget of approximately $75 billion for the fiscal year beginning in July 1972 and $3.5 billion in FY 1973.[16]

The Defense Department negotiators found support from a number of quarters on the Anderson review committee. Dr. Henry Kissinger, the president's national security adviser, and Peter Flanagan of the White House staff rejected the Gates Commission recommendation to end conscription on 30 June 1971. All proposals to end the draft hinged on a reduction in strength of 500,000 to 750,000 uniformed personnel. That troop cut depended in turn on the success of Vietnamization. Kissinger feared that an announcement fixing the end of the draft would be construed as a deadline for an American withdrawal from Vietnam. Such a move might undermine negotiations to end the war then under way with the North Vietnamese in Paris. He thus favored a three-year extension of the authority to draft along with a phased reduction in draft calls to zero by January 1973.

Nixon's budgetary advisers also opposed ending the draft in the summer of 1971 because they knew it would entail adding significant personnel costs to the defense budget. All parties to the debate agreed that a pay hike was crucial to the success of any scheme to shift from the draft to an all-volunteer force. But ending the draft in 1971 entailed raising pay for three million active duty service members, whereas a phased reduction in strength over a two- or three-year period represented a substantial savings in money. Anderson compiled the arguments and presented them to Nixon as a range of alternatives.[17]

The Department of Defense proposal steered a middle course between the fast-paced solution offered by the Gates Commission and the drawn-out and less expensive plans of the National Security Council and Office of Management and Budget. It favored a two-year extension of induction authority beginning in mid-1971, which pushed retention of the draft beyond the 1972 election but not, as would a three-year extension, into the 1974 election year. Thus, the administration could capitalize on the issue in two more elections; in 1972 it could point to substantial progress in ending the draft and in 1974 it could point to a promise fulfilled. The draft reforms Laird requested went as far as possible toward making the Selective Service System equitable. Indeed, virtually everything Laird proposed had been urged on Lyndon Johnson by the Marshall Commission in 1967. All of the reforms and the extension served to defuse opposition to the draft and give the services time to ease into an all-volunteer force. If, as Laird's manpower experts predicted, everything worked smoothly, he could end draft calls altogether before induction authority expired at the end of June

1973. This assurance fit nicely with Laird's personal agenda. He had accepted the post of secretary of defense with the understanding that he would serve four years. He wanted the two major objectives of his tenure—ending the Vietnam War and ending the draft—completed before he left office in January 1973. Laird recalls, "I gave Roger Kelley his charge, and I told him I was walking out of the [Pentagon] and a cab was picking me up on the 21st of January 1973. I wanted to walk out and there wouldn't be a draft call."[18]

Results

Nixon reviewed the alternatives presented by the Anderson group and accepted the middle course offered by Laird. The White House announced the decision on 23 April 1970. The president agreed with the basic conclusions of the Gates Commission, but concluded that the draft could not be ended on 30 June 1971. He ended occupational and paternity deferments and asked for legislation placing the draft on a uniform national lottery basis and granting authority to end undergraduate student deferments. To begin moving to a zero draft Nixon asked Congress for a 20 percent pay increase for military personnel with less than two years' service and an additional $2 billion in fiscal year 1972 for volunteer force initiatives. He further directed Laird to expand "programs designed to increase enlistments and retention" and "to review the policies and practice of the military services to give new emphasis to recognition of the individual needs, aspirations, and capabilities of all military personnel." Nixon did not request an extension of the draft immediately. The existing Selective Service Act continued in effect until 30 June 1971, over a year away. On Anderson's advice, he saw no need to be specific on an extension request; to do so might stir up opponents of the draft in society and of the all-volunteer force in Congress.[19]

As far as the White House was concerned, Nixon's announcement ended the debate on the subject and established the parameters for implementation. But since reduction of draft calls depended on events in Vietnam, and especially on progress in the Vietnamization program, the timetable remained tentative to some extent. This uncertainty, combined with the compartmentalization of the decision-making process in the Nixon White House, resulted in some ironic coincidences.

The week prior to making public his decision on the draft Nixon announced that the initial success of Vietnamization of the war would enable the United States to withdraw 150,000 troops over the course of 1971. Opinion makers responded favorably to the combination of troop withdrawals and draft reform. The *New York Times*, an outspoken critic of the war and the draft, for example, welcomed the news as a sign that the administration would be able to turn its attention to "domestic social problems that have long been starved for funds by the war." But a week after the White House announcement on the draft U.S. and South Vietnamese troops invaded Cambodia. The *Times* called the move a "Military Hallucination" and declared that it marked the demise of "the 'new' Nixon who campaigned on a platform pledged to peace." The *Washington Post*, another of the president's severe critics, had similarly greeted the troop withdrawal and draft announcements warmly, but now questioned both the wisdom of the invasion and Nixon's handling of the announcement, which, the *Post* charged, fanned the flames of student unrest in the country.[20] Had Nixon's support of an all-volunteer force been motivated solely by a desire to mollify the youth vote, and had the troop withdrawal and draft announcements merely been a smoke screen prior to the Cambodian invasion, the suspicions of the *Post* and *Times* might have been correct. However, Nixon had made the decisions independently of one another and had relied on a completely different set of advisers. Indeed, Martin Anderson knew nothing of the Cambodian incursion until the night Nixon announced it on television. Politics entered into the equation during the presidential election. Initially, Nixon said, "what really tipped the balance in my decision to support the voluntary army was the unrest over the draft because of the Vietnam war. But I would not have followed through after the election had I not become convinced that a voluntary army was economically feasible and militarily acceptable."[21]

The end of the draft and the U.S. withdrawal were linked but on courses of their own. Cambodia did not affect the program to implement the all-volunteer armed force. "The whole thing had been decided by then," Anderson said later. "The draft was going to end; it was just a question of when and how."[22]

In the eyes of the public, and indeed in most subsequent accounts of the volunteer force, the Gates Commission appeared to furnish the basis for the "when and how" of which Anderson spoke. In fact, the efforts of Roger Kelley's Project Volunteer committee contributed more to the eventual decision by President Nixon to end the draft. The significance of the Gates Commission lay in its ability to pull together and articulate a unanimous justification for replacing peacetime conscription with an all-volunteer system, and the importance of the commission's role cannot be overstated. In terms of the mechanics of the implementation, the Department of Defense alternative to the commission's recommendations proved more useful. And Colonel Butler's Project PROVIDE group and report, the essence of which was established and approved by General Westmoreland even before the creation of the Gates Commission, contributed significantly to the development of the Defense Department plan. Indeed, the Project PROVIDE study continued to form the intellectual basis of the Army's implementation of the program long after its name and origins were forgotten.

Nixon's decisions and legislative and budgetary requests in April 1970 set the stage for lengthy congressional debate and authorization and appropriation actions that consumed most of the remainder of the year. Up to now the exercise had been an affair of the mind. Now the services would develop detailed plans and compete with one another for money to finance those plans. All of this would occur while Congress debated and finally approved the administration's proposals. In the process the whole subject of military manpower and its relationship to the president's war-making powers received exhaustive attention from the Congress and, through the media, the interested public. Not since the end of World War II, when Congress considered and rejected President Truman's proposal for universal military training, had the nation's system for raising and maintaining uniformed personnel for the armed forces been subjected to such scrutiny. But the services, especially the Army, could not wait on that outcome. Work on the first budget to enable transition from draft dependency to all-volunteer status had already begun.

Notes

[1] *Public Papers of the President, Richard Nixon, 1969* (Washington, D.C.: Government Printing Office, 1971), pp. 258–59; Intervs, author with Martin Anderson and Gus Lee. Other members of the Gates Commission were: Thomas Curtis, former congressman from Missouri and vice president and general counsel, *Encyclopedia Britannica*; Frederick Dent, president, Mayfar Mills; Crawford Greenwalt, chairman, Finance Committee, E.I. du Pont de Nemours and Co.; Alan Greenspan, chairman of the board, Townsend Greenspan & Co., Economic Consultants; Theodore Hesburgh, president, University of Notre Dame, chairman, U.S. Commission on Civil Rights; Jerome Holland, president, Hampton Institute; John Kemper, headmaster, Phillips Academy; Jeanne Noble, professor, New York University, vice president, National Council of Negro Women, and former member, National Advisory Commission on Selective Service; W. Allen Wallis, president, University of Rochester; and Roy Wilkins, executive director, NAACP.

[2] Memo, Laird for Secys of the Mil Depts, Chairman of the JCS, and Asst Secys of Defense, 10 Apr 69, file 327.02, Volunteer Army, HRC, CMH; MFR, Col Bennet, 23 Apr 69, sub: Project Volunteer Committee Meeting, in DAMH Background Material, RG 319, WNRC; Gus C. Lee and Geoffrey Y. Parker, *Ending the Draft: The Story of the All Volunteer Force* (Alexandria, Va.: Human Resources Research Organization, April 1977), pp. 50–54.

[3] Ltr, William Meckling to Laird, 21 May 69, OSA file 202.10, Volunteer Army, RG 335, WNRC.

[4] Memo, DCSPER–XO for multiple addressees, 17 Jun 69, sub: Briefings for Presidential Commission on an All-Volunteer Armed Force, HRC, CMH; Transcript of Army briefing to Gates Commission, n.d., Herbits Papers; Brehm Interv.

[5] Memos, Lt Gen Connor thru CofSA for Brehm, ASA (M&RA), 10 Jul 69, sub: Ongoing, Planned, and Other Actions to Reduce Reliance on the Draft; and Brehm for Kelley, ASD (M&RA), 12 Jul 69, same sub, both in OSA file 202.10, Volunteer Army, RG 335, WNRC; Brehm Interv.

[6] Lee and Parker, *Ending the Draft*, p. 53.

[7] Memos, Charles O. Rossetti for SecDef, 22 Sep 69, sub: Reducing Reliance on the Draft; and Paul Wollstadt for Roger Kelley, 22 Dec 69, sub: All-Volunteer Force, both in OSD file 340, RG 330, WNRC.

[8] Ltrs, Thomas Gates to Melvin Laird, 29 Jul 69, and Laird to Gates, 7 Aug 69, both in OSD file 340, RG 330, WNRC; MFR, Lt Col Butler, handwritten on DCSPER Comment Sheet of 12 Aug 69, sub: Questions and Answers for CSA Interview; and DCSPER Approval Memo, 28 Oct 69, sub: Draft Speech for CSA on the Subject of the All-Volunteer Army, both in DAMH Background Material, RG 319, WNRC.

[9] *Army Times*, 5 November 1969, pp. 12–13; 12 November 1969, pp. 1, 26; 3 December 1970, p. 13; and 4 February 1970, p. 11. Fact Sheet, DCSPER to CSA, n.d., sub: Premature Disclosure of Close Hold Information, HRC, CMH; Andrew S. Effron, "Challenge to Conscription, 1963–1970: The Politics of Ending the Draft," unpublished honors thesis, Harvard College, April 1970, pp. 176–77. Note: Effron cites an interview with Herbits.

[10] Lee and Parker, *Ending the Draft*, pp. 65–67. MFR, John G. Kester, 31 Dec 69, sub: Gates Commission Progress Report, Personal Papers of John G. Kester (hereafter cited as Kester Papers). Note: John Kester was deputy assistant secre-

tary of the Army (M&RA) from March 1970 to March 1972. Agenda and Minutes of the 806th Meeting of the Army Policy Council, 7 Jan 70, RG 335, WNRC. No transcript of Meckling's briefing exists. The following reconstruction of the briefing is based on Kester's aforementioned MFR, Ltr, Resor to Gates, 10 Jan 70, and Intervs, author with Butler, Resor, Brehm, and Kester on 24 May, 21 Jun, 13 Apr, and 14 Jul 83, respectively.

[11] Summary and all quotations are from the official edition of the final report *President's Commission on an All-Volunteer Armed Force* (Washington, D.C.: Government Printing Office, 1970), pp. vii, 38, 40–43, 49, 57, 60, 62–63, 65, 126 (hereafter cited as Gates Report). See also Lee and Parker, *Ending the Draft*, pp. 55–61.

[12] Lee and Parker, *Ending the Draft*, pp. 66–67; Ltr, Resor to Gates, 10 Jan 70, w/att (9pp), OSA file 202.10, RG 335, WNRC; Memo, DCSPER–PSRD thru CSA for ASA (M&RA), 3 Feb 70, sub: Analysis of the 1964 DOD Study on an All-Volunteer Force and Comparison to the Gates Commission, file 327.02, All-Volunteer Army, HRC, CMH; Anderson, Butler, Brehm, Resor, and Kester Intervs; Effron, "Challenge to Conscription," p. 176.

[13] Memo, Paul Wollstadt for Roger Kelley, 14 Jan 70, sub: All-Volunteer Force—Report of Program Evaluation Group on Project Volunteer, w/Incl, Findings and Recommendations of Program Evaluation Group, OSA file 202.10, Volunteer Army, RG 335, WNRC.

[14] Memo, Roger Kelley for multiple addressees, 22 Jan 70, sub: Project Volunteer, OSA file 202.10, Volunteer Army, RG 335, WNRC; Interv, author with Roger Kelley, 19 Oct 83.

[15] Memo, Lt Gen Kerwin for Gen Westmoreland, 20 Feb 70, sub: DOD Position on an All-Volunteer Armed Force, file 327.02, All Volunteer Army, HRC, CMH.

[16] Memo, Laird for the president, 11 Mar 70, sub: Future of the Draft, OSD file 340, RG 330, WNRC; Lee and Parker, *Ending the Draft*, pp. 68–69, 72.

[17] Analysis of the deliberations of the Anderson Committee is based on Brehm and Anderson Intervs; Memo, Martin Anderson for multiple addressees, 17 Mar 70, sub: Draft Memorandum on All-Volunteer Armed Force, OSD file 340, RG 330, WNRC; and Lee and Parker, *Ending the Draft*, pp. 71–72.

[18] Laird Interv.

[19] Weekly Compilation of Presidential Documents, Monday, 27 April 1970, pp. 571–75; Anderson Interv; Lee and Parker, *Ending the Draft*, pp. 72–74.

[20] *New York Times*, 24 April 1970, and 1 May 1970; *Washington Post*, 1 and 3 May 1970.

[21] Ltr, Richard Nixon to the author, 29 Jan 85. Nixon added that he no longer supported the volunteer force concept "even though the quality of the service has improved somewhat.... It simply is not a healthy situation to have our defenses in peace time manned almost exclusively (except for those from the service academies and ROTC) by those who have not attended college."

[22] Anderson Interv.

CHAPTER IV

Slicing the Pie

The Battle of the Budget, 1970

President Nixon's public decision to end the draft did not affect the Army immediately. Since the beginning of its investigation of the all-volunteer force issue in September 1968, Army thinking on the subject assumed that the draft would not end until fighting in Vietnam ended; transition to an all-volunteer Army, when it began, would be gradual, and induction authority would be retained. In May and June of 1970, preoccupied by the invasion of Cambodia and distracted by the domestic uproar that it precipitated, the Army failed to realize that Nixon's decision had shattered those comfortable assumptions.

The New Budget

The Department of Defense timetable dictated that the winding down of the Vietnam War and the phasing out of conscription occur simultaneously. Secretary of Defense Laird's private stipulation that draft calls end before he left office in January 1973 implied that an all-volunteer force must be functioning by that date even if troops remained in Vietnam. Furthermore, the as yet unannounced decision to ask for only a two-year extension of induction authority beginning in July 1971 signaled the administration's willingness to abandon peacetime conscription altogether. Although Army manpower planners had participated in the development of the Project Volunteer report, realization that the administration plan provided less time to achieve a zero draft dawned only gradually. This realization came about as the Army seriously began to turn the Project PROVIDE recommendations into a coherent program and prepare a budget request in support of its objectives.

The task of translating the PROVIDE recommendations into an approved Army program initially rested with Task Group PROVIDE, the successor of Colonel Butler's study group. The task group, although containing representatives from key elements of the Army staff, remained subordinate to the deputy chief of staff for personnel, General Kerwin, who in turn needed guidance on what to expect in the way of financial resources. Not until the start of the fiscal year 1972 budget cycle, which began in mid-1970, did the Army actively seek fiscal guidance from the Defense Department on all-volunteer force issues.

Two reasons account for the Army's failure to seek funds earlier to reduce reliance on the draft. First, long-range Department of Defense plans contained no provisions for the additional monies necessary for an all-volunteer force. Second, until President Nixon made public his decision on the broad outlines of the program to achieve an all-volunteer force (AVF) in April 1970, many of the Army's top leaders questioned the true depth of the administration's commitment to the goal and its willingness to spend money on such a project.

Even after Nixon announced that he would ask Congress for $2 billion in fiscal year 1972 for AVF initiatives, the Army remained skeptical. Most of the senior generals on the Army staff as well as Secretary of the Army Resor and Assistant Secretary Brehm continued to view Nixon's commitment to the AVF as politically motivated. They knew that several key congressional figures, notably John Stennis, chairman of the Senate Armed Services Committee, and F. Edward Hebert, chairman of the House Armed Services Committee, shared their opinion. All realized that a volunteer force would be expensive, perhaps too expensive in the long run. Some speculated that if Nixon succeeded in ending American involvement in Vietnam to the point that force reductions could be made, draft calls could be cut to tolerable levels. In that case, the reasoning went, the president, who also wanted to reduce the defense budget, would not press his request for AVF money.[1]

The Planning, Programming, Budgeting Systems, introduced by Secretary of Defense Robert S. McNamara during the Kennedy administration, governed the development of the defense budget of which the Army's budget was a part. The Five-Year Defense Program, which, as the name implied, contained a five-year projection of personnel requirements and costs necessary to support defense programs, served as the foundation of the annual budget.

In 1970 the five-year program contained no provisions for an all-volunteer force. Furthermore, the budget request for fiscal year 1971, already before Congress, contained no requests for funds in support of AVF goals. The budget cycle normally began 14 to 16 months preceding the beginning of the fiscal year when the Office of Management and Budget provided the secretary of defense with the president's fiscal guidance. Defense and service programs in the five-year plan were then reviewed and reconciled within the terms of the president's budget constraints; the services presented their requests to the Defense Department in the fall, and the secretary of defense, after consolidating those requests, presented his budget to the president in December or January for incorporation into the administration's budget submission to Congress.[2]

Since neither the five-year program nor the existing budget request contained provisions for an all-volunteer force, the services had no basis for initiating requests for AVF programs until Nixon, by his decision of 23 April 1970, provided the necessary fiscal guidance.

The planning cycle for the first AVF budget got under way in May 1970. The Project Volunteer report served as the starting point at the Defense Department level. Wollstadt's Project Volunteer Program Evaluation Group, assisted by budget analysts from the Department of Defense comptroller's office, estimated that the programs proposed in the Project Volunteer report for fiscal year 1972 would require $2.563 billion, nearly $600 million more than the president was willing to spend. Thus from the start it was evident that choices would have to be made. Kelley informed the services of this information on the morning of 9 June and told them they should prepare their input for the AVF budget with the $2 billion constraint in mind.[3]

That afternoon General Westmoreland met with key staff representatives to discuss the direction the Army should take in preparing its volunteer force budget request for fiscal year 1972. General Kerwin, fresh from the morning meeting with Kelley, told the group of the $2 billion planning figure, but expressed doubts that the administration would ultimately spend that much. As everyone knew, most of the $2 billion was for pay increases. Kerwin reasoned that the administration would postpone the pay increase until the anticipated post-Vietnam force reduction occurred. Lt. Gen. William DePuy, the assistant vice chief of staff, agreed. He related a conversation with unnamed contacts in Secretary Laird's office who doubted that Nixon would go through with the requested 20 percent across-the-board pay increase. If that were the case, DePuy suggested, the Army ought to build a case for funds for increases for recruiting, improving housing, and other measures designed to make service more attractive irrespective of a pay increase. Brig. Gen. J. B. Adamson, Kerwin's director of policy, plans, and studies, then briefed Westmoreland on the proposed plan for achieving an all-volunteer Army. The plan involved "taking the initiative for implementing those actions which the Army desires instead of waiting and risking the possibility of being told by higher authority what actions DA will have to take." He reviewed the PROVIDE recommendations and told the chief of staff that the Army should focus on increasing and improving the recruiting force, eliminating job dissatisfaction, and improving conditions of life in the service.

Westmoreland agreed. He said that if the administration set aside the pay increase it "would be receptive to expenditures of lesser amounts of money that would improve service attractiveness and recruiting." He directed his staff to "develop financially reasonable projects" and be ready to submit them "to OSD when a decision is made to eliminate the pay increase." General DePuy added that he thought the Army could make a case for about $700 million in non-pay items using this approach.[4]

Events in July seemed to confirm the Army's skepticism about the administration's willingness to support an all-volunteer force. That month the Defense Program Review Committee of the National Security Council told the Defense Department to prepare for a $6 billion reduction in its estimates of nearly $80 billion for the fiscal year 1972 budget proposal; the AVF was not exempted from the reduction. On receipt of this news Westmoreland reportedly told a member of Kelley's staff, "The story of my life in this building has been to be promised the resources to do a job and then to get short changed."[5]

Westmoreland was under pressure to devote greater attention to the all-volunteer force effort from other quarters in the summer of 1970. Not everyone involved in the effort to launch the Nixon administration's zero-draft program shared the Army's self-congratulatory view that it was moving forward forthrightly and vigorously in support of the president. On 18 August Westmoreland briefed Nixon on the state of the Army as part of a routine Joint Chiefs of Staff review of defense matters. In the course of his remarks, Westmoreland dwelled on the Army's well-known dependency on conscripts for the combat arms. The Army chief concluded, "for the next several years the Army will be heavily dependent upon the draft, and I believe that all of the other Services are also greatly dependent. I am concerned that Congress and the public may have the impression that we have an alternative to the draft in the short run."[6]

Westmoreland's statement was neither new nor inconsistent with previous Army positions. But when Martin Anderson, the key figure on the White House staff concerned with ending the draft, learned of Westmoreland's remarks, he considered them an attempt to reopen debate after the decision by the president. When, later in the month, Assistant Secretary of the Army Brehm made a similar statement at the annual conference of the Armed Forces Management Association, Anderson was incensed. He recommended to Nixon that Laird be directed to tell Westmoreland that "He could be Chief of Staff of the Army in support of an all-volunteer force or the ex–Chief of Staff of the Army in opposition to the AVF."[7] Westmoreland never received such a warning from Laird, but the message that the White House was unhappy with the lack of alacrity in the Army's all-volunteer program filtered down.

The Army Staff

Through the summer and into early autumn the Army staff worked closely with Assistant Secretary Brehm's office, laboring to meld the recommendations of the Project PROVIDE report into an action program. In the process the organizational structure of the Army staff elements working on the all-volunteer force issue underwent a dramatic metamorphosis. In August Westmoreland abolished the Project PROVIDE Task Force and established the All-Volunteer Army Division within the Office of the Deputy Chief of Staff for Personnel. The creation of yet another office to coordinate the effort to reduce reliance on the draft was intended in part to dramatize the Army's official support of the project. Many of the individuals who had worked on Project PROVIDE, including Lt. Col. Jack Butler, stayed on the job to assure continuity.

As development of the Army's fiscal year 1972 budget request progressed, problems began to arise. It soon became evident to the people closely concerned with the all-volunteer force issue that normal bureaucratic arrangements for coordinating the actions associated with developing the program were insufficient. Three considerations led to the conclusion that the All-Volunteer Army Division was not up to the task. First, as the individuals charged with putting together the budget request quickly realized, the actions necessary to achieve consensus on a budget cut across normal Army staff lines. The deputy chief of staff for personnel had many responsibilities besides the all-volunteer Army and was but one among equals with the other assistant and deputy chiefs of staff. He could not resolve budget disputes over programs outside his purview. Furthermore, once an approved and funded action plan was set into motion it would affect the activities of the Army in the field. There field commanders had their own priorities regarding such matters as training and construction.

As they began to consider the timetable for achieving zero reliance on the draft, a sense of urgency overtook the Army planners. Fiscal year 1972 would begin in July 1971. By then it was common knowledge that the Nixon administration would ask for only a two-year extension of the draft. That meant the Army would have only twenty-four months to achieve the all-volunteer force goal, a difficult task if money did not become available until the beginning of fiscal year 1972. And Laird's desire to end reliance on the draft by the time he left office cut six months off even that timetable. The Army thus could not wait until July 1971 to set its program into motion.

Brehm and Kerwin, the two men in the Army leadership charged with the day-to-day development of the all-volunteer Army program and budget, discussed the dilemma of insufficient time and inadequate organization frequently as the summer of 1970 wore on. They decided that the Army needed a full-time advocate for the AVF supported by a special staff charged with coordinating plans, budget, and implementation. Brehm and Kerwin realized that ending the Army's thirty-year reliance on the draft would be similar to introducing a major new weapons system; the task required a program manager. They discussed the concept with Secretary Resor and General Westmoreland, who agreed.[8]

The concept of a program manager for the all-volunteer Army appealed to Westmoreland for a variety of reasons. It elevated the office responsible for developing and implementing the program above the often parochial internal disputes over resources and priorities within the Army staff. The idea also appealed to Westmoreland's flair for the dramatic. A project manager had visibility; he could serve as tangible proof that the Army was serious about achieving an all-volunteer force. Westmoreland could have taken the role on himself, and he considered it. Chief of Naval Operations Admiral Elmo Zumwalt publicly supported ending the draft and was leading his service's zero-draft program. But Westmoreland chose not to follow Zumwalt's lead. He did not want to appear to be imitating the Navy. He also rejected the idea of designating the vice chief of staff project manager; such a move could be misconstrued as lack of interest on his part. The solution was to bring in a senior field commander, make him special assistant to the chief of staff and secretary of the Army, and give the program publicity.

Westmoreland discussed the idea with his deputies in September. Vice Chief of Staff General Bruce Palmer tried to dissuade him. Palmer saw the all-volunteer force "as a political decision and [said] that it was wrong for the Army to get out in front publicly." But Westmoreland had made up his mind. It was obvious that the White House wanted evidence of progress by the

Army. Unless the Army stepped up its level of activity it risked having policies dictated by higher authorities. Westmoreland decided to create a special project manager for the all-volunteer Army. He announced his decision at the annual conference of the Association of the U.S. Army (AUSA) in Washington on 13 October 1970.[9]

"I am announcing today that the Army is committed to an all-out effort in working toward a zero-draft—a volunteer force," Westmoreland declared. He reviewed the problems facing the Army and said that success required coordinated action in several areas. The Army must end personnel practices that discouraged enlistments and reenlistments. At the same time, he noted, improving service attractiveness must not lead to or be construed as a relaxation of professional standards. The effort demanded dedicated and imaginative leadership at all levels of the Army, Westmoreland said, but it could not be accomplished on the basis of good intentions and hard work alone. "[We] will not achieve our goal without the application of resources, and I mean money," Westmoreland told the audience. The Army would also need support from the leaders of American society—in business, the churches, education, the news media, and politics. Money was necessary to increase pay, rebuild barracks, and hire civilians to free soldiers from menial labor "so that our helicopter mechanics are not cutting grass and our radar technicians are not washing dishes." Public support was also essential to the success of the program to eliminate peacetime conscription because "We cannot attract the kind of soldier we need into an organization denigrated by some, directly attacked by others, and halfheartedly supported by many."

Westmoreland used the occasion formally to commit the Army to improve the climate of service and to challenge the nation to reciprocate with the money and moral support necessary to complete the task. He announced the appointment of a special project manager to oversee the Army's effort and to coordinate it with the other services and society.[10]

Westmoreland's speech to the AUSA conference accomplished several things. First, it represented a positive public statement of support for the all-volunteer concept and goal by the chief of staff of the Army. Westmoreland thus could be satisfied that he had answered his critics in the White House. Even so, he had not really recanted, if that was what Anderson expected. In the speech Westmoreland restated his conviction that retention of selective service legislation remained essential "as national insurance," and he again worried rhetorically about the prospects of the reserve components in a draft-free environment. Furthermore, by using the AUSA forum Westmoreland both informed and appealed for the support of one of the Army's most influential booster organizations. The association's membership consisted of active duty and retired officers and senior noncommissioned officers as well as civilian businessmen and civic leaders with ties to the Army. Westmoreland knew he needed the understanding and support of all of these groups to bring about the shift to an all-volunteer force. AUSA members and chapters located throughout the United States could spread the word that the Army was serious about ending its reliance on the draft. The membership of the AUSA also could lobby Congress in support of Army efforts to obtain money for volunteer force initiatives. The timing of the AUSA conference and Westmoreland's address facilitated this last point. Not coincidentally, the annual convention occurred in October 1970 as the Army was putting the finishing touches on its budget request for the coming fiscal year. Westmoreland's emphasis on the need for resources, "and I mean money," was a not-so-subtle message to the Defense Department, the White House, and Congress that if they truly wanted an all-volunteer force they needed the Army's cooperation and would have to pay for it.

SAMVA

Westmoreland handpicked Lt. Gen. George I. Forsythe, Jr., commanding general of the Army Combat Developments Command, to be the special assistant for the Modern Volunteer Army. Westmoreland considered Forsythe, who had commanded the Army's first airmobile division, the 1st Cavalry Division, in Vietnam, to be an innovator and capable of independent thought and action, qualities he deemed necessary in a project manager. Forsythe soon became known throughout the Army by the acronym for his position, SAMVA.

Forsythe accepted the job from Westmoreland with the understanding "that I was not going to be a 3-star recruiter and that I would have a role in reforming the Army." He demanded and received authority to establish objectives and set priorities for both the Army staff and Army commands to assure a smooth transition to an all-volunteer force. Forsythe also received review powers over staff and major command actions and programs as well as the authority to coordinate troop and public information programs related to the Army's effort to end reliance on conscription. He enjoyed direct access to Westmoreland and Resor and authority to coordinate directly with all command levels and staffs working on AVF matters. Thus, for example, Forsythe became a member of Roger Kelley's Project Volunteer committee as well as a member of all program and budget review committees that worked on volunteer Army money requests.[11]

The Army's request for fiscal year 1972 funds was virtually complete by the time Forsythe entered the picture. He shared the sense of urgency that led to the creation of his office and plunged into the final deliberations on the Army's budget proposal. He and Colonel Butler, who had moved from Task Group PROVIDE to the All-Volunteer Army Division and now to the newly created Office of the Special Assistant for the Modern Volunteer Army, helped write the justification for the Army request that Resor formally delivered to Laird on 3 November. In crafting the request they focused on the Army's greatest concern, the shortage of "true volunteers" for the combat arms.

Less than half of the men entering the Army in 1970 were considered true volunteers (as opposed to draft-motivated volunteers). But only 4 percent of those true volunteers joined the combat arms (Infantry, Armor, Artillery); only 2½ percent volunteered for the Infantry. In order to make the volunteer force successful, the Army had to increase enlistments for the combat arms 300 percent by June 1973. Enlistment and compensation specialists on General

Kerwin's and Assistant Secretary Brehm's staff wanted to try incentive pay to attract volunteers to the combat arms. In addition, Brehm's office accepted a Recruiting Command proposal, also recommended by Project PROVIDE, for a massive increase in recruiting advertising. As early as 1968 Butler's PROVIDE Task Group had pressed for money for quality-of-life experiments at an Army post. Now, in October 1970, Butler estimated that about $5 million would be necessary to end KP, rebuild barracks, and introduce labor-saving devices for miscellaneous duties at one test post. Forsythe agreed with all these schemes but, faced with the task of ending the Army's dependency on the draft in less than two years, considered Butler's experimental approach beginning in the new fiscal year insufficient. The SAMVA urged that the Army begin the experiments immediately and on a larger scale. He reasoned that successful initiatives could be continued on an even larger scale and new ideas tried when more money became available in fiscal year 1972.[12]

The Army Budget

Secretary Resor formally presented the Army's budget proposal for implementation of AVF initiatives to the secretary of defense on 3 November 1970. Exclusive of the across-the-board pay increase for all military personnel and a 20 percent raise for soldiers with less than two years' service contained in the president's fiscal guidance, Resor told Laird that the Army needed $718 million in fiscal year 1972 for the AVF program. In addition, he requested $131 million immediately in order to begin proposed experiments in fiscal year 1971. The former amount, Resor said, should be allocated from funds promised by the administration beginning in July 1971. The latter monies, he noted, "are not in the Army budget and cannot be provided by reprogramming without the self-defeating result of reducing or deleting other programs." Resor stressed the urgency of beginning all-volunteer Army experiments at once and asked Laird to provide the $131 million needed in fiscal year 1971 from Defense Department resources. His request for fiscal year 1972 was about $718 million. The breakdown of the request was as follows:

Category/Fiscal Year	FY 71	FY 72
I. Recruiting	15,450,000	96,600,000
II. Proficiency Pay for Combat Arms	90,000,000	302,000,000
III. Service Attractiveness	20,775,000	259,240,000
IV. Program Flexibility & Contingencies	5,000,000	60,000,000
TOTAL	131,225,000	717,840,000

Resor explained that the Army intended to focus on attracting and retaining men for the combat arms, its most difficult task. Money for recruiting was aimed at increasing the size of the Recruiting Command, providing additional pay and benefits to recruiters, and advertising. Combat arms proficiency pay would be managed in two ways. First, the Army would offer $150 per month to men with infantry, armor, and artillery skills to encourage them to stay in the combat arms. Second, it would extend the incentive pay to enlistees who volunteered for those skills for thirty or more months. Improvements in service attractiveness were necessary because "There is no way to keep good men in the Army if they cannot find satisfaction in their day-to-day work, and a moderate degree of comfort for themselves and their families."[13]

The substance of the interservice debate that took place over the all-volunteer force budgetary allocations for the coming year occurred in the Project Volunteer committee where the Army's request immediately ran afoul of budgetary limitations imposed by the Defense Department and objections from the other services. At the first Project Volunteer committee meeting in November 1970, Kelley told the services to plan on only $1.3 billion in fiscal year 1972 instead of the $2 billion originally identified by Nixon in his message of 23 April. Kelley's scheme for dividing the funds included $945 million for pay, allowances, and benefits increases and $415 million for everything else. The Army had thus asked for more for its non-pay initiatives than Kelley was prepared to offer everybody. Three days later the Army came back with a scaled-down request.

Under Secretary of the Army Thaddeus R. Beal, acting for Resor, prepared the revised request. His arguments on behalf of the Army revealed both the logic by which the Army approached the task of ending reliance on the draft and its determination to buck the norms of budget bargaining to obtain what it believed necessary to accomplish the task. The Army, Beal said, could cut its proposal for proficiency pay for armor and artillery volunteers to $100. This action shaved $60 million from its requirement for the rest of fiscal year 1971 and $195 million in fiscal year 1972. Beal went on to suggest that if Kelley reduced the amount proposed for additional pay and allowances, enough money could be found within the $1.3 billion to cover the 20 percent raise for enlisted members under two years of service and a variable housing allowance. Give the Army what it wanted, and the Defense Department would still have $270 million left for the other services' programs.

Beal justified the Army's "hard-ball" proposal with an argument that would form the bedrock of the service's request for all-volunteer force funds for the duration of the transition. He acknowledged the reality of limited funds but emphasized that "The task is not to give a share of the funds to every program, or to every service. It is to reduce draft calls to zero by July 1973." Beal went on to point out that only the Army relied on the draft. In fiscal year 1970, he wrote, only 4,000 true volunteers joined the combat arms; the Army needed that many combat arms volunteers a month in FY 72. He strongly urged Laird to approve the Army's proposal and warned, "there is... skepticism in some quarters as to whether the zero-draft effort is mere rhetoric, or we really mean business." Allocating limited funds in a pragmatic fashion would signal to skeptics in the services and Congress that the Army was serious.[14]

The Navy and Air Force objected. Both wanted a piece of the proficiency pay proposal or something like it. The Army proposed using proficiency pay as an incentive for combat arms enlistments and retention by withholding it until a recruit qualified for it after basic training. The Air Force opposed this plan on the grounds that it lacked visibility. According to the Air Force representative to the Project Volunteer committee, "A bonus is far more visible, provides an immediate larger reward, and we think will have a greater effect on enlistments at a lower cost." If, however, proficiency pay was approved, "the Air Force has combat and other skills which would qualify for pro pay under this proposal." The Navy, on the other hand, voiced no specific objections to the proficiency pay concept, but insisted that, "If it is decided to apply it to the Army, it must also be applied to the Marine Corps in the same manner; and... an improved sea pay program must be applied to the Navy."

The Air Force voiced other criticisms as well. While willing to support modest expenditures for a paid recruiting advertising experiment, the Air Force argued that the Army should not be permitted to proceed on its own; a common approach was preferred. The Air Force also complained that the Army's request for barracks rehabilitation funds left nothing for the other services. Throughout its critique of the Army's proposal the Air Force argued for equity; the Navy, though not as strident, also demanded its fair share of the $1.3 billion Kelley had to offer.[15]

Army planners viewed the other services' demands for an equitable share of Project Volunteer funds with scorn and their arguments on behalf of equity as disingenuous. None of the other services, including the Marine Corps, relied on the draft to supplement their enlisted needs in 1970. Unquestionably many of the volunteers for those services were draft motivated. The Navy, for example, estimated that over half of its enlistees in 1970 were true volunteers and concluded that it could meet its fiscal year 1972 manpower requirements without a pay raise. The Air Force had, since its inception, attracted both the quantity and quality of youths it needed for its enlisted ranks. Thus, when the Air Force chief of staff demanded an equal share of funds available for Project Volunteer recruiting initiatives on the grounds that the Army to Air Force ratio of nondraft enlistments was less than two to one, Army manpower planners were incensed.

The Army also greeted an Air Force request for equity in barracks rehabilitation funds with disdain. With few exceptions, the Air Force boasted the most modern barracks and facilities throughout the world. Many Army enlisted men in the United States lived in barracks constructed during World War II that remained in use ten years beyond their life expectancy. Army barracks in Europe which, with few exceptions, had been taken over from the German armed forces in 1945 dated to the late nineteenth or early twentieth centuries and were in wretched condition. When Vietnam War exigencies cut funds for facilities maintenance to the bone in the middle and late 1960s, these antiquated facilities had become only worse.[16]

Assistant Secretary of Defense Kelley attempted to resolve the differences. Negotiations over the division of the nonpay portion of the all-volunteer force portion of the fiscal year 1972 budget took place within the context of the Project Volunteer committee, over which Kelley continued to preside. He had been pleased with the degree of consensus achieved by the committee during the formulation of the Defense Department alternative to the Gates Commission report recommendations. Now Kelley saw the Army separating itself from the rest of the services, trying to "achieve more budget dollars that would be taken out of the hides of the other services." He attempted to broker the budget, but the other services retaliated. Only partial consensus was restored. All agreed that waiting to initiate actions until the beginning of FY 72 was unwise. No one agreed on what actions should begin immediately or from where the funds would come. The services achieved consensus on a 20 percent pay raise for enlisted men with less than two years' service, the need for increased recruiting and an experiment with paid advertising, barracks improvement, and special initiatives for increasing enlistments and retention through a reduction in service life irritants. They also agreed that the active forces needed immediate attention while problems facing reserve components could wait. The issues of proficiency pay for hard-to-fill skills and the Army's plans to try prime-time television and radio recruiting advertising and substituting civilians for soldiers on KP remained unresolved.

Secretary Laird broke the impasse in December. He gave the Army substantially what it wanted for nonpay items. Laird agreed to include $105 million for experiments to improve service quality of life and for stepped up recruiting (including advertising) and $209 million in the fiscal year 1972 budget request. In each case the distribution of funds favored the Army. Laird also approved money for a combat arms enlistment incentive, but opted for a bonus instead of proficiency pay to soothe Air Force objections. Only the Army could pay the bonus initially. Laird retained $446 million in funds and directed Kelley to allocate them so as to reduce reliance on the draft to zero by the end of calendar year 1972.

In reaching his decisions in favor of the Army, Laird drew on the conclusions of a study prepared by Philip Odeen, his assistant for system analysis. Odeen told Laird that except for the Army the services "have had more potential volunteers than they have enlisted." The planned 20 percent pay increase for entry level enlisted personnel combined with force reductions "should preclude the possibility of a manpower gap occurring for the Air Force, Navy or Marine Corps." The Army had the problem and, therefore, should get the bulk of the money. He proposed creating a contingency fund to offset shortages in the other services should they develop. On the subject of combat arms incentives Odeen favored bonuses over proficiency pay. A larger lump-sum bonus had more visibility and would attract more enlistments. He calculated that "where $100 million in Army proficiency pay would draw 7,500 new accessions, the same amount in first-term Army bonuses would draw 15,500 new accessions."

Laird's decision on the structure of the fiscal year 1972 budget allocations for volunteer force initiatives also reflected Odeen's analysis. High draft calls in fiscal year 1972 would bring in two-year men (draftees and draft-motivated volunteers) who would leave uniform in large numbers in 1973 and 1974. Odeen argued that allocation of funds to emphasize recruiting, bonuses, and unexpected shortages in fiscal year 1972 would support a strategy of lower draft calls and reduce problems in fiscal year 1973 and beyond. He cautioned, however, that any plan to hold down inductions be kept internal, "thus reserving the use of higher calls as insurance."

Odeen also noted the relationship between the draft and the war in Vietnam. Large draft calls in fiscal year 1972, especially in the first half of the fiscal year (July–December 1971) raised the concern that draftees would continue to be sent to the war zone. Two-thirds of the Army's combat arms enlisted men were draftees. Laird's schedule for Vietnamization of the war envisioned about a 50,000-man force in Vietnam by June 1973, 30,000 of whom would be Army personnel. It was preferred that all be volunteers.[17]

The revised Project Volunteer budget proposal went to Dr. Henry Kissinger, the national security adviser in the White House, in mid-January as part of the Department of Defense request for fiscal year 1972 funds. Under Secretary of Defense David Packard summarized the rationale for Laird's request, highlighted problems, and analyzed alternative proposals to distribute the large contingency fund Laird had established. Packard made clear the point that long-term success of the all-volunteer force effort depended to a large extent on how the $1.3 billion allocated for fiscal year 1972 was divided. The general strategy, he said,

is to invest heavily in programs with known effects, focus on the critical problem areas (principally the Army enlisted manpower gap), provide limited initial funding for some of the long lead time problems (e.g., officers, doctors), and undertake a number of limited experimental programs.

Packard acknowledged that the proposal as advanced did not solve all of the problems envisioned in implementing an all-volunteer force even in fiscal year 1972. He reminded Kissinger that "we cannot afford to look only at FY 72, since our success in reducing the FY 72 draft affects the size of our FY 74 problem." It is not clear whether the "FY 74 problem" to which Packard referred was the size of the defense budget, which, presumably, would be affected by the cost of ending the draft, or the ability of the Nixon administration to end the draft prior to the 1974 congressional election. In either case, the Defense Department preferred to proceed cautiously in fiscal year 1972 and evaluate the effects on the manpower gap of the 20 percent pay raise, the increases in recruiting activities, and the Army's combat-arms bonus experiment before committing itself to a larger increase in basic pay or an across-the-board raise in military compensation. "Although we hope to achieve a low draft in '72, we plan to begin '72 with conservative draft calls. This provides a hedge against unanticipated problems since it would be undesirable to start low and then be forced to increase draft calls in FY 72," Packard explained. If problems did develop, Packard reasoned, maintaining a sizable contingency fund was advisable. On the other hand, he noted, the strategy "provides the option of a rapid phase down during FY 72, if the results of the Zero Draft spending programs warrant." Alternative uses for the contingency fund included offering unrestricted enlistment bonuses for all new enlistees in fiscal year 1972 or an additional basic pay raise. Packard, who preferred retaining a contingency fund to deal with unforeseen problems, counseled against the alternative options.[18]

The Defense Program Review Committee, of which Kissinger was a member, approved the basic strategy outlined by Packard, but recommended that the Defense Department place greater emphasis on increasing new enlistments in all services in fiscal year 1972. The committee wanted greater assurance that draft calls in 1972 would be lowered as far as possible.

Following the Defense Program Review Committee's guidance, the final version of the all-volunteer force portion of the fiscal year 1972 defense budget that Laird sent to the White House requested $1.52 billion for Project Volunteer initiatives. Instead of a 20 percent increase for all enlisted men with less than two years' service beginning in January 1971, Laird asked for an average pay raise of 36 percent for junior officers and first term enlisted personnel effective July 1971. This change reflected Laird's desire to boost new entries in the first year of the transition and his emphasis on increasing accessions immediately as opposed to a more gradual shift to volunteerism. Laird took the money for the additional pay from the contingency fund, but left Kelley over $106 million for emergencies. Of the nonpay items, the Army, which had 52 percent of the requirements, received 64 percent of the funds.

Despite its success in arguing its case, the Army continued to voice preference for proficiency pay instead of a combat arms enlistment bonus. The Army wanted to begin offering proficiency pay immediately and was prepared to do so with reprogrammed funds. Legislative authority for proficiency pay already existed, and it could be expanded under current law. A bonus, on the other hand, would require congressional approval. That could take months, the Army argued, and the delay in lost volunteers could be costly. Furthermore, the Recruiting Command was preparing to feature the special combat arms proficiency pay in a paid, prime-time radio and television advertising experiment. The Army's arguments failed to move Laird and irritated Kelley, who did not want the consensus achieved in December disturbed. Reluctantly, Laird agreed to let the Army argue its proficiency pay case before Congress, but he passed the word to the White House and Capitol Hill that he preferred the bonus.[19]

Nixon incorporated the package in his annual budget message to Congress on 28 January 1971 without alteration. At the same time the president finally made public his intent to ask for only a two-year extension of induction authority. It was now up to the Defense Department and the services to convince Congress that an all-volunteer force was desirable, practical, and affordable.

Thereafter Congress spent eight months in 1971 conducting hearings, preparing legislation, debating, and finally approving a two-year extension of induction authority and raising military pay to attract more volunteers. In the end, the Nixon administration received more than it asked for—or wanted—in some areas. The administration had requested $908 million in pay raises for 1972 as phase I of a two-part pay package with the intention of asking for more in 1973. Congress, which apparently arrived at the same conclusion as did Laird, reasoned that a larger pay raise in the first year of the transition would give the process a better chance of success and doubled the pay hike by authorizing $1,825.4 million. Congress also approved $276 million for nonpay Project Volunteer programs in 1972.[20]

The Army received one very rude surprise from Congress during consideration of the volunteer force legislative package. The Senate reduced the authorized average strength of the armed forces for 1972 by 56,000. The Army's share of the cut came to 50,000. Senator John Stennis justified the action on the grounds that withdrawals from Vietnam and modest reductions in support troops in Europe made the strength cuts possible. Senator Peter Dominick of Colorado suggested other motives. By reducing military end strength in 1972, Congress reduced the potential margin for failure of recruiting in the first year without a draft. If a deficit did occur it would be smaller and could be reduced or eliminated at lower cost by yet another pay increase in the following year.[21]

Except for the reduction in strength, the implementation of which caused considerable turmoil, the Army fared well with the Congress in 1971. The Army's success at influencing the Defense Department's input to the administration budget request paid off. But the process had taken precious time, and the end of induction authority was less than two years away. Fortunately the Army, particularly General Forsythe and his "SAMVA Warriors," had not been idle. While Congress deliberated the future of peacetime conscription through the summer of 1971, Forsythe had already begun to wean the Army away from the draft.

Notes

[1] Resor, Brehm, Palmer, and Kerwin Intervs.

[2] For a good description of the PPBS, see Lawrence J. Korb, *The Joint Chiefs of Staff: The First Twenty-Five Years* (Bloomington: Indiana University Press, 1976), pp. 111–28, especially pp. 121–28, for the system during Laird's tenure as secretary of defense. See also Amos A. Jordon and William J. Taylor, Jr., *American National Security: Policy and Process* (Baltimore: Johns Hopkins University Press, 1981), pp. 185–87, 192–95.

[3] MFR, Lt Col O'Connor, 11 Jun 70, sub: Implementation of the Volunteer Army Concept, All-Volunteer Army file, HRC, CMH. See also Lee and Parker, *Ending the Draft*, p. 75.

[4] MFR, Lt Col O'Connor, 11 Jun 70, sub: Implementation of the Volunteer Army Concept, All-Volunteer Army file, HRC, CMH.

[5] The Defense Program Review Committee consisted of the president's national security adviser, deputy secretary of defense, under secretary of state, chairman of the JCS, director of the Office of Management and Budget, and chairman of the President's Council of Economic Advisers; see Korb, p. 124. The announcement of the $6 billion reduction and Westmoreland's reaction are in Lee and Parker, *Ending the Draft*, pp. 75–76.

[6] "Notes for JCS Discussion with President Nixon," 18 Aug 70, History File, Westmoreland Papers, HRC, CMH.

[7] "The Volunteer Army," Address by William K. Brehm at the Annual Conference, Armed Forces Management Association, Los Angeles, Calif., 21 Aug 70, All-Volunteer Army file, HRC, CMH; Anderson Interv. In an interview with the author Laird dismissed Anderson's charge that Westmoreland spoke against the AVF after Nixon's decision. "There's one thing about Westy," Laird said, "When he got the word, he marched." Laird did recall asking Westmoreland to keep his views on the long-term need for a draft to himself for a while. Westmoreland denies being pressured into more open support. "The decision was made by the President and transmitted to me by the Secretary of Defense; I complied." Rumors that a confrontation between Laird and Westmoreland occurred at an Airlie House Conference on 18–19 September 1970 circulated among the Army staff that fall. Former Secretary Resor and Assistant Secretary Brehm, both present at that conference, deny the allegation. Laird, Resor, and Brehm Intervs; and telephone Intervs, author with Westmoreland, Forsythe, and Butler, 28 Feb 83.

[8] Brehm and Kerwin Intervs.

[9] Based on Interv, author with Forsythe, 24 Oct 80, and Palmer Interv.

[10] Westmoreland to the Annual Luncheon, Association of the United States Army, Washington, D.C., 13 Oct 70, Speeches files, Westmoreland Papers, HRC, CMH.

[11] Forsythe and Palmer Intervs; Draft CSM, 25 Oct 70, sub: Special Assistant for the Modern Volunteer Army (SAMVA), All-Volunteer Army file, HRC, CMH.

[12] Brehm, Kerwin, Forsythe, and Butler Intervs. As previously noted, this chapter deals largely with the development of the Army's budget request and interaction with DOD on the subject. Detailed development of the Modern Volunteer Army Program is treated in Chapter VI.

[13] Memo, Resor for Laird, 2 Nov 70, sub: Volunteer Army Actions, OSA file 202.10, RG 335, WNRC.

[14] Memo, Beal for Laird, 6 Nov 70, sub: Volunteer Army Actions, OSA file 202.10, RG 335, WNRC. See also Lee and Parker, *Ending the Draft*, pp. 78–80.

[15] Memos, Assistant Secretary of the Air Force for Kelley, 5 Nov 70, sub: Project Volunteer, and 8 Dec 70, sub: Air Force Comments on Project Volunteer Actions; and Assistant Secretary of the Navy for Kelley, 9 Dec 70, sub: Project Volunteer. All in OSD file 340, RG 330, WNRC.

[16] Memo, Chief of Staff of the Air Force for Sec AF, 21 Dec 70, sub: Project Volunteer, OSD file 340, RG 330, WNRC; System Analysis and Long Range Objectives Division, Office of the Chief of Naval Operations, "Impact of an All-Volunteer Force on the Navy in the 1972–1973 Time Frame," Dec 70, p. iii; Brehm, Kester, and Forsythe Intervs.

[17] Phillip Odeen, "Implementation of A Zero Draft Program," n.d., forwarded to Laird 14 Dec 70, in OSD file 340, RG 330, WNRC; MFR, Brig Gen R. E. Pursley, 4 Jan 71, sub: Decision from the December 15, 1970, Volunteer Service Meeting with Messrs. Laird and Packard, OSD file 340, RG 330, WNRC.

[18] Memo, David Packard for Kissinger, 15 Jan 71, w/four attachments, OSD file 340, RG 330, WNRC. This memo and its attachments formed the basis for the administration's final review of the all-volunteer force budget for FY 72 before it went to the president for inclusion in the annual budget message.

[19] Memos, Packard for Secretary of the Army, 12 Jan 71, sub: Army Zero Draft Request for FY 71; and Laird for Kissinger, 26 Jan 71, both in OSD file 340, RG 330, WNRC; see also Lee and Parker, *Ending the Draft*, pp. 83–87.

[20] U.S. Congress, *Congressional Quarterly Almanac*, 27, 92d Cong., 1st sess., 1971, p. 293.

[21] U.S. Congress, Senate, *Congressional Record*, 92d Cong., 1st sess., May 6, 1971, pp. 13913, 13917–18; Senate Armed Services Committee Report 92–93, May 5, 1971, pp. 64–67.

CHAPTER V

The Manpower Laboratory
SAMVA And the Modern Volunteer Army Program

The Army could not wait to see how Congress responded to the selective service extension and military pay increase bills that formed the heart of the Nixon administration's program to end the draft by 1973. The urgency that led to the creation of a special assistant for the modern volunteer Army (SAMVA) in the autumn of 1970 did not flag. General Forsythe threw himself into the job and was involved almost immediately in virtually every aspect of Army activities. Like the men who created his position—Westmoreland, Brehm, and Kerwin—Forsythe harbored grave concerns about the institutional health of the Army. He too saw in the all-volunteer force concept an opportunity to reestablish order and professional standards in the military.

SAMVA Planning

Forsythe's charter directed him to develop a comprehensive program and implementation plan for achieving a volunteer Army by mid-1973. He viewed the task as a twofold project. To meet the zero-draft goal, the Army recruiting system needed a total overhaul. After a generation of reliance on selective service, recruiters had lost the knack for seeking out potential volunteers and selling the Army to them. Recruiters had become order takers. True volunteers and draft-motivated volunteers came to the recruiter and essentially accepted what limited choices the Army offered. The recruiting force for an all-volunteer Army would have to be larger, innovative, and dynamic. It would also need a different product to "sell" to potential volunteers, and improving the product—making the Army attractive to prospective volunteers—was Forsythe's second task.

Forsythe believed that the success of the volunteer force concept depended on creating the kind of Army young people would want to join. To make the Army attractive involved increasing pay, reducing irritants of service life, and, most important to Forsythe, restoring professionalism. The pay initiative represented the least controversial aspect of the program as Forsythe began his work. He would focus his attention on internal improvements.

Project PROVIDE suggested numerous ideas for eliminating unproductive tasks and dehumanizing practices associated with Army enlisted life, and

Forsythe had thoughts of his own on how to enhance the professional image of soldiering. What he lacked was empirical data. Thus, Forsythe concluded that his first order of business was to conduct experiments with the various proposals to make the Army attractive to volunteers. Only then would he have a basis for developing a true program for ending reliance on the draft. Forsythe's dilemma lay in the fact that the Army had only thirty months to accomplish everything. He would have to conduct his experiments, overhaul the recruiting system, and develop his program simultaneously.

Forsythe faced one more problem as he began his assignment as SAMVA. Many career and noncommissioned officers in the Army harbored grave reservations about the volunteer force concept. As the congressional debate over draft extension and the pay raise began and Forsythe launched his experiments, expressions of dissent over ending the draft began to be heard from the career ranks and auxiliary circles such as retiree and veterans groups. Thus Forsythe soon found himself on the road explaining and justifying his evolving program as much to the Army itself as to foes and skeptics outside of the service.[1]

The first month proved especially hectic. As the head of a previously nonexistent office, Forsythe had to create his organization from scratch. Initially he leaned heavily on Colonel Butler, who provided a valuable link between the study and the experimental phases of the transition. Butler's tenure, however, was shortlived. Recently selected for promotion to colonel, he would soon depart to attend the Army War College. Thus, although Butler was a valuable source of information and continuity, Forsythe needed his own people in the new organization.[2]

One of Forsythe's first actions on assuming the role of SAMVA was to name his deputy and begin to pull together a staff. The off-line nature of his organization allowed Forsythe to range widely in his search. He wanted Col. Robert M. Montague, Jr., with whom he had worked as a member of Ambassador Robert W. Komer's personal staff during the latter's direction of the Civil Operations and Revolutionary Development Support (CORDS) program in Vietnam. Montague served as an aide to Komer in both the White House and Saigon where the CORDS chief gained the reputation for using unconventional means for solving problems. Forsythe, who served as Komer's deputy, frequently found himself smoothing waters between the CORDS staff and military and other civilian agencies in Washington and Vietnam.[3] Now Forsythe sought Montague for the same role in his new organization.

Montague joined SAMVA in November 1970 and brought with him a wealth of ideas about how to make the all-volunteer concept work. He came directly from commanding the 5th Infantry Division Artillery at Fort Carson, Colorado, where he had dealt with soldiers on a daily basis, observed their living and working conditions, and knew firsthand of the frustrations they faced. His assignment at Fort Carson coincided with Maj. Gen. Bernard Rogers' tenure as commander of the 5th Infantry Division (Mechanized). Under Rogers' leadership the division experimented with several nontraditional approaches to solving personnel problems that Montague would later commend to Forsythe as they launched the Modern Volunteer Program.

When Rogers had taken over the 5th Division in September 1969 the division suffered from all of the problems associated with the U.S. Army of that period: high personnel turnover, crime, absences, drug abuse, and racial conflict. Discipline, morale, and combat readiness dropped steadily. Resorting to traditional Army methods such as investigations and punishment aimed at isolating and eliminating "troublemakers" or vigorous training to instill soldier pride and unit esprit failed to stem the decline.

In February 1970 Rogers took a new approach. Recognizing that the soldiers in his division—like the soldiers throughout the Army—were mostly draftees and Vietnam returnees with little commitment to the service, Rogers rejected further attempts to compel or intimidate them into acceptable behavior and chose to co-opt them. He established an Enlisted Man's Council. Junior enlisted soldiers (grade E–4 and below) elected company representatives who met regularly with their battalion commander. The company representatives elected a battalion representative who became part of a brigade council. Brigade representatives, in turn, constituted the division council that met with Rogers. The council brought the views, complaints, and suggestions of the lowest ranks—who constituted the largest number of soldiers at Fort Carson—directly to Rogers' attention, unfiltered by layers of intervening command levels.

The council generated ideas immediately. Rogers adopted 70 percent of the council's early suggestions for improving enlisted living and working conditions at Fort Carson. He ended Saturday morning inspection and daily reveille and retreat formations. Soldiers received permission to partition their barracks and decorate them to taste. Bright colors, black lights, and psychedelic posters blossomed. Enlisted clubs on post took on the appearances of coffee houses, and officers were encouraged to drop in and "rap" with the men. Traditionalists decried the experiments, charged that the council undermined authority, and predicted disintegration of the chain of command.

Nothing of the sort happened. Within ten months reenlistments at Fort Carson increased 45 percent, absences and criminal activities declined, and morale among junior enlisted soldiers went up. Rogers said the new system merely forced the Army to "give a damn about the soldier." Col. David Hughes, Rogers' chief of staff, concluded that the approach worked because "when mistrustful soldiers saw that their complaints and suggestions actually got a hearing, and they got an answer, they began to trust." Furthermore, a sense of reciprocity developed. As the soldiers received more discretion over their daily affairs, they accepted the responsibility of self-discipline. Peer pressure often brought into line soldiers who deviated from the new standards and abused newly won privileges.[4]

Montague's experience at Fort Carson convinced him that changes in lifestyle could make the Army more attractive to volunteers and, moreover, were necessary even if the draft was retained. His experience on Ambassador Komer's staff convinced him that innovative programs often required unorthodox means of implementation to assure success. Montague combined his attitudes and experience in a zealous determination to push SAMVA initiatives without regard to normal Army staff procedures. He expected resistance not out of ulterior motives but due to bureaucratic inertia and traditionalism. The former would involve requirements to coordinate things fully throughout the staff with all the attendant delays, budgetary squabbles, and misunderstandings or misinterpretations. Traditional resistance would come from those in the Army who feared that change would undermine discipline and readiness.

Montague developed a system to overcome resistance. General Westmoreland and Secretary of the Army Resor, as well as Resor's successor, Robert F. Froehlke, all supported the all-volunteer force. Montague figured out which one was more likely to support a specific idea and, using Forsythe's unique access, first approached the office most likely to give him a favorable hearing. If he failed to get past the vice chief of staff or secretary of the General Staff on an issue, "we'd go to Mr. Resor or Mr. Froehlke and have them walk through the door of the Chief of Staff and announce what they had decided to do."[5]

Montague also identified and "made friends" with those people who supported the volunteer force concept elsewhere in the defense establishment and Washington. Within the Army Montague worked closely with Clayton Gompf, a retired colonel on Assistant Secretary of the Army Brehm's staff who was a confidant of Secretary Resor. He developed a similar relationship with Gus Lee, a career civil servant on Roger Kelley's defense manpower staff. Later Montague established contacts with aides to members of Congress supportive of the all-volunteer force, notably Andrew Effron of Congressman William Steiger's staff and Stephen Herbits, the former Gates Commission member who as a member of Senator Robert Stafford's staff was considered the chief theoretician of the antidraft forces on Capitol Hill.

Montague used these contacts in a variety of ways. Through Gompf and Lee he could bypass normal staff procedures and obtain information or send requests directly into the Army and defense secretariats. Informal contacts on Capitol Hill proved useful when the Army needed to build support for programs unpopular with key members of the Armed Services Committee or defense appropriations subcommittees.[6]

With Montague on board Forsythe worked out a method of operations. Initially he, Montague, and Butler would put together a tentative program. Forsythe would sell it to the senior leadership and go on the road to help build support within the Army and before Congress. Montague would push it through the staff. "Montague was my bulldozer," Forsythe later recalled. From Butler the SAMVA acquired what Forsythe termed his list of "'670 Jim Dandy things' that had come up in these previous studies as to what you could do to have a volunteer Army." The proposed innovations included changes in everything from personnel policies, training systems, and logistics management to regulations governing soldiers' off-duty time, hair styles, and even how they decorated their living spaces.

With Westmoreland's concurrence Forsythe decided to launch the Modern Volunteer Army Program (MVAP) dramatically by having the chief of staff announce several innovative changes Army-wide. The next step would be the inauguration of a series of experiments at various Army bases in the United States. The purpose of the former initiative was to display immediate Army action on behalf of the all-volunteer effort following Westmoreland's speech to the AUSA convention in October 1970. Launching the experiments at selected Army posts would also demonstrate action as well as gather needed empirical data, but it would do so without shocking the institution. Forsythe knew that many in the Army were uneasy over the volunteer force concept. By experimenting first he hoped to reassure doubters that "it's not going to happen all over until it's tried."[7]

Forsythe's operation began to develop its proposals for Army-wide initiatives, field experiments, recruiting reorganization, and an overall master plan to integrate the volunteer Army effort simultaneously in November 1970. Each of these efforts represented a major undertaking and promised to have a significant impact on the Army. What would become the Master Program for the Modern Volunteer Army was only dimly visible. It was like a jigsaw puzzle made up of blank pieces. Many ideas would yield unacceptable or unintended consequences and ultimately be rejected. From the start it was a trial-and-error effort.[8]

The Modern Volunteer Army Program

The broad outline of what became the Modern Volunteer Army Program was already visible when Forsythe assumed his role as SAMVA. The all-volunteer Army would be achieved by simultaneous action along three fronts: development of incentives designed to attract new recruits; improvement of service attractiveness; and adoption of new recruitment practices aimed at informing prospective volunteers about the "new" Army. Low- or no-cost initiatives in support of the three components of the program were to be implemented Army-wide as they were approved. Initiatives that required funds were to be tried on an experimental basis first. If these experiments yielded promising results, funds for full-scale implementation would be requested.

What the program lacked was a conceptual framework acceptable at once to the Army, the supporters of the all-volunteer force, and the congressmen who held the purse strings. Ending reliance on the draft was an obvious goal, but emphasizing that aim contained risks. Many career soldiers and key members of Congress openly doubted the value of ending peacetime inductions. Forsythe thus chose to emphasize professionalism as the goal of the Modern Volunteer Army Program. The idea was not new. From the beginning of the Army's internal examinations of the all-volunteer concept members of the study groups and leaders who reviewed their efforts agreed that the post-Vietnam Army needed substantial improvements regardless of whether the draft ended or not. Westmoreland and Palmer established the basis for a philosophical framework for the Army's all-volunteer effort when they approved the PROVIDE recommendations in October 1969.

Forsythe, Montague, and Butler roughed out the program in a series of day and night sessions between mid-October and 6 November 1970. The stated goal of the Modern Volunteer Army Program was "to create a professionally challenging and personally rewarding Army," which, as a salubrious by-product, could get along without conscription.[9]

Initially Forsythe intended to increase professionalism by a mixture of actions aimed at improving training and job satisfaction. Many measures were targeted at the individual soldier. Efforts to upgrade service life, such as higher pay and better housing, also contributed to enhanced professionalism. A more professionally attractive Army represented the product that Forsythe expected recruiters to sell to volunteers. The second major component of the program would involve rebuilding and reorienting the sales force.

But the exigencies of the situation that set the zero-draft goal at 31 December 1972 demanded a significant increase of voluntary enlistments almost immediately. As noted earlier, Department of the Army manpower experts had estimated that enlistments of true volunteers would have to increase 300 percent overall to sustain an active force of 900,000; the combat arms required a 1,200 percent increase. In order to attract volunteers immediately, before improvements in service attractiveness took hold, Forsythe added a third component—enlistment incentives—to the program.

Consistent with his recognition of the needs of the combat arms, Forsythe emphasized actions to improve professionalism and incentives to attract volunteers to the Infantry, Armor, and Artillery. No-cost or low-cost initiatives were to be applied throughout the Army, but initiatives requiring money would for the most part be aimed at the combat arms initially and on an experimental basis only.

Westmoreland authorized experiments in each of the three component areas of the Modern Volunteer Army Program. To test combinations of ideas aimed at improving service attractiveness and military professionalism, Forsythe proposed a series of field experiments at four Army posts in the United States and in Europe. Essentially he planned to adopt the ongoing experiment at Fort Carson and, beginning in January 1971, to expand it to include a basic training facility (Fort Ord), an installation oriented toward junior officers and noncommissioned officers (Fort Benning), a second troop location in the United States (Fort Bragg), and selected troop centers in Germany (USAREUR). Forsythe dubbed the experiments Project VOLAR (*Vol*unteer *Ar*my). He intended to use the initial VOLAR posts as test beds. Each post commander would receive $5 million with which to try out ideas aimed at improving training, living and working conditions, and career attractiveness. Successful ideas would be tried elsewhere beginning in July 1971 (fiscal year 1972). Following further refinement Forsythe intended to inaugurate worldwide application of proven actions in fiscal year 1973.

Westmoreland also approved the SAMVA's proposal to seek authority to offer proficiency pay to volunteers for the combat arms. During the planning stage of this proposal in late October 1970 General Forsythe justified the concept as "special pay for special people." Although the other services and Defense Department manpower experts continued to oppose the proficiency pay, he wanted to avoid offering enlistment bonuses, which he considered bounties. Proficiency pay had to be earned through meeting prescribed standards. Enlistment bonuses, on the other hand, required nothing more than the act of volunteering for specific hard-to-fill positions. Laird had overruled Westmoreland and requested money for enlistment bonuses in fiscal year 1972. But Forsythe persisted, and Laird reluctantly permitted the Army to request permission from Congress to reprogram $25 million for a proficiency pay experiment beginning in April 1971. Forsythe planned to compare the results of the proficiency pay experiment with those obtained from the enlistment bonus requested for fiscal year 1972. Confident that he would succeed in convincing Congress to release the funds for proficiency pay, Forsythe included the special pay incentive in the Modern Volunteer Army Program.[10]

The third component of the Modern Volunteer Army Program also received money for experimental projects. Forsythe requested and received authority to increase the strength of the recruiting force of approximately 3,000 by 536 and to raise the recruiting advertising budget from $3.1 million to $18.1 million for the remainder of fiscal year 1971. He asked for 3,000 additional recruiters and a $30 million advertising budget for fiscal year 1972. He intended to put all of the additional recruiters on the streets looking for volunteers. Meanwhile his office and the Recruiting Command began to develop an advertising campaign designed to feature the changes that were taking place in the Army. The theme of the campaign would be "The Army Is Changing—For the Better." The Recruiting Command prepared a test to determine the potential of paid radio and television advertising during prime broadcast time.[11]

Consistent with his charter, Forsythe retained considerable control over the execution of the Modern Volunteer Army Program. Each Army staff agency and all elements of the chain of command received instructions to "give full support and priority attention to MVAP and its goals." Westmoreland gave Forsythe authority to communicate directly with posts and organizations participating in the various experiments while informing intermediate commands. Westmoreland also agreed to launch the Modern Volunteer Army effort personally. He used the occasion of the Army Commanders' Conference, an annual meeting of the senior leaders of the service, to outline the program and direct compliance with it. At the same time Westmoreland announced the immediate Army-wide implementation of a series of no-cost actions aimed at improving service attractiveness.

High-Impact Actions

The first overt Army action on behalf of the all-volunteer force effort following Westmoreland's speech to the AUSA on 13 October 1970 and the appointment of Forsythe as SAMVA was the announcement of the implementation of a package of "High Impact Actions Toward Achieving A Modern Volunteer Army." Westmoreland unveiled these actions on 30 November at the Army Commanders' Conference, the annual gathering of the Army's top leaders who reported directly to the chief of staff. The occasion was appropriate. Rumors of policy changes had been circulating throughout the Army since the *Army Times* had published portions of the Project PROVIDE recommendations in November 1969. A year later, following his dramatic speech to the Association of the U.S. Army convention committing the Army to support the all-volunteer effort, it was time for Westmoreland to be specific.

The Army was already actively seeking money for long-range programs such as eliminating KP and renovating barracks. The actions Westmoreland announced to his key commanders on 30 November cost nothing and could be implemented immediately. They included ending traditional daily reveille formations and liberalization of pass policies to include the elimination of the requirement for soldiers to sign in and out of their units, bed checks, and locally imposed restrictions on travel distance while on pass. Westmoreland announced that henceforth the Army staff would not work on Saturdays "except for 'crash' actions" and directed his field commanders to follow suit.

The chief of staff also told his subordinates of Army staff efforts to revise the system of formal inspections, eliminating the emphasis on "spit and polish" harassment of troops. Unannounced inspections of unit maintenance and administration programs had evolved into a major irritant and a source of fear and loathing at the battalion and company levels. Additionally, Westmoreland continued, all Army regulations would be reviewed and revised to simplify language and eliminate outmoded policies. Nonessential and repetitive mandatory training was to be eliminated and basic training improved to allow soldiers to progress according to performance.

Westmoreland directed his key commanders to make better use of their noncommissioned officers in communicating to the soldier and in identifying areas of discontent. He alluded to the ongoing experiments with enlisted men's councils and brought in General Rogers to talk about the results he had achieved at Fort Carson. "Every commander can do as well," Westmoreland said. To do less "will not be sufficient."

The unifying focus of the high-impact actions was to eliminate unnecessary irritants and give the soldier more personal freedom without lowering discipline. With an eye toward the latter Westmoreland also announced the relaxation of restrictions on alcoholic beverages in noncombat areas on a trial basis. Commanders could serve beer in mess halls and install beer vending machines in barracks at their discretion. Westmoreland asserted that if the Army stopped treating the soldier as a juvenile and started dealing with him "like a responsible man he will act like one." The elimination of restrictions on personal movement and the beer in the barracks experiment represented gestures in support of that assumption.

Taken together, the new policies Westmoreland announced on 30 November aimed at improving the attractiveness of service life. He warned his commanders that the changes were just beginning and that "much inertia must be overcome." He challenged them to double reenlistments by 1 July 1971 and triple them by 1 January 1972. The draft, he warned, was no longer an "open-end manpower account"; the Army had "been spoiled by the draft" and it was going to end. "The time for debate on whether this is a good idea is over...the decision has been made...I expect your full support."[12]

Westmoreland's support of the all-volunteer force concept at the November 1970 Army Commanders' Conference set the stage for future initiatives and, through his demonstration of personal support, lent a necessary legitimacy to Forsythe and the Modern Volunteer Army Program. But the high-impact actions did not spring full grown from Westmoreland's brow. The actions Westmoreland announced on 30 November were drawn from a list prepared by Forsythe's office earlier in the month, and most of those ideas had been thrashed about the Army staff since the chief of staff approved the Project PROVIDE recommendations a year earlier. Proposals such as ending routine reveille formations, liberalization of pass restrictions, and the five-day workweek already had been approved.[13] Staff review and approval of these actions was complete by the end of September 1970. Butler, Montague, and Forsythe added only those proposals ending inspections and permitting beer in the barracks and also urged the chief of staff to direct the establishment of enlisted men's councils Army-wide. Westmoreland approved Forsythe's package in principle on 13 November and directed the Army staff to review it to identify "any serious pitfalls" before he gave his final approval.[14]

The staff posed numerous objections. Beer in the barracks and in the mess halls proved to be a major issue. All elements of the staff either opposed the idea outright or urged a "go slow" approach. Forsythe argued that over-control of alcohol was a major irritant with troops. Westmoreland agreed to give commanders discretionary authority to test the idea and directed his subordinates to report on the results by 1 July 1971.

The proposed directive establishing enlisted men's councils Army-wide also encountered opposition. The assistant chief of staff for force development considered the proposal tantamount to creating a union. The deputy chief of staff for personnel offered an alternative approach including noncommissioned officers. Forsythe argued that councils had proven their worth where they already existed. Voluntary adoption of the concept was unlikely, he warned; only by ordering their establishment throughout the Army could Westmoreland assure their acceptance. Westmoreland overruled Forsythe and decided merely to allude to the concept and suggest it be tried on an ad hoc basis.

The chief of staff also backed off from directing outright cessation of the odious inspections. Instead, on the advice of his deputy chief of staff for logistics and the inspector general, he elected to announce only that the procedures governing the unpopular inspections were under review and new policies would be forthcoming.[15]

The manner in which the chief of staff and Army staff decided on the high-impact actions bothered Forsythe. He worried constantly about the lack of time available to accomplish the transition. Although he respected Westmoreland, Palmer, and other key figures on the Army staff and the senior commanding generals in the field, Forsythe complained of "fearful leadership." From Forsythe's perspective many people in decision-making positions were simply too cautious. They wanted to go slowly on every proposal: "let's think about this, let's study it some more, let's have somebody do a research project on it," Forsythe recalled. Meanwhile, "the clock is running and guys out there were being drafted." Westmoreland helped by issuing directives from the top. But Forsythe found that often the word did not filter down the chain of command. Intermediate commanders who disagreed with the new direction the Army was taking ignored change or looked the other way when subordinates failed to ensure compliance.

Forsythe's solution was to establish "SAMVA points of contact" throughout the Army. Using his authority as a special assistant to the chief of staff, Forsythe ordered the establishment of modern volunteer Army liaison positions on major staffs. He notified these officers of new policies and changes directly. Field commanders complained that the system represented a dual communications network that subverted the chain of command. Palmer agreed and ordered Forsythe to use established notification procedures.[16]

Montague considered General Palmer and elements of the Army staff major roadblocks. He characterized Palmer as a "reluctant dragon" who cared deeply for the Army, passionately supported efforts to rebuild it, but urged caution. Palmer, Montague observed, feared that the changes necessary to create a volunteer force might upset discipline and readiness if pushed too fast.

Montague had less respect for the Army staff, especially after seeing how it handled the first set of high-impact actions proposals. As the all-volunteer Army effort gained recognition the SAMVA office began to receive unsolicited suggestions. Later Forsythe issued an open invitation for ideas. Montague screened every recommendation. Then he passed them to the Army staff for comment. But, as he told a contact in the secretary of the Army's office in a moment of despair, "Farming them out to the Staff will not likely result in any positive action." He considered turning promising ideas over to consultants or researchers. Once outsiders developed programs "your office and ours can instruct the Staff to carry them out."[17]

Montague's frustration with Palmer and the Army staff was a natural function of his perspective. Driven by the seemingly impossible deadline to end reliance on the draft by the end of 1972, Forsythe, Montague, and the rest of the "SAMVA Warriors," as Forsythe's people began calling themselves, focused their sights solely on the goals and programs of the Modern Volunteer Army Program.

Westmoreland and Palmer had broader horizons. Charged with the responsibility for leading and managing the whole Army, they looked on Forsythe's innovations more cautiously. Palmer, who ran the Army on a day-to-day basis, thought that Forsythe and his people served a useful purpose. "They got the attention of the whole Army," he said later, but he had problems with SAMVA too. As he reviewed Forsythe's proposals he concluded at least half were "half baked," and he succeeded in quashing them.[18]

Ideas that Palmer and Westmoreland screened went to the Army staff which, despite Montague's analysis, also served a useful purpose. Not noted for its generation of new ideas, the staff system helped by identifying potential unintended consequences of many of SAMVA's schemes. The tension between Forsythe's people and the Army staff was thus natural. Occasionally Forsythe became directly involved. "George and I used to blow fire at each other more than once in a while," recalled General Walter Kerwin, the deputy chief of staff for personnel.[19] It was a necessary product of the dynamic process aimed at changing personnel practices and assumptions that had been in place for nearly thirty years.

Forsythe recognized the necessity to get along with the Army staff. His small office did not have the personnel to research each idea thoroughly. But as soon as Westmoreland announced the first set of high-impact actions, SAMVA began preparing another. Westmoreland and Palmer approved some of the proposals immediately. For example, Forsythe pushed again for an announcement ending Command Maintenance Management and Annual General Inspections. The new, less onerous procedures for the CMMI were ready, so Westmoreland had no trouble approving their immediate release as a high-impact action. On receipt of the news Montague was jubilant. "C/S [chief of staff] has approved elimination of CMMI! Victory!" he scrawled across the message slip.[20]

The haircut issue in many ways typified the problem of change in the Army at the unit level. Westmoreland had approved the release of a statement announcing a review of regulations governing hair styles and directing commanders not to establish local haircut standards more severe than those currently in force. Along with restrictions on personal freedom during off-duty hours and on alcoholic beverages, soldiers resented Army haircut rules intensely. Existing regulations left much discretion to local commanders and standards varied from unit to unit, often on the same post. A deputy assistant secretary of the Army, returning from a trip to Europe in October 1970, considered troop unhappiness over haircut regulations sufficiently demoralizing to bring it to the attention of Secretary of the Army Resor. The nub of the issue, he reported, lay in disagreements between noncommissioned officers and soldiers over what constituted "looking good": "The NCO wants the soldier to look good, which to him means short hair. The young soldier also wants to look good, but to him good means long hair."[21] The Army released its new haircut regulations in April 1971 and the following month published a poster illustrating "various hair styles, mustaches and sideburns which are acceptable."[22]

Westmoreland refused outright to approve a proposal to eliminate standard wall and footlocker arrangements required of troops living in barracks. "This is a loser!" he wrote on the list Forsythe offered. He also considered the idea of ending "bad check" lists—names of soldiers who bounced checks were regularly circulated to local concessionaires—on posts to demonstrate the

Army's increased trust in its soldiers "another loser." Palmer agreed on the latter proposal, and Forsythe abandoned both quickly.[23]

Other proposals survived Palmer's and Westmoreland's pens and went on to the Army staff. The staff, in turn, killed a proposal to eliminate registration of personal vehicles on Army posts on the grounds that local authorities would lose their ability to control vehicles on their installations. The Army staff also quashed a recommendation to release draftees returning from Vietnam up to three months early. However, proposals requiring offices that performed personal services to remain open during lunch periods, the reduction of nonessential guard requirements, and the creation of new enlistment options passed the Army staff's review and were announced later in the spring of 1971.[24]

SAMVA and the Media

The Modern Volunteer Army opened to mixed reviews. Typically, the *Army Times* obtained an advance copy of Forsythe's "High Impact Actions" list. " 'Chicken' Dead," the *Army Times* crowed, as it prematurely reported reduced inspections, an end to unrealistic training, and five-day work weeks.

Following Westmoreland's announcement of the high-impact actions at the Army Commanders' Conference of 30 November 1970, the *Army Times* highlighted the more sensational changes just ordered. "Beer Can Now Flow In Barracks, Messes," proclaimed the bold headlines. The article noted that only 3.2 beer was permitted and observed that if the action led to major disciplinary problems the policy would be "scrubbed." The *Army Times* article also reported on the new liberalized pass policies and the end of routine reveille formations and quoted Westmoreland correctly on the purpose of the changes—improvement of service attractiveness and the elimination of irritating aspects of Army life. But the emphasis was on change.

Time magazine also reported on Westmoreland's announcements of 30 November in a feature article that highlighted changes in the Navy and implied that the Army was steaming into the present in its rival's wake. *Time* also suggested that the Army expected great resistance to the Modern Volunteer Army changes from within, especially from the noncommissioned officers corps.[25]

Information often reached commanders and troops alike in piecemeal fashion and without explanation of the intended purposes of the changes. The reactions to the new policies came swiftly. Because of the rapid succession of events leading to the formulation and announcement of the Modern Volunteer Army Program and high-impact actions most soldiers in the field learned about them from the *Army Times* or by word of mouth. Copies of Westmoreland's remarks to the Commanders' Conference circulated through command channels slowly. The Master Program for the Modern Volunteer Army, which included a detailed explanation of the philosophy, goals, and component programs of the implementation plan, was available for distribution in January 1971 but was withheld because it had not been thoroughly staffed through the Department of the Army. A coordinating version approved by the Army staff reached field commanders in March, but the final revised master plan was not released Army-wide or to the public until October. By that time the damage had been done.[26]

Barely a month after Westmoreland launched the Modern Volunteer Army Program, the *Army Times* began to receive and publish a stream of letters on the subject. One of the first, written by retired Air Force Lt. Gen. Ira C. Eaker, the highly decorated and respected commander of the Eighth Air Force during World War II, asked, "Military Going Mod?" Eaker quoted a sergeant who complained about the "hippie crew" that would result from the liberalization of the Army. The former Air Force general worried that the effort to make the Army more appealing to the "modern youth culture" would "alienate the loyal, dedicated men and women who had always been the backbone of the military service."[27]

Others agreed. "Patriot," writing from Vietnam, praised the purpose of the Modern Volunteer Army plan but charged that "the intent of the program seems to have been lost in the hustle and bustle, over-enthusiasm, and mad, headlong rush to get there 'fustiest with the mostest' in an effort to 'prove' that the program will work." The result, "Patriot" continued, was the "damaging impression that military discipline is to be all but abolished." Another writer, "Sergeant Major," agreed, asking "Why such overriding concern for first termers?" and "Does the Army really believe that by relaxing discipline, standards and quality that it will be for the better?"[28]

Not everyone shared the negative reaction to the changes taking place. Sfc. Kenneth Cannady was sufficiently irritated by General Eaker's letter to reply. Cannady called the "'New Army' Unalarming," and said the "biggest cause for alarm" was not change but traditionalists like Eaker who failed to appreciate the purpose behind the volunteer Army plan. "If he would look past the tradition and scratch the surface of this subject, Gen. Eaker would discover that the intent of the Modern Volunteer Army concept is not to turn the Army into a 'hippie crew,'" Cannady argued. He went on to define the real purpose of the program as well as Westmoreland or Forsythe ever did: "Anyone with open eyes and a half-way open mind can tell that neither of these fine officers is aiming at a 'mod force,'" he continued, "but they recognized that basic reform in living and working conditions must come if the Army is to attract the men needed to form a modern force." Fortunately, Cannady concluded, Eaker was retired and could not do much damage. But, he warned, there were many traditionalists still in the ranks "doing everything they can to insure that the reforms instituted by Gen. Westmoreland flop."[29]

The debate on the pages of the *Army Times* reflected a much broader argument that occurred within the Army itself in the first months of 1971. To bolster supporters like Sergeant Cannady and allay the fears and suspicions of "Patriot," "Sergeant Major," and retirees like General Eaker, Forsythe went on a speaking tour that took him around the country. He addressed gatherings of officers and noncommissioned officers on post and veterans and retiree groups off post with the same message. He told his audiences that the volunteer Army program would result in higher, not lower, standards and discipline.

Freeing soldiers from KP, post clean-up details and grass cutting would give them back to the sergeants, he said. The result would be more training. Furthermore, he added, units would be able to train at full strength. "Soldiers join the Army to soldier," Forsythe told the *Army Times*. His program intended to "free the soldier of non-soldier duties." Forsythe defended the beer in the barracks experiment. It did not represent permissiveness, he said. Soldiers already drank beer. He preferred that they drink in the barracks rather than off post or in cars. He revealed that the idea came from a sergeant major in an infantry unit, and added, "If a man is old enough and man enough to be a soldier in his country's Army we ought to trust him enough to have a couple of cans of 3.2 beer in the barracks."

Over and over Forsythe emphasized that the point of VOLAR was "to treat the soldier like a man—to place our trust in him (as we do on the battlefield)." To make his point he quoted George Marshall:

> The soldier is a man; he expects to be treated as an adult, not as a schoolboy. He has his rights; they must be made known to him and thereafter respected. He has ambition; it must be stirred. He has a belief in fair play; it must be honored. He has need of comradeship; it must be supplied. He has imagination; it must be stimulated. He has a sense of personal dignity; it must be sustained. He has pride; it can be satisfied and made the bedrock of character once he is assured that he is playing a useful and respected role.
>
> To give a man this is the acme of inspired leadership. He becomes loyal because loyalty has been given to him.

To Forsythe these "Old Army" ideas represented "the very guts of our MVA program." In later years he expressed frustration at his inability to get that point across.[30]

In order to counter the perception that noncommissioned officers opposed the volunteer Army plan, the Third Army command sergeants major called a special conference to emphasize their support of Forsythe's program. Command Sgt. Maj. Donald Meyer of Fort McPherson said, "the only thing wrong with the modern volunteer Army is that we are 13 or 14 years too late in starting." The problem, another asserted, was not reforms but "the lackadaisical NCO who won't accept it."

Forsythe also got some needed help from other quarters. The Association of the U.S. Army published a thoughtful essay by a rifle company commander that echoed Sergeant Major Meyer's sentiment. "My men are the ones we're trying to keep," wrote Capt. Robert Killebrew. "And we aren't keeping them." Pay raises and combat arms bonuses would help, he said. Some men served for money. But they stayed out of pride, and "they're leaving because they find no tradition, no pride in their job, no sense of identification with the Army they see." He applauded programs under way to improve service attractiveness and return soldiers to training.

The American Legion, which staunchly opposed ending the draft, also praised the Modern Volunteer Army Program. In a lengthy article that analyzed Westmoreland's high-impact actions, the Legion concluded that "Westmoreland's reforms make as much sense in a draft army as in a volunteer army." In response to charges that the reforms would lead to a breakdown of discipline, the writer replied, "if we have intelligent officers who understand leadership, this writer fears nothing from the reforms that have been ordered so far. If we lack enough such officers, God help us in any case." [31]

At times efforts to mollify critics of the Modern Volunteer Army Program backfired. General Ralph E. Haines, Jr., commanding general of the Continental Army Command, which oversaw all units in the United States as well as the Army's training establishment, granted a two-hour interview to the *Army Times* to explain the program and his command's role in its implementation. Haines covered all aspects of the program and carefully explained its philosophy and goals. Media emphasis on life-style improvements created confusion and fostered negativism, he charged. Sensational headlines created false impressions among veterans, retirees, and career officers and noncommissioned officers that the Army "is seeking to gain 'popularity through permissiveness.'" The reactions by "old sarge," he added were critical and had to be reversed. The *Times* ran the story with a headline reading: "'Old Sarge'—Big VOLAR Hang up."

The interview set off a new debate within the Army as "old sarges" responded to the charge that they stood in the way of progress. "SFC E–7," writing from Fort Meade, exploded: "sure treat the troops as human beings: they are. Remove necessary irritants but don't turn an Army into civilians or you will lose that next war." He resented the suggestion by "a general officer of some prominence" that "NCOs should either adjust or get out of the Army." "Concerned NCO" from Fort Monroe also interpreted Haines' remarks as a condemnation of noncommissioned officers. He charged that the real problem rested with General Haines, who demanded compliance with the new volunteer Army guidelines without providing the resources to accomplish them. Troops were being freed from guard duty that still had to be done, for example, and noncommissioned officers were standing guard in their place. "Captain MVA" poured gasoline on the fire in a letter from Germany that accused old sergeants of opposing long hair because they had forgotten what it was like to be young. "Old soldier, do you really have a good justified reason why the young soldier can't have long hair, sideburns, beards and mustaches," the captain asked, "or are you saying to yourself 'If I had to do it when I came in the Army, so does the young soldier coming in today.'" M. Sgt. James Guyton retorted from Fort Lewis that "Capt. MVA and all his cronies depend on us (noncommissioned officers) for getting their work done whether they care to admit it or not." [32]

By May a new tone began to creep into the open debate. "Change is life," argued Sp4c. Richard Tietjens. "The Army must change to remain viable," he continued, or, like the dinosaurs, it would die. And, he noted significantly, "Discipline is not relaxed. Some unreasonable practices have been deleted, but this does not indicate wholesale mutiny." S. Sgt. Charles Gerrald went further. He called the changes engendered by the Modern Volunteer Army Program "welcome," and wondered why anyone could be against "any changes that can benefit the military and its missions." Sfc. Theodore Evans was even more frank. He called the "bickering" over the merits of the volunteer force changes "non-professional" and deplored what he characterized as a new tendency among noncommissioned officers: "fighting AGAINST benefits being offered their men; open conflict with the Army; open conflict with their men; outright greed for personal benefits." He called charges that the Volunteer Army Program hurt discipline "Poppycock," and told the nonprofessionals to "catch up—now—before it's too late."[33]

The Modern Volunteer Army Program was six months old by the end of June 1971. By that time the debate slackened. The *Army Times* published fewer and fewer letters on the subject. The decline in volume of letters did not signal an end to discussion. It did, however, suggest that some of the confusion of the early heady days of the program had passed, and, as Specialist Tietjens observed, the mutiny had not occurred. Beer in the barracks did not result in any major riots. Indeed, as Captain Killebrew revealed, beer consumption did not increase. Most of his men opposed the idea because "spilled beer smells." Having exhausted the pros and cons of the issue the army in the field got on with its business. As one general officer, who was an assistant division commander in 1971, recalled, "we were so very busy that one more staff section [to oversee the implementation of Modern Volunteer Army initiatives] didn't seem to bother anybody." His attitude was, "if that's what they want to do, good luck to them."[34]

Meanwhile new ideas continued to pour into the SAMVA office. Forsythe reported that he received between four and five hundred suggestions a month from soldiers all over the Army ranging in rank from private to general. His office asked the *Army Times* to publish its address and urged anyone with an idea on how to make the Army more attractive "to send it in."[35] The experiments had only begun.

Notes

[1] Interv, author with Forsythe, 11 Feb 83.

[2] Ibid.

[3] Thomas W. Scoville, *Reorganizing for Pacification Support* (Washington, D.C.: U.S. Army Center of Military History, 1982), pp. 28, 30n, 60–66; Forsythe Intervs.

[4] Col. David Hughes, "Fort Carson Debrief," undated briefing manuscript, c. Nov 72, Background Material, HRC, CMH; "Humanizing the U.S. Military," *Time*, 21 December 1970, pp. 16–22.

[5] Interv, author with Montague, 11 Mar 83.

[6] Montague Interv; Interv, author with Andrew Effron.

[7] Forsythe Interv.

[8] As noted, the Modern Volunteer Army Program contained many components that evolved simultaneously beginning in November 1970 under the auspices of SAMVA. For the sake of clarity the remainder of this chapter deals with early Army-wide initiatives, the development of the tentative MVA Program, and initial reactions within the Army. Ensuing chapters cover the VOLAR experiments and recruiting initiatives, concluding with an overall summary of the SAMVA effort.

[9] "Master Program for the Modern Volunteer Army," Office of the Special Assistant for the Modern Volunteer Army, 1 Mar 71 (hereafter cited as "MVAP–March 71"), HRC, CMH. Unless otherwise noted the following section on the master plan is based on the above reference and the author's interview with General Forsythe.

[10] See Chapter IX for further discussion of this issue.

[11] See Chapter VIII, pp. 111–14 and Chapter IX, pp 129–36, for a detailed discussion of the paid advertising experiment.

[12] Edited transcript, Address by Westmoreland at Army Commanders' Conference, 30 Nov 70, HRC, CMH.

[13] See, for example, Memo DCSPER for CofSA, 22 Sep 70, sub: Reveille Troop Formations; and Memo, DCSPER for CofSA, 24 Sep 70, Army Training/Work Week, both in Background Material.

[14] Memo, SAMVA for SAMVA Points of Contact, 13 Nov 70, sub: High Impact Actions Towards Achieving a Modern Volunteer Army, Background Material.

[15] Action Memo, SAMVA for Westmoreland, 25 Nov 70, sub: High Impact Actions Towards Achieving a Modern Volunteer Army, Background Material. The memo summarizes Army staff comments on SAMVA's sixteen actions and contains General Kerwin's handwritten notes of Westmoreland's decisions on each action.

[16] Forsythe Interv.

[17] Montague Interv; Memo, Montague for Gompf, 4 Jan 71, sub: Letter from Maj Gen Forbes, Herbits Papers.

[18] Oral History Intervs, Lt Col Edward Smith with General Bruce Palmer, Jr., 23 Apr 76, MHI; Dr. James Hewes with General Bruce Palmer, Jr., 24 Nov 81, CMH.

[19] Kerwin Interv.

[20] Memo, ODCSLOG for CofSA, 16 Jan 71, sub: Maintenance Assistance & Instruction Team Program, w/ handwritten notes by Montague, Background Material.

[21] Memo, John Kester for Secretary of the Army, 23 Oct 70, sub: Trip Report—Visit to USAREUR, provided by John Kester (hereafter cited as Kester Papers).

[22] AR 600–20, 28 Apr 71, and DA Poster 600–20, May 71.

[23] Memo, SAMVA thru Palmer for Westmoreland, 26 Jan 71, sub: High Impact Actions for Improving Service Attractiveness, containing Westmoreland's handwritten notes, Background Material.

[24] Staff Comments on "Further Actions for Improving Service Attractiveness" appended to Memo, Montague for Col B. F. Harmon III, Office of the Deputy Chief of Staff for Personnel, 27 Jan 71, sub: High Impact Actions (Request #103), Background Material.

[25] *Army Times*, 28 October 1970, pp. 1, 20; 16 December 1970, pp. 1, 24; *Time*, 21 December 1970, pp. 19–20.

[26] Jack R. Butler, "The All-Volunteer Armed Force—Its Feasibility and Implications," U.S. Army War College Research Paper, unpublished, 3 Jan 72, pp. 33–34; Butler Interv.

[27] "Commentary," *Army Times,* 20 January 1971, p. 12.

[28] "Letters to the editor," *Army Times*, 17 February 1971, p. 13; 3 March 1971, p. 12.

[29] *Army Times*, 3 February 1971, pp. 13, 18.

[30] "Removal of Irritants to Up VOLAR Caliber," *Army Times* interv with Gen Forsythe, 10 February 1971, p. 10; Ltr, Forsythe to author, 1 Sep 85.

[31] "Noncom Role Vital in VOLAR Program," *Army Times*, 17 February 1971, p. 8; Capt. Robert B. Killebrew, "Volunteer Army: How It Looks to a Company Commander," *Army* 21, no. 3 (March 1971): 19–22; Lewitt A. Knight, Jr., "What the Army Is Doing To Make Out Without the Draft," *American Legion Magazine*, April 1971, pp. 4–9, 42–46.

[32] "'Old Sarge'—Big VOLAR Hang-up," *Army Times*, 7 April 1971, p. 4; "Commentary," *Army Times*, 14 April 1971, pp. 12, 24; Letter to Editor, *Army Times*, 28 April 1971, p. 20; "A Letter to Sarge," *Army Times*, 5 May 1971, p. 13; "The NCO's Function," *Army Times*, 21 May 1971, pp. 12, 20.

[33] "Army Must Change," *Army Times*, 19 May 1971, p. 13; Letter to Editor, *Army Times*, 2 June 1971, p. 20; "The Non Professionals," *Army Times*, 9 June 1971, pp. 12, 20.

[34] Killebrew, "Volunteer Army," p. 20; Interv, author with Maj Gen George S. Patton, Jr., USA (Ret), 1 Jul 83. Patton was the assistant division commander of the 4th Armored Division in Germany in 1970 and 1971.

[35] "Volunteer Army Ideas Pour In," *Army Times*, 5 May 1971, p. 3.

CHAPTER VI

VOLAR: The Volunteer Army Field Experiment, 1971

"VOLAR was a test," General Forsythe remembered. "I never should have put a label on it. Everybody thought 'Oh, this is the Volunteer Army.' In fact it was just a test of certain things."[1] The "certain things" Forsythe referred to were a series of experiments begun at four Army installations in the United States and selected posts in Germany in January 1971 aimed at testing methods of increasing enlistments and reenlistments in the combat arms, those branches of the Army that research showed were crucial to the eventual success or failure of the volunteer effort. Like the overall Modern Volunteer Army Program, Project VOLAR's origins dated to the recommendations of the PROVIDE report, which assumed a lengthy transition to an all-volunteer armed force after the end of the U.S. involvement in Vietnam.

Initial Proposals

The Army staff had begun to consider a modest test of no- or low-cost experiments early in 1970 before Forsythe came on the scene. In the almost crisis-like atmosphere of October–November 1970 that attended the creation of SAMVA, the pace of action quickened. The experimental phase of the program was expanded first to three posts, then to four and to Europe. Money to pay for more expensive innovations was reprogrammed from other Army accounts. Representatives from the installations affected were called to Washington hastily to discuss their part in the program, and in a matter of two weeks the first experiments were approved and announced to an unprepared Army along with the high-impact actions. The urgency that drove Forsythe and Montague was real, and they communicated it to the people from the field who were drawn into the effort. But for the rest of the Army VOLAR became another crash project that bred confusion, misunderstanding, and, for some, resentment.

Initially the idea of testing innovative changes in Army policy applied only to practices relating to attractiveness of service life. To the PROVIDE study group and those on the Army staff and in the field interested in pursuing the subject, this meant eliminating "irritants" of service life such as reveille and additional duties of a nonmilitary nature—KP, window-washing, grass-cutting, and so forth. As early as January 1970 the PROVIDE task group had proposed a field experiment to develop quantifiable data on improvements to Army life.

Essentially, the PROVIDE group intended to co-opt General Roger's ongoing innovations at Fort Carson. Colonel Butler proposed making approximately $5 million available to the commander of Fort Carson beginning in fiscal year 1971. When General Forsythe became SAMVA at the end of October 1970 and absorbed Butler and the PROVIDE recommendations, he quickly concluded that a larger, more comprehensive test was needed, beginning immediately. Forsythe agreed that the experiments with life-style innovations should continue at Fort Carson, but he saw Fort Carson as the end of a series of experiments.

The logical place to begin an overhaul of Army policies and practices should be where the civilian first encountered the Army—basic training. Improve basic training at one of the Army's training centers, Forsythe reasoned, and send a better trained and motivated soldier on to either specialty training or directly to a unit at a location that was also participating in the experiment and compare the results in terms of attitudes toward the Army, reenlistments, and other measurable indicators such as undiscipline rates to those of soldiers trained under existing systems and assigned to other posts.

Forsythe proposed to conduct the expanded experiment at three posts. Fort Ord, in California, would serve as the foundation by providing basic trainees. They would then be assigned to Fort Benning, Georgia, for advanced training or to Fort Carson, Colorado, for assignment to a combat unit. At each post administrative and training practices, regulations, and policies governing individual life-style and living and working conditions would be adjusted to foster individual development and personal freedom.

Forsythe intended to involve the commanders of the selected posts by allowing them to follow their own initiatives within the broad parameters of the Modern Volunteer Army Program philosophy. He asked for $15 million, $5 million for each post, to launch the program beginning in January 1971. The secretary of the Army approved the concept late in October.[2]

Once he obtained conceptual approval of the experimental program Forsythe involved the selected installations in the planning stages of the VOLAR project. He notified the commanding generals of Forts Benning, Carson, and Ord that they were to participate and would receive $5 million each with which to make life-style improvements or to use for other purposes consistent with program concepts. Forsythe directed each commander to prepare a proposal and send representatives to Washington for a working conference on 2 December 1970.

Selection of the three posts had not been random. Except for Fort Benning, planning, though not specifically devoted to volunteer Army goals, was already under way. Under General Rogers Fort Carson already had an ongoing program. The VOLAR funds would permit Carson to expand its program by making possible the initiation of projects previously too costly to consider. Fort Ord had been studying and trying ways to improve the quality of instruction for basic trainees on its own initiative since mid-1969, and, in fact, was selected for the VOLAR experiment because Forsythe knew of the training center's independent efforts in that direction.

Forsythe selected Benning because it was the Infantry Center and, as such, the proponent for training the largest of the Army's combat arms. He notified the commandant of the Infantry Center, Maj. Gen. Orwin C. Talbot, personally during a visit to Fort Benning on 2 November 1970. Since Benning had to start from scratch, Forsythe suggested that Talbot employ seminars drawing from soldiers at all levels and from all post activities to develop ideas. He asked for Talbot's initial plan by 19 November.[3]

General Talbot appointed Col. William B. Steele, director of the Leadership Department of the Infantry School, as the project officer for the Benning study. Steele created a planning staff, six committees, and twelve sub-study groups drawn from all of Fort Benning's activities. Those involved included representatives of the noncommissioned officer students, units assigned to the Infantry Center, and officer, noncommissioned officer, and enlisted wives. He asked each sub-study group to conduct brainstorming sessions and make recommendations for improving service life and military professionalism at Fort Benning. Ideas generated by the groups went to the six committees that evaluated them, determined funding requirements, and arranged them into categories that ranged from proposals that could be implemented immediately at no cost on General Talbot's approval to actions that required regulations changes, special waivers, or legislative authority and funds.

The sub-study groups generated over 250 proposals. Most dealt with removing irritants, enhancing personal dignity, increasing personal freedom, or improving individual well-being. The only criteria that General Talbot set for acceptability was that a proposal had to be feasible for implementation at Fort Benning and contribute to the achievement of the volunteer Army goal in a demonstrable fashion. The Benning study group also developed a control plan to oversee implementation and execution of the program once approved and an evaluation plan to determine to what extent the actions taken under the Benning phase of the VOLAR experiment influenced attitudes toward the Army, intentions to remain in the service beyond initial obligations, or public impressions about the Army.

Colonel Steele presented his study group's proposal—the Benning Plan—to General Talbot on 12 November, ten days after Talbot had received word that his post would participate in the VOLAR experiments. Talbot reviewed the plan and approved it, and Steele delivered it to General Forsythe on 19 November.

Many of the ideas expressed in the Benning Plan anticipated those under study as high-impact actions. They involved no monetary cost. For example, on General Talbot's authorization Fort Benning immediately eliminated reveille formations and ordered Saturday training and work details cut to a minimum. Talbot also established an enlisted men's council, following the lead of Fort Carson, and an enlisted wives' club to allow that previously unrepresented group input into the installation's affairs.

The Benning Plan Study Group also proposed changes in training that Talbot approved without waiting for review. He abolished the practice of requiring lieutenants attending the Infantry Officers Basic Course to march to class. He ordered that classes on mornings following night training start at 0900 hours to allow students time to prepare for their lessons, and scheduled classes on common subjects for captains, lieutenants, and noncommissioned officers together to permit a sharing of ideas and experiences.

In the area of community services Talbot accepted recommendations to keep the post exchange and commissary open late at least one night weekly, and he established customer relations courses for their employees in an effort to improve relationships between military customers and the civilian personnel working in the stores. The study group wanted to revise regulations that required service members to salute when either or both persons were riding in automobiles or when either or both were wearing civilian clothes, long-standing conventions that created universal confusion throughout the Army. The Benning Plan also contained proposals to hire civilians to perform KP, post cleanup, and grass-cutting details; contract for free charter bus service for soldiers living off post; partition troop barracks to provide for individual living space and privacy; offer free laundry service for all enlisted men; and arrange for free cleaning of quarters of departing families.[4] None of these innovations were considered radical, and in retrospect they appear self-evident. The same was true of most recommendations that required funding or higher approval.

Lengthy lists of recommendations similar to the Benning Plan were also prepared at Forts Carson and Ord. Planners at Carson, who had a head start on thinking about ways to improve the Army by eliminating irritants and increasing professionalism, also wanted to hire civilians to free soldiers from KP and other menial jobs unrelated to their military duties and wanted to complete their program of subdividing barracks to ensure that every soldier enjoyed privacy. Under the heading of "professionalism," the commanding general at Fort Carson recommended establishing a program to identify and use soldier-civilian skills and education in a systematic fashion. He also requested that Fort Carson be guaranteed stabilization of personnel assigned to its units to eliminate the personnel turbulence that plagued the Army and detracted from individual and unit training effectiveness.[5]

A survey of personnel at Fort Ord was conducted to establish a basis for recommendations other than revision of basic training. The survey results revealed significant differences between trainee and cadre desires. Trainees wanted more livable barracks above all else, a fact that was "not unusual since 61% of the troop billets on this post are World War II type barracks which have suffered for years from a deprivation of maintenance funds." Next the trainees wanted more and better food. Better pay ranked a distant third.

The training cadre, consisting of career soldiers of all ranks, wanted pay increases first, followed by free dental care for their families, improvements in the cadre rooms in the barracks, and more vocational and educational courses after duty hours.

Both trainees and cadre wanted "more and better training and modern training equipment." Fort Ord asked for money to renovate or repair thirty-one World War II–type barracks and to purchase new barracks furniture. It also initiated "short order" food lines in mess halls to give soldiers an alternative to standard menus and installed soft drink dispensers in the mess halls. Ord also requested a 10 percent increase in the ration allowance of 4,600 calories a day for trainees to provide more milk, steak, and ice cream. But even more than money and a rations increase, Fort Ord urged that the Army staff its kitchens with the full "number of mess personnel authorized and in the right grades."

Consistent with the views of its career personnel as revealed by the survey, officers at Fort Ord requested that the Army consider extending dental care to dependents and added to that request the suggestion that medical care further be expanded to include providing complete eye care to include glasses for dependents. The Fort Ord commander also proposed paying soldiers twice monthly on an optional basis and providing a variable housing allowance keyed to actual local housing costs of service members forced to live off post due to chronic shortages of government family quarters.[6]

The major contribution to the VOLAR experiment coming out of Fort Ord was the Experimental Modern Volunteer Army Training Program. Until 1970 Army recruit training had consisted of a fairly standard eight weeks of basic training followed by advanced individual training in a wide variety of military occupational specialties (MOS). In the combat arms, that segment of the Army at which Forsythe targeted VOLAR, the Infantry took most of the recruits.

Following basic combat training an infantry recruit remained at the training center and received an additional eight weeks of training at the end of which he received the Military Occupational Specialty (MOS) 11B (light weapons infantryman) or MOS 11C (indirect fire crewman), the two basic infantry classifications. All recruits moved through the sixteen-week program of basic and advanced individual infantry training at the same pace.

When General Forsythe notified the Fort Ord commanding general, Maj. Gen. Phillip B. Davidson, that his training center would participate in the VOLAR test, Davidson created a task force of military and civilian experts in the fields of training, psychology, and testing to develop the new training program. Based on guidance from Forsythe's office, the task force designed a program oriented to the individual and based on the principles of self-paced instruction and performance-based advancement. Recruits in the Fort Ord program could progress through a unified sixteen-week training cycle and, depending on their ability and initiative, earn up to three infantry MOSs, 11B, 11C, and either 11H (heavy weapons crewman) or 11U (mechanized infantry vehicle driver). Recruits who passed through the program quickly would receive rewards. Officers at Fort Ord proposed to accelerate promotions for recruits who performed well, making it possible to advance as high as the grade of E–4 by the end of the sixteen-week program. Recruits were to be promoted to grade E–2 upon completion of the 11B training, grade E–3 following 11H or 11U training, and grade E–4 if they successfully completed all three. The Fort Ord task force envisioned an even more ambitious program for exceptional trainees who completed the entire program ahead of schedule and demonstrated leadership qualities. The very best trainees, the task group suggested, should proceed immediately to educational and vocational training at Army schools or local high schools and community colleges. Fort Ord's training program was to be conducted within the context of a five-day, forty-hour training week.[7]

All three plans reached Forsythe by late November. On 2 December 1970, representatives from each of the posts participated in a working conference attended by representatives of all the Army staff sections and the Continental Army Command, the headquarters which supervised the three installations. The working conference reviewed each proposal and either approved it, approved it in concept pending changes in Army regulations or statutory limitations, deferred it for further study, or disapproved it. The group approved immediately virtually all proposals not prohibited by statute. Forsythe notified the installations that proposals approved for one could be implemented at all three without further staff review subject only to funding limitations.[8]

The Department of the Army also approved Fort Ord's Experimental Volunteer Army Training Program, although it made some changes. Fort Ord wanted to gear up for the experiment by bringing in a full complement of officers and noncommissioned officers with training experience and spending a full three months preparing them for the new venture before implementing the experimental system in all of its three training brigades in April 1971. Continental Army Command disapproved involving all three training brigades and recommended that Ord begin more modestly with only one brigade.

Continental Army Command also ruled that trainees from Fort Ord's program would be available for worldwide assignment, including Vietnam, and not just for assignment to Benning or Carson as was originally proposed. The decision meant that Fort Ord had to add a forty-hour block of instruction on counterinsurgency warfare to its program. Further revision of the plan resulted in the elimination of MOS 11H training and substitution of mechanized infantry vehicle driver training for those trainees who progressed furthest in the program. MOS 11H training involved firing the 106-mm. recoilless rifle, which was no longer in use throughout the Army. On the other hand, the Army had an increasing need for soldiers capable of driving and maintaining the M113A1 armored personnel carrier.

Forsythe accepted the changes requested by Continental Army Command and made one of his own. He directed the commander of Fort Ord to begin the first cycle of training under the experimental program on 11 January 1971, three months before Ord's proposed start date.[9]

In planning VOLAR Forsythe and the SAMVA staff conceived of a true experiment with control and test populations. They intended to assign graduates from Fort Ord through Fort Benning to Fort Carson or directly to Carson and to compare their attitudes toward the Army and reenlistment rates with those of recruits trained and assigned elsewhere. But events quickly conspired to undermine the grand scheme of VOLAR. The continued demand for infantrymen in Vietnam and the personnel turbulence generated by the policy of rotating men through Vietnam on a twelve-month basis made it impossible to isolate the VOLAR participants from the Army's worldwide manpower requirements. Continental Army Command's decision that VOLAR trainees would be available for assignment anywhere thus did more than add an additional training requirement to Fort Ord's experimental program.

The decision forced Forsythe to expand the number of VOLAR sites in an effort to follow Ord trainees around the world. In December he notified Fort Bragg and United States Army, Europe (USAREUR), that they too would participate in the experiment, and he directed them to develop plans immediately. Forsythe also intended to establish scientific control populations by comparing VOLAR trainees with regular trainees graduated from the Army Training Center at Fort Jackson and assigned through Fort Knox, the Armor equivalent to Benning, to Fort Riley. This portion of the plan fell through entirely because of the demands of the personnel assignment process, but Forsythe was able to track graduates from Forts Jackson and Knox as they were assigned to other non-VOLAR posts worldwide.

The announcement of the high-impact actions and beginning of the Modern Volunteer Army Program in November 1970 and January 1971, respectively, also negated some of the effects of the VOLAR initiatives at Carson, Benning, and Ord. Soon virtually every post in the Army was conducting volunteer Army experiments of one sort or another with their own limited resources. Soldiers everywhere enjoyed more personal freedom on and off duty. Thus, it proved difficult to identify a true control group against which to compare the soldiers trained and assigned to VOLAR posts.[10]

VOLAR Funding

The initial VOLAR experiments begun in January 1971 could not be paid for with programmed funds. Fiscal year 1971 monies had been approved and appropriated early in 1970 before the conception of a volunteer Army field experiment surfaced. The bulk of the money for VOLAR 71 thus had to come from existing funds, mostly by reprogramming the Operation and Maintenance, Army (OMA), account of the Army budget. The Army spent nearly $30 million on VOLAR during the last six months of fiscal year 1971 (January to June 1971), with $25 million coming from OMA funds. The remaining money for VOLAR 71 projects came from the Family Housing Management (FHMA) and Major Construction (MCA) accounts.[11]

The fast pace of VOLAR planning and the ad hoc nature of its funding arrangements for fiscal year 1971 created problems from the start and threatened to bring the more visible aspects of the program to a halt before they began. Such an outcome would have discredited the experiment, Forsythe's operation, and the Army's entire commitment to the volunteer force effort. In this area two subprograms were especially critical: the rehabilitation and partitioning of barracks to provide decent individual living space and the hiring of civilian food service attendants—the Army's euphemism for ending KP. Both ranked high on every list of soldiers' desires. Both the Army and SAMVA had promised action to eliminate these irritants, and all VOLAR posts had indicated their intention to address these two areas. Failure to deliver on these promises would be viewed by the soldier as a breach of contract.

Most posts still maintained large numbers of World War II mobilization barracks that had been built hastily during the vast expansion of World War II and then retained as a reserve. The Vietnam expansion brought these old wooden barracks into full-time use again. Built with a planned life of seven years, they were poorly insulated, blazing hot in summer, drafty and cold in winter, and twenty-five years past their prime by 1970. In most cases maintenance consisted of an occasional fresh coat of paint.

Most young unmarried soldiers lived in these World War II–vintage barracks. Typically they consisted of large open rooms called platoon bays that held up to forty men. Standard platoon bay arrangements called for ten double-deck bunks on each side of a central aisle. Each man had a wall locker and a foot locker for his military and personal belongings. Noncommissioned officers who lived in the barracks enjoyed semiprivate or private rooms at the end of the bays.

In USAREUR soldiers lived in casernes taken over from the Germans at the end of the war. Some dated back to the nineteenth century, and most were marred by peeling paint, falling plaster, leaking plumbing, and faulty wiring. Limited maintenance funds, reduced by the exigencies of the Vietnam War, made it impossible for the Army's facilities engineers to keep up with the deterioration. A soldier living in Merrell Barracks, Nuremberg, Germany, said of his living conditions, "If we repaired them 100 percent they would only be half as good as they were when Hitler's troops lived in them." He added that the local zoo was in better condition than troops barracks in Germany.[12]

Efforts to improve troop living conditions predated the Modern Volunteer Army Program and VOLAR in USAREUR. In late 1968 the European command budgeted funds to begin complete renovation of 120 barracks. By 1971 work on 26 buildings was complete. In 1970 the Army began the first of 800 selected rehabilitation projects in Germany. Emphasis on improving living conditions, sparked by the Nixon administration's interest in achieving an all-volunteer force, helped accelerate these programs, as the Army justified requests for more funds to speed completion by 1973 and 1974 in terms of their contribution to the zero-draft goal.

Under VOLAR barracks improvements took a different form. Commanders at the VOLAR posts authorized the construction and erection of partitions in the platoon bays creating private and semiprivate "rooms" for the occupants. Troops were then permitted to decorate these rooms to taste. The troops did most of the labor on these projects, while facilities engineers did the electrical work and plumbing. Project VOLAR also provided money for barracks furnishings such as drapes, scatter rugs, individual beds with innerspring mattresses, desks, and chairs. Institutional style wall lockers and Army issue foot lockers gave way to dressers and closets. Barracks became dormitories.[13] But these changes did not occur immediately. The nature and size of the jobs exceeded the authority of the local commands to authorize the expenditure of the OMA funds necessary to accomplish them. While the Army struggled to free other funds for the projects, a credibility gap developed.

All of the VOLAR posts in the United States began to design partitions for barracks as soon as Forsythe and the Department of the Army approved their plans. The designers chose one of two routes. Some planned semipermanent construction of wood and gypsum panels; others elected to purchase standard room dividers that the Government Services Administration developed and offered to the Army early in 1971. In both cases the posts expected to finance the barracks modifications from Major Construction, Army (MCA), funds. Problems developed almost immediately.

Approval to expend MCA funds for minor construction came from the Department of Defense. But the assistant secretary of defense for installations and logistics, Barry Shillito, the approving authority, balked. Shillito supported the aim of barracks rehabilitation, but he objected to "frittering away" money on projects that would increase privacy in substandard barracks without raising the standards of the buildings. He argued that the Army's major effort in barracks rehabilitation should be directed toward a program that would improve "our permanent plant." Shillito refused to approve VOLAR 71 minor construction requests until a related matter, the Army's request for $48 million in fiscal year 1972 for the same purpose worldwide, was approved. He feared that Congress would object to the latter request and did not see any point in proceeding until the whole issue was settled. Meanwhile plans to partition 99 old barracks at Fort Benning and 170 at Fort Carson languished, and the troops who had been promised private rooms with so much fanfare began to question the sincerity of the Army.[14]

Forsythe immediately took the problem to Secretary of the Army Resor, who in turn met with Shillito's deputy Edward Sheridan to iron out the problem. Sheridan explained that the Army's approach of using the MCA funds to accomplish a series of minor projects that added up to a sizable program without prior consent of Congress risked a backlash which could result in cancellation of the whole scheme. As an alternative, Sheridan suggested the Army use its authority under section 103 of the annual Military Construction Act to authorize "unforeseen construction" up to $10 million with only notification of Congress. By proceeding under section 103 the Army could begin barracks rehabilitation in fiscal year 1971 without having to wait on the outcome of its request for funds for 1972. Resor agreed, but even that process took time. Meanwhile the barracks partitions waited.[15]

For the next six weeks Forsythe, Montague, and representatives from the Army Corps of Engineers and the Office of the Deputy Chief of Staff for Logistics traveled back and forth between the Pentagon and Capitol Hill visiting members of Congress and staff members of the four committees that had to agree to let the Army use major construction funds for barracks partitions. One by one the committees agreed; the Senate Appropriations Committee was last because its staff expert on military construction was traveling. Finally, on 30 March Forsythe gained approval and immediately notified the comptroller of the Army, who released the funds to the field. Construction began on 2 April, and on 8 April Forsythe notified Secretary Resor that the program on VOLAR posts would be completed by 15 July. Congress subsequently approved the Army's entire request for $60 million for barracks rehabilitation in fiscal year 1972. At the troop level, however, the delay hurt. A later report from Fort Benning, for example, stated that "The time lag involved in completing this very visible, high-impact project caused many soldiers to become cynical about the entire MVA effort."[16]

A different problem delayed the start of another highly visible VOLAR initiative in USAREUR, the replacement of soldier KPs by civilian food service workers. The stateside VOLAR posts hired civilians immediately to free soldiers from KP and return them to training. Fort Benning let a $1.2 million contract for civilian KPs before it formally received the funds to pay them and commenced operations on 2 January 1971. In Germany the problem was not money but a labor shortage. United States armed forces normally obtained unskilled labor overseas from the local economy. In West Germany unemployment was so low that the Army estimated that it could not fill all of the estimated 3,600 positions needed to civilianize food service with local citizens. USAREUR headquarters requested permission to hire U.S. citizens living in Europe—specifically family members of military personnel—to make up the shortage. Since statutes limited the authority of the military to create jobs for U.S. citizens overseas or offer them to a limited category of citizens, the Army needed permission from the Civil Service Commission to proceed.[17]

Under Secretary of the Army Thaddeus Beal forwarded the Army's formal request for permission to hire U.S. nationals living in Germany to perform KP at the end of March. He spelled out the Army's dilemma clearly and specified that the Army would hire Americans only after all the supply of local nationals ran out. He further noted that the Army wanted to hire dependent family members of service members already in West Germany. The purpose of this restriction was twofold. First, it avoided creating jobs for transient Americans abroad. Furthermore, and of greater importance to the Army, limiting employment to military family members created jobs for low-skill Americans who most needed the income and otherwise could not find employment in the Federal Republic's economy. The Army proposed to pay civilian KPs $1.60 an hour.

The Civil Service Commission took two months to reply to the Army's request, a short time in the bureaucratic context but a lengthy delay for soldiers in Germany who had been promised relief from such duties and for the family members who anticipated supplementing their income by applying for the food service jobs. Writing for the commission, Raymond Jacobson, director of the Bureau of Policies and Standards, informed the Army on 3 May 1971 that its request was approved. Henceforth dependents of military personnel could be hired as food service workers. The commission limited appointments under the exception to policy to three years to coincide with the length of a normal overseas tour of duty. With approval in hand the Army released funds to the command in Germany to begin hiring civilians.

Because of the decentralized nature of the European command, a further vexing delay ensued while the staff at USAREUR headquarters determined how much money each caserne and unit needed. Actual hiring did not begin until June, and the command did not report completion of conversion to civilian food service until July 1971, at the beginning of the new fiscal year. Thus six months elapsed between the time the Army announced an end of soldier KP and the time it was realized for troops serving in Germany. The delay again strained the credibility of VOLAR and the Modern Volunteer Army Program.[18]

Evaluation

Perhaps too much can be made of the delays in starting up the more expensive and highly visible VOLAR programs. At the time the bureaucratic hurdles that had to be overcome within the Army, between the Army and other agencies, or with Congress frustrated Forsythe and Montague. Some members of the SAMVA staff were even persuaded that the delays were deliberate and designed to discredit the effort. Later, with the advantage of perspective, one SAMVA "warrior" recognized that the pace of Forsythe and the others working on the problem on a daily basis contributed to the problem. "Because of the urgency of time," he concluded, "[SAMVA] came into being by caesarian and grew to maturity before its musculature was developed enough to support it."[19] In the rush to show progress, Forsythe had announced programs that could not be implemented immediately. Like the high-impact actions that Westmoreland sprung on the unprepared units of the Army in the field, the announced VOLAR initiatives created confusion and some unrealistic expectations in those units designated to participate in the program.

By mid-1971 the hurdles had been cleared, exceptions to policy granted, and money released. Just as the hue and cry over the Modern Volunteer Army Program settled down by summer, so did the confusion over VOLAR begin to abate. The timing proved fortunate. The start of the new fiscal year brought with it more money for expansion of VOLAR to eleven additional posts in the United States and additional locations overseas. During fiscal year 1972 the Army would spend $73.7 million on VOLAR projects. That figure did not include monies appropriated separately in fiscal year 1972 for barracks partitions and rehabilitation or barracks furniture purchases Army-wide. By the end of fiscal year 1972 Project VOLAR involved over 300,000 active duty Army personnel and touched the lives of 334,000 active duty family members. VOLAR projects on the additional posts duplicated, for the most part, experiments begun at the initial VOLAR sites. By that time the emphasis had shifted from starting new experiments to evaluating the effects of the existing programs on soldier attitudes toward the Army.[20]

Notes

¹ Interv, author with Forsythe, 24 Mar 83.

² Capt. Grant L. Fredericks, "The Modern Volunteer Army Field Experiment: An Analysis of the Modern Volunteer Army's Field Experiment on Soldier Attitudes and Army Career Intentions," Report Number 72–1, Office of the Special Assistant for the Modern Volunteer Army, Washington, D.C., 1 June 1973, pp. 1–5 (hereafter cited as VOLAR Final Report); Butler and Forsythe Intervs.

³ Hughes, "Fort Carson Debrief"; Lt. Gen. Harold G. Moore and Lt. Col. Jeff M. Tuten, *Building a Volunteer Army: The Fort Ord Contribution* (Washington, D.C.: Department of the Army, 1975), pp. 18–27, 51–53; Brig. Gen. Willard Latham, *The Modern Volunteer Army Program: The Benning Experiment, 1970–1972* (Washington, D.C.: Department of the Army, 1974), pp. 11–12; VOLAR Final Report, p. 1.

⁴ The Benning Plan, pp. 8–41 passim.

⁵ Memo, Commanding General, Fort Carson, for SAMVA, sub: Revision of Fort Carson Plan for a Modern Volunteer Army, (c. Jan 71), Background Material. This memo included revised fund estimates for proposals in the original plan dated 29 November 1970 and proposals added on 4 January 1971.

⁶ "Fort Ord Plan for Modern Volunteer Army," (c. Nov 70), Background Material.

⁷ "Experimental Volunteer Army Training Program (EVATP)," pt. D, sec. II, Fort Ord Plan, pp. 1–3; Moore and Tuten, *The Fort Ord Contribution*, pp. 59–67.

⁸ Memo, Montague for Forsythe, 9 Dec 70, sub: Project VOLAR 71, Background Material.

⁹ Ibid.; Moore and Tuten, *The Fort Ord Contribution*, pp. 68–71.

¹⁰ VOLAR Final Report, pp. 4–5; Moore and Tuten, *The Fort Ord Contribution*, p. 68.

¹¹ VOLAR Final Report, pp. 12–13. For fiscal year 1972 the Army included VOLAR projects as part of its budget request; Congress authorized $72 million for VOLAR 72 as a separate item in the Department of Defense Project Volunteer budget.

¹² Haynes Johnson and George C. Wilson, *Army in Anguish* (New York: Pocket Books, 1972), pp. 14, 16 (originally published as a series in the *Washington Post* in September and October 1971).

¹³ Westmoreland, *Report of the Chief of Staff*, pp. 85–86; Latham, *The Benning Experiment*, pp. 47–48; Moore and Tuten, *The Fort Ord Contribution*, p. 92.

¹⁴ MFR, 1 Feb 71, sub: SA/SAMVA Meeting, 28 Jan 71, w/attached Talking Paper, sub: MVA Funding, contained in binder, "Modern Volunteer Army Program SA/SAMVA Meetings and Memos, Jan–Apr 71," (hereafter cited as SA/SAMVA Meetings, Jan–Apr 71), HRC, CMH; Memo, John Kester for Dr. Fox, 1 Feb 1971, sub: Volunteer Army—Privacy in Barracks, OSA file 202.10, RG 335, WNRC.

¹⁵ MFR, 19 Feb 71, sub: Conference with Secretary Resor Concerning Proposed Construction to Support PROJECT VOLUNTEER, w/attached Talking Paper, sub: 1391 Status, SA/SAMVA Meetings, Jan–Apr 71, HRC, CMH.

¹⁶ Memoranda for Record of SA/SAMVA meetings of 25 Feb, 4 Mar, 18 Mar, 1 Apr, 8 Apr, and 1 Jul 71, SA/SAMVA Meetings, Jan–Apr 71 and Apr–Jul 71, HRC, CMH; Latham, *The Benning Experiment*, p. 55.

[17] Installation Evaluation Report, "Modern Volunteer Army Experiment, 1971," Fort Benning, Georgia, 26 Jul 71, Tab C–42, Background Material. Memo, DCSPER for CofS, 23 Mar 71, sub: Request for CSC Authority, Employment of Dependents in Low Skill Jobs in Europe, OSA file 202.10, RG 335, WNRC.

[18] Ltr, USA to Chairman, USCSC, 31 Mar 71; Ltr, Director, Bureau of Policies and Standards, USCSC, to SA, 3 May 71, OSA file 202.10, RG 335, WNRC; MFRs, SA/SAMVA Meetings of 20 May and 25 Jun 71, SA/SAMVA Meetings, Apr–Jul 71, HRC, CMH.

[19] Butler, "The All-Volunteer Armed Force—Its Feasibility and Implications," p. 35.

[20] VOLAR Final Report, pp. 14, L–1.

Richard M. Nixon, President of the United States (1969–1974). His support for an all-volunteer force during the 1968 presidential campaign energized the Army to seriously study the issue (NARA); right, *Congressman F. Edward Hebert (D-La.) presiding over a session of the House Armed Services Committee. As chairman of this powerful committee, Mr. Hebert was initially skeptical about the administration's intentions and the advisability of ending the draft, but later became a supporter of legislation that affected the MVA Program* (F. Edward Hebert Papers, Tulane University); below left, *Lt. Gen. George I. Forsythe, Jr., Special Assistant for the Modern Volunteer Army (1970–1972)* (TRADOC); below right, *Brig. Gen. Robert M. Montague, Jr., Deputy Special Assistant to the Secretary of the Army for the Modern Volunteer Army (1970–1972) and Special Assistant to the Assistant Secretary of Defense (Manpower, Reserve Affairs, and Logistics) (1972–1973).* (MHI)

Enlisted quarters at Camp Zama, Japan, renovated with funds from the Modern Volunteer Army Program. The press often highlighted images such as this in its reports about the all-volunteer Army. Quarters that looked more like a college dormitory than soldiers' billets scandalized veterans and worried senior military personnel about the Army's image and future discipline (NARA)

Soldiers of the 503d Supply and Transportation Battalion at Edwards Kaserne in Frankfurt, Germany, renovated an old shower room to create a "Trucker's Lounge" in early 1972 (NARA).

Soldiers were given considerable latitude in decorating parts of their barracks. At Fort Carson, Colorado, a small area of the barracks has been configured as an informal lounge, where a unit commander (left) conducts a "rap session" with some soldiers in his command. (NARA); below, a company commander at Fort Carson joins his troops for a game of pool in their barracks at the height of the VOLAR project in January 1971 (NARA).

Trainees from Company B, 2d Battalion, 5th Training Brigade, at Fort Polk, Louisiana, dine outside as part of the MVA Program, February 1972 (NARA).

CHAPTER VII

The Permissive Army
Evaluating VOLAR, 1971

The VOLAR experiment began in January 1971. The initial confusion that attended its beginning, which coincided with the start of the High Impact Action and the Modern Volunteer Army Program worldwide, and the delays in funding for high-visibility VOLAR projects already cited settled down by spring. Because VOLAR began at only three posts in the United States (Fort Bragg's program began in April), the rest of the Army looked on with curiosity, and in some cases resentment, at what took place at Forts Benning, Carson, and Ord. The public too showed an interest in the changes apparently sweeping the Army. To satisfy that curiosity various segments of the media examined VOLAR and how the changes affected the soldiers living and working at the VOLAR posts.

Media Reaction

Life magazine went to Fort Carson as soon as the Army announced VOLAR because Carson's experiments in a freer life-style were already well advanced. Its editors commissioned Bill Mauldin, the celebrated artist who had created "Willie and Joe" in World War II, to "take a dubious look" at Fort Carson. Mauldin found troops in one infantry company that proclaimed itself "the most liberated unit in all of Fort Carson" living in individualized barracks where the decor ranged from contemporary hippie to gay nineties. The cover of the issue set the tone. A perplexed Willie and Joe looked on as a Fort Carson infantryman in uniform buckled on a psychedelic motorcycle helmet emblazoned with a peace symbol. The article featured photos of Carson GIs drinking beer in the barracks, enjoying go-go girls dancing topless in the enlisted men's club, and "rapping" with the assistant division commander at the on-post coffeehouse.

Life quoted Chairman of the House Armed Services Committee F. Edward Hebert, who said, "when you turn the military into a country club, discipline goes out the window." But Mauldin observed that absences in Fort Carson's most "liberated" company were down 90 percent, and he expressed little concern that soldiers were painting the barracks in bright colors. The Army at Fort Carson is "way ahead of the rest of the country," he said, in learning from young people. "This experiment might even save the poor old Army from coming apart at the seams." "As for Willie and Joe," *Life* concluded, "... well, call it envy."[1]

Life covers linking soldiers wearing peace symbols to VOLAR sensationalized the experiment and gave a false impression of what the program involved in terms of its impact on the troops themselves. To get a firsthand look, the publisher of *Army* magazine, the journal of the Association of the United States Army, visited Fort Benning. Writer L. James Binder reported that Fort Benning had declared "open season on sacred cows," and the results were not nearly as scary as critics contended. Binder talked to Fort Benning soldiers of all ranks. He found that young soldiers were most concerned about hair length and privacy when they came into the Army. They welcomed the more liberal haircut standard, but it appeared that some would never be satisfied. Of greater significance, Binder noted, was the progress toward barracks privacy. The troops eagerly participated in barracks rehabilitation and quickly purchased items of furniture, decorations, and other items of a personal nature to individualize their new 12-by-16-foot rooms. Benning soldiers especially appreciated the civilianization of KP and other post details such as grass cutting and garbage collection. Married soldiers who lived off post no longer had to rush to reveille formations and then spend the next two hours waiting for work to start. The brigade commander reported that soldiers willingly worked longer hours during the week knowing that their weekend was guaranteed free. As for the much-touted beer in the barracks and mess hall innovation, Binder reported that only 20 percent of the troops bought beer in the mess halls; most preferred milk or soft drinks with their meal. Of beer in the barracks, he quoted another commander who observed, "In the old days one of my men would go down to the PX, buy a six-pack, and then have to sit on the curb someplace to drink it." Smart commanders ignored beer in the barracks as long as there was no trouble. "Now the record says we can bring that soldier from the parking lot or curb into his home." Uniformly, Binder found that officers at Fort Benning favored most of the changes and, contrary to expectations, reported that discipline and job performance improved.[2]

The vice chief of staff of the Army, General Palmer, was concerned enough by stories about Fort Carson to send a trusted aide there on a fact-finding tour. Lt. Col. John Seigle visited Carson in November 1971. On the subject of the "so-called life-style improvements," Seigle concluded that he found nothing among them "either revolutionary or startling." He pointed to the addition of "fast food" lines in the troop messes as an example. "The improvement in troop messes is so striking that we should be embarrassed not to have instituted a choice of meals years ago." He added that new arrivals to Fort Carson expressed surprise at the notion that good food was supposed to motivate them positively. They assumed that the food should be good. He applauded the Enlisted Men's Council at Fort Carson and noted that it was "at least as useful to the commanders as it is to the junior soldiers." He found no evidence that the enlisted men's councils circumvented the chain of command. Overall Seigle concluded that VOLAR at Fort Carson had created "a more positive attitude on the part of the members of the team." But he doubted whether improved attitudes alone could contribute greatly to better training. Seigle believed that the root cause of poor training—personnel turbulence—remained unsolved and, indeed, could not be solved at the installation level.³

As VOLAR continued and expanded to more locations, a number of patterns developed. Among the experiments designed to increase professionalism, civilianization of KP and other menial duties that consumed soldier labor and detracted from training stood out as the single most important success. Barracks privacy, a so-called life-style measure, ranked second. Fort Ord even reported an exception to the trend toward more barracks privacy. Trainees tried movable partitions to break platoon bays up into smaller living spaces and quickly went back to the open forty-man arrangement. They found that during the hectic pace of basic training open bays proved easier to clean. Trainees also preferred close-cropped hair even when given a choice. Among soldiers with families, improvements in medical services and dental care stood out. Highly visible innovations such as beer in the barracks and mess halls flopped. Indeed, after about a year the Army removed beer vending machines from most barracks for lack of patronage.

Other VOLAR initiatives also ranked high with soldiers. In the area of leadership and supervision, soldiers responded favorably to measures that reflected respect and fair treatment. Enlisted men preferred to be called "soldier" instead of "EM," the universal term for enlisted man that had replaced "GI" between the Korean and Vietnam Wars. Soldiers expected stabilized assignments, the chance for educational and vocational development, fair treatment on the job, and the chance to participate in their own career development. On the other hand, they were unimpressed with other VOLAR initiatives such as increased sports, on-post entertainment, and opportunities for a more diverse social life.

In the specific area of training, the Experimental Volunteer Army Training Program developed by Fort Ord proved a major success. Soldiers trained at Ord consistently outperformed men trained in the traditional methods used at other basic training centers, and Fort Ord's methods soon spread to the other combat arms training centers. In 1973 the commander of the combat support training brigade at Fort Ord adapted the program to courses under his purview. Within a year proponent schools of the combat service and service support arms of the Army were adapting the concepts developed for infantry basic and advanced individual training for use in their programs.⁴

It quickly became obvious that much of the VOLAR experimental program appealed to the soldier. In retrospect, as Colonel Seigle noted, no one should have been surprised that actions such as improving menus, ending KP, rehabilitating barracks, giving soldiers more individual freedom consistent with responsible behavior, ending lock-step training, and treating individuals with respect should have had anything but a positive effect on troop morale. But improving Army life was only half of the VOLAR equation. The whole point of the Project VOLAR experiments was to see what effect innovations in training, professionalism, and life-style would have on combat arms soldiers in terms of their attitudes toward the Army and their willingness to stay in the service beyond one enlistment. Evaluating the results of VOLAR and determining what aspects of the experiment to apply Army-wide remained the most important part of the project.

Evaluating VOLAR

As General Forsythe frequently told audiences on his tours of the country, he was not running a popularity contest for the Army with the MVA Program or the VOLAR experiments. The ultimate goal of the former was to reduce the Army's requirement for draftees to zero by the end of 1972. The purpose the latter was to determine what kinds of professional and life-style changes facilitated the MVA Program goal by increasing retention. Higher reenlistments reduced pressure on recruiters and allowed them to be more selective. Likewise, improved service attractiveness could be featured in recruiting advertisements. Thus, while VOLAR primarily was aimed at people already in the Army, the reciprocal relationship between service attractiveness, reenlistments, and recruiting made the experiment crucial to the overall success of the Modern Volunteer Army Program.

The SAMVA office evaluated and analyzed the effect of VOLAR actions in several ways. First, commanders at VOLAR test sites collected attitude and opinion data which were compared with similar data taken from soldiers at non-VOLAR posts and Army-wide samples. The Human Resources Research Organization (HumRRO), a civilian contractor, developed questionnaires for SAMVA to collect data from soldiers, officers, family members, trainees, and commanders. HumRRO provided direct support to each VOLAR installation to design and evaluate the data collection tests and assisted SAMVA in developing the Army-wide tests. The tests asked three types of questions: Did the respondent notice changes in the quality of the modern volunteer Army? Were those changes positive, negative, or of no consequence? Did the changes affect the respondent's intent to remain in the Army beyond his initial service obligation? Second, Forsythe conducted cost effectiveness analyses of VOLAR actions that the survey data revealed to be of significance in terms of their effect on soldier attitudes. Finally, the VOLAR evaluation correlated attitudinal and cost data with other data on soldier performance, retention rates, and traditional indicators such as courts-martial, nonjudicial punishment, absenteeism, and other delinquency rates to see if VOLAR actions influenced behavior as well as attitudes.

VOLAR questionnaires were administered throughout the approximately eighteen months of the experiment. Sample sizes varied. Tests aimed at trainees, for example, were given to all basic trainees at Forts Ord and Jackson. Approximately 450 enlisted and 50 officer personnel represented the permanent part of the military population at each VOLAR installation. Army-wide attitudinal surveys reached about one percent of all active duty service members not including trainees, personnel in Vietnam, and VOLAR participants.[5]

The surveys administered in support of the VOLAR evaluation made it possible for the SAMVA office to develop a composite profile of the Army enlisted soldier in the 1971–72 time frame. The soldier was a white male, age 23.1, between the grades E–4 and E–5. He had spent slightly less than two years in the Army. Some differences existed between the composite enlisted man assigned to VOLAR versus non-VOLAR posts. More soldiers at VOLAR posts tended to be young and unmarried. The surveys revealed no difference in educational levels between VOLAR and non-VOLAR participants; educational attainment ranged from an average of 11.4 years at Bad Kitzingen, West Germany, to 15.0 years at Fort Benning. Subsequent evaluation of the survey results revealed significant correlations between personal background characteristics and retention potential among enlisted personnel.[6]

The VOLAR evaluation surveys indicated that only 40 percent of enlisted personnel liked being in the Army, and that among soldiers with less than two years' service only 18 percent liked it. Over 77 percent considered their jobs important but only about 40 percent found them interesting, and less than half reported being challenged by their jobs. Although discouraging, the levels of satisfaction showed positive trends between 1971 and mid-1972. The improving trends suggested that as more "true volunteers" replaced draftees and draft-motivated volunteers, more soldiers would find greater satisfaction in the Army and their jobs. Survey findings on career intent reinforced the optimistic outlook. Among soldiers with less than two years of service the percentage of those indicating "Yes" and "Not Sure" to reenlistment questions increased between March 1971 and June 1972. Army-wide only 15 percent of enlistees polled registered an interest in continuing their careers in early 1971; a year later the figure rose to 22 percent. The increase at VOLAR posts was gratifyingly more significant: in March 1971 only 12 percent of the soldiers with two years' or less service expressed positive or neutral opinions toward reenlistment; by the end of the VOLAR test 36 percent considered remaining on active duty. Among soldiers with more than two years' service—including draft-motivated volunteers but not draftees—reenlistment intent was higher, and the surveys revealed less difference between VOLAR and non-VOLAR posts. By the end of the experiment 67 percent of VOLAR post soldiers with more than two years' service indicated at least a willingness to consider staying on; the figure for non-VOLAR post respondents in the same category was 64 percent.[7]

When the analysts compared actual reenlistment behavior with expressed intent, they found that "expressed reenlistment intent is a reasonable, but not uniformly accurate, predictor of later reenlistment action, at least within a year of such action." Of VOLAR soldiers surveyed between January and June 1971, over 81 percent of those who responded "Yes" when questioned on their reenlistment intentions did in fact reenlist by the end of February 1972; 37 percent of those who replied "Not Sure" actually reenlisted. An analysis of background characteristics of reenlistees revealed several interesting points: the longer a soldier remained in the Army the more likely it was that he would reenlist; married soldiers with families were more likely to reenlist than single soldiers; blacks tended to reenlist at slightly higher rates that did whites; the higher a soldier's grade at the time of eligibility for first reenlistment, the more likely it was that he would reenlist; and soldiers who had completed high school were more likely to reenlist than high school dropouts or soldiers with college degrees. Not surprisingly, draftees and draft-motivated volunteers normally did not reenlist.[8]

The VOLAR evaluation surveys confirmed what Forsythe and commanders at the VOLAR posts already knew intuitively—VOLAR initiatives indeed resulted in more favorable soldier attitudes toward the Army and higher retention rates. After the initial confusion that accompanied the entire program died down, commanders began reporting favorably on most aspects of the endeavor. In his review of the second six months of the program, General Ralph E. Haines, Jr., commanding general of the Continental Army Command, told Westmoreland that the initiatives were "beginning to pay off." Haines reported that innovations in the areas of professionalism and training showed the greatest promise, especially the programs designed to replace soldiers with civilians, thereby releasing the former for training. Barracks improvement programs in general and those funded by VOLAR in particular also proved effective, according to Haines, once the funds caught up with the promises. Problems with Army credibility also declined during the reporting period, and Haines noted "no indication of erosion of discipline as a result of the MVA program." Indeed, he reported, "military courtesy and appearance continue to improve."

Haines' generally favorable report contained one pointed criticism of VOLAR. Reflecting on the early confusion over the goals of the Modern Volunteer Army Program and the VOLAR experiment and the constant interchangeable use of the terms by the press and soldiers alike, he noted "the term 'VOLAR' is frequently associated with extremes, whether good or bad, and whether or not they are part of the MVA effort." He recommended discontinuance of the use of the term as soon as the experiment ended.[9]

Others ratified Haines' views. General Michael S. Davison, commander of troops in Europe and the Seventh Army, told Westmoreland that he and his subordinate commanders "are encouraged by the progress made thus far." He did admit some setbacks. The program of decentralized training, for example, "resulted in junior leaders conducting some very poor training." However, Davison added, the inexperienced officers were learning from their mistakes, "especially where brigade and battalion commanders are intelligently playing their appropriate roles." Davison praised VOLAR, especially the programs that freed soldiers for training and provided employment to civilian family members. He noted that only 42 percent of approved VOLAR projects had begun, while all funds had been obligated. Obviously much remained to be done. Like Haines, Davison reported that the freer life-style arrangements did not affect discipline adversely. Indeed, statistics on crime and absences were "encouraging." Absences without leave, serious incidents, and crimes of violence dropped during the six months covered by the report. The positive trends associated with the volunteer Army experiments continued during the last six months of the VOLAR experiment. In his next report to the chief of staff Davison concluded, "We have seen many areas of improvement over the past six months. Appearance, military courtesy and conduct of our soldiers are better. Training shows heartening improvement," and the "back to basics" programs such as releasing soldiers from nonmilitary duties continued to be "ranked by soldiers as the most significant morale builder."[10]

The commanders also reported positive trends in enlisted retention, although the requirement to reduce the Army by approximately 100,000 soldiers by the end of fiscal year 1972, dictated in late September 1971 by the final passage of the Military Pay and Selective Service Extension Act, clouded the effect of VOLAR and Modern Volunteer Army actions on reenlistments. Third U.S. Army commander Lt. Gen. Albert O. Connor reported that reenlistments in his command declined overall between June and December 1971 compared to the same period in 1970. But he also pointed out that standards for reenlistment had been raised to facilitate the reduction in strength. Furthermore, Connor noted, reenlistments among soldiers assigned to VOLAR posts in his command exceeded objectives. At Fort Benning, for example, 1,098 soldiers reenlisted, 124.21 percent of Benning's six-month objective. In the final six months of the VOLAR test reenlistments among first-term soldiers in the Third Army increased despite higher standards and the imposition of an involuntary early release program forced on the Army by the necessity to meet lower end-strength requirements by June 1972. The new Third Army commander, Lt. Gen. Melvin Zais, attributed the increase in first-term enlistments during the first half of 1972 to "the combined effect of MVAP actions and command emphasis."[11]

Other commanders also noted the adverse impact of the forced reduction in strength on reenlistments. Brig. Gen. Thomas K. Trigg, commanding general of the Army Security Agency, concluded that the Army's manpower reductions and an early release program for Vietnam returnees "led to an atmosphere which is directly counter to the MVA goal of retention of personnel to build a volunteer force." Trigg reported that following announcement of the strength cut and early release programs, a "'get out of the Army as soon as possible' philosophy quickly dominated and dampened the spirit of the MVA." Reenlistments plummeted in his command, and the trend would not improve until the programs ended. The Army urgently needed to reestablish a credible reenlistment atmosphere to assure the soldier that he still was wanted, Trigg concluded. General Davison also reported a drop in reenlistments in Europe following the beginning of the early release programs. Although he acknowledged the requirement to reduce strength, he warned that the accompanying decline in reenlistments would lead to significant losses among skilled enlisted men which, in turn, would limit training and support capabilities.[12]

Commanders in the field and civilian and military analysts who evaluated the VOLAR surveys also agreed on those measures that contributed most to improved attitudes toward the Army and, by extension, to higher reenlistments. Generally the survey results indicated, and commanders concluded, that efforts to make the Army more professionally stimulating furthered the goals of the volunteer force more than did improvements in life-style. The analysts who performed the formal VOLAR evaluation rated VOLAR and MVA programs in terms of three categories: soldiers' awareness of the innovation; the influence of the innovation on soldiers' attitudes toward the Army; and the influence of the innovation on soldiers' intent to reenlist. Overall, the single most positive innovation was civilianization of KP—a professionalism initiative. The program, designed to "return soldiers to soldiering," achieved "very high" soldier awareness levels on all surveys and according to the samples had a "very high" impact on attitudes and a "moderate to high" effect on retention. The formal VOLAR evaluation considered the program "among the most promising actions for Army-wide implementation" and recommended continuation of the program and expansion of the concept to roads and grounds maintenance.

Commanders agreed. General Haines told Westmoreland that "the program for the civilianization of detail labor forces appears to be the most effective Army life [sic] innovation." Like others, Haines at first misunderstood the point of civilianization and saw it as a program aimed at eliminating irritants. Certainly soldiers saw KP as an irritant of Army life, but unit commanders regarded troop labor details as a drain on training strength. General Davison reported that nonmission troop labor requirements—that is, the diversion of troops from training to post maintenance—consumed an average of 2,800 soldiers per day in Europe. He welcomed the civilianization initiative and told Westmoreland it was immensely popular with the soldiers too.[13] Equating civilianization with enhancing military professionalism instead of Army-life improvements satisfied both commanders and soldiers. The objectives of civilianization and what it accomplished were not necessarily the same. In effect it was both a professional and a life-style enhancement measure, regardless of how it was intended.

Both the survey-supported VOLAR analysis and the subjective reports of major commanders concluded that life-style innovations had little impact on retention. The notable exception to the lack of success of actions aimed at improving living conditions was in the area of barracks renovations and furniture programs. The VOLAR analysis and commanders agreed that these programs should continue despite the fact that survey data indicated that barracks improvements had only a "moderate to low" impact on retention. Innovations in the area of life-style did, however, achieve widespread recognition and had a positive impact on overall attitude. Analysts of the VOLAR experiments thus concluded that improvements in fundamental living conditions should continue despite low direct return in terms of reenlistment on the grounds that decent living conditions constituted a minimum norm for a volunteer Army and contributed to an improved image with the general public. The thrust of the analysis was that while decent living conditions would not hold soldiers to service, the absence of them surely would drive them away. Army commanders and the Army staff concurred, and throughout the period of the VOLAR test field commanders commented favorably on the barracks renovation projects and furniture programs. Noting the lag between authorization and commencement, they urged the Department of the Army to authorize more funds for rehabilitation of existing buildings and recommended eventual replacement of aging structures with new contemporary design "dormitory" style barracks. In a similar vein, analysts and field commanders agreed on the need for more and better housing for married service members and their families.[14]

Recognition that success of the volunteer force depended indirectly on greater attention to basic human needs appears self-evident in retrospect. That the Army required survey data to confirm it in the early 1970s suggests the extent to which senior commanders and the Army staff had become preoccupied with their missions during Vietnam when selective service assured a constant flow of replacements. In the process soldiers had become an abstract resource. In the same vein, the confusion in the minds of senior commanders over the distinction between "professionalism" and "life-style" VOLAR initiatives suggests that the distinctions were artificial. Eliminating KP enchanced professionalism in the eyes of the commander; to the soldier it improved his life-style.

The formal evaluation of the VOLAR experiments required time-consuming collection and correlation of survey and statistical data, and, although installations and contractors issued interim reports, the final report was not finished until March 1973. This study, prepared by Capt. Grant L. Fredericks, a member of the SAMVA staff from its inception, consisted of a documented history of the VOLAR phase of the MVA Program, an analysis of the contract and commanders' evaluations of the experiment, and recommendations to expand and continue successful VOLAR projects on an Army-wide basis in support of the Modern Volunteer Army effort.

Fredericks reported that VOLAR programs in the professionalism category showed the most promise of stimulating retention and recommended that in the future MVA Program emphasis should be placed on that area. At the same time he urged that the Army pursue "a balanced program" which continued initiatives in the areas of life-style and retention. In terms of future administration of volunteer Army projects, Fredericks recommended that local commanders receive wide latitude in selecting, implementing, and modifying innovations in view of the fact that his analysis revealed significant differences in the impact of specific actions on soldiers' attitudes and reenlistment intentions from one post to another. Fredericks also recommended that the Army expand and refine its ability to manage and evaluate the volunteer Army program at local and Department of the Army staff levels using the existing system of installation and contract reports as the basis for further development.[15]

Form and Substance

By the time Fredericks rendered the final VOLAR evaluation report events had passed him by. As is so often the case with fast-moving programs, the Army's thinking on VOLAR and the MVA Program evolved more quickly than the projects themselves. The VOLAR experiment terminated as scheduled at the end of June 1972. In theory, the Modern Volunteer Army Program was supposed to continue beyond that date, but by the time the VOLAR evaluation was complete, the MVA too was a thing of the past. Army field commanders and elements of the Army staff had recommended an Army-wide transition to a volunteer force early in the course of the experiments. They considered the off-line nature of the Modern Volunteer Army Program and the VOLAR experiments confusing, divisive, and an administrative burden. Commanders and senior officers on the Army staff also worried that continued use of the terms VOLAR and Modern Volunteer Army, which acquired negative connotations in the press and in the field, would be counterproductive. Thus, even before the end of the VOLAR experiments the Army staff had begun working on plans to phase out a separate and distinct Modern Volunteer Army Program.[16] As a result Fredericks' report had little influence on the subsequent course of events.

In contrast, it was the interim reports supported by survey analyses provided on a periodic basis by contract evaluators that influenced the VOLAR experiments and led to a major shift in the emphasis of the overall Modern Volunteer Army Program. As earlier noted, commanders at all levels had recommended shifting the emphasis of these actions from Army life to professionalism. The former area was often misunderstood and too easily trivialized. Media coverage of the changing Army focused on go-go girls in servicemen's clubs and beer in the barracks. During the first six months of 1971 the *New York Times*, CBS, and NBC did several stories each on Fort Carson that emphasized permissiveness themes, according to General Haines. One of Haines' subordinates stated the problem best: "much of the initial MVA publicity was slanted toward service attractiveness features which tended to submerge the objective of creating a highly professional Army with a strong chain of command." Haines and the field army commander under him also complained that Army advertising excessively focused on life-style improvements. The adverse results were twofold. Commanders and noncommissioned officers who read the newspaper stories and watched the television coverage of the Fort Carson experiment saw in the Army advertisements confirmation of their fears that the Army was becoming permissive. Soldiers, on the other hand, expected immediate delivery on the improvements promised by the ads, and when these were not forthcoming due to bureaucratic and budgetary delays they doubted the willingness or ability of the Army to deliver on its pledges. As the commanding general of the Fifth Army put it, "Our advertising has gotten ahead of our accomplishments." Like others, he suggested placing greater emphasis on professionalism rather than on life-style measures. Above all he pleaded for "a breathing spell to assimilate the many changes to date in the MVA program."[17]

Forsythe was extremely receptive to the analyses and recommendations that flowed in from the field commands. The first series of commanders' comments arrived in late July 1971 and proved especially timely. At the time the

SAMVA staff was engaged in revising the Master Plan for the Modern Volunteer Army for final publication and general release. Frustrated by the initial reaction to the MVA Program and VOLAR in and out of the Army, Forsythe seized on the recommendations that professionalism be emphasized over improvements in life-style. The idea was compatible with his own evolving thoughts on how best to express the goals and objectives of the volunteer force effort. Under his guidance the SAMVA staff revised the master program and shortly produced a slick brochure featuring a combat infantryman on the cover entitled "The Modern Volunteer Army: A Program for Professionals." The new description and justification for the several components of the Modern Volunteer Army Program emphasized that its ultimate purpose was to "Expedite the development of a capably led, highly competent fighting force which attracts motivated, qualified volunteers." Improvements in Army life were subordinated to strengthening professionalism throughout; combining the two would lead to a better Army. Whereas the original version of the master program devoted most of its space to a bland explanation of Modern Volunteer Army Program funding arrangements, the VOLAR experiment, and the high-impact actions, most of which were low- or no-cost life-style innovations, the revised "Program for Professionals" employed dynamic language and located the discussion of programs aimed at fostering professionalism up front, relegating Army life programs and the VOLAR experiment to later pages.[18]

The new pamphlet clearly was aimed at a general audience and was designed to sell the program to the Army and public rather than explain it to a narrower audience. The actual balance of the program really did not change in terms of component projects or allocation of funds. But the members of Congress who had to authorize and appropriate funds for volunteer Army initiatives and the senior officers who administered them were more amenable to changes that enhanced professionalism. Life-style changes smacked of coddling and were thus deemphasized or shown to contribute to professionalism. In this sense the revised publication was a new label on an old bottle designed to market the product in terms that appealed to Forsythe and others of his generation in and out of the Army.

"Program for Professionals" received wide distribution. Secretary of the Army Robert F. Froehlke sent copies to members of the Senate and House Armed Services Committees and Appropriations Committees and to other interested members of Congress. Predictably the reaction was mixed. Senator Robert T. Stafford, a leading supporter of the volunteer force concept, praised the publication and "those responsible for developing this far-reaching program." Congressman Louis C. Wyman, a fiscal conservative on the House Defense Appropriations Subcommittee, wrote personally to Froehlke of his worry that the higher salaries and fringe benefits necessary to attract and retain volunteers would increase personnel costs to 60 percent of the overall defense budget. When Froehlke replied that he did not consider providing the individual soldier a decent living "the purchase of defense through wage comparability," Wyman shot back, "all well and good, but where in the hell are we going to find the money?" [19]

Redirection of MVA Program and VOLAR emphasis toward professionalism measures received a favorable response from commanders in the field. In their subsequent semiannual reports commanders, still reflecting the confusion between professionalism and life-style initiatives, praised the new direction and claimed that the focus on efforts to enhance professionalism paid bigger dividends than did the earlier attention devoted to life-style changes. General Haines singled out "our initiative toward improved professionalism" as showing the greatest promise in his analysis of developments between July and December 1971. And the survey data compiled by the VOLAR evaluation teams at the test installations and in the SAMVA office confirmed the subjective judgments of Haines and his colleagues.

In terms of its ability to provide the Army with the data necessary to identify the category of innovations that offered the greatest return in improved soldier attitudes and retention, the VOLAR experiment can thus be judged a success. On the other hand, it can be argued that the success of the professionalism measures was little more than a self-fulfilling prophecy. It was never a secret that commanders and noncommissioned officers were uneasy about the host of life-style changes associated with both VOLAR and the overall MVA Program. Many expressed open hostility and more probably gave only lukewarm support to the programs consistent with the dictates of the Department of the Army and their responsibilities as leaders. These same officers and noncommissioned officers could more easily support efforts to improve professionalism. When the focus of the Modern Volunteer Army Program and its field experiment changed to emphasize professionalism, latent opposition declined; nobody could be opposed to professionalism, which was the Army's equivalent of motherhood. Officially the emphasis of the MVA Program and VOLAR had always been on making the Army a more professionally rewarding and effective force. Because of the frantic pace of events at the onset, undue attention had been given to some of the more sensational examples of changing Army life-style. The inability of Forsythe and the Army leadership to emphasize and articulate the true purpose and goals of the programs correctly from the beginning compounded the confusion and reinforced latent hostility to any sort of change in the field. Forsythe's recognition of these problems and his ability to capitalize on the early success of professionalism measures and redirect the focus of the program helped repair the early damage. At the same time, the early success of professionalism measures occurred mainly because they began quickly and were not held back by delays in funding or bureaucratic squabbles over authority and reprogramming. Furthermore, the most successful professionalism measure, ending KP, was seen by most soldiers as an improvement in life-style even if the Army classified it differently. Whether VOLAR "proved" that a more professional Army had greater appeal to soldiers than did a more comfortable one is therefore debatable but not the point.

VOLAR's real contribution lay in its role as a catalyst. Again, because of the rapidity with which the Army launched the overall MVA Program, there simply was not enough money to permit experiments everywhere. Neither would it have been prudent to experiment everywhere throughout the Army. Despite the confusion, the limited nature of the VOLAR experiment was appropriate. By its very existence it stimulated change elsewhere in the Army. Commanders at non–VOLAR posts quickly imitated successful VOLAR initiatives, often without formal Department of the Army approval. VOLAR was necessary, according to General Palmer, who admitted to disagreeing with Forsythe on numerous occasions. "George Forsythe and his people did serve a useful purpose. They got the attention of the whole Army," Palmer concluded. "They stirred us up, made us think the impossible and, on balance, I think they did a good job." [20]

Notes

[1] "Willie and Joe Visit the New U.S. Army," *Life*, 5 February 1971, pp. 2A, 20–27.

[2] L. James Binder, "The Now Is Very In at Fort Benning," *Army*, April 1971, pp. 22–29.

[3] MFR, 10 Nov 71, sub: "What the Hell Is Going on at Fort Carson?" Both Less and More than Some Think, Background Material. Note: Forsythe received a copy and passed the report on to the deputy chief of staff for personnel, General Kerwin, who ordered every director on the DCSPER staff to read it.

[4] VOLAR Final Report, pp. 81–86, 90–91; Latham, *The Benning Experiment*, pp. 81–106; Moore and Tuten, *The Fort Ord Contribution*, pp. 92–95, 103–05, 113–17, 123.

[5] MVAP–March 71, pp. B–2, 7–B–1 to 7–B–3; VOLAR Final Report, pp. 25–35.

[6] VOLAR Final Report, pp. 50–52.

[7] Ibid., pp. 58–60.

[8] Ibid., pp. 64–69.

[9] Ltr, Haines to Westmoreland, 14 Feb 72, w/incl, Reports from the four Army commands subordinate to CONARC, Background Material.

[10] Ltrs, Davison to Westmoreland, 11 Feb 72, and to Palmer, 14 Aug 72, Background Material.

[11] Ltrs, Connor to Haines, 31 Jan 71, Zais to Haines, 27 Jul 72, Background Material.

[12] Ltrs, Trigg to HQDA, 14 Aug 72, Davison to Westmoreland, 11 Feb 72, Background Material.

[13] VOLAR Final Report, pp. 73–74, 76, 127; Ltrs, Haines to Westmoreland, 14 Feb 72, Davison to Westmoreland, 26 Jul 71 and 14 Aug 72, Background Material.

[14] VOLAR Final Report, pp. 106–15, 118, 127; and Memos, Lt Col Jacoby for ADCPER and DCSPER, sub: Evaluation of Field Command Progress Reports for the Period 1 July–31 Dec 1971, and Maj Gen Seitz for CofSA, 14 Nov 72, sub: Major Commands' MVA Progress Reports for the Period 1 Jan–30 Jun 72, both in Background Material.

[15] VOLAR Final Report, pp. 121–26.

[16] Memo, Maj Gen Seitz for CofSA, 12 Nov 72, sub: Major Commands Progress Reports for the Period 1 Jan–30 Jun 72; Memo, Maj Gen Forrester for CofSA, 20 Mar 73, sub: VOLAR Wrap-Up Report, both in Background Material; Forsythe and Palmer Intervs.

[17] Ltrs, Haines to Westmoreland, 19 Jul 71; Lt Gen Hutchin to Haines, 13 Jul 71; Lt Gen Underwood to Haines, 13 Jul 71, all in Background Material.

[18] Forsythe Interv; "The Modern Volunteer Army: A Program for Professionals," c. Oct 71, 52 pp.; "Modern Volunteer Army: Master Program" (Washington, D.C.: OSAMVA, 1 March 1971), 14 pp., w/10 annexes.

[19] Ltrs, Stafford to Froehlke, 17 Nov 71; Wyman to Froehlke, 13 Oct 71; Froehlke (reply) to Wyman, 6 Nov 71; and Wyman (reply) to Froehlke, 15 Nov 71, OSA file 202.10, RG 335, WNRC.

[20] MHI Interv with Palmer.

CHAPTER VIII

The Bottom Line Recruiting, 1969–1971

Between the world wars, the last time the United States relied exclusively on volunteers for enlistments for its armed forces for a sustained period, military personnel managers understood well the relationships between recruiting and service attractiveness, pay, changes in the economy, and the amount of money and people available for recruiting. The General Recruiting Service constantly badgered the War Department for more recruiters, believing that the correct ratio of Recruiting Service strength to Regular Army strength was 1:100. The Army experimented with paid recruiting advertising as early as 1919 and maintained a Recruiting Publicity Bureau throughout the interwar years. Experience during the period ratified the General Recruiting Service's assumptions about enlisted procurement. Economy measures that reduced the size and budget of the recruiting force inevitably were followed by a drop in enlistments. When Regular Army enlisted strength was increased and large numbers of new recruits were needed quickly to fill the ranks, the proven method for meeting the requirement was to increase the numbers of recruiters in the field and advertise widely.[1]

The Organization Base

By 1970 when the Army faced the real prospect of having to rely on true volunteers again for the first time in a generation, most of the experience and expertise of the earlier all-volunteer Army had been lost. Indeed, only a handful of senior officers on active duty served before World War II and none had direct recruiting experience. The U.S. Army Recruiting Command (USAREC), the successor of the General Recruiting Service, was commanded by a major general under direction of the deputy chief of staff for personnel and consisted of over 8,000 military and civilian personnel.

USAREC performed two major functions. As the executive agent for the Department of Defense, it administered the seventy-four armed forces examining and entrance stations that processed draftees and volunteers into all of the armed forces. USAREC's other function was recruiting for the Army. Approximately 3,000 enlisted men and women, all noncommissioned officers, formed the field recruiting forces. The recruiters worked out of more than 950 offices located throughout the United States, Guam, Puerto Rico, and the Virgin Islands.[2]

In fiscal year 1970, the last year before volunteer Army initiatives began, the recruiting force enlisted 177,300 men and women. Based on studies done for the Project PROVIDE study group during the same period, less than half of those enlistees were considered true volunteers. In the same time frame 198,700 men entered the Army involuntarily as draftees. Thus recruiters accounted for less than one-quarter of the total. In the absence of a draft they would have needed over 30,000 volunteers a month to meet fiscal year 1970 requirements instead of the 7,300 true volunteers actually recruited per month that year.[3]

USAREC had contributed a full-time participant to the Project PROVIDE study group. The input from the Recruiting Command identified the problems the recruiting force faced in an all-volunteer environment, especially shortcomings in organization and personnel, and offered suggestions for solutions. The PROVIDE report refined these initial USAREC proposals. Thus by the end of 1970, when Westmoreland openly committed the Army to achieving the all-volunteer goal and Forsythe arrived on the scene, the basic program for remaking the Recruiting Command into an aggressive sales force for an all-volunteer Army had already begun. Forsythe, who personally was more interested in using his charter to reform the Army, left most of the details of the recruiting effort to USAREC. His main task with respect to recruitment would be acting as an advocate on behalf of the recruiting proposals before Congress and assuring that the recruiting program was compatible with and integrated into the Modern Volunteer Army Program.

Army Planning

The U.S. Army Recruiting Command began serious consideration of what it would need to keep the Army's enlisted ranks filled in a zero-draft environment early in 1969 when Westmoreland ordered a full-fledged study of the problem in response to the creation of the Gates Commission. USAREC detailed a full-time representative to the PROVIDE study group in January 1969. Colonel Butler, the study director, asked the Recruiting Command to examine its organization and staffing, enlistment options, incentives and benefits for recruiters, training programs, the potential of its recruiting markets, and budget and to make recommendations in each area with regard to the command's ability to meet the needs of an Army of between 800,000 and 1.2 million officers and enlisted men.[4]

The USAREC staff furnished its input to the PROVIDE study group by the end of May 1969. USAREC concluded that its basic organization and staffing arrangements were sound. The quality of officers assigned to the organization and level of training of recruiters, on the other hand, left something to be desired. USAREC found "serious qualitative deficiencies among officer personnel assigned [to] this command" during the Vietnam buildup and complained that "increased overseas levies" which curtailed the normal three-year tour of duty for recruiters had resulted in a "training backlog" and the assignment of unqualified personnel to the field. While it would not go so far as to acknowledge that the Recruiting Command had become a dumping ground, USAREC noted that the assignment of "only the highest caliber officers" to the command would ensure motivation of the recruiting force which, if stabilized and fully trained, the report implied, could meet the demands of the Army without draft pressure.[5]

Nothing in the USAREC recommendations to the PROVIDE study suggested that the Recruiting Command was considering an increase in the number of recruiters necessary in early 1969. Instead, USAREC proposed to squeeze more out of its existing force through an incentive program similar to those offered to civilian salesmen and a significant improvement in the level of benefits and reimbursable expenses. In the case of the former, USAREC argued for a combination of proficiency pay to recruiters based on production and "monetary awards or awards of items of useful and continued value...to show recognition for outstanding performance." Benefits too should be increased. USAREC pointed out that many recruiters assigned to high-cost areas had to absorb housing and other living expenses in excess of standard Army allowances from their pay. USAREC requested leased housing for recruiters and larger allowances for meals. Furthermore, the Recruiting Command proposed that recruiters be furnished an additional dress uniform and a monthly allowance of $20 for out-of-pocket expenses related to their duties.

USAREC also commented on attractions that it could offer to potential volunteers. It concluded that the current enlistment options available to volunteers generally were sound but found fault with the basic four-year enlistment option. In 1969 volunteers had to agree to a minimum of four years' active duty. Draftees served only two. USAREC argued that tying length of service to the skill or assignment for which one enlisted would give recruiters more flexibility when dealing with prospective volunteers. It found no justification for requiring a minimum four-year enlistment of all volunteers. Furthermore, the Recruiting Command concluded that better attention should be paid to assure that volunteers who enlisted for a specific option in fact received training and assignments commensurate with their contract. Shorter enlistments and guaranteed assignments would stimulate more true volunteers.

The most significant recommendation from USAREC came in the area of advertising. At that time the Recruiting Command spent approximately $3 million annually on advertising. Most of the expenditures were for the development and placement of posters, brochures, and advertisements in the print media. Advertising on radio and television was minimal and inexpensive; stations provided air time free as part of their public service obligation as FCC license holders. USAREC proposed to enter the unknown territory of paid broadcast media advertising on a limited basis and asked for $36 million to begin.[6]

The PROVIDE Report repeated the Recruiting Command's recommendations, in some cases verbatim. One area covered by Butler's report that the Recruiting Command input did not address was enlistment standards. Peacetime standards, according to the PROVIDE study group, "are presently at the lowest practical level; therefore, any further reduction... is not considered feasible." Thus, looking forward to the advent of the all-volunteer force from the perspectives of the Recruiting Command and of the PROVIDE study group in mid-1969, the proposed course the Army set for itself involved achieving over a 400 percent increase in enlistments of true volunteers with the existing recruiting force and with no reduction in standards. USAREC thought it could meet the challenge with a more generous compensation and incentives package for recruiters and an aggressive public relations campaign.[7]

The Department of Defense Project Volunteer committee, which reviewed the services' programs for the transition to the all-volunteer force, found little fault with the Army's proposal. In its report to the secretary of defense the committee supported efforts by all services to provide their recruiters with modest expense accounts and an increased package of benefits and incentives. The Department of Defense group agreed that standards for enlistment could not be lowered to assure requisite numbers and endorsed increases in funds for advertising to include money "for a carefully-designed pilot project to assess the cost effectiveness of paid TV/radio advertising in a particular area, and to measure its impact upon availability of public service time." No mention was made of increasing the number of recruiters in the field.[8]

Sometime between May and November 1970 the Army and the Department of Defense modified their thoughts on the need for additional recruiters. The Gates Commission, which made a draft of its recommendations available to the Defense Department and the services as early as December 1969, suggested that "there seems to be substantial opportunity for the productive addition of more recruiters," but made no specific proposal as to numbers.[9] In September 1970, Assistant Secretary of Defense Kelley visited USAREC headquarters at Fort Monroe, Virginia. During the course of his discussions with the USAREC staff Kelley expressed concern about the number of recruiters. "Might not we be able to make a significant gain in enlistments by increasing the number of recruiters, in addition to pressing the existing recruiters to work harder?" he asked. He suggested an experiment in which USAREC would "saturate" a recruiting district with recruiters to see what effect, if any, such an increase would have on enlistments.[10]

The record is unclear on the origin of the sudden interest in increasing recruiting personnel. Kelley's visit to USAREC came a month following his notification that the fiscal year 1972 Project Volunteer budget was not immune to reduction. Kelley and the services had been thinking in terms of $2 billion. Perhaps he reasoned that personnel resources could make up for a loss of money programmed for recruiting advertising or other initiatives. Although additional recruiters also cost money, their pay and allowances came from the personnel portion of the Army's budget, not the limited funds available for experimenting with volunteer force recruiting initiatives.

Kelley's interest in increasing recruiters also coincided with the increased anxiety within the offices of the Army's deputy chief of staff for personnel and assistant secretary for manpower that summer. Apparently everyone involved in planning for the all-volunteer force realized that not enough money or time was available and concluded that the dedication of additional people to the task of increasing voluntary enlistments offered possibilities.

Whatever the source of the idea to increase recruiters, Kelley's suggestion had a direct effect on Army plans. USAREC immediately developed a test to measure the impact that increasing the number of recruiters in an area would have on voluntary enlistments. The Army was so confident of the positive outcome of the test that it incorporated plans to double the size of the recruiting force in its fiscal year 1972 budget request that went to Secretary of Defense Laird on 3 November 1970 and asked permission to reprogram funds to enable the immediate reassignment of 536 noncommissioned officers to recruiting duty. About the same time the deputy chief of staff for personnel alerted the Army's major commanders that he would shortly announce a program to obtain volunteers for recruiting duty and urged their support. He noted that if sufficient volunteers failed to step forward it would be necessary to transfer noncommissioned officers with previous recruiting experience to USAREC to fill the requirement. In an emergency the Army was clearly not above "drafting" recruiters to obtain volunteers.

In November 1970 USAREC dispatched recruiter selection teams to Europe and Vietnam to interview noncommissioned officers identified as having previous experience as potential candidates for the recruiting force buildup. Many of these individuals were serving as career counselors or reenlistment NCOs in units. Commanders feared that their involuntary transfer to USAREC would cut down on reenlistments. Kerwin acknowledged these fears but reminded commanders in the field that the chief of staff and secretary of the Army had made achievement of the zero-draft goal a top Army priority.[11]

During his visit to Fort Monroe in September 1970 Kelley also directed USAREC to plan and host a meeting of representatives of all the services' recruiting organizations, along with their respective military chiefs of personnel and assistant secretaries for manpower, and his own assistants to discuss and coordinate plans and programs for eliminating dependency on the draft. Kelley's purpose was to achieve consensus and unity of effort among the service recruiters. But, as events developed, once again the Army perceived opposition and resistance from its rivals for recruits and its nominal superiors in the Department of Defense manpower office.

In preparing for the Joint Recruiting Conference that Kelley directed, the Army's personnel and recruitment planners refined their proposals one more time before finally moving from plans to action. During the ensuing conference, held at Fort Monroe on 5 and 6 November 1970, Army spokesmen vigorously aired their ideas for increasing recruiter benefits and incentives, expanding enlistment options, and conducting an experiment with paid television/radio prime-time advertising. They also formally unveiled their plan to expand the size of the field recruiting force; the Army would double the strength of its 397 one-man recruiting stations; add a full-time administrative noncommissioned officer to its 139 four- and five-man stations immediately; and ask for an additional 3,000 recruiters for an expanded effort at all levels beginning in July 1971.

Consensus and Dissent

Differences of opinion over the appropriateness of some of the Army's proposals surfaced immediately. The Army found little resistance to those ideas that did not directly affect the other recruiting organizations. Indeed, all the services agreed on the need for increased or improved recruiting resources such as better office furniture, relocation of recruiting stations to sites better situated to support the mission, modern sedans for recruiters, adequate housing or increased compensation for housing for recruiters assigned to high-cost areas, and so forth. The services also agreed on the need for increased incentives for recruiters. In both instances differences were over specifics and priorities, not principles. For example, Navy and Marine Corps recruiters, through a quirk of Department of Defense regulations, received $50 a month proficiency pay while Army and Air Force recruiters did not. All agreed that everyone should get proficiency pay and that everyone should receive the same amount. But, perhaps because the Navy already had proficiency pay, it argued harder for upgrading the vehicle fleet for recruiters in the field. Rear Adm. William Greene, director of Navy recruiting, related the story of his service's "red fleet" in Oklahoma. The Navy required its recruiters to wear white uniforms in the summer. "When you drive 50 miles without air conditioning in this red clay desert of Oklahoma, your uniforms turn to pale red or maybe a pink by the time you reach your destination."

The Navy also inclined toward pushing for a variable housing allowance for recruiters, which would allow recruiters working in high-cost areas greater flexibility in finding and acquiring housing. The other services and Department of Defense manpower specialists favored expanding the current practice of leasing housing for recruiters and held out for variable housing allowance as a long-range goal which recruiters could offer prospective volunteers as an inducement to which all service members authorized government quarters but unable to occupy them could aspire.[12]

Differences at Fort Monroe arose over the merits of the Army's paid television/radio prime-time recruiting advertising, and, despite the Project Volunteer committee's willingness to sanction a controlled pilot project, the other services even opposed the Army's proposal to conduct a test to gather data on the effectiveness of the scheme. The Army scheme involved the purchase of prime-time radio and television advertising time in both local and national markets; the conduct of a full-fledged advertising campaign in those media; and a follow-up program to measure the results in terms of viewer awareness and voluntary enlistments. According to Col. Henry Beuke, director of advertising and information, USAREC, the Army believed that "to achieve the goal of increased voluntary accessions, it will be necessary to greatly increase the reach and frequency of our advertising delivery, particularly against the prime target audience of young men."

The Army and Air Force used paid advertising in magazines. The Navy and Marine Corps relied on public service space for their limited print media ads. All services depended on public service time for local radio and television advertising. Studies for the Army suggested that most stations aired their public service messages "in such time periods as 6:05 AM, between the morning 'Thought for the Day' and the farm news, or at 3:30 AM in the 'Late, Late, Late Show'" when few recruiting prospects were apt to be watching or listening. "Free air time is welcome," Beuke said, "but when the need exists to strongly increase reach and frequency against our young men target audience, clearly, public service broadcast cannot be expected to deliver. We must follow the lead of the razor blades, shaving creams, and automobiles, and buy the time necessary to deliver the audiences we need to reach."[13]

The Navy, Marine Corps, and Air Force recruiting representatives opposed the Army's plan. They feared that the use of paid broadcast advertising, even on a test basis, might undermine their claim to public service time and were unwilling to risk what they had for the sake of an Army experiment. Furthermore, the other services doubted that the limited funds available for recruiting advertising could purchase enough prime time to offset the lost public service time. Finally the opponents of the advertising test worried that once one service paid for air time the stations and networks might refuse to give it public service time after the experiment ended. Admiral Greene urged caution. He suggested that the secretary of defense meet with the National Association of Broadcasters to discuss the problem before any pilot program was developed. Greene's counterpart from the Air Force, Brig. Gen. William McGlothlin, professed an "open mind" on the subject, but he urged more study. McGlothlin apparently sensed the Army's desire for a quick decision, however, and urged "don't piddle with the study but get on with it."[14]

The Department of Defense representatives at the Joint Recruiting Conference concurred, generally, with the Navy and Air Force. Gus Lee, deputy assistant secretary of defense for manpower, told the conferees he would urge Kelley to press for a meeting with the National Association of Broadcasters and the National Advertising Council to try to squeeze more free time out of the television and radio stations. Lee added that the free air time route ought to be exhausted first. Only then, he said, should planning begin for some sort of test, and he emphasized his conviction that such a test should be a joint venture jointly planned.[15] The differences over paid broadcast advertising had to be settled at a higher level.

Not surprisingly, the Army's commitment to paid broadcast advertising remained firm. Indeed, the Recruiting Command's desire to push ahead with the idea merged with the Army's campaign to capture the lion's share of the fiscal year 1971 Project Volunteer budget, then in the final stages of drafting, and its efforts to obtain proficiency pay for combat arms soldiers instead of the general enlistment bonus for all volunteers that other services and the defense manpower specialists in Kelley's office favored.

As finally articulated, the Army's argument revealed some circular logic. Recruiting in a zero-draft environment required a substantially expanded recruiting force. The expanded recruiting force needed a product to sell. That product consisted of two major parts: improved service attractiveness and better pay, including proficiency pay for the combat arms. In order to carry its message of a new product to the "consumer," the Army needed to greatly expand its advertising. All of these programs had to be approved and begin simultaneously, according to the proponents' reasoning, and they had to begin immediately, not in the summer of 1971 when the fiscal year 1972 budget went into effect. This was the message that Forsythe and Assistant Secretary Brehm urged on Secretary of the Army Resor in November and that Resor, in turn, pressed on Laird.

The Army's civilian leadership hammered on the point that its program was a package that had to be considered as a whole. Brehm provided Resor with memos and talking papers to press the message on Laird. On 17 November, for example, Brehm suggested to Resor that "you stress to Mr. Laird the urgency of the effort and the need for [a] decision on the actions proposed" now. Brehm also expressed to Resor his sense that Kelley's subordinates were blocking the Army's program out of a desire to "spread the available money proportionately to each Service and to avoid approving all-volunteer actions/funding for one Service where another Service has raised a serious objection."

Meanwhile, Brehm's deputy, John Kester, worked on Kelley. "We have a package approach," Kester reminded Kelley on 10 December. "The heart of our package is a new and dramatic pay differential for combat arms *now*. This is supported by a massive effort to improve service life. The full and immediate potential of these actions, however, cannot be realized unless the public is informed through an extensive and innovative advertising campaign which includes paid radio and TV [advertising]."[16] Nevertheless, the decision went against the Army. Although Laird approved much of the Army's request, he sided with the other services on the issues of enlistment bonuses versus proficiency pay and withheld his decision on an advertising test. The Army, however, remained determined to have its whole package, and the issues of proficiency pay and paid advertising quickly became linked together in the minds of its leaders. Secretary of the Army Resor immediately authorized the reprogramming from Army funds of money for a proficiency pay experiment beginning in April 1971 and for the development of an advertising test to begin at an earlier unspecified date. Resor reiterated his conviction that both were essential elements of the Army's program:

Special pay, aimed at attracting new accessions and extensions of service, is an essential part of our balanced program of interdependent items. It will give our recruiters something new to say, our advertisements something dramatic and tangible to announce. It will complement the efforts underway for FY 72 and beyond. And it will be paid for from Army funds.[17]

Roger Kelley prepared the Defense Department reply which Deputy Secretary of Defense David Packard signed. Kelley again opposed proficiency pay as a "road with no return." Once some specialties were opened to proficiency pay, all could be opened later. The budgetary implications were obvious (although Kelley apparently overlooked the fact that the same argument could be applied to enlistment bonuses). Yet, despite his strong feelings on the subject, Kelley gave the Army the chance to appeal by agreeing to allow either General Westmoreland or General Forsythe to discuss the matter with the chairmen of the Armed Services Committees later in January when he was scheduled to testify before them. "The army will have an opportunity... to tell its story on behalf of using pro pay as an incentive to attract combat personnel and to enhance professionalism in combat units," Packard wrote, but, "It will be Roger Kelley's responsibility to tell the overall story." Packard and Kelley were confident the congressional leaders would see their side of the argument.

On the subject of the advertising test, Packard informed the Army tersely that he understood that, according to an agreement reached at the Joint Recruiting Conference, any advertising test would be conducted under the supervision of Kelley's office "to ensure that there would be reasonable balance and selectivity in the tests made." Kelley's office wanted to be sure that the test did not favor one service over the others and that the tests did not undermine the availability of free public service time the services already received from the networks and the local stations.[18]

The Army's efforts to win the largest possible share of the fiscal year 1972 Project Volunteer budget underscored the concern with which its top military and civilian leaders viewed the zero-draft requirement. More than just interservice rivalry over funds was involved. Finally convinced that the Nixon administration was serious about ending the draft, the Army's leaders realized that they had only about 30 months to accomplish the task. Westmoreland's speech to the Association of the U.S. Army and appointment of Forsythe as SAMVA had then galvanized the Army staff. Brehm's staff, which as appointed representatives of the administration was already predisposed to work for the all-volunteer force, quickly joined forces with the new SAMVA organization to pull the several components of the program together and articulate the Army's case.

All of the elements of the Army program except increased numbers of recruiters had been discussed since 1969. In October 1970 the program gelled. But by defining its program as an interrelated package the Army backed itself into a corner. Thus, when the Defense Department and sister services opposed proficiency pay and paid advertising, the Army concluded that it had to take extraordinary steps to gain the entire package and launch its program immediately. Westmoreland and Forsythe would carry the fight for proficiency pay to Congress while the Recruiting Command laid the groundwork for an advertising test with or without the approval of the Defense Department. Meanwhile the Recruiting Command and Forsythe's office began a series of field experiments with increased recruiters and new enlistment options geared to the

VOLAR experiments. As was the case with the overall Modern Volunteer Army Program, of which expanded recruiting efforts were but a part, these initiatives all began in late 1970 or early 1971 and proceeded simultaneously.

USAREC Acts

USAREC represented the leading edge of the Army's effort to penetrate the volunteer market. During 1971 and 1972 the command conducted numerous experiments to test concepts aimed at increasing the effectiveness and productivity of recruiters and at attracting more recruits to the Army. The innovations took two general forms. The first category included organizational changes and innovations within USAREC designed to establish the best mix of recruiters for an all-volunteer Army. The second group of innovations involved experiments aimed at the potential recruits themselves such as increased enlistment options, enlistment bonuses, and offering volunteers the chance to try the Army before actually joining it. Many of the experiments in the latter category were planned in anticipation of the success of the Army at obtaining proficiency pay for volunteers and approval for paid broadcast media advertising. Subsequently, when these efforts failed or were curtailed, the Recruiting Command had to modify its plans and those experiments already under way.

The most obvious effect of the volunteer Army transition on the Recruiting Command was the immediate increase in USAREC's strength. To determine the best way to employ its new personnel, the Recruiting Command quickly planned and conducted a test, dubbed "Operation FLOOD," to determine the feasibility of doubling the number of recruiters in the field. USAREC selected two recruiting stations—one rural, one urban—in each of its five recruiting districts to receive additional recruiters for ninety days beginning 1 November 1970. The personnel selected were all experienced recruiters. Men assigned to augment urban stations were drawn from like situations elsewhere; similarly, rural recruiters went to rural stations. All personnel involved in the test received orientations on the purpose of the test and the characteristics of the areas to which they were assigned. Working hours and routines remained unchanged. USAREC doubled the objectives of each of the ten stations for the period of the test.

Operation FLOOD produced mixed results. Only one station, Marysville, California, achieved its FLOOD objective. Eight of the ten stations recruited at a rate higher than what normally would have been their objective, but two urban stations failed even to meet their pre-FLOOD quotas. Overall Operation FLOOD resulted in a quantitative increase of 61 percent over normal objectives; rural stations exceeded normal objectives by 84 percent and urban stations by 48 percent. Clearly enlistments did not increase proportionately with recruiters. Furthermore, analysis of the data generated by FLOOD revealed that individual recruiter production declined when more recruiters were added to stations, especially those in urban areas which may have been squeezed dry already. But aggregated enlistments did increase, and on this basis USAREC considered the test a success and began immediate plans to increase the strength of recruiting stations Army-wide beginning in fiscal year 1972.[19]

USAREC initiated two other recruiting experiments early in 1971. The first, known as the recruiter assistant program, involved sending selected top advanced individual training graduates back to their hometowns for four weeks as recruiter assistants. The idea behind the plan was that local youths who had recently excelled in Army training would better appeal to their civilian friends than a recruiter. The initial test ran from April to October 1971. USAREC was so pleased with the results that it expanded the test Army-wide immediately. In fiscal year 1972, 1,912 recruiter assistants were sent to the field. They contacted almost 40,000 prospects and received credit for enlisting 1,585 volunteers. By May 1972 USAREC was sending 100 new soldiers back to their hometowns each week for 28 days' duty as assistant recruiters.[20]

The Recruiting Command and selected units of the Continental Army Command jointly participated in a unit-of-choice enlistment option, a recruiting experiment developed by Forsythe's SAMVA office. The original unit-of-choice option had begun on 1 February 1971 and offered qualified male applicants assignment to one of seven combat arms units in the United States. The Army guaranteed volunteers a stabilized tour of duty with their unit of choice before or following an assignment in a short-tour area such as Vietnam or Korea. Under USAREC guidance the units involved established recruiting teams and developed touring displays that featured their history, unique missions, and training opportunities or the appeal of their geographic location. The teams and the information developed were then dispatched to designated recruiting districts.

USAREC also developed an advertising campaign that stressed the unit-of-choice option and assisted unit recruiters in developing local advertising programs. Initially only combat units participated. In 1972 the Army expanded the program to include noncombat units and added a station-of-choice option as well. By the end of fiscal year 1972 virtually every unit in the Army was open to volunteers, and qualified male and female applicants could sign up for over 300 and 80 military occupational specialties, respectively. As the number of full-time recruiting personnel increased through 1971 and 1972 the Army cut back on the use of special recruiting teams from the units themselves. However, it continued the practice of sending bands, displays, and demonstrations to high schools, state and county fairs, and other suitable places to attract attention to the all-volunteer Army and to create interest among potential enlistees in the civilian community.[21]

The rapid growth of the Recruiting Command and the simultaneous proliferation of its activities strained the organization. Initially USAREC planned to absorb the nearly 3,000 additional recruiters coming on board in fiscal year 1972 within its existing structure. The bulk of the manpower increase would be used to augment existing recruiting stations or to create new stations to better exploit the potential of a particular area. Under the existing organization noncommissioned officer recruiters operated out of one-, two-, or three-man stations located within the communities that they canvassed. These neighborhood stations, in turn, were commanded by a lieutenant colonel whose headquarters was in a centrally located recruiting main station. In 1971 there were 37 main stations. As the number of recruiters grew, the number of stations supervised by a recruiting main station commander grew from an average of 27.3 to 40.6. The supervising reach of the station commanders was quickly stretched thin by the expansion. In late 1971 USAREC headquarters thus concluded that additional recruiting main stations were needed and requested funds and personnel to create 27 additional intermediate supervisory headquarters. The new recruiting main stations became active over a two-month period beginning in May 1972.[22]

At the same time USAREC began an experiment employing officers in neighborhood recruiting stations as "recruiting area commanders." In the USAREC field organization, recruiting areas represented the level of organization below the recruiting main stations. Heretofore master sergeants had commanded recruiting areas, which consisted of several one- and two-man stations satellited off a central five-man facility. Recruiting long had been considered the noncommissioned officer's domain in the Army, but USAREC headquarters was concerned with a number of trends that indicated potential trouble for both recruiting and the smooth management of such a large and still growing decentralized organization in a changing market.

During the height of the Vietnam War many high school guidance counselors opposed permitting recruiters access to their schools to talk to graduating seniors about the Army. The practice persisted into the 1970s and, given the Army's poor standing in the public eye relative to the other services, threatened to deprive recruiters of one of their most promising sources of potential volunteers. Furthermore, with the existing arrangement of noncommissioned officers supervising each other at the grass roots level of USAREC, something of an "old boys network" had grown up. Recruiters became set in their ways and resistant to change. After years of depending on the draft to provide the bulk of the Army's combat arms soldiers, the reasoning went, few recruiters effectively "sold" prospects on enlisting in the Infantry, Armor, or Artillery. Instead, recruiters "filled orders" and met their quotas with draft-motivated volunteers. Finally, USAREC leaders worried that noncommissioned officers at the area level of the command would not be able to keep up with the administration required in the rapidly changing recruiting environment. Officers, combat arms captains specifically, with leadership and administrative experience might be the answer. First, an officer area commander might bring a higher level of managerial and administrative expertise to the job and free the noncommissioned officer to concentrate solely on recruiting tasks. Second, as an officer the captain area commander would inject a degree of formality and distance between the supervisor and the recruiters and, it was expected, break up the old boy network that some observers believed was plaguing the recruiting service. Finally, USAREC hoped that the captains, who possessed college degrees, would be better able to penetrate the high schools and reopen them to recruiters.[23]

On 1 May 1972, five combat arms captains began 120 days of duty as recruiting area commanders in the Chicago Recruiting Main Station (RMS) jurisdiction. The areas to which the captains were assigned had recently experienced declining production rates and several were under investigation by the Army inspector general for recruiting malpractice. Within three months the fortunes of the Chicago RMS reversed. Production increased, and in October the RMS achieved 106.3 percent of its objective and moved from seventh of eight to fifth of fifteen in the Fifth Recruiting District, centered in the upper Midwest. Nevertheless, the commander of the Chicago RMS, Col. John Hougen, downplayed the direct role of the officers in the turnaround. Hougen emphasized the officers' contribution to improved command management and administration. He reported that after an initial reluctance to accept the officers "because they felt jeopardized," the recruiters "accepted the Captains as area commanders primarily because they found they could receive immediate decisions to everyday type recruiting problems" that noncommissioned officer commanders previously had to refer to higher headquarters. Hougen also reported that administration, particularly the maintenance of official files and records, improved significantly in the affected areas.[24]

The captains themselves also downplayed their direct influence on production. Most criticized the conditions they found and expressed frustration at their perceived inability to effect change. Their reports offer a revealing glimpse into the world of the recruiter during the early stages of the buildup of the Recruiting Command. Capt. John Lewis concluded that he had little impact on station or recruiter production and none on the market; "the same number [of civilians] still went to college, still waited out the draft...." He found the recruiters assigned to his area plagued with personnel and personal problems which consumed half of his time. In addition Lewis complained about the "inexperience, laziness, attitude, etc.," of recruiters, which led him to conclude that "the greatest part of the [men assigned to the] area could be classified unsuitable or undesirable," and he regretted that he lacked sufficient authority to promptly rid the recruiting area of its deadwood.

Capt. Arthur Schulcz reported similar findings. He found no training program in effect for new station commanders and recruiters, no supervision, and little evidence of "prospecting or salesmanship." He instituted a training program, eliminated individual quotas, and established a team concept in his area. Schulcz concluded that much of the problem derived from management practices higher up the chain of command. Inspections by higher headquarters emphasized the negative without offering suggestions, he observed. Furthermore, Schulcz complained, "The stations most visited by higher headquarters are those having problems.... The successful recruiter is slighted." He also recommended that field recruiters receive more advance warning of impending changes and implementation instructions.[25]

After evaluating the captains' and Colonel Hougen's reports the director of recruiting operations at USAREC headquarters concluded that the test demonstrated the effectiveness of officer area commanders. The officers "were more responsive and had better control over their areas than did the enlisted commanders," Col. James Lay reported. The captains proved more responsive to their recruiters' needs and established a "more business-like" relationship in their commands. Colonel Lay also noted the improved production in the areas of the experiment and concluded, "since intensified management raised production and morale" in the RMS Chicago, the use of officers elsewhere "might be beneficial." USAREC's personnel branch concurred and recommended assigning captains as area commanders "as a means of invigorating the recruiting force and providing stronger leadership at the critical area commander level." The following year 152 captains were assigned as commanders of metropolitan recruiting areas.[26]

Most of the experiments that USAREC conceived and conducted beginning in 1971 involved increasing the ability of field recruiters to penetrate the youth market or improving the organizational efficiency of the command. Operation FLOOD, the Recruiter Assistant Program, and the unit-of-choice option represent examples of the former, while the Chicago experiment is an example of the latter.

The Selection Center Experiment, conducted between February and November 1972, attempted both to reach more youths and to test a new organizational concept for potential use by Army recruiting. General Forsythe proved to be the motivating force behind the experiment. During a visit to England in June 1971 to investigate British volunteer army recruiting techniques, Forsythe was particularly impressed by the British selection center concept. At such centers youths interested in military service spent several days receiving briefings and orientations on the army and enlistment options, taking physical and mental tests designed to determine their qualifications, and making their choice of career options before formally enlisting.

The British system, which had evolved over thirteen years of all-volunteer experience, permitted the interested prospect to consider the army on a trial basis and make a sound judgment about his military service. The British found that this process resulted in the placement of the individual in a field of interest suited to his aptitude to the mutual benefit of both the army and the soldier. Forsythe returned from England determined to try the concept in the United States Army.[27]

The Department of the Army directed USAREC to plan and conduct a selection center experiment with support from the Continental Army Command. The Recruiting Command saw great potential in the concept. At that time enlistees passed through three stations before arriving at a basic training facility: the recruiting station, an armed forces examination and entrance station (AFEES), and a U.S. Army reception station. The recruit experienced wasted time, duplication of tests and exams, and confusion in the process of moving from one stop to the next. A selection center that combined all three functions would save the Army time, personnel, and money. Furthermore, as the Recruiting Command developed the idea, the concept promised to improve both the quantity and quality of Army enlistees in the zero-draft environment because

"Peer group pressure is strong among young people and the word would get back to their contemporaries regarding the sincere effort by the Army to place the right man in the right job." During the three-day period the Army planned to hold applicants for enlistment at the selection center it would have sufficient "time to detect those traits and characteristics of the enlistee that might result in later unsuitability separations from the army, i.e., apathy and behavior disorders." Finally, USAREC predicted that the experiment might even result in increased reenlistment rates: "if the Selection Center's emphasis on matching the enlistee's desires with his qualifications is successful, then more soldiers would request extension of service." [28]

The Recruiting Command activated the U.S. Army Selection Center (Provisional) at Fort Jackson, South Carolina, in November 1971. The center commander, Col. John Kean, received orientations and briefings from Forsythe; Maj. Gen. John Henion, the USAREC commander; General Smith, the assistant deputy chief of staff for personnel; and a host of Recruiting Command experts. Some of the advice was conflicting. General Smith told Kean that the Army had not decided whether the purpose of the experiment was "to benefit primarily the volunteer or the Army," but told him to emphasize "the right thing." General Henion told him the Army needed a "better environment" that got away from the mass-production-of-recruits image. Forsythe emphasized that the governing concept of the test "is the Army must be a 'good employer,'" and added that he and the chief of staff expected Kean to reject applicants. Forsythe too counseled Kean to "do the thing right." [29]

Colonel Kean spent November and December 1971 interviewing and selecting his cadre. In January the assembled selection center personnel prepared their facility at Fort Jackson, and in February they conducted a dry-run with 100 junior ROTC cadets from a nearby high school. The first group of soldier candidates arrived from the Atlanta Recruiting Main Station on 28 February 1972.

The plan called for the selection center to receive approximately 100 civilians per week who had indicated an interest in enlisting. During a three- to five-day stay at the center the soldier candidates would undergo medical and mental screening to determine their fitness for service and the enlistment options for which they were qualified. Subsequently they would receive orientations on their options and personalized professional counseling designed to help them make the best choice. Candidates who declined to enlist would be returned home. Youths who enlisted could go directly to their first training assignment or return home under a delayed entry program. During the first three weeks of the experiment over half of the candidates were disqualified for mental or medical reasons. Kean and a general officer advisory council quickly decided to expand the area from which the selection center drew its candidates to encompass the entire Third Recruiting Region, which comprised the southeastern United States, and to prescreen them at the armed forces examination and entrance stations.

During the next twenty-one weeks the center processed 2,072 candidates. Of that number 170 (8 percent) were disqualified, and 1,585 (83 percent of those qualified) enlisted. Survey data compiled during the experiment revealed that over half of the candidates who enlisted made their final decision to do so after they arrived at the selection center. Nearly 90 percent of those who declined reported favorable impressions of the experiment; about 60 percent said they "just weren't ready to enlist," or had come to the center to "get the feel of the Army." Of those who declined to enlist at the selection center, 20 percent subsequently did so. The data revealed no significant differences between men who enlisted and those who did not.

Phase I of the selection center experiment ended in October. Thereafter the Army tracked selection center enlistees through training and their first assignments expecting to find that they displayed higher levels of job satisfaction and performance compared to men who entered the Army through the AFEES–reception center route and did not receive personalized job counseling and placement. So confident was the Army that the Phase II evaluation would substantiate its preconceived notion about the worth of the selection center that it requested $10 million in the fiscal year 1974 budget to expand the program Army-wide.[30]

To the surprise and disappointment of its proponents, the selection center concept failed to meet expectations. The Third Recruiting District reported that production declined during the experiment; local recruiters saw prospects committed to enlisting leave the selection center only to return a week later unwilling to sign up. Even more discouraging were the revelations that selection center enlistees did not perform significantly better on the job than did volunteers who entered the Army through the traditional route and that the selection center process did not result in greater job satisfaction. The key to job satisfaction was accurate information about the Army and the extent to which volunteers found what recruiters told them about the Army to be true. In addition the selection center evaluation found that job satisfaction and performance depended on recruits' immediately receiving the training and assignment they agreed on enlisting for when they talked to recruiters. Finally, the proposed method for expanding the selection center concept by creating a separate career orientation facility near each of the seventy-four armed forces examination and entrance stations duplicated the existing recruiting-examination-reception station system rather than replacing it (as the initial concept implied) and resulted in an increased cost instead of a savings.

The selection center concept was quietly scrapped. Meanwhile, the Recruiting Command continued to use the results of the experiment to improve the ability of recruiters and job counselors within the existing system to provide prospective recruits with comprehensive information about the Army and its career fields in a "digestible form" and to give potential volunteers "more personalized treatment." Thus, the substance of the experiment survived even as the Army discarded the form.[31]

Notes

[1] Griffith, *Men Wanted for the U.S. Army*, pp. 30–31, 86–91, 199, 205–07.

[2] Brig. Gen. Donald H. McGovern, "History of Army Recruiting Parallels Nation's Growth," *Recruiting and Career Counselling Journal* 22, no. 4 (April 1969): 16–17 (McGovern was Commanding General, USAREC, 1969–70).

[3] *Department of the Army Historical Summary, Fiscal Year 1970* (Washington, D.C.: U.S. Army Center of Military History, 1973), pp. 54–55 (hereafter cited as DAHSUM).

[4] DCSPER Memo, 4 Feb 69, sub: All-Volunteer Army, w/attachment, "Study Plan—All-Volunteer Army," Background Material. The memo, attributed to Lt. Col. Butler, forwarded the draft study plan to interested parties within the office of the DCSPER.

[5] "Project 'PROVIDE' A Summary," 28 May 69, Background Material, hereafter cited as USAREC PROVIDE Summary). Authorship is attributed to Mr. T. Wilkinson, the USAREC representative to the PROVIDE study group. Organization and wording of the summary suggest it is a synthesis of reports provided the author by the USAREC staff for input to the PROVIDE study.

[6] Ibid.

[7] PROVIDE, vol. 2, 6–1 to 6–15.

[8] "Project Volunteer: Plans and Actions To Move Toward an All-Volunteer Force" Draft Report, 29 Apr 70, OSA file 202.10, RG 335, WNRC. The Draft Report cited is the secretary of the Army's coordination copy of the final draft of the Project Volunteer report.

[9] Gates Commission Report, pp. 82–83.

[10] MFR by John Kester, 4 Sep 70, sub: USAREC Visit, Kester Papers.

[11] Recruiting Operations, Historical Summary 1971, vol. 1, HQ, USAREC, n.d., "Plans and Training Division," p. 2, USAREC Archives; Memo, Resor for Laird, 3 Nov 70, sub: Voluntary Army Actions; Msg, DA–DCSPER 291932Z Oct 70, sub: Volunteers for the United States Army Recruiting Command; Msg, DA–DCSPER 162351Z Nov 70, sub: Assignment of Qualified Noncommissioned Officers, MOS 00E to the United States Army Recruiting Command, Background Material. The results of the test led to an increase in the number of recruiters in an area—Operation FLOOD.

[12] "Facilities and Equipment," transcript of briefing by Cmdr Moody, USN, and closing comments by Rear Adm William Greene at Joint Recruiting Conference, Ft. Monroe, Va., 5–6 Nov 70 (hereafter cited as JRC), USAREC Archives.

[13] "DOD Advertising," transcript of briefing by Col Henry A. Beuke, JRC.

[14] Ibid., and transcript of Admiral Greene and Brig Gen William McGlothlin's closing remarks, JRC.

[15] Transcript of Lee's summary remarks, JRC.

[16] Note for Secretary Resor by William Brehm, 17 Nov 70; Memo, Kester for Kelley, 10 Dec 70, sub: Volunteer Army Actions, OSA file 202.10, RG 335, WNRC.

[17] Memo, Resor for Laird, 4 Jan 71, sub: Army-Funded Zero-Draft Actions for FY 1971, OSA file 202.10, RG 335, WNRC.

[18] Memo, Kelley for Packard, 8 Jan 71, sub: Army Zero Draft Requests for FY 71; Memo, Packard for Resor, 12 Jan 71, sub: Army Zero Draft Requests for FY 71, both in OSD file 340, RG 330, WNRC.

[19] After-Action Report, Operation "FLOOD," 1 November 1970–31 January 1971, 25 Feb 71; Historical Summary—FY 71, Recruiting Operations Directorate, USAREC, n.d., p. 2, both in USAREC Archives.

[20] Historical Summary—FY 71, Recruiting Operations Directorate, p. 4; Historical Report, Director of Recruiting Operations, USAREC, 1 July 1971–30 June 1972, n.d., both in USAREC Archives.

[21] U.S. Continental Army Command/U.S. Army Forces Strike Command Annual Historical Summary, FY 1971 (hereafter cited as CONARC Annual History FY 71), Ft. Monroe, Va., July 1972, pp. 237–38; CONARC Annual History FY 72, vol. 1, July 1973, pp. 320–21; "Unit of Choice Option Implemented," *Recruiting and Career Counseling Journal* 24, no. 2 (February 1971): 5.

[22] HQ, USAREC, Operation Order: Increase in Military Personnel Authorization, United States Army Recruiting Command (USAREC) (Project BRIGADE), 26 Feb 71; HQ, USAREC Operation Plan: Creation of 24 Additional RMS (OPLAN REMAST), 3 Feb 72, both in USAREC Archives.

[23] In the early days of the transition to the all-volunteer Army, the impression that noncommissioned officer recruiters were "order takers" rather than "salesmen" and were resistant to change was widespread and shared by many of the senior leaders of the Army. Generals Forsythe and Kerwin mentioned the need to reinvigorate USAREC, as did Assistant Secretary of Defense Kelley. The author also recalls from his own experiences of the period a general decline in the officer corps' implicit faith in the noncommissioned officer corps—a vague feeling which was part of the professional malaise troubling the Army after Vietnam and one that was reciprocated by NCOs. The solution—to place officers in charge—was not unique to USAREC. The notion that officers could fix any problem because they were better educated, had more management training or leadership experience, and were better motivated was common. The specific situation in USAREC was exacerbated by rumors of recruiter malpractice.

[24] Rpt, Hougen to Cdr, USAREC, 18 Oct 72, sub: Evaluation of Officer Area Commander Test, USAREC Archives.

[25] After Action Report of Capt John L. Lewis, 11 Oct 72; After Action Report of Capt Arthur A. Schulcz, 11 Oct 72, attachments to Rpt, Hougen to Cdr, USAREC, 18 Oct 72, sub: Evaluation of Officer Area Commander Test, USAREC Archives.

[26] Memo, Col Lay for DCG/CofS, USAREC, 16 Nov 72, sub: After Action Report on the Chicago Experiment, USAREC Archives; "Captains as Area Commanders," *Recruiting and Career Counselor Journal* 26, no. 11 (November 1973): 8.

[27] Memo, Col Love, Chief, Procurement Division, USAREC, no addressee, 20 Aug 71, sub: Selection Center Experiment; Ltr, Maj Gen Henion to Lt Gen Kerwin, 30 Sep 71, sub: Selection Center Experiment, both in USAREC Archives; Forsythe Interv.

[28] Ltr, Henion to Kerwin, 30 Sep 71, sub: Selection Center Experiment, USAREC Archives.

[29] MFRs by Col Kean of intervs with Forsythe and Smith, USAREC Briefings, 15 Oct 71, USAREC Archives.

[30] "Report on the Selection Center Experiment," Test and Evaluation Division, U.S. Army Selection Center, Ft. Jackson, S.C., 15 Sep 72; Fact Sheet, 27 Oct 72, sub: United States Army Selection Center (Provisional), HQ, USAREC Final Report on the Selection Center Experiment (Phase II), 26 Jul 73, USAREC Archives.

[31] HQ, USAREC, Final Report on the Selection Center Experiment (Phase II), 26 Jul 73, USAREC Archives; Ltr, Henion to DCSPER, 2 Aug 73, sub: House Appropriations Committee on Selection Center Experiment in FY 74 Budget; Ltr, Brig Gen Tice to Cdr USAREC, 28 Aug 73, sub: Final Report on the Selection Center Experiment, Fact Sheet, no author or date (post 29 Oct 73), sub: MVA and Soldier-Oriented Programs, Report and Analysis: Exploitation of the Selection Center (SC), USAREC Archives.

CHAPTER IX

Today's Army Wants To Join You
Military Salesmanship, 1971

From the beginning of their examination of the feasibility of replacing the draft with a volunteer force, Army manpower analysts accepted as axiomatic that military pay would have to rise substantially to induce sufficient enlistments to make up for the loss of draft-motivated volunteers and conscripts. The PROVIDE Study, for example, revealed that about half of potential volunteers would consider enlisting if pay were raised to levels comparable with prevailing civilian wages; two-thirds if pay exceeded expected civilian wages. The group also found that offering prospective recruits a $2,000 preenlistment bonus produced an additional 28.9 to 36.6 percent volunteers. Butler's analyst concluded, however, that a bonus was in reality a bounty, then prohibited by statute (Section 514(A), Title 10, U.S. Code). The bar on bounties dated to World War I, when Army Judge Advocate General E. H. Crowder, drawing on the lessons of the Civil War, included a prohibition on enlistment bounties in the Selective Service Act of 1917. The PROVIDE group also reasoned that preenlistment bonuses contained a hidden cost. Soldiers enlisting for a bonus who subsequently became dissatisfied with Army life or low pay would likely become malcontents, convinced they had been lured into uniform. Sustaining a volunteer Army on this basis could become a liability in the long run. Alternative incentives would have to be found.[1]

From the beginning the Army recognized that higher pay alone would not attract volunteers to the more arduous branches of the service, the combat arms. In his critique of the Gates Commission recommendations, prepared with the help of the PROVIDE group, Secretary of the Army Resor had observed that if pay schedules were raised so high as to theoretically attract volunteers to those jobs hardest to fill, the Army, not to mention the other services, might end up paying more than necessary to fill more desirable positions in the technical branches of the services that attracted other enlistees seeking skill training or educational benefits.[2] Thus while the Army supported a general increase in pay for all soldiers as essential to making the transition from draft dependency to the volunteer force and recognized a need for some form of incentive to attract people to the combat arms without paying too much for other volunteers, it remained wary of bonuses. For these reasons Army leaders continued to favor, as an alternative to enlistment bonuses, proficiency pay for critical skills.

Under the pro-pay scheme the Army proposed to pay three-year volunteers for the combat arms $150 a month above their other pay and allowances as long as they maintained proficiency in the skills associated with their assignment. Draftees already serving in a combat arms assignment who volunteered for a third year of service and who passed the proficiency test could immediately qualify for the incentive. The proposal appealed to the Army's leaders on two counts. It avoided the taint of a bounty associated with the bonus: soldiers had to *earn* proficiency pay. More important, in the context of the growing urgency that infused the Army on the volunteer force issue in late 1970, proficiency pay did not require special legislation before it could be offered. Army leaders, especially Assistant Secretary Brehm and General Forsythe, wanted to begin all of the zero-draft experiments as early in 1971 as possible. All they needed to announce proficiency pay for combat arms volunteers was approval from the secretary of defense and permission from Congress to reprogram the funds to finance the program through the end of fiscal year 1971. Moreover, proficiency pay appealed to General Westmoreland and those senior officers who saw in the all-volunteer force concept an opportunity to reestablish a sense of professionalism in the Army.

The alternative to the Army's pro-pay proposal was the Department of Defense combat arms enlistments bonus. This plan, contained in the Fiscal Year 1972 Project Volunteer Budget, offered a $3,000 to $5,000 bonus to combat arms volunteers in three installments. It provided nothing for two-year volunteers or draftees already in the service or for first-term reenlistments. The Army's proposal provided incentives for non–prior-service volunteers, for draftees and draft-motivated volunteers already in the service, and for reenlistees and career servicemen who volunteered for combat arms assignments and qualified for proficiency pay. Soldiers who failed to maintain standards could lose their proficiency pay; no such provision existed for bonus recipients. As the Army saw things, its proficiency pay plan offered more for improving voluntary enlistments and strengthening the quality of the career force. Furthermore, by beginning the program immediately the Army could gather data which could be compared with that generated by the Defense Department's bonus when and if Congress approved it.[3]

The Army insisted on proceeding with its request to try a proficiency pay experiment in the last half of fiscal year 1971 after it lost its attempt to have the scheme included in the Fiscal Year 1972 Project Volunteer Budget request. With Assistant Secretary Kelley's concurrence Secretary of Defense Laird gave his approval for General Westmoreland and Mr. Kelley to discuss the proposal with F. Edward Hebert, the chairman of the House Armed Services Committee. The meeting took place on 19 January 1971. Westmoreland asked for their approval to experiment with proficiency pay for three months beginning 1 April.

At the same meeting Kelley explained the Department of Defense enlistment bonus proposal for fiscal year 1972. Reactions were mixed on all sides. Hebert seemed responsive to the idea of an experiment with some kind of combat arms enlistment incentive. Frank Slatinshek, the personnel and compensation expert of the House Armed Services Committee, expressed misgivings about the

Army's proposal, while John Blandford, the staff director, was disposed to let the Army try. Kelley came away from the meeting convinced that Hebert favored the bonus. John Kester, the deputy assistant secretary of the Army who attended with Westmoreland, complained bitterly that Kelley had confused Hebert by discussing the bonus option for 1972 while the chief of staff was trying to sell the pro-pay experiment for 1971. "Mr. Hebert was close to agreeing," Kester told Secretary of the Army Resor later. Kester implied that Kelley's office was undercutting the Army's effort to secure congressional permission for the pro-pay experiment and urged Resor to intervene with Secretary of Defense Laird.[4]

With both sides convinced that Hebert favored their viewpoint, not much happened initially after the meeting in January. Kelley, who continued to press for unity of purpose among the services on the volunteer force initiatives, proposed a compromise package; the Army's zero-draft people, notably Kester and Forsythe, kept urging Resor to go to the secretary of defense to break the log jam. Laird took Kelley's side. Based on advice from Gardiner Tucker, his assistant for systems analysis, Laird stalled the Army until the prospects for the bonus initiative in the fiscal year 1972 budget clarified. The Army's reprogramming request thus remained bottled up in the Office of Management and Budget. Meanwhile, Forsythe and Brehm's offices stewed. They wanted to use the pro-pay initiative in the advertising test that was about to begin and faced the prospect of having nothing tangible to offer prospective recruits beyond promises of a better Army in the future.

Montague, who monitored the pro-pay issue for Forsythe, charged that Kelley "screwed it up again by asking some relatively low level guy in OMB what he thought" of the proposal. "As a result, the top dogs—Mr. [George P.] Schultz and Mr. [James R.] Schlesinger, who do not understand our proposal, have reacted negatively." Schultz expressed concern that pushing the Army's proposal for a proficiency pay experiment might undercut the Defense Department's bonus proposal. In taking that position Schultz merely echoed the position of Kelley's office. Clearly, as long as the bonus option remained viable, the Army's scheme would not get a hearing.[5]

The House Armed Services Committee ended the impasse on 22 March when it voted to reject the administration's enlistment bonus proposal. Within three days Laird advised the Office of Management and Budget of his support for the Army's proposal. On 26 March Kelley advised all interested parties that "the Administration supports the Army's pro pay proposal and urges its early approval by Congressional Committees so that it can be used to attract May and June high school graduates." Kelley added that the Defense Department would continue to pursue bonus legislation and if it were approved would phase out the Army's program. Army spokesmen were given a week's notice to be ready to present their case to Congress. Having blocked the Army's program for three months the administration now wanted it to be ready to proceed in a matter of days.[6]

On 1 April the key members of the Army's leadership concerned with implementing the all-volunteer force program met to discuss the next step. Secretary of the Army Resor told the group he wanted to push the special pay program hard even though some of his advisers cautioned that one or more of the congressional committees involved might balk and kill the whole scheme. General Forsythe wanted to start pro pay as soon as possible so it could be featured in recruiting advertisements. He urged action before the congressional Easter recess. Forsythe said he was prepared to brief any committee. Meanwhile the assistant secretary for manpower would send fact sheets stressing the experimental nature of the proficiency pay proposal to the staffs of the committees involved.

Forsythe appeared before the defense subcommittees of the House and Senate Appropriations Committees on 6 and 7 April, respectively. Both referred action on the reprogramming request to their respective Armed Services Committees. The chief counsel of the Senate Armed Services Committee, Edward Braswell, was in the hospital. Thus the crucial test for the Army's case would be before the House Armed Services Committee, which had so recently killed the bonus plan. Prior to the hearing, scheduled for 20 April, Forsythe and Kester met with Frank Slatinshek of the committee staff. Forsythe came away discouraged. "He understands our plan and the fact that it is a test," Forsythe reported to his colleagues on 14 April; "however, he is not particularly sympathetic." In an effort to overcome Slatinshek's bias and to demonstrate the seriousness with which the Army viewed the request, General Westmoreland decided to lead off the testimony on 20 April.[7]

The hearing on the Army's request to reprogram $25 million from funds appropriated for procurement of equipment and missiles to the pay and allowances account in order to provide special pay for combat arms soldiers began on a discouraging note. Hebert convened the House Armed Services Committee in executive session and, after reviewing the agenda, launched into an indictment of the principle of reprogramming. "I believe in giving [the services] every dollar needed, and not one cent less," Hebert declared. "But they must justify it properly, and not justify it on Monday and come in on Tuesday with a reprogramming act which indicates they really didn't need what they said they needed on Monday." He then recognized Westmoreland and Forsythe and advised the committee that he and the Army witnesses had already discussed the matter now before the committee. Hebert implied that he disagreed with the Army's request, but professed his desire that the committee give it a fair hearing and make up its mind. Hebert then gave Westmoreland the floor.[8]

Westmoreland stressed three points in his testimony: the need for combat arms volunteers, the urgency of the situation, and the belief that the program would also improve professionalism. The proficiency pay proposal was a test intended to develop data on the effectiveness of a directed special pay program in attracting volunteers to branches of the service that needed 6,500 men a month and at that time received only 250 to 300 true volunteers monthly. Draftees comprised two-thirds of the riflemen in the Army's infantry companies. The situation was obviously unhealthy, he said. If the Army was to meet the president's goal of ending reliance on the draft, volunteers had to be attracted to the combat arms. "Time is running out," Westmoreland warned, "but it is not too late to improve the situation."

The chief of staff also expounded on his view that Vietnam had undermined the professionalism of the Army. The war was "a traumatic experience for the Army," he lamented. "The stresses and strains on our institution have been severe." He wanted to use the proficiency pay to reinvigorate the crucial combat arms core of the Army by recognizing that combat soldiers were special people deserving of additional remuneration.[9]

Forsythe elaborated. The proficiency pay test was necessary "to make a dramatic change in the relative attractiveness of service in the combat arms" at a time when the Army was trying to quadruple its level of volunteers. Thus the proposal offered $100 a month to three-year volunteers for the Infantry, Armor, and Artillery. Draftees or two-year volunteers could qualify by extending their enlistment. Furthermore, "we need to retain more of the best soldiers we now have in the combat arms," Forsythe said. Career soldiers proficient in the three combat skills who reenlisted or extended for service in a unit requiring those specialties also qualified for the extra pay. "We want to reduce the leakage out of these very tough branches," he emphasized. "Infantry, Armor, and Artillery ask more of a man," Forsythe added, "more stamina, more teamwork, and a greater commitment. When a young man has this much extra to offer, we want to provide an extra reward." But the program was not a giveaway. Volunteers would not begin to receive the extra money until they completed training; they would have to maintain proficiency and serve in combat arms units to continue to draw the pay. Soldiers who transferred out of combat units, became disciplinary problems, or failed to pass annual qualification tests would lose their special pay.[10]

The committee members questioned Westmoreland and Forsythe on three points. Several confused proficiency pay for the combat arms with hazardous duty pay, which all soldiers assigned to a combat zone received regardless of their specialty, and worried about possible inequities. Otis Pike of New York noted that a draftee serving in Vietnam got $65 a month "combat pay" while a combat arms volunteer in the United States would receive $100 a month just for completing training. Others saw the Army proposal as another form of the bounty-tainted bonus that they had so recently rejected. "Why wasn't this suggestion incorporated in the administration [request]—or the recommendations we had before us a month ago?" asked Michael Harrington of Massachusetts. The question forced Westmoreland to explain that, while the special pay proposal was his and the Army's first choice, the Defense Department and the other services opposed it and that defense consented to the Army's advancement of the scheme only after the failure of the bonus initiative.

The committeemen also raised questions about the termination costs of the experiment and the potential cost of the pro-pay plan if it became permanent. The test itself would cost $25 million. Termination costs would run between $20 and $28 million, Forsythe explained, because volunteers who enlisted in the combat arms to qualify for the special pay would have to receive it for three years. Likewise draftees and two-year volunteers who extended to qualify would continue to receive the proficiency pay after the test ended. Fairness demanded that, he said. And if the program proved successful in increasing enlistments and retention in the hard-to-fill combat branches it would cost about $90 million a year to continue.[11]

Hebert's committee rejected the reprogramming request out of hand. The vote, taken in executive session a couple of days after the hearing, was not recorded, but the Army learned it was decisively against the proposal. On 29 April Forsythe informed the biweekly meeting of senior military and civilian leaders working on the volunteer force that special pay was a dead issue. The Senate Armed Services Committee had approved the administration's bonus plan, and the Army would now bend every effort to support passage by the full Senate. Clearly a bonus was better than nothing in the Army's eyes. The issue was finally resolved in September when the Selective Service Extension and Military Pay bill containing the bonus authorization finally passed and was signed by President Nixon. But by then it was too late for the Army's purposes. The experiments in recruiting volunteers in fiscal year 1971 had to proceed without either proficiency pay for the combat arms or enlistment bonuses. Forsythe and the others were bitter. From their perspective the Defense Department and Congress had blocked the Army's carefully developed integrated program.[12] But there was no time for remorse or recrimination. The other elements of the Modern Volunteer Army Program had been launched in the spring of 1971 and needed attention. The advertising test held special promise, but that too would soon encounter roadblocks.

The Advertising Issue

The debate over the role of paid broadcast media advertising for volunteers reemerged in January 1971 when the Army unilaterally produced and proceeded with its plan to conduct an advertising experiment as part of its Modern Volunteer Army Program. The Army plan was prepared by the Recruiting Command and its advertising agency, N.W. Ayer & Son of Philadelphia, and refined by John Kester of Assistant Secretary of the Army Brehm's office. In its final form it centered on a radio and television advertising campaign built around a new theme aimed at attracting the attention of potential recruits and their parents and friends. The campaign was to begin in March and run for thirteen weeks, after which the Army and N.W. Ayer would evaluate the results. Total cost of the test would be $10.6 million.

On 12 January Kester informed Paul Wollstadt of Kelley's office of the Army's intention to plan and conduct the test, and on 26 January he forwarded an outline of the plan to Wollstadt. In his letter of transmittal Kester informed Wollstadt of the Army's intent to begin the test on 1 February. Kester worded the letter carefully. "We welcome your suggestions and shall of course keep your office and the other services informed as to progress and evaluation," he said. In timing and tone he left Kelley's people little opportunity to respond negatively. By the time Wollstadt replied, Kester informed him that the Army had already purchased the air time. There was no turning back.[13]

On 20 February Kester and representatives from N.W. Ayer briefed the other services and the Defense Department manpower office on the program. Few present were happy. After the briefing James Hittle, assistant secretary of the Navy for manpower, complained to Kelley, "I think we all agree that the Army's advertising plan exceeds the scope and density of coverage required for 'test' purposes." Hittle reported that his recruiting and advertising people were already reporting loss of public service time and expressions of "deep resentment" from radio and television stations not receiving contracts from the Army. He warned of severe repercussions and suggested that the Department of Defense inform the public and news media that the "unilateral Army campaign is a 'test program' only" that would be evaluated by the Defense Department and that no further experiments of a similar (paid) nature were contemplated. Kester agreed to the Navy proposal when Kelley relayed it to him. "If there has been any misunderstanding regarding the [advertising test]," he told Kelley's deputy, "I hope that it is clarified. We look for your continued support."[14]

N. W. Ayer developed the advertising campaign for the Recruiting Command with input from Forsythe, Kester, and the Army's leadership. The Recruiting Command planned to blanket the United States with radio commercials for thirteen weeks beginning 2 March. During the same period the Army would buy prime-time commercial space to air ten television commercials daily on national networks and more concentrated television ads in eight regional areas. Ayer's role was to develop a completely new approach and theme for the campaign designed to attract public attention, inform the viewers and listeners of the new direction the Army was heading in, and at the same time "go for accessions."

On 26 January representatives from Ayer's creative department met with Forsythe, Westmoreland, and other representatives from the Army staff and USAREC. Ayer had just revised the Army's existing low-budget advertising program around the theme "Your Future, Your Decision, Choose Army." In view of the changes taking place Ayer's people considered the line uninspiring and of low visibility. Ted Regan of Ayer, one of the members of the team that developed the new program, asked, "What does the Army have to say to people at this time?" Kester and Forsythe pointed to Project VOLAR, which was just beginning. "VOLAR became for us a U.S.P. [unique selling proposition]," Regan recalled. "We saw an Army changing to accommodate a different kind of young prospect. I heard the Army saying, 'The Army is changing; the Army wants to meet you half way.'" Regan and his team went back to Philadelphia. Two weeks later they returned to brief Westmoreland and the others on their proposal.[15]

Ayer's creative staff considered the task of developing a new advertising campaign for the Army a brutal assignment. The Army's image was low and prospects for refurbishing it were not good. Furthermore, by entering the prime-time market the Army's ads would be competing with Coke and Volkswagen, for example. The whole level of creativity had to come up. The advertisements had to be "interruptive" in the jargon of the trade; they had to grab and hold the attention of the listener or viewer. After explaining the dilemma to the generals, Regan and his team unveiled the "Today's Army Wants To Join You" theme. "God, I just wanted to vomit," General Palmer remembered. "Do you have to say it that way?" Westmoreland asked. Regan explained his position. If the Army hoped to attract youths with enthusiasm, vigor, and talent it had to emphasize its willingness to enter into a partnership with them. "OK," replied Westmoreland, "We'll try it and see what it does." "We were surprised that the Army bought it," Regan remembered.[16]

The experiment began on 2 March 1971. Ayer bought time on 581 television stations (including networks) and 2,200 radio stations. Because of depressed market conditions and the recent ruling of the surgeon general banning cigarette advertising by the electronic media, Ayer purchased the time at lower than usual rates. For the money spent, the company developed and aired twenty-two commercials; eleven emphasized combat arms directly and others were "theme" ads that stressed the new directions the Army was taking. Some commercials dealt with specifics such as the unit-of-choice and station-of-choice options being offered at VOLAR posts. Others featured skill training available to volunteers. Ayer also prepared, but obviously never used, a commercial featuring proficiency pay (as yet unapproved) for the combat arms. The commercials that did run included a toll-free telephone number for prospects to call for more information. Ayer subcontracted with the LISTFAX Corporation to receive calls for information and provide the callers' names to Army recruiters.[17]

The Army found much with which to be pleased when the initial results of the advertising test began to come in. Enlistments increased by 4,000 compared to the same three-month period in 1970. Voluntary enlistments for the combat arms jumped tenfold. Coupon returns from print media ads that employed the same themes as the radio and television ads rose from 3,000 to 22,000 compared to the previous year. N.W. Ayer was also gratified. Before-and-after telephone surveys conducted for Ayer by Rome, Arnold, & Company revealed that awareness of Army advertising increased significantly among young men, and their fathers recalled specific aspects of the campaign. Especially significant was the fact that 35 percent of the target audience remembered the "Today's Army Wants To Join You" theme. Ayer noted that traffic through recruiting stations increased from 87,000 between April and July 1970 to 129,000 in the same three months of 1971. But the advertising agency cautioned that too much could be made of the results. During the period of the test national economic conditions were poor and youth unemployment was high. Furthermore, draft pressure continued during the test. Ayer also pointed out that no control group existed against which to measure the effectiveness of the test because of the Army's desire to conduct the experiment nationwide and to use it to seek increased enlistments as well as to provide data on the effectiveness of paid advertising.[18]

So pleased was the Army that Secretary Resor asked Laird for permission to conduct a six-week follow-up beginning in late August, a period when recruiters normally expected to pick up additional volunteers from the ranks of high school graduates who took the summer off and were looking for work. Resor was all the more enthusiastic in his request because the preliminary evaluations of the test indicated that enlistments in the other services also increased during the experiment. Indeed, the Army's paid broadcast media advertising program had not adversely affected the other services' recruiting advertising programs. Resor discussed these findings with his counterparts in the Navy and Air Force and reported to Laird that "they had no objection to the Army's planned follow-up."[19] But the Army's request to continue paid recruiting advertising ran into a stone wall in the summer of 1971. The program, now no longer controversial within the Department of Defense, met with criticism from outside sources the minute the first ad aired.

Station managers from radio and television stations that failed to receive contracts to broadcast the test advertisements were incensed. Immediately they began complaining to their congressional representatives, who in turn referred the matter to the Defense Department for explanation. William Ewing, vice president of WTUX, Wilmington, Delaware, wrote to Senator William Roth to say that his station had "contributed generously" of its public service time for twenty-four years to the Army and Army Reserve, but was "completely by-passed" by the paid campaign. He considered the neglect an "unfair disposition of public money," and asked Roth to look into the matter "and see if some fair disposition might not be made!"

Some stations that received contracts from N.W. Ayer refused to accept them. Ward Quaal returned a sales order for $50,000 to Ayer with the message that the WGN Broadcasting Company, based in Chicago, would not accept it but would continue to air messages for the armed forces as a public service "as long as I am steward of these precious resources." Quaal forwarded a copy of his letter directly to Secretary of Defense Laird. "My dear Mel:" he wrote, "While I haven't the slightest idea who initiated the paid advertising campaign...I feel I have an obligation to you as a longtime friend...to tell you of the posture of our company in this regard." Quaal considered it the "obligation of every licensee to act totally in the public interest and that means to help keep America 'strong' from those who would work against its best interests...and certainly that involves recruiting personnel for our Armed Forces." Thirteen stations informed the Army they would no longer carry recruiting ads free as a public service. KCLB of Libby, Montana, tersely canceled all Army programming and sent Resor a copy of its standard rate schedule.[20]

The Army quickly issued a fact sheet on the subject emphasizing the experimental nature of the advertising test. But the congressmen were not mollified. Lionel Van Deerlin, chairman of the Subcommittee on Communications and Power of the House Committee on Interstate and Foreign Commerce, introduced a resolution prohibiting expenditure of public funds for advertising and began holding hearings on the issue. Kester and Wollstadt testified on 21

April and, while the committee continued to express reservations about the ad campaign, the resolution was not pushed thereafter.[21] The issue, however, was far from dead, as new revelations kept it alive.

When the campaign began, the trade journal *Broadcasting* published a factual analysis of the experiment and N.W. Ayer's involvement in preparing it. Shortly thereafter, competitors and critics of the defense contracting process raised questions over how the Army awarded Ayer the $10.6 million contract to develop and conduct the test and campaign. The *Armed Forces Journal*, for example, wrote that the Army had failed to open the contract to competitive bidding and hence "awarded" Ayer a windfall which, the *Journal* implied, was unfair. According to the *Journal* Ayer, one of the smaller companies in the trade, began 1971 with only a one-year $3 million contract with USAREC. When the Army awarded N.W. Ayer the $10.6 million contract for 1972, the *Journal* pointed out, only four other companies competed, and none of the four understood that they were bidding on anything more than "a straightforward renewal of the regular $3 million-a-year recruiting ad effort." John Kester defended the apparent "sweetheart deal" on the grounds that the contracting procedure had been "overtaken by events" in the rush to launch the Modern Volunteer Army Program as soon as possible. The issue blew over, but surely did not help when the Army began talking about extending the advertising campaign.[22]

As was the case with any request pertaining to the expenditure of funds for projects not contained in congressionally authorized programs, the Army had to obtain Congressman Hebert's approval before going ahead with its plan to run a follow-up advertising test in the summer of 1971. Hebert, who was a former newspaperman known to have strong opinions about the electronic media, had been embarrassed and angered by the CBS production "The Selling of the Pentagon" that aired in January 1971 and that implied that he used his relationship with the military services to advance his political fortunes in his district. He was also known to harbor deep suspicions about the advertising industry.

Not surprisingly, Hebert had followed the ad campaign closely. During hearings on the Project Volunteer budget request in February he asked Roger Kelley how much money CBS received from the Army for its portion of the advertising experiment. He used the occasion to express his opinion that FCC licensees should furnish the armed forces free advertising as needed as part of their agreement for use of the public airways.[23] When Kelley and Hadlai A. Hull, the new assistant secretary of the Army for manpower, visited Hebert to advise him of the Army's plan, Hebert stopped them cold. "Polite but closed mind," Hull recorded of Hebert, and "suspicious of any material that came from Ayers [sic] agency." His answer to the Army's request to extend the paid advertising program was "Positively 'no' "; and according to Hull's memo of the meeting Hebert threatened "to use all power within his command to prevent any advertising, and if we do so, to make things difficult."[24]

By July 1971 the Army leaders concerned with achieving the zero-draft goal were convinced that advertising was absolutely essential to the success of the enterprise. They were willing to risk angering the powerful chairman of the House Armed Services Committee by asking for another chance to change his mind on the subject. On 13 July, at the biweekly meeting of the secretary of the Army/SAMVA staff, the SAMVA representative argued that advertising was essential to maintain momentum, especially in light of the fact that Congress had failed to extend the draft by the 30 June 1971 deadline and induction authority had lapsed. Until Congress renewed the draft the Army had to depend solely, if briefly, on volunteers in the summer of 1971. "Despite Mr. Hebert's opposition, which probably results from his personal feelings about the media, especially CBS, we in DOD must make the independent judgment to proceed." [25]

The new secretary of the Army, Robert F. Froehlke, agreed. On 26 July he sent his under secretary, Thaddeus R. Beal, and Forsythe back to Hebert. The chairman remained unmoved. He told Beal and Forsythe that he "respected the Army for attempting to convince him of the merit of this plan and would have been disappointed if we had not attempted to persuade him," they reported to Froehlke, but "he was adamant in adhering to his position of opposition and he doubted that he would ever change his mind on this question." Hebert advised them to try to have the FCC put pressure on the stations to give more free public service time in prime viewing and listening hours.[26]

The next day a discouraged Froehlke told Laird of the outcome of the meeting. Froehlke informed the secretary of defense that Hebert's refusal to sanction paid advertising "makes it extremely difficult for us to maintain the momentum of our current effort ... and diminishes the Defense Department's prospects for a volunteer force in the longer term." He suggested that Kelley's office was the proper one to pursue Hebert's suggestion that the services try to get more public service advertising. Froehlke also asked for guidance on how to proceed. Should the Army defy Hebert and go ahead with the additional ad campaign in August and September, or should he "accede to Chairman Hebert's views?"

Laird would not defy Hebert. The Defense Department chief knew he needed the goodwill of the chairman of the House Armed Services Committee more than he needed paid advertising. Laird thus directed Froehlke to draft a letter for him to send to the president explaining that Hebert's truculence jeopardized the administration's goal of an all-volunteer force by June 1973. If Nixon wanted to expend political capital to override Hebert, he was free to do so without hurting other defense programs.

On 29 July Froehlke notified Hull, Forsythe, and the other Army leaders close to the issue that "using paid radio/TV advertising was dead for the time being." General Kerwin complained that it would be impossible to achieve the zero-draft goal without advertising. Froehlke agreed, but reiterated, "for the time being we would have to defer to Congress." [27]

Hebert's unbending opposition to paid advertising on television and radio was a severe blow and the second the Army received from the autocratic chairman. Like its response to Hebert's refusal to permit the proficiency pay test, the Army would do no more than pick itself up and press on. Forsythe and the others involved simply did not have time to worry about lost battles.

Interim Evaluations

Failure to achieve renewal of the ad campaign ended the Recruiting Command's last major initiative of the experimental phase of the transition to the all-volunteer Army. Success had been achieved in the areas of expansion and reorganization of the Recruiting Command and its field force. The use of new enlistment options was also proving worthwhile. The advertising test proved what could be achieved, and the Army's new recruiting theme, "Today's Army Wants To Join You," continued to be used and enjoyed high recognition and acceptance among youths even if many career soldiers disliked it. The lessons learned from the experiments in recruiting organization and techniques in 1971 were applied, to the extent they could be given Hebert's attitude, in the revised Modern Volunteer Army Program and fiscal year 1973 budget request that Forsythe and the Army unveiled in October 1971.

Following the experiments of 1971, the Army's plan was straightforward: discard failure, reinforce success, and where roadblocks could not be overcome find alternate routes to the objective. When Congress approved enlistment bonuses, the Army was ready with an advertising program to get the information to the prospects, but it was an ad campaign based largely on print media, public service messages, and news releases. Prudently, the Recruiting Command and N.W. Ayer continued to plan for and urge the Army leadership to request funds for paid advertising. But as long as F. Edward Hebert remained in the chair of the House Armed Services Committee those plans remained on the shelf. The brunt of the burden of carrying the Army's message to potential volunteers remained with the expanded field recruiting force.

Notes

[1] PROVIDE, vol. 2, pp. 10–1 to 10–2, 10–5 to 10–7.

[2] Ltr, Resor to Gates, 10 Jan 70, w/att (9pp), OSA file 202.20, RG 335, WNRC.

[3] Note, Kester to Resor, 16 Jan 71, sub: Special Pay versus Bonuses, Kester Papers. The internal debate over the inclusion of the Project Volunteer bonus proposal is covered in Ch. 4, pp. 20–23. Kester's note to Secretary Resor summarized positive and negative points of each proposal.

[4] Memo, Kelley for Secretaries Laird and Packard, 20 Jan 71, sub: Meeting with HASC Leadership, Background Material; Note, Kester to Resor, 21 Jan 71, sub: Volunteer Army Roadblocks, Kester Papers.

[5] Memo, Montague for Forsythe, 19 Feb 71, sub: Special Pay, HRC, CMH; Memo, Kester for Resor, 23 Mar 71, sub: Special Pay; Memo, Kester for Secretary of the Army and Under Secretary of the Army, 24 Mar 71, sub: Special Pay, both in Kester Papers; Memo, Gardiner Tucker for Secretary of Defense, 9 Jan 71, sub: Army Revised Proficiency Pay Proposal, in OSD file 340, RG 330, WNRC; and Memo, Kelley for Resor, 13 Feb 71, sub: Incentive Plan for Army Combat Arms, HRC, CMH.

[6] Memo, Kelley for Multiple Addressees, 26 Mar 71, sub: Administration Position on General Pay Increases and Proficiency/Enlisted Bonus, HRC, CMH.

[7] MFR, 6 Apr 71, Forsythe, sub: SA/SAMVA Meeting, 1 Apr 71; Ibid., 9 Apr 71, sub: SA/SAMVA Meeting, 8 Apr 71; Ibid., 19 Apr 71, sub: SA/SAMVA Meeting, 15 Apr 71, all in Modern Volunteer Army Program SA/SAMVA Meetings & Memos file, Jan–Apr 71, HRC, CMH.

[8] U.S. Congress, House, Committee on Armed Services, Stenographic Transcript, Hearings, Army Reprogramming, 20 April 1971, 92d Cong., 1st sess., 1971, pp. 1–6. (Transcripts provided by General Forsythe to author.)

[9] Ibid., pp. 6–8.

[10] Ibid., pp. 9–14.

[11] Ibid., pp. 22–24, 35, 42–44, 46, 52–59.

[12] MFR, Forsythe, 3 May 71, sub: SA/SAMVA Meeting, 29 Apr 71, MVAP SA/SAMVA Meetings & Memos file, Apr–Jul 71, HRC, CMH; Forsythe Interv.

[13] Memo, Kester for Resor, 7 Jan 71, sub: Paid Radio and TV Advertising; MFR, Kester, 12 Jan 71, sub: Volunteer Army Advertising; Memo, Kester for Wollstadt, 26 Jan 71, sub: Army Advertising; Memo, Kester for Wollstadt, 12 Feb 71, all in Kester Papers.

[14] Minutes of Meeting: Presentation of Army's Recruiting Advertising Program, 20 Feb 71; Memo, Hittle for Kelley, 24 Feb 71, sub: Project Volunteer—Paid Advertising, both in Herbits Papers; and Memo, Kester for Admiral Mack, 6 Mar 71, sub: Test Program in Paid TV/Radio Recruiting Advertising, Kester Papers.

[15] Talking Paper by Lt Col Broady, OSAMVA, 28 Jan 71, sub: Advertising, SA/SAMVA Meetings and Memos file, Jan–Apr 71, HRC, CMH; Minutes of Meeting: Presentation of Army's Recruiting Advertising Program, 20 Feb 71, Herbits Papers; Interv, author with Ted Regan, 25 Aug 83.

[16] Regan and Forsythe Intervs; MHI Interv with Palmer.

[17] Memo, Kester for Admiral Mack, 6 Mar 71, sub: Paul Wollstadt's Memo dated 2 March (1 March ?), sub: "Comments on Army TV/Radio Commercials"; Memo, Kester for Wollstadt, 23 Mar 71, sub: Army Advertising Program, both in Kester Papers; Rpt, D. Ackerman et al., "Effectiveness of the Modern Volunteer

Army Advertising Program" (Menlo Park, Calif.: Stanford Research Institute, December 1971), p. 100.

[18] Historical Rpt, n.d., Director of Advertising and Information, USAREC, 1 July 1970–30 June 1971, USAREC Archives; Rpt, "U.S. Army Recruiting Advertising Test" (Chicago: Rome, Arnold, & Company, September 1971).

[19] Ackerman et al., "Effectiveness of the MVA... ," p. 7; Memo, Resor for Laird, 28 Jun 71, sub: Army Advertising Program, OSD file 340, RG 330, WNRC.

[20] Ltrs, Ewing to Senator Roth, 5 Mar 71; and Quaal to Laird, 21 Apr 71, both in OSD files, RG 330, WNRC; Ltr, Robert Knickerbocker, Manager KCLB, to Sec Army, 3 Mar 71, in attachment D, SA/SAMVA Meeting, 18 Mar 71, SA/SAMVA Meetings and Memos file, Jan–Apr 71, HRC, CMH.

[21] Ltr, Van Deerlin to Laird, 26 Feb 71, OSD file 340, RG 330, WNRC; Copy of House Concurrent Resolution 215, in attachment D, SA/SAMVA Meeting, 8 Apr 71; Talking Paper, 29 Apr 71, sub: Advertising, attachment E, SA/SAMVA Meeting, 29 Apr 71, both in SA/SAMVA Meetings and Memos file, Apr–Jul 71, HRC, CMH.

[22] "Army Enlists Ayer for Ad Blitz," *Broadcasting*, 22 February 1971, pp. 38, 40; "Will Fate of President Nixon's All-Volunteer Force Hinge on 'Competition' for Nation's 50th Largest Ad Contract?" *Armed Forces Journal*, 15 March 1971, pp. 40–41; Memo, Kester for Dr. Fox, 22 Apr 71, sub: Army Recruiting Advertising Contract, Kester Papers.

[23] Lee and Parker, *Ending the Draft*, pp. 160–62.

[24] MFR, Hull, 9 Jul 71, sub: Advertising—8 July 1971 Meeting with E. Hebert, Roger Kelley, Frank Slatinchek, John Ford, and Jack Redden, Herbits Papers.

[25] SAMVA Talking Paper, 13 Jul 71, sub: Status of Advertising, 12 Jul 71, attachment C to SA/SAMVA Meeting, SA/SAMVA Meetings and Memos file, Apr–Jul 71, HRC, CMH.

[26] MFR, SAMVA, 26 Jul 71, sub: Discussion with Congressman Hebert on Army Plans for Recruiting Advertising, August–September 1971, OSD file 340, RG 330, WNRC.

[27] Memo, Froehlke for Laird, 27 Jul 71, sub: Recruiting Advertising, OSD file 340, RG 330, WNRC; MFR, Forsythe, 2 Aug 71, sub: SA/SAMVA Meeting, 29 Jul 71, SA/SAMVA Meetings & Memos file, Apr–Jul 71, HRC, CMH (Froehlke's draft letter for Laird to Nixon is attached at Tab C).

CHAPTER X

A Pilgrim's Progress
The Transition Begins, 1971

During fiscal year 1972 (from July 1971 to June 1972) the transition to an all-volunteer force began in earnest. At the beginning of the period the Army was still in an active experimentation phase under the auspices of General Forsythe and his SAMVA office. One year later both Forsythe and Westmoreland had retired. But before they did they presided over a final experimentation phase that reflected efforts to stabilize and institutionalize the successful initiatives begun by Forsythe. At the same time they also developed criteria for the management of Army manpower procurement in an all-volunteer environment and made provisions to pass the day-to-day control of the Modern Volunteer Army Program over to the Army staff.

Continuity and Change

In August 1971 Congress finally passed and President Nixon signed the Selective Service Extension and Military Pay Act of 1971 permitting inductions for an additional two years, through 30 June 1973. The extension law also provided for the military pay increase that everyone agreed was essential to a successful transition to an all-volunteer armed force. The number of men being inducted had already begun to drop—47,000 fewer in 1971 than in 1970. Whether this was a result of early successes of the experiments by the Army to end draft dependency, a reduction in requirements as a result of the gradual winding down of the war in Vietnam or in the size of the Army, or a combination of all three remained to be determined.

William K. Brehm, who with General Kerwin was instrumental in creating the position of Special Assistant for the Modern Volunteer Army, left the Office of the Assistant Secretary of the Army (Manpower and Reserve Affairs) at the end of 1970 just as the experimentation phase was getting under way. Hadlai A. Hull, a Minnesota business executive, succeeded Brehm in May 1971. During the interval Kester, who remained until March 1972, handled most of the issues pertaining to the volunteer Army program within the secretariat assisted by Clayton Gompf, a retired Army colonel who joined the manpower and reserve affairs staff in 1970. Stanley R. Resor left the office of secretary of the Army in June 1971. Robert F. Froehlke, the assistant secretary of defense (financial management), replaced Resor as Army secretary in July.

About the same time Paul D. Phillips, a retired Army brigadier general, became deputy assistant secretary of the Army (manpower and reserve affairs).

While the Army's civilian leadership changed, the military figures concerned with the volunteer force remained stable. So too did the makeup of the Defense Department civilian leadership structure. As Froehlke, Hull, and Phillips became familiar with the problems and issues facing the Army in the manpower arena they found conflicting opinions on the direction they should take.

Kelley's office wanted to continue to move toward the zero-draft goal on a unified front using the equitable distribution of the Project Volunteer funds provided in the annual budget to assist the services as needed. The Army staff, led by the Office of the Deputy Chief of Staff for Personnel and backed by General Palmer, the vice chief of staff, urged an end to experimentation and stabilization of the all-volunteer effort on terms favorable to the Army. Forsythe's office wanted to continue some experiments and pressed for new initiatives, especially in the area of bonuses. Within the secretariat Clay Gompf and soon Paul Phillips began to express concern that too much emphasis was being placed on quantity alone and that the Army needed to look at the quality of volunteers enlisting.

All of these arguments had to be considered within the context of the development of the Army's request for fiscal year 1973 funds and the distribution of unexpended FY 1972 Project Volunteer funds. Further complicating the decision on how to proceed were two provisions of the Selective Service Extension and Military Pay Act of 1971 and the final approval and publication of the Master Plan for the Volunteer Army, which all parties within the Army agreed would form the basis for immediate and future program requests. As usual these decisions were made under the pressure of the day-to-day management of ongoing projects and on the basis of incomplete information. Manpower and budget forecasts were vastly complicated by unanticipated requirements or unintended consequences of congressionally mandated programs. Differing bureaucratic perspectives further muddied the waters. By the end of June 1972, as the Army embarked on its last full year of draft dependency, despite cautious optimism it remained to be seen whether the goal truly could be achieved.

The Revised Master Plan

The absence of a clear statement of the purpose and goals of the Modern Volunteer Program dogged Forsythe and the SAMVA organization through the first half of 1971. Army staff opposition to the original version of the Master Program led to its withdrawal in March. While Forsythe's office revised the document to conform with staff recommendations on wording and emphasis, the VOLAR experiment, the reorganization and expansion of the Recruiting Command, and the paid recruiting advertising including the new Army theme began. As noted, the attendant publicity generated confusion and bred resentment in the field; many career soldiers perceived the programs as pandering to populism and faddishness, and they worried that the Modern Volunteer Army would lead to permissiveness and undiscipline in the ranks. The *Life* article on Fort Carson confirmed their deepest fears.

To counter these perceptions and capture the support of the professional strata of the Army, Forsythe directed his staff to completely revise the master program. While the original document had been a compilation of papers describing Modern Volunteer Army actions, the new publication offered a totally new statement of the program's philosophy. The final document emphasized professionalism. Improvements in Army life-style, advertising, and experiments were deemphasized or presented in terms of their importance to the accomplishment of the overall objective, "the development of a capably led, highly competent fighting force which attracts motivated, qualified volunteers."

The original version, prepared hastily and under pressure in the first frantic days of the SAMVA operation's existence, focused perforce on those aspects of Army work and life that created dissatisfaction among soldiers. Only vaguely did it reflect the nagging concern that senior leaders such as Westmoreland, Palmer, and Forsythe shared about the professional health of the Army. By the time he ordered the master plan revised in March 1971 Forsythe could see that the program was misunderstood in the field and had identified the points of opposition to his program from within elements of the bureaucracy and Congress. The revision of the master plan thus became an attempt to repackage the Modern Volunteer Army Program and present it to both the Army and outsiders in terms that would emphasize positive change without threatening traditionalists who valued continuity. General Palmer circulated the draft of the revision to Army staff agencies late in July. They reviewed it favorably. Westmoreland approved it the following month. He and Froehlke immediately began sending copies of the master program, entitled "The Modern Volunteer Army: A Program for Professionals," to commanders in the field and members of Congress.

In his cover letter Westmoreland candidly admitted that the program initially "moved ahead without a comprehensive program for action" due to the urgency of the situation. The revised program "incorporates lessons learned from our early experience," he assured. Froehlke employed a similar tone. He acknowledged that the Army's initial efforts had attracted "widespread criticism" but added his conviction that "you will be reassured by the objectives which the Army has established for itself and by the approaches being taken to achieve them."[1]

The Soldier-Oriented Budget

The publication and release of the revised master plan was hardly random. Since June the SAMVA office, the Army staff, and the secretariat had been hard at work preparing budget requests, to include the initial proposal for fiscal year 1973 funds and a claim for a share of fiscal year 1972 Project Volunteer funds still controlled by Kelley's office. In the summer of 1971, as the Army prepared these requests, the overall status of funding for volunteer force programs remained cloudy. Congress still had not approved either the administration's selective service extension and military pay request or the fiscal year 1972 budget. The services were operating under the provisions of a continuing resolution. Thus it was imperative that the Army still opposition to the Modern Volunteer Army Program within its own ranks as well as on Capitol Hill before it proceeded to ask for more money.

Vice Chief of Staff of the Army General Bruce Palmer formally kicked off the fiscal year 1973 budget cycle in June 1971 when he directed the Army staff directors and program chiefs to take a close look at the "extent to which base programs meet or fail to meet the need for increased emphasis on the human requirements of the Army." The base budget was that portion of the Army's annual request that it considered absolutely essential for smooth and continuous operation of the service in the coming year. More specifically Palmer told Army staff members to be prepared to report on the extent to which their programs contributed to the fulfillment of Modern Volunteer Army goals of enhanced professionalism and improved service life.

Here was the germ of the Army's strategy to ensure that successful volunteer force initiatives did not end up being cut from the budget during Department of Defense or Office of Management and Budget reviews prior to being incorporated into the president's budget. Incorporation of volunteer Army costs in the base budget also freed the Army from dependency on the Project Volunteer fund controlled by Roger Kelley's office. Palmer's guidance also suggested that he was preparing to phase out the semiautonomous SAMVA operation. It was no secret that Palmer had doubted the need for or wisdom of creating an off-line organization to manage the transition from the draft to the volunteer Army. Turning budget authority for the Modern Volunteer Army Program over to the Army staff would eliminate the need for Forsythe's office.[2]

About the same time Forsythe briefed the secretary of the Army and other senior civilian and military leaders concerned with the Modern Volunteer Army Program on his projections of fiscal year 1973 needs. His office identified Modern Volunteer Army Program requirements totaling $3 billion in FY 73. These funds, the SAMVA admitted, represented additions to the base budget, as dictated by Defense Department instructions which directed the services to request money to support volunteer force programs separately. Other Defense Department budget officials, who were struggling to cut the overall defense budget in response to broader guidance from the Nixon administration, placed strict ceilings on base budget programs, preventing the inclusion of Modern Volunteer Army Program initiatives into those portions of the request.

Forsythe acknowledged that the $3 billion figure he had identified as Modern Volunteer Army Program needs in FY 73 was "more than we can logically expect to receive." After all, only $1.3 billion had been allocated for the same kinds of programs for all services in FY 72. He agreed to meet with Assistant Secretary Hull and General Kerwin to work out priorities. Kerwin also worried that the Army ought not to propose programs that could not be supported in the future without cutting into the base budget. No one knew for sure how long the administration or Congress would continue to fund volunteer force add-ons to the defense budget. All parties recognized the wisdom of shifting the costs of the volunteer force from supplementary budgets to the base budget. The problem was identifying and sticking to priorities and successfully defending them to the cost-conscious administration and congressional committees. Forsythe estimated that funds for professionalism programs, improvements in service attractiveness, additional field experiments, and the as yet unaddressed problems of converting the reserve components to a draft-free basis would total an additional $1 billion for FY 74, $3.3 billion for 1975, $3.2 billion for 1976, and $3.3 billion for 1977.[3]

Secretary of the Army Froehlke accepted the logic of those who argued that the Army should include as much as possible of the funding for the Modern Volunteer Army Program in the base budget or as add-ons to the base budget rather than continue to treat it as a supplementary request, which required separate negotiations with the White House followed by additional congressional actions. As the fiscal year 1973 budget request took shape Froehlke began referring to it as the "people or soldier oriented budget." Successful Modern Volunteer Army Programs such as civilianization of KP and replacement of enlisted soldiers by civilians on other work details were rolled into the base budget. All told $532.4 million of support for MVA programs was shifted out of the supplemental request to the base budget. Forsythe developed a further request for $612.6 million from the Project Volunteer funds controlled by Kelley, although he anticipated receiving less than $500 million. An additional $1,067.6 million to cover the cost of the Army's share of pay raises contained in the Selective Service Extension and Military Pay Act would come from the Project Volunteer budget in fiscal year 1973. Thus the total Army request for funds to continue the momentum toward achieving the zero-draft goal came to approximately $2.2 billion, nearly $800 million less than Forsythe and the other manpower planners preferred. But they considered their estimate responsible and reasonable within the context of the administration's expressed interest in economy.[4]

While the Army staff was preparing the fiscal year 1973 budget request, Forsythe and the assistant secretary of the Army for manpower and reserve affairs were trying to have Kelley's office release funds from the fiscal year 1972 Project Volunteer budget to the Army for its ongoing MVA program. (Congress had failed to authorize the expenditure of funds for Project Volunteer before the beginning of FY 72, and the services were still operating under a continuing resolution.) Nevertheless, the director of the Army budget ruled that in the absence of an explicit statement from Congress prohibiting the expenditure of funds for volunteer force projects, programs begun in or projected to begin in FY 72 could proceed. To do this, the Army needed access to the money from the Project Volunteer budget that it had been promised. Thus in August Assistant Secretary Hull sent Kelley the Army's list of claims against the Project Volunteer fund. The request totaled $102.6 million.[5] The bureaucratic struggle that ensued reveals much about how the different levels of management within the defense establishment viewed the challenge of ending the draft and the means to accomplish it.

After a month of silence to Hull's request to Kelley for Project Volunteer funds, the Army tried again. This time it received an answer. According to officials in Kelley's office, because funds had to be set aside to cover the higher-than-requested pay raise working its way through Congress, "there really was no contingency fund left" unless the Army was prepared to support its portion of the increased pay through reprogramming. Froehlke decided the Army would have to take the matter over Kelley's head to Secretary of Defense Laird and urge him to retain the funds for their original purpose. The new under secretary of the Army, Kenneth E. Belieu, would take the issue up with David Packard, Laird's under secretary of defense. Forsythe briefed Belieu on the fund impasse and his view, widely shared in Army manpower circles, that the Office of the Secretary of Defense represented "one of our major obstacles to achieving Modern Volunteer Army goals."

Armed with information provided by Forsythe's office, Belieu met with Under Secretary of Defense Packard on 19 October 1971. Forsythe had pared down the Army's request to $277 million, which represented the absolute minimum "necessary to sustain the momentum of the Modern Volunteer Army effort." He attacked claims by unnamed sources that because of the higher pay raise the Army did not need to spend as much as originally planned on MVA projects and reasserted the position that ending reliance on the draft depended on a balanced program to strengthen professionalism, improve service attractiveness, and modernize recruiting. The pay raise certainly would improve service attractiveness, Belieu said, but it did not contribute to the other aspects of the program. If the money was not forthcoming the Army would shortly be forced to "stop ongoing programs that are critical to the Modern Volunteer Army effort." Following the meeting Kelley's office agreed to support Forsythe's list of "critical projects/activities," and the Army got its money.[6]

The outcome of the fiscal year 1973 budget request proved equally frustrating. After submitting a request for $612.6 million for Project Volunteer funds in FY 73, the Army refined its requirement to $513.8 million and proposed that it be permitted to roll the difference into its base budget. The Department of Defense comptroller disallowed the latter request, and, after the Office of Management and Budget notified the Defense Department that it would have to hold $360 million of Project Volunteer funds in reserve to defray the cost of another pay raise, the Army trimmed its bid to $345.4 million "for essential, priority programs." Then the Office of Management and Budget recommended to the White House that it cut $400 million from the Project Volunteer budget. Faced with such a loss, Secretary of Defense Laird decided to forgo creating a contingency fund for volunteer force projects in fiscal year 1973 altogether. On 23 December Laird postponed all new starts until FY 74 "when the problems to be solved will be more fully identified." The Army allocation of the remaining Project Volunteer funds came to $189.4 million. The Defense Department also cut an additional $236.7 million from the soldier-oriented programs of the Army's base budget request.

The logic behind all these actions was both econometric and political. In the fall of 1971 when the defense budget for fiscal year 1973, of which volunteer force initiatives represented a relatively small part, was being prepared, the Nixon administration had been aggressively reducing federal spending. Defense spending was hardly immune from this effort. With the U.S. role in Vietnam winding down, the administration wanted to reduce active duty strength. A smaller active force, White House economists reasoned, would be easier to recruit and the higher rates of pay authorized by Congress would make recruiters' jobs that much easier. Thus expensive experiments to improve service attractiveness and enhance professionalism, such as those the Army wanted to continue, were unnecessary. This was essentially the argument of the Gates Commission report—higher pay for fewer volunteers would do the job. The White House was not concerned with how the services ended the draft, only that they did so and contributed to Nixon's promise to reduce spending as well.

These decisions angered many volunteer force supporters who had labored so hard to craft their budget request to support the president's goal of a zero draft by 1973. Some took the decision as evidence that White House support for the all-volunteer force was waning. But despite the setback, the Army's program was still viable. Because of the decision to incorporate many of the ongoing Modern Volunteer Army Program expenses in the base budget the Army eventually received relatively more of its request than did the other services, who had continued the practice of including all-volunteer force funding initiatives in their Project Volunteer requests. Thus the Army was able to maintain, and in some cases expand, its programs in FY 73 despite the so-called "no new starts" decision by Laird.[7]

Forsythe's role in the development of the Soldier-Oriented Budget for fiscal year 1973 proved to be the last major contribution of SAMVA. Even before Laird rendered his judgment on the FY 1973 budget General Palmer told Forsythe of his desire to transfer planning and management of volunteer Army programs back to the Army staff. Forsythe agreed that "my office's involvement in the details of the VOLAR experiments and the sponsoring of new programs and policies related to the MVA has achieved what was desired by the Chief of Staff." Palmer asked Forsythe to revise the SAMVA charter. Forsythe replied that he would shift his efforts to the areas of "training, motivation, and other related aspects of professionalism" while continuing to "assist you and the Chief of Staff in monitoring staff work in the areas of recruiting, retention, and career attractiveness." He continued to speak on behalf of the Modern Volunteer Army Program as did other members of his staff, especially his deputy, General Montague. But, as Westmoreland formally advised him on 15 January 1972, Forsythe's office began "to phase out of activities whenever we are confident that desirable new initiatives are fully set as lasting Army practices."[8]

Progress and Problems

By the end of 1971 the Army had accumulated a year's worth of experience with actively seeking increased numbers of true volunteers and higher retention among serving soldiers through its three-pronged program of enhanced professionalism, improvements in service attractiveness, and a revamped acquisition system. In October Forsythe reviewed the events and accomplishments of the previous twelve months beginning with the creation of his office. "Since the formal inception of the [Modern Volunteer Army] program in October 1970," he told the secretary of the Army and others assembled for a weekly meeting on all-volunteer force issues, "rather substantial progress has been made." He summarized seven major accomplishments: the announcement of the all-out effort to achieve the zero-draft goal, followed by the Army Commanders' Conference on the Modern Volunteer Army; announcement and implementation of the "high impact actions"; development and implementation of the Army-funded experimental Modern Volunteer Army Program in early 1971; expansion of the recruiting force; development and execution of the highly successful recruiting advertising program; development and implementation of the fiscal year 1972 programs that expanded on and reinforced successful initiatives; and the development of the fiscal year 1973 program, especially the Soldier-Oriented Budget, which would carry the Army through the end of the draft era. The results of the effort, Forsythe reported, were an increase in enlistments "despite declining draft pressure, continued public criticism of the military, Calley publicity [referring to the inquiry of Army Lt. William Calley's role in the My Lai massacre], Laos [the U.S.–supported invasion of South Vietnamese forces into the Laotian panhandle], and congressional debate to limit [the] draft. . . ." In the crucial category of combat arms volunteers, he noted enlistments in that category rose tenfold, from 315 to 3,865, between January and September 1971. Forsythe reported that the "entire Army is geared up for continuous and increasing efforts to build a better Army and in the process reduce reliance on the draft," but, he cautioned, much remained to be done. Overall the Army needed to increase the number of true volunteers 200 percent; the combat arms required 6,000 volunteers a month.[9]

Forsythe sounded a more cautious note in his public statements. In his formal report to the Association of the United States Army, published in the October 1971 issue of *Army* magazine, known as the "Green Book," he reviewed the objectives of the Modern Volunteer Army Program and VOLAR Experiment but said "it may be too early for a precise evaluation. . . ." Enlistments were up, he noted. But he could not say whether they were up because of Army initiatives or because the war was winding down and youth unemployment was up. Furthermore, he was not prepared to answer what to him was the crucial question: "Have we in fact created a more professional Army since the inception of MVA?" The most that could be said, Forsythe went on, was that the effort to move the Army from draft dependency to an all-volunteer basis had stimulated a "process of self examination" and created the need for the Army to "seek a meaningful relationship with the young Americans on whom the Army depends for its very existence." The end result of these developments would be an improved Army, he added. Indeed, the results of the self-examination and establishment of new links with America's young people were "necessary if our Army is to survive and prosper as an institution in the 1970s." The process, he predicted, required more hard work.[10]

The caution Forsythe expressed proved well founded. Beginning in October, enlistments began to drop off. The Army needed 19,000 new enlistees in October; it expected to recruit 13,900, but only 10,900 actually volunteered. Combat arms recruits also dropped. Nearly 4,000 men signed up in September while only 1,933 joined in October. In November the decline continued. Only 10,200 youths volunteered out of an anticipated 13,800; 1,770 of these enlisted for the combat arms.[11] The quality of those that volunteered also came under scrutiny.

Over the course of the year since the Modern Volunteer Army Program began, manpower analysts in the Office of the Assistant Secretary of the Army (Manpower, Reserve Affairs, and Logistics) and on the Army staff worried that as the Army increased its intake of true volunteers quality would suffer. The anticipated problem finally began to rear its head in the fall of 1971.

The issue of quality versus quantity in an all-volunteer environment had deep roots. Prior to World War II the old Regular Army understood the problem well. During the relative prosperity of the 1920s recruiters took just about every able-bodied applicant for enlistment. Officers in line units who received these volunteers complained bitterly of the poor quality of the recruits, who frequently became disciplinary problems and deserters. In the late 1920s the Army began to administer intelligence and mental tests to recruits in an attempt to weed out misfits before they enlisted. Completion of the eighth grade became established as the minimum acceptable education level.

By the beginning of World War II the Army had refined its tests. All recruits and inductees took a series of exams designed to determine adaptability for service and trainability. The Army General Classification Test (AGCT) was designed to measure the combination of an individual's common sense, experience, and formal education—in short, his "intelligence" in the colloquial sense. The test grouped soldiers into five classes—Class I represented the highest, Class V the lowest. Classes I and II proved to be the source of most officer and noncommissioned officer candidates during the war. In theory all services were to receive a proportionate share of men from each group. In fact, the more technical arms and services laid successful claim to a greater share of Class I and II men while the nontechnical branches, especially the combat arms, received more Class IV and V men. The unintended consequence of this practice soon manifested itself in combat. Casualties among Class IV and V men were higher, especially in units where junior leaders were also of lower intelligence. One observer concluded it was "murder" to assign a Class V soldier to an infantry unit. After the war Congress agreed. The Army continued to employ the AGCT and the Class I–V system, but when it extended selective service legislation Congress prohibited induction of Class V men.[12]

Following World War II the Army refined its test, renamed the Armed Forces Qualification Test (AFQT), and the other services adopted it. However, the practice of grouping scores into five classes continued, and Congress continued to forbid the enlistment or induction of Category V personnel, a practice which suited the services anyway since their experience with these "marginal men" proved unsatisfactory. Nevertheless, during the mid and late 1950s and early 1960s all the services experimented with training and education programs designed to increase the capabilities and utility of Category IV personnel. The Army especially conducted experiments in the training of "marginal men" because, although it could and did set high standards for volunteers, selective service standards were lower and in some years more than 50 percent of the Army's inductees were Category IV.

In 1966 the Department of Defense launched a major program, designated Project 100,000, expanding opportunities for marginal performers. Troubled by the knowledge that one-third of the nation's military age men failed to meet minimum education or medical standards for induction, Secretary of Defense Robert S. McNamara directed the services to revise their standards and take in 100,000 formerly disqualified men a year. To compensate, he also ordered them to develop training programs designed to offer additional assistance to these "new standards" personnel. The aim of the program was twofold: to open "the opportunity to serve in the armed forces to a broader spectrum of the Nation's youth" and to teach them "new skills and disciplines" that would enable them to perform military service and return to civilian life better equipped to become "productive members of society." The program, which was seen as the Defense Department's contribution to President Lyndon Johnson's "Great Society," was viewed with misgivings by many defense manpower managers who questioned the use of the armed forces for "social engineering" and feared its consequences.[13]

Using the services for social purposes was hardly new. Following World War I the Army had briefly accepted the enlistment of illiterates and non–English-speaking immigrants and trained them in special "Americans All" units to demonstrate the social utility of a peacetime military establishment as well as to encourage volunteers seeking to improve themselves. Subsequently, during the debates over Universal Military Training in 1920 and again following World War II, Army spokesmen argued that UMT would uplift the nation's youth as well as provide for the common defense. Project 100,000 was thus one more attempt to use the military to augment social programs. Furthermore, although it was never so stated, the program increased the pool of men eligible for induction even as the buildup for Vietnam was getting under way.

Project 100,000 (dubbed "McNamara's 100,000" by its opponents) required the Army to accept Category IV personnel totaling up to 24 percent of its annual enlisted accessions. In addition, the program specified that 50 percent of Category IV accessions come from the lower half of the quintal. The aim of this action was to assure that sufficient numbers of men from the lowest mental category permitted to serve were included in the program. The Army accepted the program grudgingly and found, to the surprise of many opponents of the effort, that 95 percent of the soldiers accessed under the program completed their training, that most did not become disciplinary problems, and that those who served in Vietnam were judged "very good soldiers."

Nevertheless, with the shift to an all-volunteer force the Army and the other services quickly began urging the Defense Department to end the program. The services argued that reduced strength ceilings dictated by the drawdown after Vietnam would eliminate many of the "soft skill" jobs they had for the least trainable Category IV personnel.

Kelley agreed. Although he considered the requests "difficult to justify on the basis of the performance record of Mental IVs and the number of military jobs they are able to do," he revised the standards slightly in February 1971. The percentage of the lowest group of Category IV men was reduced from 4.5 percent of total accessions to 3.5 percent for the Navy and Air Force and from 6 to 4 percent for the Army and Marine Corps. Kelley also reduced the overall percentage of Category IVs that the Air Force, Marine Corps, and Navy had to accept, but he continued to insist that the Army take in 24 percent Category IVs annually. The Army objected strenuously. "We cannot wait until July 1973 to cast an improved quality mold for the Army," argued an Army staff manpower analyst. "A 24 percent ceiling is too high for the needs of VOLAR." A smaller volunteer Army needed greater flexibility. Project 100,000 research showed that Category IV men could be trained in one skill area; the smaller volunteer Army needed soldiers capable of performing at least two and often more skills. Assistant Army Secretary Hull asked Kelley to adjust the Army's Category IV ceiling to 20 percent, the same as that of the Marine Corps. Kelley relented. The new standard went into effect in October 1971.[14]

The Army responded immediately by reducing its recruiter quotas for Category IV enlistments. Furthermore, in an internal move designed to discourage recruiters even from considering Category IV volunteers, the Army announced to the Recruiting Command that recruiters would not receive credit for volunteers who scored in the Mental Category IV range on the AFQT unless they had a high school diploma or its equivalent. Secretary of the Army Froehlke personally endorsed the move when Forsythe explained it to him. "Recruiters have been doing a good job so far in obtaining more volunteer enlistments," Froehlke stated, but "now is the time to stress quality."

Unfortunately, recruiters swung too far in the direction of searching for quality. Category IV accessions in October and November plummeted from 24 to 4 percent. Overall quantity also fell. On the other hand, the quality of recruits entering the Army, as measured in terms of volunteers scoring in the upper three mental categories or possessing high school diplomas or their equivalent, rose from 54 percent in September to 88 percent by December. Analyzing the data, Forsythe concluded, "results indicate that the Army can enlist its share of quality men."

In December 1971, in an effort to balance the quality-quantity equation, the Army relaxed quality controls again by restoring recruiter credit for Category IV enlistments who were not high school graduates. The percentage of Category IV volunteers rose immediately to the new ceiling of 20 percent of total accessions. The message to Forsythe was clear. "This indicates that there are probably sufficient Category IV individuals who will enlist to meet the

Army's Category IV requirements," he reported. Quality enlistments dropped slightly, but did not return to the pre-October level. Army manpower analysts attributed the new level of quality accessions to the final approval by Congress of the military pay raise included in the Selective Service Extension and Military Pay Act of 1971.

The Army's optimism was short lived. Personnel analysts soon found to their chagrin that the increased quality of recruits between October 1971 and February 1972 was illusory. Recruiters, the Army discovered, were spending much of their time obtaining, sometimes fraudulently, high school diploma equivalency certificates (General Education Development or GED certificates) for volunteers. In March the Army "put the recruiters out of the GED business" by requiring high school diplomas as a prerequisite for enlistment.[15] But the Army was no closer to solving either its quantity or its quality problem after nearly six months of tinkering with the controls.

Extension of the Draft

In 1971 the debate over draft extension and the all-volunteer force cut across party and ideological lines. More was at issue than intellectual differences over how best to raise armed forces in a democratic society. Debate over selective service extension in 1971 was inexorably linked to the debate over the war in Vietnam and the breakup of the bipartisan consensus on foreign policy that had existed in the United States since the late 1940s. It was also part of the broader effort by Congress to regain a more active role in the foreign and national security policy-making process. The outcome was both more and less than the Nixon administration wanted. The exercise offers a classic example of the American legislative process at work.

The chairmen of the two armed services committees, Senator John C. Stennis and Congressman F. Edward Hebert, opposed the volunteer Army on both philosophical and practical grounds. Neither objected to pay raises for the military, but both favored a four-year extension of induction authority. Yet they introduced the Nixon administration's bills to extend the draft for only two years and to facilitate the transition to an all-volunteer force, and they pledged to give the issue a full and open hearing. Pressure from two directions motivated them. The president requested the action; as key members of the bipartisan coalition on foreign and national security policy they could not refuse him. Second, congressional sentiment demanded action. Resentment lingered over the handling of debate on the issue in 1967; an attempt to block change in 1971 risked legislative revolt and changes more radical than those proposed by Nixon.

The forces for change made strange bedfellows. Antiwar congressmen such as Senator Mark Hatfield, who urged an immediate end of the draft as a way to derail the war effort, found a measure of support from Senator Barry Goldwater, who supported the war effort but opposed the principle of conscription. Goldwater cosponsored Hatfield's bill to enact the recommendations of the

Gates Commission immediately, but voted against his resolution to repeal the Selective Service Act altogether. At the other extreme, Senator Edward M. Kennedy, a leading critic of the Vietnam War, opposed the all-volunteer force proposals of the administration and his antiwar colleagues. Kennedy did not oppose the volunteer concept per se. At the core of his rejection of both Nixon's and Hatfield's proposals lay a fear that a shift to volunteerism before the war ended would result in a mercenary force of racial minorities and the economically disadvantaged. Kennedy favored immediate draft reform to ensure that the middle class did not escape the fighting and modest pay raises; volunteer force legislation could wait until the end of the war.

The House Armed Services Committee devised a formula for eventual success. Unable to agree on how long to extend induction authority, the pro- and antidraft congressmen joined ranks on increasing pay. Hebert's committee doubled the size of the administration's pay hike request and voted to pay it all immediately (the administration wanted to spread the raise over two years to reduce the impact on the budget). The logic proved flawless. It allowed everyone to support the bill. Antidraft congressmen could vote for a large pay increase because it increased the chances for a successful, and perhaps even faster, transition to an all-volunteer armed force. Prodraft forces could support the bill because it did justice to draftees and volunteers alike who, all agreed, had been underpaid for years. After much pulling and hauling, which included considerable debate over nongermane amendments dealing with the war, the bill passed. Nixon signed it into law in September 1971.[16]

Agreement to end peacetime conscription over a two-year period by reducing the size of the active duty armed forces and providing a major pay raise to stimulate voluntary enlistments was possible in 1971 because all major parties in the decision found something good in the arrangement. The Nixon administration wanted to reduce the size of the defense establishment and overseas commitments without sacrificing security. Nixon also wanted to reduce spending. Opponents of the war saw the end of the draft as way to force the government out of direct involvement in Vietnam. Even the Army found benefit in ending the draft after its role in the war in Vietnam was resolved. Whether it could build a truly better Army on what seemed to many to be the ruins of an existing one remained to be seen.

Notes

[1] Memo, SAMVA for VCofSA, 21 Jul 71, sub: Modern Volunteer Army Master Program; Memo, VCofSA for Heads of Army General Staff Agencies, 23 Jul 71, sub: Modern Volunteer Army Master Program, Background Material; Ltr, Westmoreland to ASA(R&D), 7 Sep 71; Ltr, Froehlke to Senator Allott, 5 Oct 71, both in OSA file 202.10, RG 335, WNRC. Westmoreland sent similar letters to all major commanders and members of the Army secretariat, while Froehlke sent identical letters to key members of both houses of Congress.

[2] Memo, VCofSA for major staff agencies, 19 Jun 71, sub: Presentation of POM Program, Background Material.

[3] MFR by Forsythe, 25 Jun 71, sub: SA/SAMVA Meeting, w/ SAMVA Talking Paper, 30 Jun 71, sub: Program Objective Memorandum, both in SA/SAMVA Meetings and Memos file, Apr 71–Jul 71, HRC, CMH; Memo, SAMVA for Points of Contact, 22 Jun 71, sub: Modern Volunteer Army's Program Objective Memorandum Submissions, Background Material.

[4] SAMVA Talking Papers, 7 Oct 71, sub: Soldier Oriented Aspects of the FY 73 Budget; Soldier Oriented Programs, 3 Dec 71; Status of FY 73 Budget, 29 Dec 71, all in SA/SAMVA Meetings and Memos file, Jul–Aug 71, and Dec 71–Jun 72, HRC, CMH.

[5] Memo, Comptroller for SAMVA, 24 Jun 71, sub: Fiscal Year 1972 Funds for the Modern Volunteer Army, Background Material; Memo, Hull for Kelley, 24 Aug 71, sub: Claims Against the FY 72 DoD Project Volunteer Contingency Fund, OSA file 202.10, RG 335, WNRC.

[6] SAMVA Talking Papers, 23 Sep 71, sub: Status of Funding Actions, and 7 Oct 71, sub: Possible Ways in Which the Under Secretary Can Assist the Modern Volunteer Army Effort, SA/SAMVA Meetings and Memos file, Jul–Nov 71, HRC, CMH; Memo, Forsythe for Belieu, 19 Oct 71, sub: Talking Paper in Connection with Claims Against the FY 72 Project Volunteer Contingency Fund, w/enclosures, OSA file 202.10, RG 335, WNRC. The claim against the FY 72 Project Volunteer fund and Belieu's role in resolving the impasse are traced in Forsythe's memorandums of the meetings between his office, and representatives of the Army staff and the secretariat. By 14 October the issue of FY 72 Project Volunteer funds had reached the top of the SA/SAMVA meeting agenda. Belieu did not record the specifics of his meeting with Packard, and Kelley's files are equally mute on the subject. But after the meeting between Belieu and Packard on 19 October the topic disappeared from the Army's volunteer force agenda and the FY 73 budget moved to the fore.

[7] Memos, Hull for Kelley, 22 Oct 71, sub: Claims Against the FY 73 Project Volunteer Contingency Fund, 8 Dec 71, sub: Army Project Volunteer Priority List, 11 Dec 71, sub: Allocation of FY 73 Project Volunteer Funds, all in OSA file 202.10, RG 335, WNRC; OSA Program/Budget Decision Memorandum 319, 23 Dec 71, sub: All-Volunteer Armed Force, OSD file 340, RG 330, WNRC; SAMVA Talking Paper, 29 Dec 71, sub: Status of FY 73 Funding, 29 Dec 71, SA/SAMVA Meetings & Memos file, Dec 71–Jun 72, HRC, CMH. See also Lee and Parker, *Ending the Draft*, pp. 179–87, for the OSD perspective.

[8] Draft Ltr, Forsythe to Palmer, 3 Jan 72, sub: Revision of SAMVA Charter; Ltr, Westmoreland to Forsythe, 15 Jan 72, sub: Guidance for the Special Assistant for the Modern Volunteer Army, provided by General Forsythe.

⁹ SAMVA Talking Paper, 7 Oct 71, sub: MVA Concept and Accomplishments, SA/SAMVA Meetings and Memos file, Jul–Nov 71, HRC, CMH.

¹⁰ George I. Forsythe, "The Impact of VOLAR," *Army* 21, no. 10 (October 1971): 29–32.

¹¹ SAMVA Fact Sheets, 3 Nov and 2 Dec 71, sub: Recruiting Progress, Enclosure 1, sub: Objectives & Enlistments, SA/SAMVA Meetings and Memos file, Jul–Nov 71 and Dec 71–Jun 72, HRC, CMH.

¹² For the "quality v. quantity" debate of the interwar years and the development of intelligence tests for recruits, see Griffith, *Men Wanted for the U.S. Army*, especially ch. 4, "Maintaining the Volunteer Army During Peace and Prosperity." On the use of the AGCT in World War II and the casualty experience of Class IV and V men, see Robert R. Palmer et al., *The Procurement and Training of Ground Combat Troops* (Washington, D.C.: Department of the Army, 1948), especially pp. 4–6, 10–12, 15–28, 48–53. See also Department of the Army, *Marginal Man and Military Service* (Washington, D.C.: Government Printing Office, 1965), pp. 9–16, 29–36.

¹³ *Marginal Man and Military Service*, ch. 10, "Training and the Marginal Man"; *Annual Report of the Secretary of Defense, Fiscal Year 1967* (Washington, D.C.: Government Printing Office, 1967), p. 67.

¹⁴ Memo, Kelley for Assistant Secretaries of the Military Departments (Manpower and Reserve Affairs), 26 Feb 71, sub: Project One Hundred Thousand Quotas; DCSPER Fact Sheet, 19 Apr 71, sub: New Standards Program; DCSPER Summary Sheet, 2 Aug 71, sub: Mental Standards of the Volunteer Army; Memo, Hull for Kelley, 25 Aug 71, sub: Mental Standards of Inductees; Memo, Hull for Kelley, 29 Sep 71, sub: Mental Standards of Army Accessions, OSA file 202.15, RG 335, WNRC.

¹⁵ MFR, Montague, 14 Oct 71, sub: SA/SAMVA Meeting, SA/SAMVA Meetings and Memos file, Jul–Nov 71; SAMVA Talking Papers, 3 Dec 71, sub: Other Recruiting Initiatives; Analysis of December Enlistments/Accessions, 20 Jan 72; Analysis of January 1972 Enlistments, 9 Feb 72; Other Recruiting Information, 9 Mar 72, SA/SAMVA Meetings and Memos file, Dec 71–Jun 72, HRC, CMH; Historical Report, Director of Recruiting Operations, 1 July 1971–30 June 1972, USAREC Archives.

¹⁶ For a concise summary of the legislative history of the selective service extension and military pay bills of 1971, see *Congressional Quarterly Almanac*, 27, 92d Cong., 1st sess., 1971, pp. 257–96. For a detailed analysis of congressional action on the bills, see Lee and Parker, *Ending the Draft*, ch. 3, "Legislative Debate and Decision."

CHAPTER XI

The Washington Battlefield
Pushing the AVF in 1972

Changing an army's entire manpower procurement policy in time of peace is a major undertaking. Making such a transition during a major war is even more complex. Outwardly the war speeded up the transition, while the transition itself forced changes in American strategy and policy that otherwise might have been adopted earlier and with more success. Vietnamization, or at least some of its components, is one example. Yet despite the Vietnamization program, which had greatly reduced U.S. troop requirements in South Vietnam, U.S. worldwide security commitments, especially in Europe and Korea, remained substantial, and the U.S. Army could not simply close its doors for renovation until all its internal problems were resolved. Instead it would have to make the leap from one manpower procurement system to another without losing any of its essential military capability during the passage.

Reduction in Force (RIF)

While it wrestled with the correct balance between its quantitative needs and qualitative standards, the Army faced a more immediate problem that threatened to undermine many of the gains achieved thus far by the Modern Volunteer Army Program. When Congress finally passed the Selective Service Extension Act in September 1971, it contained a provision requiring the Army to cut its average strength of 1.23 million men by 50,000 by the end of fiscal year 1972. The Army fought the measure all the way through the legislative process, but passage of the law occurred well into the fiscal year, forcing the Army to accelerate discharges to accomplish the lower strength authorization.[1] Beginning in September it thus announced that draftees assigned in the continental United States would be released from the service up to 120 days ahead of their discharge date. In October the Army also established a 60-day voluntary early release program for Regular Army volunteers finishing their first enlistment. It planned to eliminate 86,000 enlisted personnel under this program. But in October it became apparent that the required reduction in strength could not be achieved by these means alone, and the early release for draftees and volunteers was extended to soldiers serving in all theaters except Vietnam. The reduction in force (RIF) also affected career soldiers. The Army forced 5,000 reserve officers on extended active duty assignments and 4,500 retirement-eligible noncommissioned officers to terminate their careers involuntarily. The programs worked too well—the Army ended the fiscal year nearly 10,000 men understrength.[2]

The reduction in strength created havoc in many Army programs. The rapid discharge of personnel stripped units and overloaded the personnel management system as finance clerks, personnel noncommissioned officers and clerks, medical corpsmen, and supply sergeants worked overtime to out-process soldiers leaving the Army or being transferred to Europe and Korea to replace soldiers being discharged from units there; overseas units had to be maintained at 95 percent strength. Many of the personnel management specialists were themselves being reassigned or released. Critical shortages soon developed in areas such as clerical personnel, medical specialists, military police, and cooks. The reduction in strength also affected people remaining in the service. Statutory limits on the number of people who could hold a specific rank or specialty grade led to promotion lags, and in some cases men experienced reductions in grade on the basis of seniority. Personnel turbulence increased as the Army cut short the assignments of soldiers stationed in the United States and sent them to Europe in order to maintain units there at required strength. While personnel turbulence had characterized the whole Vietnam era, the dislocation brought on by the congressionally mandated reduction in force in late 1971 and early 1972 seemed to add insult to injury, especially in the career ranks. The human dimension of these abrupt changes weighed heavily on families; wives had to leave jobs, pack household goods, and take children out of school. Readiness suffered also. Following the rapid reduction in strength with its attendant disruption of the assignment process only three of the Army's thirteen active divisions reported themselves combat ready for worldwide missions.[3]

The Modern Volunteer Army Program suffered indirectly from the personnel reduction of fiscal year 1972. Rapid and unexpected discharges and reassignments that strained administrative systems or left units shorthanded forced an extension of work hours and heavier workloads among remaining personnel. Experimental programs under the auspices of VOLAR, such as night clinics, had to be curtailed due to a shortage of personnel. Soldiers who wanted to reenlist could not because of the mandatory nature of the early-out program. As a result the Army's attempt to build a new image of credibility with soldiers, especially young soldiers, eroded. An analyst in the office of Assistant Secretary of the Army Hull observed that young people who experienced the conditions created by the reduction and the young leaders who had to cope with the attendant problems became disenchanted with the Army and returned to civilian life with a negative attitude. "These attitudes become voiced and thus impair our ability to achieve a volunteer force."[4]

The irony of pushing people out one door while recruiting replacements through another was not lost on Congress. When Assistant Secretary Hull reported on the results of the strength reduction during hearings on the fiscal year 1973 authorization bill, his aim was to plead for personnel stability in the coming year. His explanation of the Army's efforts to accomplish the congressionally ordered cuts was not greeted sympathetically. "I do not see how you can say this is a move toward a Volunteer Army when we are separating people who are volunteers in the sense of career motivation," chided Alexander Pirnie of New York. Pirnie expressed the hope that the Army's conduct in battle exceeded that in the personnel office. Hull, however, considered his role in the management of the traumatic reduction one of the more successful actions of his tenure. Reducing the Army's strength simply by limiting accessions would have inevitably left the service top-heavy in rank and unneeded specialties.

Despite Pirnie's cynicism Congress recognized the Army's need for personnel stability. The House Armed Services Committee recommended no further manpower cuts in fiscal year 1973, but in words that reflected Pirnie's critique of the way in which the reduction was managed and Hebert's opinion of recruitment advertising, the committee report concluded, "We find it inexplicable that the Army is forcing out of the service qualified officers and denying enlisted personnel the opportunity to reenlist... while at the same time using Madison Avenue approaches to secure young men for service in the Army."[5]

Kitchen Police

Congressional criticism of the Army's management of the reduction it had previously ordered was followed by an attempt by some members to roll back one of the more successful innovations of the Modern Volunteer Army Program—civilianization of KP. The Army requested $99 million to civilianize KP in fiscal year 1973, an increase of $70.6 million over the previous year. The Subcommittee on Defense Appropriations of the House Appropriations Committee balked at the request on two points. First, members questioned the cost. Why had the cost of civilians performing KP more than doubled in only a year? Brig. Gen. Leslie R. Sears, Jr., assistant director of the Army budget, explained that the previous year's program had been experimental (under the auspices of Project VOLAR) and did not reflect the cost of such a program Army-wide. The Army estimated that 1.5 civilians would be needed to replace one soldier on KP because of the necessity for two shifts of civilians in the mess halls. Based on an average annual cost of $6,300 per civilian, the Army arrived at its total cost of $99 million.

More than cost bothered the congressmen. To many with previous military service the odious KP represented part of the rite of passage of life in the ranks. Drawing on his own military experience, Congressman John J. Flynt of Georgia, who chaired the hearing, observed that "most soldiers, certainly most good soldiers, did not complain so much about KP as they did when they thought the program of KP was being unfairly administered and being used as punishment." He implied that the Army was coddling the troops.

General Sears and General Montague, Forsythe's deputy, argued strenuously to the contrary. Civilianization of KP was necessary as a professionalism measure. The Army lost as many as 45,000 junior enlisted soldiers daily to such labor details. Civilianization of these jobs would free troops for more productive military activities such as training or maintenance. The Army's justification was, after many previous hearings, by now well known, and it did not move the committee. The full Appropriations Committee recommended against civilianization. In its report the committee doubted the Army's assertion that KP hurt morale and esprit and complained that the Army presented no empirical evidence to show that the pilot program conducted at the VOLAR posts had any effect on "reducing AWOL's, desertions, disturbances in the service, or [an] overall effect on the 'esprit de corps' in the service which could encourage reenlistments." The committee also complained that the Army, although planning to increase civilian employee strength or civilian contract hirees, offered no comparable reduction in military strength. The committee recommended appropriations of $34 million to facilitate termination of the program.[6]

Congressional insiders learned that Congressman George Mahon of Texas, the powerful chairman of the House Appropriations Committee and a skeptic on the volunteer force concept, was the moving force behind the committee's attempt to scuttle civilianization of KP. The Army and the other services, which also were affected by the termination of the program, were reluctant to press Mahon on the issue because of his influence over all military appropriations. Thus the effort to have the funds for civilian KP restored took an indirect approach. On Capitol Hill congressional friends of the all-volunteer force, led by Congressman William Steiger in the House and Senator Robert Stafford in the Senate, took up the cause. Steiger's aide, Andrew Effron, learned that Congressman Robert L. Sikes of Florida, the number two man on the House Appropriations Committee, personally favored civilianization of KP if it released servicemen for better training. With Steiger's prodding the Army prepared detailed arguments in support of civilianization which Effron distributed to each member of the Appropriations Committee over Steiger's signature. Secretary of the Army Froehlke helped by meeting with members who asked for more information. Meanwhile, Stafford's assistant, Stephen Herbits, mounted a grass-roots lobbying effort. Herbits contacted the companies that provided contract KP work on bases in the United States. The employers brought pressure to bear on their members of Congress while the workers went through the unions to complain about loss of jobs. Because many of the firms involved were minority owned and employed low-skilled minority workers, the Congressional Black Caucus also became involved in the effort to preserve civilianization.

When the 1973 defense appropriation bill came to the House floor, Sikes offered an amendment to the committee bill restoring authority for the services to continue toward civilianization of KP and other nonmilitary details currently performed by service members but requiring the services to absorb the cost from other accounts. A lively debate ensued on the floor of the House. Members such as John Rhodes of Arizona declared that a little KP never hurt anybody; "Certainly it did not hurt this former soldier when he was on active duty." Louis Wyman of New Hampshire added that he saw no reason why "housekeeping chores, as they are called, whether KP or cleanup details, should be considered beneath the dignity of members of the Armed Forces." Steiger defended Sikes' amendment. He pointed out the problems of getting men to volunteer for service in a professional force when they were still expected to perform menial labor. He quoted company commanders and generals who complained to him of the frustrations of training with understrength units. Additional support came from Congressman Dan Daniel of Virginia, the highly respected member of the Armed Services Committee who had conducted special hearings on the progress toward the zero draft. Daniel stripped the issue of its rhetoric. "It may very well be that some Members do not feel that an all-volunteer force is feasible or desirable," he said. "If that be the case, let us abandon the objective, because it is not realistic to enact expensive programs to make service careers more attractive on the one hand, and then on the other negate that action by adopting a policy which runs counter to the objective." Sikes' amendment carried by a vote of 265 to 116. His was the only successful effort to amend the defense appropriations bill for 1973.[7]

The Senate Appropriations Committee accepted the services' rationale for continuing their programs of civilianizing KP and other enlisted details when it received the amended House bill. But the Senate committee disagreed with the House over the requirement that the armed forces absorb the cost of continuing the programs and added nearly $100 million to the bill to cover the cost. When the bill reached the Senate floor, a debate similar to that in the House occurred. Some senators, such as William Proxmire of Wisconsin, complained about "maid and butler service" for enlisted service members. "Who does KP for the taxpayer?" he asked. They do it themselves, he answered, and argued passage would result in increased idleness in the ranks. Senator John O. Pastore of Rhode Island worried about the 600 Rhode Islanders who would lose their jobs if civilianization was halted. "They would go on welfare. Where's the savings there?" Pastore asked. "It's a $74 billion bill," he declared. "If Senators want to cut it down, cut it somewhere else." Senator Stafford, one of the volunteer force's staunchest allies, brought the argument back to cases. "A vote to restore the funds will mean that the Army did not break its word to the young recruits and potential recruits who are impressed with the modernization of our armed services," he said. "To revert back to the old system now will take much of the momentum out of modernization of the forces and deal a severe blow to progress towards an All-Volunteer Force." As in the House, civilianization of KP survived in the Senate as pro–volunteer force senators pulled together a coalition with members concerned about jobs in their states. In conference the two bodies agreed to appropriate $118.2 million for all services to continue civilianization of KP functions.[8] The single most successful initiative of the Modern Volunteer Army Program had been saved.

Bonuses

Although Congress proved it could be flexible on issues related to the all-volunteer force, in 1972 the Army continued to encounter bureaucratic roadblocks in other areas. Having failed in its attempt to secure authorization for combat arms proficiency pay in 1971, it threw its support behind Kelley's proposal for a combat arms enlistment bonus. Congress approved authority for a $3,000 bonus on an experimental basis when it passed the Selective Service Extension Act in September 1971. Immediately Army manpower specialists began pressing Defense Department managers for permission to begin using the bonus. In November 1971 Forsythe told Hull that the Army required prompt action on the subject in order to determine quickly how many volunteers a bonus actually attracted and because he feared that by spring 1972 pressure by the other services for a "hard skills" bonus aimed at attracting recruits to other unglamorous positions might result in competition. Hull took the request to Kelley, who procrastinated. White House pressure to hold down expenditures delayed implementation of the program in part, but Kelley expressed other reservations. His office was preparing a more comprehensive pay package eventually enacted as the Special Pay Act of 1972, and he did not want the Army to initiate a program that would soon be overtaken by events. Furthermore, the Army wanted to offer $3,000 for combat arms volunteers, the maximum bonus allowable, and members on Kelley's staff advocated a lesser amount initially in the range of $500 to $1,000.

The date the Army wanted to begin offering the bonus, 1 January, passed. In February the Army tried again. This time General Kerwin initiated the request to the secretary of the Army through General Westmoreland. Again the response was negative. Secretary of Defense Laird quietly informed Army Secretary Froehlke that "he was getting flack from Congress on going ahead with the enlistment bonus." At Laird's urging Froehlke withdrew the request. Montague took the news to Forsythe. "So we are back in the dugout waiting for the rain to stop," he declared ruefully. "Nothing officially has transpired. All pretty neat—and sneaky."[9]

Undeterred, the Army tried again. In April Westmoreland personally urged Froehlke to ask the secretary of defense to initiate the use of a combat arms enlistment bonus on a test basis until the Special Pay Act cleared Congress. He noted that despite a "massive effort," during which recruiting for the combat arms received "command emphasis, priority of recruiting resources, attractive geographic/unit-of-choice options, and intensive advertising," the Army achieved only 64 percent of its combat arms accessions goal for the first three months of 1972. "We have had no experience with this type of incentive," Westmoreland observed, "and theoretical estimates do not provide a sound basis for decision in this case." The Army needed early use of the bonus to develop data on its effectiveness, he concluded.

Again the effort went nowhere. Finally, in conjunction with passage of the Special Pay Act, the Army and the Marine Corps received authority to offer a combat arms enlistment bonus of $1,500 for a four-year enlistment. Between 1 June 1972 and 1 May 1973, 35,110 men enlisted in the Army combat arms; 23,172 joined for four years and received the bonus. In a report prepared for Kelley's office, the General Research Corporation concluded that most of those who enlisted for the bonus would have joined anyway, but that the bonus was effective at directing volunteers to the combat arms. Further analysis revealed that nearly 60 percent of those who volunteered for the combat arms bonus were not high school graduates. In May 1973 the Defense Department increased the amount of the bonus to $2,500 for high school graduates who scored in mental categories I–III and volunteered for four-year enlistments in the Army combat arms. Subsequent experience showed that this higher bonus did draw "quality" enlistees into the combat arms. Thus, by 1973 the Army at last obtained a combat arms incentive approximating the original amount it had sought in late 1970. By then all those who had initially advocated the incentive had passed from the scene.[10]

Changing the Guard

The process of ending the experimentation phase of the Modern Volunteer Army Program began even before General Forsythe agreed to the revision of his charter as SAMVA in January 1972. A month earlier Roger Kelley had asked the services to provide his office with their proposals for experiments they wanted to conduct between January and October 1972. Assistant Secretary of the Army Hull replied for the Army. He reminded Kelley that the Army's approach toward achieving the zero-draft goal had been experimental from the start. Hull believed that insufficient time remained before the actual end of induction authority to initiate new experiments beyond those already proposed and still awaiting funds or authorization to commence. The Army's philosophy was to complete its experiments well before June 1973 so it could be in a position to request funds for successful programs in fiscal year 1974, the first year it would be on its own without the draft.[11] The subsequent decision to turn over to the Army staff management of the successful Modern Volunteer Army Program initiatives was consistent with that approach.

When the chief of staff modified Forsythe's charter in January 1972, directing him to devote more attention to professionalism and training in the Army, he set the stage for the eventual abolition of the SAMVA office altogether. Several factors contributed to the decision. Westmoreland's tour of duty as chief of staff of the Army ended on 30 June 1972, the same day that Project VOLAR, the field experiment of the Modern Volunteer Army Program, terminated. As related earlier, the vice chief of staff of the Army, General Palmer, had been cool toward the concept of a project manager for the transition to the all-volunteer force and believed that management of the transition was an Army staff function. The end of the VOLAR experiment offered a convenient place to disestablish the Office of the Special Assistant for the Modern Volunteer Army. The new chief of staff would not have to review or terminate the operation, Westmoreland and Froehlke agreed. No formal decision was made until late spring 1972, but between February and May Palmer reviewed all Modern Volunteer Army actions with an eye toward determining which should be continued and which should end on 30 June along with VOLAR and the SAMVA office itself.[12]

New Battle Plans

One of the first subjects reviewed was the advertising program. On 26 February Westmoreland, Palmer, Forsythe, and several other officials met to discuss the continued use of the terms MVA and VOLAR and the content of the recruiting advertising campaign. General Haines, commander of the Continental Army Command, had proposed that use of the term VOLAR be discontinued. Haines' recommendation, along with a general unhappiness in the Army with the theme "Today's Army Wants To Join You," led to the meeting. The group agreed to discontinue use of the term VOLAR, which had acquired a negative connotation because of its association with permissiveness in the ranks; it was to be dropped at the end of the field experiments in June. But Forsythe argued that the advertising theme continued to be popular with recruiters and, more important, received favorable reviews from the target audience. "Today's Army Wants To Join You" committed the Army to offering potential recruits the opportunity to acquire a skill and assuring them of "mature personnel policies" and an "attitude of respect for the individual soldier." Disregarding the possibility that the theme might be misinterpreted, Westmoreland agreed. The theme would not be changed. He directed Forsythe to prepare a *Weekly Summary* article notifying commanders that the Army policies underlying the MVA program remained valid and should continue to receive command emphasis. This reemphasis of support for the program was necessary because of the turbulence attending the reduction in strength still under way. Forsythe also noted that the press erroneously reported the abandonment of civilian KP programs at Army basic training centers and removal of beer vending machines from barracks as signs of Army backsliding from its commitment to the MVA program. In the *Weekly Summary* message that Westmoreland dispatched, the chief of staff enjoined commanders to ensure that the policies and promises of the Modern Volunteer Army Program continued to receive priority attention.[13]

The overall review and evaluation of the Modern Volunteer Army Program was completed by early April. Paul Phillips, deputy assistant secretary of the Army for manpower and reserve affairs, compiled the findings and reported that as a result of its initiatives the Army had made progress toward the all-volunteer force and remained "hopeful" of achieving the objective. Phillips cautioned, however, that "achievement of the zero-draft goal by 1 July 1973 presents a most difficult and complex problem." He cited the fact that the pay raises, which raised entry pay above poverty levels, had not resulted in an increase in enlistments as predicted by the Gates Commission. Because the Army considered additional general pay increases "prohibitive in cost," Phillips instead urged the application of "focused pay"—enlistment and reenlistment bonuses for hard-to-fill skills such as the combat arms—as an alternative.

Phillips wanted the Army to focus its attention on those initiatives that had proved to be highly successful. These included the expansion and stabilization of the recruiting force, the use of new enlistment options, especially the unit- and area-of-choice programs, and service attractiveness and professionalism measures. Other initiatives that had also proved successful, such as paid television and radio advertising, could not be exploited because of congressional denial of authority or funds and administration unwillingness to press the issue. Phillips especially deplored this situation because it "degraded the Army's ability to rapidly bring career opportunities in the Army to the attention of prospective enlistees." He also noted that the Army's continued inability to use all media resources to the fullest impaired its effort to rebuild its image with the general public. The Army still remained lowest among the services in terms of public knowledge and esteem. He also pointed out that failure of the Defense Department and Congress to appreciate the consequences of the force reduction imposed on the Army in fiscal year 1972 seriously undermined its program to increase enlistments and reenlistments. Indeed, Phillips added, by forcing out men who might have reenlisted in a year or two, the reduction in strength had created a manpower "gap" in FY 74, the very year the zero-draft was to go into effect. He urged that greater attention be paid to the interrelationship between initiatives in the future and that the Army be given longer lead time to execute major changes.[14]

Phillips painted a grim picture for 1973, the first year of a truly draft-free Army. In his assessment of the Modern Volunteer Army Program that went to the Defense Department in mid-April 1972, he reported that the Army estimated its supply of true volunteers for the twelve-month period ending in June 1972 at 115,000 men and women; in the following twelve months, July 1972 to June 1973, the figure would rise to 135,000–140,000 assuming all currently authorized and funded incentives continued. But total accession requirements through June 1972 would exceed 160,000. The difference between requirements and supply could be made up with selectees only until the draft ended in June 1973. But for the twelve-month period beyond the end of the draft, FY 74, Phillips projected a requirement of 180,000–200,000 new accessions against an estimated supply of 123,000–134,000 volunteers. "How do we close the 46–77 thousand gap in FY 74?" he asked rhetorically. Phillips used the opportunity to again press the Army's need for directed enlistment incentives, which, as noted above, it finally received in June 1972, and support from the Defense Department for paid radio and television recruiting advertising.

Long-term solutions to close the gap included increasing the number of women in uniform and converting military jobs to civilian positions. Both options, Phillips noted, required long-range planning. In the case of the former, lead times of two to three years were involved to provide the training and housing facilities for additional women in uniform. In the latter case, congressional and administrative ceilings on civilian strength had to be raised. The point was, he said, that the Defense Department had to face the prospect of failure of the volunteer force and take additional steps ahead of time to prevent such an occurrence rather than wait until 1973 to report to the president and public that a draft remained necessary.

One final alternative Phillips offered was reduction of standards. "Experience to date indicates ample numbers of mental category IV men available in the pool," he wrote. The Army did not want to lower standards, and Phillips warned gravely, "Should quality standards be lowered to meet numerical requirements, the decision maker must realize that degradation of the competence of the force will result." [15]

Publicly the Army remained optimistic about the prospects for achieving zero-draft status by the end of June 1973. Bureaucratic caution and a sense of duty prevented its leaders from airing their unhappiness with the Defense Department and Congress over their failure to remove roadblocks to beginning the combat arms enlistment bonus and resumption of paid advertising. At the time General Montague gave an interview to *U.S. News & World Report* that emphasized progress and implied that the promise of ending the draft on schedule would be kept. Training was tougher, but soldiers enjoyed more leisure time due to the end of make-work details and routine chores, reported the news weekly. The result was a more professional, "smarter" Army. This was exactly the message the Army wanted the public to hear. The Army was not more "permissive," Montague claimed, it was better. Eliminating bed checks and KP meant that a man could join the Army to soldier and keep his individualism, he said. But, he cautioned, the new Army was not cheap. Privates' pay was up over 100 percent, from $134 to $288 a month. On the other hand, this meant the Army could insist on higher levels of performance. "The Army has made it clear that there will be no room for the 'goof-off'—not at present pay." Montague expressed confidence that the Army would reach its goal, but did conclude that, "If we fail, it won't be for lack of trying." [16]

Evaluations

Internal acceptance of the volunteer Army concept and the progress of its programs continued to be uneven. Even as momentum began to shift from his office to the Army staff, Forsythe continued to keep tabs on developments. During the evaluation of the Modern Volunteer Army Program he sent inspection teams to the field to report on how well various VOLAR and MVA initiatives were being received and working. He learned that despite exhortations from Washington many commanders followed their own lights. One team, led by Lt. Col. James Waldeck, visited Forts Benning and Bragg. Fort Benning, one of the original VOLAR posts, continued to exhibit a positive attitude and high degree of support for the principles behind the MVA program. The commanding general and post MVA/VOLAR officer "are totally involved in the Benning MVA program." But some ominous trends suggested trouble ahead.

Despite the loss of almost 500 troops because of the reductions in force or reassignment to Europe, the 197th Infantry Brigade at Benning, one of the first Army combat units to achieve all-volunteer status as a unit of choice, continued to draw the troop support requirements of a full-strength unit. The commander reported he would be forced to revert to a six- or seven-day workweek. Colonel Waldeck reported to Forsythe, "If Benning reneges on the five-day work week or is required to work personnel after having served guard, etc., the 197th might be a very short-lived all volunteer brigade."

The situation at Fort Bragg proved even more discouraging. At the post level the program looked good. "The funded actions are potentially highly visible, appear to be focused towards the troops, and constitute a well balanced set which addresses the most pressing needs of the post." But again Waldeck found evidence that all was not well. One of the most valuable members of Fort Bragg's MVA staff, an enlisted man, would soon leave the service, and, although willing to stay on the job as a civilian employee, could not do so because of a hiring freeze.

An even more discouraging situation greeted Waldeck when he visited the 82d Airborne Division, one of the Army's elite units, a prime tenant at Fort Bragg. Waldeck found the division area "shabby" despite the fact that paint for improvements was available. He described the barracks "as in a state of 'benign neglect.'" Waldeck noted that only one company of airborne soldiers had improved its barracks, and seemed to be concerned for its living areas. After a short visit with the assistant division commander, Brig. Gen. Edward C. Meyer, and members of the staff, he came away with the impression "that the 82d feels a bit smug—MVA is great, but the 82d is inherently in such good shape that it is really redundant." The division, he concluded, lacked "the level of positive enthusiasm" necessary to make the Modern Volunteer Army work. Waldeck pressed Forsythe to bring his findings to Westmoreland's attention. He suggested corrective action as well. The chief of staff of the Army should send a letter to all commanders, Waldeck urged, in which he praised the progress made toward achieving the volunteer Army, pointed out where more effort was needed, restated his personal commitment to the program, and enjoined all levels of command to keep up the momentum.[17]

Forsythe accepted Waldeck's advice. Although the focus of attention was shifting from Forsythe's office to Kerwin's Army staff in the spring of 1972, Forsythe still enjoyed access to Westmoreland and, as the recognized authority on the Modern Volunteer Army Program, his words still carried weight. He pressed Waldeck's findings on the chief of staff and told him how important a statement of his support for the effort at this critical juncture, the disestablishment of the SAMVA office, would be.

Westmoreland agreed. He used the *Weekly Summary*, a high-level distillation of news and information prepared by the secretary of the General Staff in the name of the chief of staff and sent to all general officers, as the vehicle for a final message on the volunteer Army. The article followed Waldeck's advice exactly. It reported on Westmoreland's review of the latest analyses from all major commands of their progress toward achieving the volunteer Army and his satisfaction with those aspects of the program that had proved successful. However, the *Weekly Summary* article continued, the chief of staff noted that momentum was not being maintained everywhere. Westmoreland "expects commanders at all levels not only to maintain but also, and more importantly, to increase both the momentum and the credibility of the MVA program." Westmoreland declined to speak for his successor, but he expressed his confidence that the next chief of staff would "continue to give priority support to successful MVA policies, programs and actions, which have one overriding objective—a truly professional volunteer Army."[18]

Westmoreland offered a final personal analysis of the progress toward achievement of an all-volunteer force on the eve of his retirement. On 30 June 1972, he addressed a four-page letter to President Nixon providing "a brief status report" on the "state of the Army." Most of the letter dealt with the Army's successful efforts to increase the number of volunteers through improved professionalism, service attractiveness, and the transformation of the Recruiting Command. Westmoreland noted with satisfaction that the increase in volunteers had been achieved without a loss of discipline or the acceptance of permissiveness. But, he warned Nixon, "I can give you no assurance that we will achieve our goal of a volunteer force by 1 July 1973." He cited the familiar roadblocks: congressional refusal to permit paid radio and television advertising, "largely through the personal opposition of the Chairman of the House Armed Services Committee (F. Edward Hebert)"; failure of the Defense Department to authorize the payment of combat arms enlistment bonuses in the full amount authorized and funded by Congress; and the 50,000 man-year reduction, which disrupted every aspect of the Army's personnel program in fiscal year 1972. The result of recruiting shortfalls and degraded readiness, he feared, would be an effort by Congress to further reduce strength coupled with "an increasing tendency to use money—in the form of added pay raises, pay incentives, and similar measures—to obtain the final increment of manpower needed to close the gap." Higher personnel costs jeopardized the overall defense effort, Westmoreland warned. For these reasons he wanted to see the draft continue and recommended that Nixon ask for an extension of induction authority in 1973. Keeping the draft alive would "ensure that a cross section of America is represented in its Armed Forces." At the same time, Westmoreland noted, continuation of reasonable volunteer force initiatives would limit the actual use of induction authority so that use of the draft "would not be onerous."[19]

Westmoreland did not make public the contents of his letter to the president, but his views were well known within defense circles. He had argued consistently for retention of induction authority from the beginning of the debate over ending the draft. Critics of Westmoreland charged that his statements on behalf of retaining induction authority undercut the effort to achieve an all-volunteer force. But Westmoreland had refrained from publicly advocating retention of induction authority since 1970, and his advice to Nixon did not become common knowledge until publication of Westmoreland's memoirs in 1976, three years after the draft expired. If his purpose in urging retention of induction authority was to sabotage the volunteer force concept he did not do it well by keeping his views private during the last year of the transition. Insiders knew of Westmoreland's letter to Nixon. Secretary of the Army Froehlke recalled that the letter had "relatively little effect," and further observed that "because of the controversy that continued to attend Vietnam and [Westmoreland's] close identification with that unpopular war he was not effective as a spokesman for the Army in general or the AVF in particular." General Palmer agreed. He knew about the letter in advance and tried to talk Westmoreland out of it. "It was probably not the politic time to do it," he noted. Roger Kelley concluded that Westmoreland "had more lingering reservations and doubts about the all-volunteer concept than any high-ranking military officer I encountered in my four years in Washington," but his opinions did not impede the transition.[20]

Ending the Experiment

Forsythe retired on the same day as Westmoreland. With the disestablishment of the Office of the Special Assistant for the Modern Volunteer Army he was out of an immediate job. His and his wife's parents were quite ill and needed attention. Westmoreland offered him "some interesting assignments," but Forsythe chose retirement, ending his 33-year career. More than personal reasons prompted his departure. His experience as SAMVA frustrated him. He had become an ardent champion of an effort to restore professionalism in the Army and resented what he perceived as pettiness and parochialism on the part of some senior officers who failed to support his programs fully. More generally, Forsythe's frustration stemmed from the failure of many in the Army to understand the purpose of the Modern Volunteer Army Program, the VOLAR experiments, and other specific initiatives of the effort. He later condemned what he termed "fearful leadership," in which officers resisted change and innovation lest it rock the boat which they commanded, thereby jeopardizing their future advancement. "We had to knock off some of this crap and get on with being a professional fighting Army," Forsythe observed. "I probably had an overly simplistic approach to it." He knew that with the elimination of the SAMVA operation and the absorption of its functions by the Army staff that he would be a fifth wheel. It was time to go.

But despite his frustration, Forsythe did not leave bitter. Later in life he reflected on the extraordinary opportunities the Army had offered "an ROTC graduate from a 'cow college.'" He himself had entered the Army prior to the beginning of World War II, when it more closely resembled the old Indian-fighting constabulary of the nineteenth century than the force he retired from. He commanded one of its finest divisions—the 1st Cavalry (Airmobile)—in Vietnam and served as the commandant of the Infantry School, a position also held by the likes of General George C. Marshall. And Westmoreland chose him for one of the toughest jobs the Army had to offer any general in peace or war—managing the transition from a draft to an all-volunteer force. He believed he achieved that objective, "at least our 'warriors' made the blue-prints and laid the foundation."[21]

Others already had left. John Kester, the deputy assistant secretary of the Army for manpower, who had worked on the Army's response to the Gates Commission recommendations and was an early supporter of the effort behind recruiting reorganization and paid recruiting advertising, returned to private law practice in March. Within the secretariat Paul Phillips and Clayton Gompf remained and formed the core of the civilian leadership of the volunteer force effort within the Army. General Montague departed also. He left in April to become director of the Central All-Volunteer Force Task Force, a new body in Kelley's office created to prepare contingency plans for use in the event the services came up short in their recruiting efforts. Montague's energy and commitment to the all-volunteer force concept, demonstrated in his service as Forsythe's deputy, commended him to Kelley. He enjoyed direct access to the assistant secretary and soon became a key member of Kelley's team.

With the formal disestablishment of the SAMVA office on 30 June 1972, only Capt. Grant Fredericks remained from the staff. He was assigned the task of writing the final VOLAR report. The deputy chief of staff for personnel became the Department of the Army "focal point and General Staff monitor" for the Modern Volunteer Army Program. Ongoing SAMVA actions and functions were transferred to "each appropriate Army Staff agency having staff cognizance for the soldier-oriented program functions falling within its primary area of interest." According to the Office of the Chief of Staff, "The function of SAMVA in establishing objectives, goals, and priorities for the Army Staff and Army commands in the development of an integrated MVA effort has been accomplished."[22]

Notes

[1] Congress normally regulates the size of the Army through the imposition of "man years" ceilings, a financial constraint that has to be reconciled with congressional rank structure and end-strength guidance to the service. A reduction in 50,000 man years thus does not necessarily equate to a 50,000 reduction in end-strength. Instead, the "cuts" might be taken, for example, by an even reduction of 100,000 during the course of the fiscal year, by limiting accessions, or by eliminating a smaller number of higher (and more costly) officer and enlisted grades. Ultimately, the process usually involves a combination of such measures, but the later such a reduction is begun in the fiscal year, the less flexible the methods employed. Comments of Brig Gen (Ret.) Paul D. Phillips, former DASA (M&RA), on draft manuscript.

[2] *Department of the Army Historical Summary* (hereafter cited as *DAHSUM*), Fiscal Year 1972 (Washington, D.C.: Government Printing Office, 1974), pp. 75, 79; *DAHSUM*, FY 73, p. 59; Memo, ASA (MRA&L), n.d. (c. Apr 72), sub: Impact of FY 72 Man Year (50,000) Reduction on the Army, OSA file 202.10, RG 335, WNRC.

[3] Memo, Impact of FY 72 Man Year (50,000) Reduction on the Army.

[4] Ibid.

[5] U.S. Congress, House, Committee on Armed Services, Subcommittee No. 2, Active Duty Forces and Reserve Force Strengths for Fiscal Year 1973, hearings on . . . , 92d Cong., 2d sess., 1972, pp. 11849–50; U.S. Congress, House, Committee on Armed Services, Authorizing Appropriations for Fiscal Year 1973, 92d Cong., 2d sess., 1972, H. Rpt. 92–1149, pp. 70–71; Interv, author with Hadlai Hull, 17 May 83.

[6] U.S. Congress, House, Subcommittee of the Committee on Appropriations, *Department of Defense Appropriations for 1973, Hearings on . . .*, 92d Cong., 2d sess., 1972, pp. 221–25; U.S. Congress, House, Committee on Appropriations, *Department of Defense Appropriation Bill, 1973*, 92d Cong., 2d sess., 1972, H. Rpt. 92–1389, pp. 27–29.

[7] U.S. Congress, *Congressional Record*, 92d Cong., 2d sess., 1972, Sept. 13, 1972, pp. 30533, 30538–45, 30737, 30740, 30748; Interv with Andrew Effron.

[8] U.S. Congress, Senate, Committee on Appropriations, *Department of Defense Appropriation Bill, 1973*, 92d Cong., 2d sess., 1972, S. Rpt. 29–1243, pp. 13–14; U.S. Congress, *Congressional Record*, 92d Cong., 2d sess., 1972, Sept. 30, 1972, pp. 33023, 33031–32, 33117, 33121–22; *Congressional Quarterly Almanac* 28 (Washington, D.C.: Congressional Quarterly, 1972), p. 811.

[9] Lee and Parker, *Ending the Draft*, pp. 199–204; SAMVA Talking Paper, 26 Nov 71, sub: Enlistment Bonus for Combat Arms; Memo, Kerwin thru Westmoreland for Froehlke, 9 Feb 72, sub: Enlistment Bonus for Combat Arms; Memo, Hull for Kelley, 11 Feb 72, sub: Enlistment Bonus for Combat Arms; Memo, Montague for Forsythe, 29 Feb 72, sub: Enlistment Bonus, all in HRC, CMH.

[10] Memo, Westmoreland for Froehlke, Apr 72, sub: Combat Arms Enlistment Bonus, HRC, CMH; Lee and Parker, *Ending the Draft*, pp. 340–42.

[11] Memo, Hull for Kelley, 29 Dec 71, sub: Experiments Associated with the Modern Volunteer Army Programs, OSA file 202.10, RG 335, WNRC.

[12] Interv, author with Palmer, 25 Mar 83. Palmer is unclear as to exactly when the decision to disband SAMVA was reached. When it became clear that General Abram's confirmation as Westmoreland's successor would be delayed and that Palmer would serve as acting chief of staff, Palmer told Westmoreland, "If you don't

[kill SAMVA], I will." Westmoreland answered, "I would rather do it." Interv with Palmer by Lt Col Edward P. Smith, Carlisle Barracks, PA, 23 Apr 76, MHI.

[13] ASGA MFR, 28 Feb 72, sub: MVA Themes and Recruiting Advertising; "Modern Volunteer Army Policies," *Weekly Summary* (WS), 22, no. 8 (1 Mar 72): 22–23.

[14] Memo, Phillips for Lt Gen Taber, Principal Deputy Assistant Secretary of Defense (M&RA), 13 Apr 72, sub: The Army's Volunteer Force Effort, OSA file 202.10, RG 335, WNRC.

[15] Ibid.

[16] "Building a 'New' Army: Results Begin To Show," *U.S. News & World Report* 72 (6 Mar 72): 48–50.

[17] Memo, Lt Col James Waldeck for Forsythe and Montague, 22 Feb 72, sub: Some Cursory Observations at Fort Benning and Fort Bragg, HRC, CMH.

[18] "Maintaining the Momentum of the Modern Volunteer Army," *Weekly Summary*, 22, no. 18 (10 May 72): 1–3.

[19] Ltr, Westmoreland to Nixon, 30 Jun 72, HRC, CMH.

[20] General William Westmoreland, *A Soldier Reports* (Garden City, N.Y.: Doubleday, 1976), p. 375; Froehlke, Palmer, and Kelley Intervs.

[21] Forsythe Interv; Ltr, Forsythe to the author, 1 Sep 85.

[22] Kester Interv; Lee and Parker, *Ending the Draft*, pp. 187–91; CSM 72–10–35, 15 Jun 72, sub: Special Assistant for the Modern Volunteer Army, HRC, CMH.

CHAPTER XII

Last Year of the Draft, 1972

In mid-1972 two events signaled that the transition to a volunteer force remained on schedule. In June the Nixon administration announced that henceforth no draftees would be sent to Vietnam unless they volunteered for the assignment. In August Secretary of Defense Melvin Laird reported to the president and Congress on the progress made toward achieving the all-volunteer force and assured them that the goal could be met. Successful initiatives toward achieving the all-volunteer force together with the reduction of troop strength in Vietnam obviated the assignment of conscripts to the combat zone.

The Army's programs to end its reliance on the draft made both the no-draftees-to-Vietnam policy and Laird's optimistic report possible. But behind the scenes the men in the Army who were responsible for the day-to-day management of the transition harbored doubts about their ability to deliver on Laird's promises. During the months before induction authority expired, the men in the Office of the Assistant Secretary of the Army for Manpower and their uniformed counterparts in the Office of the Deputy Chief of Staff for Personnel wrestled with two problems: how to close the gap between the supply of true volunteers and accession requirements and how to define, justify, and achieve quality enlistments at the same time as they sought sheer numbers.

The Army's search for solutions to these problems took place quietly at first. The last six months of 1972 coincided with Richard Nixon's campaign for reelection as president, and once again his pledges to end the draft and the war were features of the campaign. Army expressions of concern over its ability to meet its quantitative and qualitative needs were consequently muted during that period. Following Nixon's second inauguration, in January 1973, the Army instituted new programs aimed at resolving the continuing personnel dilemma. When these efforts proved counterproductive, supporters of the all-volunteer force effort accused the Army of attempting to undermine the transition in the waning days of draft authority in order to force an extension. The draft ended on schedule on 30 June 1973 amid public expressions of doubt that the volunteer force would survive for very long.

Optimistic Beginnings

On 28 June 1972, President Nixon announced that "effective immediately draftees will no longer be assigned for duty in Vietnam unless they volunteer." Since early 1970 Congress had pressed the Army to limit its use of conscripts in Vietnam. The Army staunchly resisted the idea on several grounds. During its years of heavy involvement in ground combat operations in Vietnam a restriction on the assignment of draftees to that region would have prevented the Army from meeting its strength requirements there, especially in the combat units where only 4 percent of enlisted soldiers were volunteers. Furthermore, restricting duty in Vietnam to volunteers would have forced the Army to increase assignment time there from twelve to eighteen months and to reduce the time between repetitive tours in Vietnam for career servicemen. Finally, the Army pointed out, institution of a no-draftees-in-Vietnam policy would result in an increase in draft calls since many volunteers who enlisted to avoid the draft would no longer do so.[1]

The Department of Defense supported the Army's position through 1971, but as early as March of that year suggested that in time, as the success of the Vietnamization program led to significant troop reductions, "we may eventually reach a point where Vietnam replacement requirements have been reduced sufficiently so that we could send only volunteers."[2] By spring 1972 Laird concluded that strength levels in Vietnam, which were projected to drop to 69,000 by 1 May 1972, had reached a point where it was possible to impose a volunteers-only policy. The North Vietnamese Easter offensive, which began on 30 March, did not interrupt the withdrawal schedule, and when the no-draftees-in-Vietnam policy went into effect in July only two maneuver battalions remained in the country.[3]

Vietnamization was not the only factor reducing the overall requirement for draftees. Since Nixon took office in January 1969 the size of the active duty armed forces had shrunk from 3.5 to 2.3 million as units redeployed from Vietnam and were inactivated, and active Army strength dropped from 1.5 million to 974,000. Lower strengths and greatly limited involvement in Vietnam, combined with the Army's vigorous efforts to attract volunteers, reduced the overall need for draftees; inductions projected for all of calendar year 1972 totaled only 50,000, compared to nearly 300,000 in 1968.[4]

As the armed forces began the final year of their direct or indirect dependency on the draft, the Department of Defense prepared a report to the president and Congress on its progress toward achieving the zero-draft goal. Laird formally presented it to Nixon on 28 August 1972. "We are within reach of achieving an All-Volunteer Force," Laird told Nixon in the cover letter of the report. The proportion of "true volunteers" had increased from 40 to 75 percent since the beginning of the effort. Laird cited the increase in military pay and improvements in living and working conditions in the services as factors contributing to the progress, but he attributed the reorientation of the recruiting program as the most significant ingredient. According to Laird's report, the gains in volunteers had not come at the expense of quality. Seventy percent of all enlistees in FY 1972 possessed high school diplomas, compared to 67 percent in 1971 when draft calls were higher. Compared to the noncollege population, military volunteers looked good in terms of their mental test scores (*see Table 2*), although the report acknowledged that enlistment bonuses were necessary to attract volunteers in the upper mental categories for "difficult jobs," and reenlistment bonuses would continue to be used to "selectively retain them."

Higher pay and the use of bonuses to attract and retain high quality volunteers cost money, Laird admitted in response to a question at the news conference following release of the report. Personnel costs had doubled between 1965 and 1972, from $21 billion to $42 billion, despite an overall decline of 300,000 people. At the same time, he noted, spending on the war in Southeast Asia dropped from $22 billion to less than $7 billion under the Nixon administration. Thus the "peace dividend"—a reference to the reduction in defense spending occasioned by the end of U.S. involvement in Vietnam—was financing the all-volunteer force.[5]

TABLE 2—MENTAL TEST SCORES OF MALE ENLISTMENTS, FY 1972, COMPARED TO NONCOLLEGE POPULATION

	Mental Groups (AFQT)	Noncollege Population, Ages 19–21	Percent of Enlistments
Above Average	I & II	25	35
Average	III	39	48
Below Average	IV	26	17
Not Accepted	V	10	0

Source: "Progress in Ending the Draft and Achieving the All-Volunteer Force," p. 22.

Laird also addressed the difficult question of racial composition of the all-volunteer force. From the beginning of the debate over the merits of transition, some critics of the volunteer concept argued that recruiting programs governed by the forces of the marketplace would draw volunteers primarily from disadvantaged sectors of the youth population, especially from the ranks of the urban poor, who tended to be racial minorities.

The Gates Commission produced analyses to refute the claim and predicted that the proportion of blacks in an all-volunteer force would rise only 0.8 percent higher by 1980 than would occur if the existing mixed force of draftees and volunteers were retained. The Gates Commission analysis estimated that the proportion of black enlisted men in the Army would rise from 12.8 percent in 1969 to 18.8 percent in 1980 while the nonwhite population of the nation would increase from 13.4 to 15 percent. The Department of Defense report on progress toward achieving the all-volunteer force supported the Gates Commission's prediction. Overall, the rate of black participation in the armed forces was 11 percent, well below the percentage of blacks of military age in the general population (13.5 percent). In the Army the figure was 15 percent, which Laird acknowledged was significantly above the current proportion of military-age blacks. Furthermore, he noted that the rate of enlistments and reenlistments by blacks in the Army also exceeded the national average. But the secretary of defense saw nothing alarming in the trend. If blacks and other disadvantaged youths found greater opportunity and better treatment in the military than in the private sector, "so much the better for them, the Armed Forces, and the Nation."[6] The specter of a predominately black enlisted force led by a predominantly white officer corps, a vision that privately haunted the minds of some Army leaders, did not intrude into the secretary's open comments.

Overall, Laird's report on the prospects for achieving the goal of an all-volunteer force by the end of June 1973 was positive. The secretary of defense sounded two notes of caution. The reserve components of the armed forces had slipped below their authorized strength, and the services projected a shortage of medical doctors beginning in 1975. Both of these deficiencies could be corrected, Laird said, with legislation that was currently before Congress. He predicted that Congress would approve the proposals. And once it did so, he implied, all the machinery to make the all-volunteer force a reality would be in place. Induction authority would expire on schedule, and the president did not intend to request its extension.[7]

The extremely positive tone of the Defense Department's report created some doubts. Prospects for ending reliance on the draft as scheduled and the timing of the report's publication with the beginning of Richard Nixon's formal campaign for reelection in August 1972 prompted some reporters at the news conference to question the purpose of the all-volunteer force program. One asked Laird what effect cuts in draft calls would have on the antiwar movement, and another queried the secretary of defense for his view on how the end of the draft would affect the youth vote in November. Laird objected to the implication that the all-volunteer force initiative was aimed at defusing campus unrest. He stressed his conviction that "we are carrying out a program here which we believe is very important for young people in America." He evinced pride in achieving draft reform and reiterated his view that peacetime military service should be voluntary and that those who served in that capacity should be properly rewarded. Laird asserted that since he left Congress, "I have tried to stay away from the partisan question," but he agreed that the president probably would reap some benefit from the program in terms of the youth vote.[8]

The question of Nixon's role in ending the draft did not figure into his electoral effort. On 3 September 1972, the day Nixon formally began his campaign, the *New York Times* dismissed the all-volunteer force as "merely a bid for the youth vote in an election year" since only induction authority would end while selective service machinery remained in place. The *Times* further charged that the all-volunteer force posed a threat to national security since inflated pay for volunteers would lead to cuts in weapons procurement. It predicted an expensive failure. Nixon did not bother to respond. His only reference to the program was a pledge to continue the quest for the all-volunteer force made in a speech at the Nassau County Coliseum, Long Island, on 24 October. Amnesty for draft evaders, a related issue raised by challenger George McGovern, drew more attention than ending the draft itself, and it was hard to tell what effect, if any, the all-volunteer force had in creating the landslide that engulfed McGovern in November.[9]

No documentary evidence exists to suggest that the Nixon White House or the Committee to Reelect the President attempted to slant volunteer force data to present a falsely optimistic impression of success coincident with the 1972 presidential campaign. But, in fact, the data contained in the All-Volunteer Force Progress Report released in August masked concerns by the Army that certain goals in the effort might not be met. For example, the report compared the mental test scores of male enlistees for all services in fiscal year 1972 to the noncollege population. The effect of the comparison was to imply that the services enlisted significantly more of the Mental Category I and II males than existed proportionately in the population. But compared to the total military-age population the services drew a considerably lower percentage of the top two mental categories into the ranks. Furthermore, the Defense Department report aggregated enlistment data for all services. The Army did not fare as well as the defense average in terms of quality enlistments as measured by mental category in the year covered by the report.

TABLE 3—MENTAL TEST SCORES OF ARMY ENLISTEES AND INDUCTEES, FY 1972, COMPARED TO REFERENCE POPULATION

	Mental Groups	Reference Population	Army Enlistees and Inductees
Above Average	I & II	36	32
Average	III	34	49
Below Average	IV	21	19
Not Eligible	V	9	0

Sources: Compiled from OSD (MRA&L) Evaluation of Army's Proposed Actions to Reorient Recruiting, October 1972, and *Profile of American Youth* (OSD[MRA&L], March 1982), p. 7.

The Search for Quality

The Defense Department report on the continuing success of the all-volunteer effort masked an internal debate between the Army and manpower analysts in Roger Kelley's office over what the qualitative requirements of the Army should be, how to establish standards to measure quality, and how to achieve the desired quality and quantity of enlisted accessions in the absence of a draft.

Congress contributed to the debate over quality in late 1971 when, as part of the defense appropriations act for fiscal year 1972, it prohibited the secretary of defense from establishing quotas for enlistments based on mental categories. This action ended the last vestiges of Project 100,000, through which the Department of Defense had required each service to induct or enlist a minimum number of Mental Category IV recruits annually. The prohibition reflected fears on the part of some congressmen that all-volunteer force advocates within the Defense Department would lower standards to ensure success. Freed from the constraints of the quotas, the services began experimenting with recruiting standards. Kelley's staff continued to monitor the services and attempted to develop guidelines on which all could agree.[10]

In an effort to establish standards for qualitative enlistments, Kelley asked the new Central All-Volunteer Task Force to study the subject. Between February and October 1972 the task force considered input from the services on their qualitative requirements and proposals for measuring and acquiring quality volunteers. Two schools of thought emerged on the subject. One group adhered to the position that service needs in each military occupational specialty should dictate the level of requisite quality; this view became known as the "requirements approach." The other school argued that the services should raise and lower qualitative standards based on the available supply of recruits and the ability of recruiters to attract them into uniform; this was dubbed the "market approach."[11]

In October 1972 the differences between the two schools emerged dramatically. Paul Phillips and Clayton Gompf of the Army manpower office began circulating a proposal to reorient Army recruiting effort reflecting a "requirement approach." As late as June 1972 Phillips' major concern had been the Army's apparent inability to close the gap between the supply of true volunteers and the Army's enlisted requirement in a totally draft free environment. That month he advised Kelley that he estimated a shortfall of approximately 67,000 men in fiscal year 1973 who would have to be supplied by the draft. By October the situation looked better in terms of overall numbers, and Phillips reported that he and Gompf now believed the Army would achieve its goal of 184,500 enlistments that year. The problem was no longer quantity but quality.[12]

Phillips told Kelley that although the Army could recruit enough men to fill its aggregate requirement, many of the volunteers did not possess the "trainability requirement" necessary to fill specific vacancies. He and Gompf calculated that not all skill areas could be filled with current enlistees. "We have been successful in increasing volunteer numbers," they noted, but the Army was "not successful in getting volunteers for the proper skills needed," including not only the combat arms, but cooks, military police, mechanics, and medical lab technicians. The shortage in fiscal year 1973 would be 49,000, Phillips reported. Shortages in recruits for "undesirable" or "shortage skill" areas could be filled with men who volunteered without specifying a preference for training or assignment. As long as the draft continued inductees could be assigned to the remaining hard-to-fill skills.

The real problem would occur after induction authority expired. Experience over the last eighteen months showed that recruiters could enlist all the Mental Category IV men they needed to achieve quantitative requirements, but these volunteers, although they proved to make good soldiers in many skill areas, simply could not assimilate the training necessary to qualify them to fill the more technical roles. In a related area Phillips noted that the Army continued to encounter difficulty recruiting sufficient numbers of high school graduates. Experience demonstrated that high school graduates presented fewer disciplinary problems during their service. Furthermore, Mental Category IV volunteers with high school diplomas who scored in the 21–30 range on the test—that is, the upper end of the Category IV scale—tended to qualify for more skill areas. In fact, Phillips asserted, research by his office showed that 65 percent of Category IV volunteers in the 21–30 test score range qualified for the shortage skill requirements, but only 46 percent of recruits in the 16–20 score range did so. A meager 33 percent in the bottom of the Category IV pool (10–15 test score) could be assigned to a shortage skill.[13]

To rectify the problem of shortages in skill areas, Phillips proposed to reorient the Army's recruiting effort. He wanted to establish subobjectives and priority goals for the Recruiting Command to encourage recruiters to actively seek volunteers for the shortage skills. He also recommended denying recruiters credit for enlisting volunteers who scored in the lower half of the Mental Category IV range on the Armed Forces Qualification Test. The effect of removing recruiter credit for enlisting recruits who scored between 10 and 21 on the AFQT would be to discourage recruiters from pursuing such prospects, Phillips said. He further argued that the impact of the proposal would be "minimal" in terms of overall numbers. "At a maximum we may lose 3,000 enlistments in FY 73 due to these actions." Phillips urged swift concurrence. "We are already late initiating this shift from numbers only to numbers and skill match," he said. "If we do not take the actions now to start to reorient the recruiting effort, our problems as soon as we stop drafting will be of such magnitude that achievement of the proper mix of volunteers to meet the All-Volunteer requirements may be impossible."[14]

Roger Kelley's office reviewed the Army proposal quickly and found fault immediately. The response by the Office of the Assistant Secretary of Defense for Manpower revealed a fundamental difference in approach to the problem of quality versus quantity between the Army and the manpower analysts in the Defense Department. The Army wanted to find the level of quality it could achieve. Kelley's office worried that emphasis on quality would result in a decline of quantity. The analysts advised Kelley that while the Army's proposal to establish subobjectives and priority goals had merit, the "Army lacks the hardware and procedures comparable to an 'airline reservation' system" for recruits. Thus, the result might be counterproductive. Kelley's adviser urged further study and advised Kelley to "cancel" the Army's scheme to deny recruiters credit for volunteers from the bottom half of the Mental Category IV population. Loss of credit for low Category IV recruits could cost the Army 10,000 volunteers in fiscal year 1973, one analyst wrote, not the mere 3,000 Phillips predicted. Furthermore, the Army proposal would not "provide any significant number of men qualified for the 'hard skill' training." Recruits for those skills came from the upper three mental categories, not Category IV. Finally, many of the shortage skills the Army reported, such as cooks, could be filled by volunteers from the lower range Category IV group. Denying recruiter credit for "lower CAT IV's could very well result in a bigger shortage of volunteers for the 'unattractive' skills."

If the Army believed it could recruit all the Category IV recruits it needed from the upper half of that population, Kelley's analysts asked rhetorically, why not do so and abandon its self-imposed limit of 19 percent Category IVs? Kelley thus asked Phillips to hold off on the directive denying recruiter credit for lower Mental Category IVs and also suggested that the Army consider raising its intake of Category IV enlistees from 19 to 21 percent. The result, he believed, would increase enlistments, thereby enabling a reduction in draft calls.[15]

The Army ignored Kelley's request and went ahead with Phillips' proposed actions to reorient recruiting. Late in October the Recruiting Command raised minimum recruiter credit for an enlistment to AFQT 21. Recruiters could continue to enlist men who scored below 21 on the qualification test, but their quotas would not be credited for such enlistments. The Army also began to assign recruiters objectives for specific skills in October. These changes remained in effect for the remainder of the fiscal year.[16]

The Women's Army Corps (WAC)

One reason that Phillips was able to turn his attention from quantity to quality in October 1972 was the Army's favorable "manpower" balance. The gap between overall requirements and recruiting capabilities was no longer significant. But the Army had closed the gap by increasing the number of uniformed women in its ranks, a measure that was itself both nontraditional and controversial.

The idea of substituting women for men was hardly new. The commanding general of the Services of Supply and the quartermaster general had proposed the creation of women's auxiliaries in World War I, and during the interwar period the General Staff prepared several contingency plans for the use of women in future mobilizations. During World War II over 100,000 women served in the Women's Army Auxiliary Corps (WAAC) which became the Women's Army Corps (WAC) in 1943. Conceived as a wartime organization, the corps was retained in part because the Army experienced difficulty maintaining its strength during the draft hiatus of 1947–1948. In 1948 Congress enacted legislation creating a peacetime WAC as part of the Regular Army.[17]

At the end of June 1968, 10,711 enlisted women served in the WAC, less than 0.8 percent of the total enlisted strength of the active Army.[18] That year the Battelle Institute was under contract to the director, Personnel Studies and Research, Office of the Deputy Chief of Staff for Personnel, to determine Army personnel requirements for the next decade. In its review of policy and program changes necessary to achieve the Army's future manpower goals, it recommended that the WAC be increased to an enlisted strength of 20,000 by June 1975.

The Battelle study—formally known as the Army 75 Personnel Concept Study, shortened to the "Army 75" study—identified two trends that, it believed, would lead to the expansion of the WAC. First, the study acknowledged the growing demands by American women for greater opportunity in the work force. "The utilization of women by the armed forces is another and special aspect of the general tendency toward opening up new areas of work for women outside the home," it concluded. But the Army 75 study also recognized that increasing the number of women in the ranks was not merely a bow to the pressures of the women's liberation movement. Citing the report of the National Advisory Commission on Selective Service, it noted that more women volunteers meant fewer male draftees: "The young women of the nation offer a broad pool of volunteers which, if more thoroughly tapped, could help to reduce the numbers of those forced to serve." Thus, the Army 75 study predicted, "In light of the current trends in society to gain greater and more effective utilization of our manpower resources through the employment of women, the Army should expand the role of the Women's Army Corps in the next decade." The figure of 20,000 women that the study recommended represented its best estimate of the appropriate strength of the WAC in a peacetime active force of between one and two million men.[19]

A key assumption of the Army 75 study had been the continuation of the draft into the 1970s. Even before the final report appeared that assumption was in doubt. But the same logic that led the Army 75 study group to recommend an increase in the WAC continued to apply in conjunction with the volunteer force concept. Lt. Col. Jack Butler's Project PROVIDE study group, which began its detailed examination of ways to achieve an all-volunteer Army in March 1969, concluded that "the woman-power pool is sufficient to provide an almost limitless source" of qualified volunteers for the Army and recommended that the WAC be increased to a strength of 22,400 enlisted women over a five-year period.

Butler believed that an expansion of the WAC in order to substitute enlisted women for men required no justification; the need was self-evident. He concerned himself rather with the impact of such an expansion on the Army and the WAC. Butler's study group could identify only 21,689 spaces Army-wide to which enlisted women currently could be assigned. Although the number of spaces exceeded the existing supply of uniformed women, Butler believed far more positions could be converted from "male only" to "male or female" in the Army as "borne out by the fact that since the buildup in Vietnam beginning in 1965, DWAC [the director, Women's Army Corps] and OPD

[Officer Personnel Directorate] have received almost daily requests for WAC officers and enlisted personnel to fill male requirements world-wide."

A thorough review of Army requirements would reveal additional spaces to which women could be assigned without jeopardizing the sustaining base. Obviously, women could not be substituted across the board for men. But Butler's recommendations were far from radical in terms of the extent to which women could replace men. Indeed, he advised against assigning women below corps level or to short-tour areas. Nevertheless, Butler suggested that further research might warrant an even greater expansion of the WAC.

The major limitation to an immediate increase of the WAC to facilitate the transition to an all-volunteer Army was not jobs for women but facilities for them. Existing training and housing facilities at Fort McClellan, Alabama, the WAC Center, barely sufficed for the 300 officer and 6,000 enlisted women the Army trained there annually. Furthermore, WAC policy prohibited the assignment of women to posts where there was no WAC unit or suitable on-post housing. Separate barracks would have to be built for enlisted women or existing barracks converted for their use. Butler estimated that the cost of construction necessary to accommodate the recommended increase in the WAC would be $8.2 million.

The PROVIDE study group identified recruiting and the image of the WAC as the other impediments to achieving the proposed increase in the number of women in the Army. "Although today's women are ranging further into fields of employment previously reserved for men, they hesitate to enter military service," Butler wrote. He attributed "traditionalism by parents, males, and women themselves," which discouraged women from entering fields that encroached on their femininity, as a major obstacle to increasing the WAC.

To overcome negative attitudes toward military service on the part of women, he proposed a major overhaul of the recruiting practices aimed at the female market. At that time 207 enlisted women served as recruiters. WAC officers were assigned as advisers at recruiting district headquarters and at recruiting main stations, but did not have enlistment quotas. This arrangement could not continue in the absence of the draft, Butler observed, when male recruiters would be hard pressed to fill their own quotas. He recommended that the Recruiting Command be required to determine the potential of each recruiting area for producing female volunteers and to subsequently assign WAC recruiters in those areas. Male recruiters would then concentrate their efforts on male volunteers and refer female contacts to WAC recruiters, who should receive special training in the Army's requirements and opportunities for women.

To overcome traditional resistance to women joining the service, Butler proposed an "all-out publicity program to extol the advantages of a career in the Women's Army Corps." The campaign should show young women that "their true value to the service is not that they are capable of replacing men, an unfeminine connotation, but that they are women and the feminine touch is required to do the job better." Butler further recommended that the WAC recruiting campaign emphasize that in the Army women "do not take a back seat to men" in terms of pay, benefits, or responsibility. Butler estimated that an advertising campaign directed at women and designed to improve the public image of the WAC would cost approximately $5 million over the five-year period coinciding with the expansion of the corps.[20]

The President's Commission on an All-Volunteer Armed Force made no mention of using military women to reduce the services' need for men. The Gates Commission did explore the substitution of civilians for military personnel and found a "substitution potential" of approximately 95,000 military spaces in an active force of 2 million that could be converted to civilian positions without harming readiness. The commission identified the vast majority of the jobs suitable for civilianization in the Air Force. Only 5,200 Army jobs were considered appropriate for conversion. Roger Kelley's Project Volunteer committee, which reviewed the recommendations of the Gates Commission and the services with respect to the all-volunteer force, expressed guarded skepticism over the merits of civilianization.

In 1966 the Defense Department began to replace 114,000 military with 95,000 civilian personnel but never completed the conversion due to a civilian hiring freeze ordered by Congress. The services expressed greater interest in converting uniformed male positions to uniformed female positions because they could retain greater control over uniformed personnel whatever their gender. Thus the Project Volunteer committee recommended that civilian substitution receive further study, but that the service's proposals with regard to women be supported.[21]

With the blessing of the Defense Department, the Army went ahead with plans to increase the WAC as part of its Modern Volunteer Army Program. Drawing on the earlier studies of the Army 75 and Project PROVIDE reports, it prepared to increase the size of the WAC by approximately 50 percent in two phases beginning in fiscal year 1973. The timing of the increase was contingent on the availability of funds for the construction of housing and training facilities. In June 1971 the deputy chief of staff for logistics requested $6.3 million additional funds in the FY 73 Military Construction Appropriation request for the necessary WAC facilities.

When Congress disapproved the request as an economy measure, the Department of the Army directed its field commands to examine no-cost and low-cost means to initiate the expansion. The Continental Army Command (CONARC) replied that it could create one additional WAC training company in FY 73 with no additional funds. The deputy chief of staff for personnel then ordered a modest expansion of the corps from 12,400 to 13,400 enlisted women by the end of FY 73 and increased the annual recruiting objective for women from 6,000 to 7,000. Meanwhile, the deputy chief of staff for logistics again requested funds for additional WAC housing and training facilities to support a 50 percent increase of the corps by FY 78.[22]

The measured pace of WAC expansion ended abruptly in mid-June 1972. On 5 June personnel analysts from the Office of the Assistant Secretary of the Army for Manpower and Reserve Affairs advised Secretary of the Army Robert F. Froehlke that the expected gap between requirements and projected true volunteers in the first year following the end of induction authority would lead to a shortage of male military personnel. The situation would make it impossible to maintain the Army's thirteen active divisions at an appropriate level of readiness. Froehlke immediately asked the chief of staff to direct a special study aimed at investigating "ways to reduce our dependence on male military manpower, or, as a last resort, to decrease the total active authorizations to be supported." [23]

Froehlke's charge to the Army staff that it find ways to reduce dependence on male volunteers or face a reduction in strength brought immediate results. The earlier plans for an increase of the WAC to upwards of 20,000 enlisted women suddenly received a fresh look. The assistant chief of staff for force development told the deputy chief of staff for personnel, "We need an increase of 5 thousand trained WACs by the end of FY 73 in order to help us get to the 13 division level." That the increase might result in a disorderly expansion of the WAC did not concern the ACSFOR. "The alternatives appear, from the viewpoint of the Army's combat capability, to be worse than a disorderly procedure." [24]

Two major obstacles stood in the way of the planners as they contemplated the requirements to expand the WAC on a crash basis. First, the problem of housing and training facilities remained. Knowledge of Secretary of the Army Froehlke's personal interest in the program helped overcome the problems associated with the physical expansion. Paul Phillips submitted an amendment to the Army's request for major construction funds for FY 73 increasing from $14.93 to $38.8 million the amount requested for WAC expansion. Phillips made clear the Army's newfound interest in the program and the high level of priority attached to the request. At the same time the director of the Army budget notified the commanding general, CONARC, that $21.334 million in his command operating budget for FY 73 would be used to fund the CONARC portion of the WAC expansion program. Where existing barracks proved insufficient or below standard, leased housing could be secured. Physical space to accommodate the increased number of WAC trainees was ultimately found by discontinuing advanced WAC training courses at the WAC Center and sending those women who required advanced training to Army training centers and schools previously closed to women that offered comparable courses.[25]

The remaining obstacle to WAC expansion centered around opening more military jobs to women. Although the Army had previously identified over 19,000 spaces appropriate for enlisted women, these positions were dominated by clerical, general technical, and medical care and treatment occupations. Indeed, over 90 percent of WAC positions clustered around these "traditional" women's jobs. If the Army expected to revamp the image of the WAC and attract more women at a time when American women in the private sector were entering the nontraditional job market in increasing numbers, it would have to provide equal job opportunities for them.

Fortunately for the action officers who hurriedly responded to Secretary of the Army Froehlke's order to rapidly reduce dependence on male soldiers, the Personnel Management Development Division of the Army's Office of Personnel Operations had recently completed a study which recommended opening all but 48 of the 482 military occupational specialties (MOS) for enlisted personnel to women. The initiative for the study had come not from within the Army but from the Central All-Volunteer Task Force created by Roger Kelley early in 1972 to provide greater control over the transition to the AVF and chaired by Brig. Gen. Robert Montague, formerly the deputy SAMVA. Early in February 1972 the task force asked the services to analyze plans to double the number of women in their ranks by 1977. Shortly thereafter the Equal Rights Amendment passed Congress and was sent to the states for ratification. In response to the former and influenced by the latter, the Personnel Management Development Division began its work.[26]

The study group, led by Harry Vavra, an occupational analyst, examined MOS closed to women and determined "on an individual basis women can satisfactorily perform in any occupation now reserved exclusively for men." Vavra concluded that "WACs can be used in all MOS excepting those associated with combat, close combat support, hazardous duty, or unusual strenuous physical demands," and recommended opening up all but the 48 MOS associated with those occupational areas to women. The director, Women's Army Corps, agreed, and the Army staff and Continental Army Command approved the recommendations unanimously. The chief of the Office of Personnel Operations urged speedy implementation to "improve the Army's image as a pioneer and leader in equal opportunities and the 'women's liberation movement,' to place the Army in a stronger recruiting position in competition with our sister services, to enrich the morale of the members of the Women's Army Corps, and, more importantly, to help the Army transition to a volunteer force."[27]

Secretary of the Army Froehlke and Brig. Gen. Mildred Bailey, director of the Women's Army Corps, announced the WAC Expansion Program and the opening up of nontraditional military occupations to women on 7 August 1972. General Bailey's office had learned that the Air Force intended to announce a similar expansion later in August, and the Army stole a march on its sister service in order to capture the most publicity possible from the move. Froehlke and Bailey told the press that the WAC would be increased from 12,400 to 15,900 in FY 73 and continue to grow until 1978 when it would reach a strength of 23,500, a 100 percent increase. Recruiting Command objectives for women were raised from 6,000 to 10,000 in 1973 and to 12,000 annually thereafter. To spur recruiting, Froehlke said that enlistment options available to men, such as the Service School Enlistment Option, the Career Group Enlistment Option, and the Training and Travel Enlistment Option, would be open to women. General Bailey pointed out that enlistment standards for women would remain unchanged, and she expressed confidence that the Army could recruit the additional numbers with ease.[28]

The lower retention rate of female volunteers had made Army leaders wary of expanding the WAC too rapidly, but this problem was solved in part by the gradual elimination of most female assignment and career restrictions.[29] Necessity had cleared the way for the rapid expansion of the Women's Army Corps.

Notes

[1] Draft Memo, General Counsel, DOD, for F. Edward Hebert, n.d. (c. Mar 71), OSA file 202.10, RG 335.

[2] Ibid.

[3] Memo, Laird for Sec Army and Chairman, JCS, 21 Mar 72, sub: Draftees in Vietnam; Memo, Hull for SGS, 28 Jun 72, sub: Draftees to Vietnam, both in OSA file 202.10, RG 335; *New York Times*, 29 Jun 72; *DAHSUM*, FY 72, pp. 30–31.

[4] *DAHSUM*, FY 69, p. 34; Ibid., FY 72, p. 75; "Progress in Ending the Draft and Achieving the All-Volunteer Force," Report to the President and the Chairman of Armed Services Committee of the Senate and House of Representatives (Washington, D.C.: Department of Defense, August 1972), pp. 12–13 (hereafter cited as "Progress Report, 1972").

[5] "Progress Report, 1972," pp. iii, 16–17, 20–24; Transcript of News Conference by Secretary of Defense Melvin R. Laird at San Clemente, Calif., 28 Aug 72, OSD file 340, RG 330.

[6] "Progress Report, 1972," pp. 24–26; Transcript of News Conference, 28 Aug 72.

[7] Transcript of News Conference, 28 Aug 72.

[8] Ibid.

[9] *New York Times*, 3 Sep 72; Ibid., 24 Oct 72.

[10] The congressional ban on quotas is contained in Section 744 of the DOD Appropriation Act for FY 72. See Lee and Parker, *Ending the Draft*, pp. 369–71, for further discussion.

[11] Lee and Parker, *Ending the Draft*, pp. 363–64. The terms are Gus Lee's. Lee served as a member of the task force.

[12] Kelley reported on 6 October that the services set a four-year record for monthly enlistments and that 83 percent were true volunteers. *New York Times*, 7 Oct 72. Memo, Phillips for Kelley, 1 Jun 72, sub: Supply of True Volunteers and Pay Elasticities, OSA file 202.10; OASA (M&RA) Point Paper, c. Oct 72, sub: Management of Enlistments, Herbits Papers.

[13] OASA (M&RA) Point Paper, Management of Enlistments; Ibid., no sub, 6 Oct 72, Herbits Papers. Both papers were attributed to Phillips. The former is a formal document which Phillips circulated; the latter is a summary of the former used for briefing purposes. Gompf assisted in the preparation of both.

[14] OASA (M&RA) Point Paper, Management of Enlistments, and Ibid., Point Paper of 6 Oct 72, Herbits Papers.

[15] Evaluation of Army's Proposed Actions to Reorient Recruiting, no author or date, c. Oct 72, and OASD(M&RA) Point Paper, no author or date, c. Oct 72, responding to Phillips' plan, both in Herbits Papers.

[16] Annual Historical Report, Directorate of Recruiting Operations, 1 July 1972–30 June 1973, USAREC Archives.

[17] The creation of the WAAC and its successor, WAC, was by no means easy or unopposed. For a detailed treatment of the controversies surrounding the origins of the WAC and its continuation after World War II, see Mattie E. Treadwell, *The Women's Army Corps*, The United States Army in World War II, Special Studies (Washington, D.C.: Government Printing Office, 1954), especially chs. 1, 2, and 34; and Bettie J. Morden, *The Women's Army Corps, 1945–1978*, Army Historical Series (Washington, D.C.: U.S. Army Center of Military History, 1990), esp. ch. X, "The End of the Draft and WAC Expansion."

[18] Strength of the Army, pt. I, Active Army (Washington, D.C.: Office of the Deputy Chief of Staff for Personnel, 30 Jun 69), p. 23.

[19] Army 75 Personnel Concept Study (Battelle Institute, 1969), see especially ch. 8, "The Women's Army Corps."

[20] PROVIDE, II, ch. 9, "Increased Use of Uniformed Women," pp. 3, 8, 10–11, 12–18, 24–25. The author wishes to acknowledge the assistance of Col. Bettie Morden, USA, Ret., who represented the DWAC on the PROVIDE study group. Colonel Morden also brought many of the documents on the implementation of the expansion of the WAC referred to in the remainder of this section to the author's attention.

[21] Gates Report, pp. 36–38; Draft Report of the Project Volunteer Committee, 29 Apr 70, OSA file 202.10, RG 335, WNRC.

[22] DCSPER Summary Sheet, 25 May 72, sub: WAC Expansion Study—A Progress Report; DCSPER Summary Sheet, 24 May 72, sub: WAC Recruiting Objective; Ltr, DCSLOG to CG, CONARC, 12 Jun 72, sub: Facility Support for the Expansion of the Women's Army Corps, all in ODWAC Ref File, Expansion 1973–1974, CMH; Memo, ASA (M&RA) for ASD (M&RA), sub: Project Volunteer Programs—Fiscal Years 1974–1978, OSA file 202.10, RG 335, WNRC.

[23] Memo, Froehlke for CofSA, 16 Jun 72, sub: Requirements for Military Manpower, in ODWAC Ref File, Background Papers on Expansion, CMH. Paul Phillips' analysis of the gap is found in Note, Phillips to DASD (Resource Analysis), 7 Jun 72, sub: Supply of True Volunteers, OSA file 202.10, RG 335, WNRC.

[24] Memo, ACSFOR for DCSPER, 19 Jun 72, sub: Expansion of the WAC, ODWAC Ref File, Background Papers on Expansion, CMH.

[25] Memo, Phillips for ASD (M&RA), 28 Jul 72, sub: Project Volunteer Funds for WAC Expansion; Msg, Assistant Director of the Army Budget to CG, CONARC, 4 Aug 72, sub: FY 73 Funding, WAC Expansion Program; Briefing Notes on WAC Expansion, 20 Sep 72, ODWAC Ref File, Background Papers on Expansion, CMH.

[26] Lee and Parker, *Ending the Draft*, pp. 187–97; "Utilization of Military Women," Central All-Volunteer Task Force (Washington, D.C.: OASD[M&RA], December 1972), Tab A, "Task Order," pp. i–iii.

[27] Study, Office of Personnel Operations, Personal Management Development Office, sub: MOS Appropriate for Enlisted WAC Use; DF, Chief, Office of Personnel Operations to DCSPER, Director of Military Personnel Policies, 31 Jul 72, DWAC Ref File, Expansion 1973–74, CMH.

[28] DF, General Bailey to Chief of Army Information, 28 Jul 72, sub: Proposed Press Conference; Information for Members of Congress, 7 Aug 72, sub: Army to Double Women's Army Corps by 1978: New Enlistment Opportunities Offered Women Recruits, Prepared by Office, Chief of Legislative Liaison; "Army Plans Larger Role for Women," *Washington Post*, 8 Aug 72, all in DWAC Ref File, CMH.

[29] See Morden, *The Women's Army Corps*, pp. 202–06, 376–77.

CHAPTER XIII

Keeping Promises
Recruiting and Retention, 1972

The Army's actions to increase the size of the Women's Army Corps as a means to reduce reliance on male volunteers and to establish higher quality criteria for male recruits coincided with the completion of the final Project Volunteer budget request and the decision by the Defense Department to end inductions in January 1973, six months ahead of schedule. The expected success of the Army's actions influenced the outcome of both decisions.

As it prepared its request for Project Volunteer funds for fiscal year 1974, which began in July 1973, the Army continued the practice begun the previous year by General Forsythe of including major portions of the funding requirements necessary to continue momentum toward ending the draft in its base budget. Thus, successful programs such as civilianization of KP and barracks improvement were rolled into the operations and maintenance and military construction accounts, respectively, under the continuing rubric of the "soldier-oriented program."

The 1974 Budget

In its fiscal year 1974 budget request the Army included funds for new barracks for over 16,000 enlisted men as the first stage of a major building program aimed at replacing the existing family of troop barracks with modern facilities by the end of the 1970s. The design of the new barracks focused on dormitory-style facilities that provided three-person rooms for soldiers in the grades E–1 through E–4 and single rooms for noncommissioned officers. The Army also embarked on a program to construct additional family housing and to rehabilitate existing units as part of its soldier-oriented budget request. Additionally, in October 1972 the Army obtained approval from the Department of Defense to proceed with plans to upgrade its recreational facilities. Subsequently new recreation centers, including indoor and outdoor facilities for swimming, skeet and trap ranges, marinas, travel camps, and picnic and athletic sites, appeared on Army installations throughout the country and overseas. All of these projects were justified on the basis of their role in contributing to the improvement of the soldier's environment.[1]

Roger Kelley's office, reflecting the shift in emphasis on volunteer force initiatives from the Defense Department to the services, developed the Project Volunteer budget for FY 1974 essentially as a contingency fund and for special programs and new starts in the coming year. Budget guidance restricted the total amount that could be requested under Project Volunteer to about $400 million. The Army asked for $168 million for "top priority" projects, nearly half of the total amount earmarked for all the services. Beyond that the Army listed additional requests for Project Volunteer funds totaling $417.55 million. Top priority requests included $10 million to exploit the selection center experiment (which was subsequently canceled due to its failure to live up to expectations), $8 million for leased housing to supplement the WAC expansion, $32.82 million for "support of soldier oriented programs" such as the purchase of washing machines and dryers for barracks and upgrading of troop messing facilities, $46.05 million for "urgent maintenance and repair of troop support facilities," and $2 million to automate the Recruiting Command's system of matching recruits with assignments.[2]

Kelley's office reviewed the Army's request and reordered its top priority requests into three categories. The first category, which Kelley's analysts also labeled "top priority programs," contained items clearly aimed at fostering increased enlisted accessions, such as the money for exploiting the selection center experiment, automation of the recruiting system, leased housing for WACs, and similar requests totalling $67.3 million.

Reflecting their continued preoccupation with accessions, Kelley's people dropped other top priority requests for Project Volunteer funds to Priority 2 or Priority 3 on the grounds that those projects, such as modernization of barracks and messing facilities and the purchase of washers and dryers, were oriented toward retention as opposed to recruiting.

As a further justification for denying the Army additional Project Volunteer funds in 1974, Kelley's analysts pointed out that through its soldier-oriented budget scheme the Army had diverted funds in its base budget toward all-volunteer force oriented programs, and, they implied, did not need the additional money. Ever concerned with holding down the size of the defense budget, Kelley's analysts recommended deferring authorizing funds for retention-oriented programs until the need for such expenditures became clearer. Kelley recommended that the Army receive only $67.3 million in Project Volunteer funds. Deputy Secretary of Defense Kenneth Rush agreed. Rush approved $205 million in Project Volunteer expansion and new initiatives funds for FY 1974, of which the Army received the $67.3 million for the programs Kelley considered top priority and accession oriented. Thus the very success of the Army at including volunteer force initiatives in its base budget through the soldier-oriented budget scheme undermined its efforts to win additional money from the Project Volunteer fund.[3]

Secretary of Defense Melvin R. Laird announced on 27 January 1973, his last day in office, that there would be no draft calls for the remainder of fiscal year 1973. The signing of the peace agreement in Paris ending the Vietnam War and a report from Secretary of the Army Froehlke that the Army could meet its accession requirements without draftees convinced him that no further need for induction existed.[4] Laird had made clear his desire to leave office having accomplished his twin goals of ending U.S. involvement in Vietnam and reliance on the draft early in his tenure as secretary of defense. The Vietnamization program contributed to the former goal and the Army's Modern Volunteer Army Program, in concert with the efforts of the other services under the guidance of Assistant Secretary of Defense Kelley, made possible the achievement of the latter.

The question of ending draft calls six months early remained open until the last minute. In September 1972 Secretary of the Army Froehlke assured his subordinates "If we cannot get sufficient manpower from the volunteer mechanism, the Secretary of Defense has informed us that we can still request the use of the draft [through the end of June 1973]." But, Froehlke continued, the Army would be better off in the long run if it could end reliance on the draft as soon as possible.[5]

Recruiting

Recruiting trends during the last six months of 1972 proved favorable, and the decision to expand the WAC promised to help close the gap between accessions and requirements. Between July 1972 and January 1973 the Recruiting Command achieved 95.6 percent of its total accession goal despite the imposition of higher qualitative standards and an increase in the requirement for WAC recruits. Indeed, recruiters brought in 102.5 percent of the increased WAC objective during the period. Overall the Recruiting Command increased non–prior-service enlistments 38 percent over the same period the previous year.[6]

Satisfied that the Army could secure the necessary volunteers to maintain its strength, Froehlke advised Laird that no draftees would be needed for the last half of the fiscal year. Once Laird made the announcement there was no turning back. The promise had been made. Now it was up to the Army to keep it.

The optimism of January faded quickly beginning in February. In the remaining months before induction authority expired, January to June 1973, the Army failed to meet its overall recruiting objectives. Recruiters achieved only 68.5 percent of their male non–prior-service quota for the last five months of the draft. Recruiters, who had exceeded the quota for WAC volunteers from July through December 1972, signed up only 71.1 percent of their quota between January and June 1973.[7]

This abrupt reversal in the fortunes of the Army's recruiting program resulted from an unintentional self-inflicted wound administered by the manpower managers in the Office of the Assistant Secretary of the Army for Manpower and Reserve Affairs, Paul Phillips and Clayton Gompf. Throughout the period October 1972 to January 1973 Phillips and Gompf had monitored volunteer enlistments in terms of quality to see what effect the higher standards imposed over Roger Kelley's objections had on accessions. As previously noted, accessions continued to increase despite elimination of recruiter credit for lower half Mental Category IV volunteers. Encouraged by their apparent success, Phillips and Gompf continued to experiment with enlistment standards in an effort to further improve the quality of the enlisted ranks. In January they further restricted Category IV enlistments by removing all recruiter credit for volunteers from that mental category who failed to possess a high school diploma. That month recruiters achieved 97.7 percent of their objective, with only 12.7 percent of the 17,527 men who volunteered scoring in the Category IV range, but all of those having high school diplomas.

Encouraged by these results, Phillips and Gompf went further. On their recommendation the Army reduced its 19 percent ceiling on Category IV enlistments to 15 percent effective 1 February. Furthermore, USAREC announced that recruiters would receive no credit for enlisting 17-year-olds who were not high school graduates regardless of their mental category. Finally, the Army established an overall limitation on non–high school graduates of 30 percent.[8]

There was nothing mysterious about their numbers. Phillips and Gompf had examined the loss rates of enlistees in basic training and their first assignments and found that high school graduates were twice as likely to complete a full enlistment as were high school dropouts. They also found that soldiers who had high school equivalency certificates had loss rates similar to the dropouts. They averaged the proportion of high school graduates during the peacetime draft years and found it was about 70 percent. Phillips recalled, "I felt to avoid the Army being criticized of making the number and ignoring the kind of people we were getting, that we ought to have an Army that was at least as good, as well as it could be measured, as we had under the draft." Recruiters had proved they could meet their quantitative quotas. Gompf saw the establishment of the 70 percent high school diploma graduate goal as a device to force recruiters further into the high school market.[9]

The 70 percent high school diploma graduate goal went into effect without the knowledge of the manpower managers in the Office of Assistant Secretary of Defense (Manpower and Reserve Affairs). General Montague, chairman of the Central All-Volunteer Task Force, considered the move contradictory to the spirit of the management of the transition to the AVF. "The Army apparently has not respected its verbal commitment to you to discuss changes in quality criteria with you prior to putting them into effect," Montague told Kelley in a memo advising him of the higher standard. He warned that "If quality standards are set too high in relation to accession requirements under existing market conditions, a premium price will have to be paid for manpower, or requirements will not be met." Montague recommended that Kelley require the services to give him thirty days' notice of quality changes and reminded him of the recommendation in the task force's report on qualitative accession requirements that permitted services to exceed recommended qualitative standards but made allocation of additional monies for advertising and bonuses from the Project Volunteer fund contingent upon their adherence to those minimum standards.[10]

The Army's decision to raise qualitative standards for the remainder of fiscal year 1973 and the subsequent drop in enlistment set off a sharp debate between manpower analysts in Kelley's office and the Army secretariat. Kelley's staff argued that the decline in Army enlistments resulted directly from the higher standards. They urged that the Army step down from its position of insisting on 70 percent high school graduates and base its standards according to the availability of volunteers. Department of Defense manpower analysts also pointed out that the Army's independent action and the less than successful results of that action demonstrated the fallacy of decentralized management of the all-volunteer force. They urged Kelley to formally centralize control over enlistment standards in his office.

The Army countered that its poor showing in winter and early spring recruiting resulted from the drop-off of draft-motivated volunteers following Laird's announcement of 27 January and the fact that the period between Christmas and high school graduation was traditionally slow for recruiters. Furthermore, the Army pointed out, the new policy did result in the enlistment of proportionately more quality recruits. Only 60 percent of all enlistees who signed up in the first half of fiscal year 1973 had diplomas; in the second half of the fiscal year the figure was 64 percent. Finally, defenders of the Army's more stringent quality standard noted that despite the fact that the Army ended the year approximately 10,000 men understrength it was able to maintain trained strength in eleven of its thirteen combat divisions. Taking all these points into consideration, Phillips, who became acting assistant secretary of the Army (manpower and reserve affairs) in April when Hadlai Hull was appointed assistant secretary of the Army (financial management), argued that the Army should be given sufficient time to work with the more stringent quality standards before abandoning them.

Kelley went along with Phillips despite reservations that the Army "was creating unreasonably high quality standards, which were almost bound to have the immediate effect of the Army not being able to achieve its recruiting quotas." Kelley gave the Army more than moral support. In spite of General Montague's recommendations to the contrary, Kelley allowed the Army to increase the amount of the enlistment bonus paid to high-quality volunteers for combat arms and related military occupational specialties (MOSs). The Army had been offering a $1,500 bonus for four-year combat arms volunteers since June 1972. Analysis of the recruits who entered under that offering revealed that it attracted more Category III than I and II enlistees. The Army asked Kelley to authorize an increase in the bonus to $2,500 on a test basis for high school graduates in the upper three mental groups. Montague objected on grounds that the proposal was hastily conceived, poorly timed, and that recruiters and the Army's advertising agency would not have enough time to implement programs to capitalize on the higher bonus. Despite these objections Kelley authorized the test and the new bonus went into effect on 1 May.

The new bonus option resulted in an increase of enlistments for the combat arms and an overall improvement in the quality of those who volunteered for the bonus. The Army concluded that "A $2,500 bonus appears to be the monetary threshold necessary to attract high school graduates in Mental Categories I and II," but overall enlistments continued to fall short of objectives.[11]

Congress soon took note of the Army's recruiting difficulties, and members of Congress who had remained skeptical about the volunteer force concept fastened on the rising cost of procuring volunteers and the declining number of enlistments to raise again questions of the wisdom of abandoning the draft. During his confirmation hearings in January Secretary of Defense designate Elliot Richardson indicated his support for the all-volunteer force concept and pledged to continue the initiatives begun by Melvin Laird. Senator Stennis expressed concern over the rising cost of manpower for the armed forces and urged Richardson to give the matter attention. Richardson said the issue of quality and the cost of manpower in an all-volunteer environment would be a major responsibility for his deputy designate, William P. Clements.

At Clements' confirmation, Stennis worried that manpower costs, which were approaching two-thirds of the defense budget according to the Armed Services Committee chairman, might force a reduction in strength. "I do not want to reduce [strength] too low," Stennis said, but if manpower continued to consume two-thirds of the defense budget, "it will get to the point where we can't buy enough of the expensive weapons." Clements agreed, but he added that the services did need quality recruits. "We cannot have our armed services just full of warm bodies, so to speak," he cautioned.[12]

Freshman Senator Sam Nunn of Georgia, a Stennis protege, made the manpower issue one of his special concerns. Nunn disclaimed dogmatic opposition to the volunteer force concept, but he persistently raised questions about the cost of the AVF and worried about the unintended consequences of ending the draft. Nunn considered the all-volunteer force "a clear result of the Vietnam War" and the natural impulse of a war-weary society "to get a little rest now." But because of higher pay, allowances, and bonuses for volunteers for hard to fill positions, "the problem of military manpower is on the verge of getting completely out of control." He doubted that sufficient numbers of "really skilled and educated men" would ever volunteer, and predicted that the AVF would instead attract "those who are the most disadvantaged in our society" and become "a collection of malcontents who may not readily be brought up to acceptable standards of discipline and professional skill."[13]

Nunn pressed his views on Secretary of Defense Richardson in the opening round of hearings on defense authorizations for fiscal year 1974. In particular Nunn drew attention to apparent disparities between Richardson's public statement that "quality objectives for military enlistments are being met," and that ending the draft would not result in "an organization of substandard volunteers," and classified documents that indicated differently. Richardson asserted that no discrepancy existed between public reports and classified documents. Overall, he expressed encouragement with respect to recruiting. He defended the Army's decision to increase quality standards and asserted his belief that the decision to end the draft was "right."[14]

Questions about the quality and cost of the all-volunteer force from members of Congress concerned Kelley. With Montague's help Kelley prepared an analysis of manpower costs that revealed that total personnel expenditures, including civilian pay, would constitute 56 percent of the defense budget for fiscal year 1974. In terms of constant dollars, Kelley claimed, personnel costs actually declined when compared to pre-Vietnam levels. Significantly, Kelley neglected to point out that military strength was approximately half a million men lower in 1974 than in 1964. Kelley also noted that all-volunteer force program costs totaled only 7.1 percent of total personnel costs, of which $2.4 billion went for the pay increases enacted since November 1971. The pay increases, Kelley insisted, corrected long-standing inequities between military and private sector compensation and would have been necessary regardless of whether the draft ended or not.[15]

On the subject of quality standards, however, Kelley would publicly break with the Army. The all-volunteer force came under close scrutiny during the House Armed Services Committee's hearings on the fiscal year 1974 authorization bill. At the opening session on manpower the chairman of subcommittee 2, Congressman O. C. Fisher of Texas, introduced into the record a newly published report by the General Accounting Office (GAO) critical of the services' efforts to achieve the zero-draft goal.[16] With regards to Army requirements and recruiting standards the GAO concluded, "The Army will not meet its fiscal year 1974 stated accession requirements and at the same time meet its quality goals." According to the report the Army needed 162,000 volunteers in FY 1974. If the Army adhered to its goal of recruiting 60 percent of its non–prior-service volunteers from above average mental groups it could expect to enlist only 129,000; if it insisted on 70 percent high school diploma graduates the figure would drop to 104,000, according to the GAO analysts.[17] When asked about the GAO's predictions, Kelley agreed that the Army probably would end the fiscal year understrength. He acknowledged his personal belief that Army standards were too high. If it relaxed its restriction on recruiter credit for low range Mental Category IV volunteers "the Army could address the numbers problem," he said. Kelley further asserted that "the Army is going to have to come down from its 70 percent high-school-graduation objectives in order to meet its numerical requirements."[18]

Kelley also began to have doubts about the true level of support the services were giving to the all-volunteer force. He had announced his decision to return to private life at the end of the month, and in his last weeks in office he reviewed the accomplishments of his tenure and prospects for the future of the all-volunteer force and came to some troubling conclusions.

On 7 May Kelley met with Deputy Secretary of Defense Clements. He told Clements that his optimism for the prospects for the AVF had waned. Kelley cited recent discouraging trends. Army enlistments were down, so too were Navy enlistments, and the Marine Corps met its April objective but 70 percent of its volunteers that month lacked high school diplomas. All of the services had unrealistically high quality standards, Kelley asserted, and "are expected to defend their inflated quality needs before Congress, making it more difficult for us to argue that lower requirements will provide the Services with men and women who can perform satisfactorily." Kelley added that the momentum of the previous years had been lost. He accused the Army of drawing a hard line and predicted that unless the situation reversed the Army would be asking for renewed induction authority by the end of the year.[19]

TABLE 4—DOD OUTLAYS IN CONSTANT FY 1974 DOLLARS
($ Billions)

	FY 1964	FY 1968	FY 1973	FY 1974
Payroll (military & civilian)	$34.7	$40.7	$32.6	$32.0
Other military personnel costs	6.9	9.5	6.6	5.9
Military retired pay	5.3	5.3	5.3	5.3
Family housing, excluding pay	.8	.5	.7	.8
Total pay and related costs	$47.7	$56.0	$45.2	$43.9
All other costs (procurement, R&D, construction, supplies & services)	$40.1	$57.4	$34.0	$35.1
Total outlays constant (FY 1974) prices	$87.8	$113.4	$79.2	$79.0

Source: Memo, Montague for Kelley, 3 April 1973, sub: Material for Congressional Meetings, Herbits Papers.

Clements responded by creating a special task force to review trends and take "timely actions" to solve the "remaining problems" of the AVF before induction authority expired. At the first meeting of the task force, which was attended by the service secretaries and the Joint Chiefs of Staff, Clements advised the group that he and Secretary of Defense Richardson believed the task force was necessary "to ensure we are meeting our All-Volunteer Force problems," to develop a "common base" from which to communicate with the people and Congress, and to demonstrate to the field "that we mean business." Kelley reiterated his belief that standards were too high. He suggested sticking with existing standards through the normally good recruiting months in the summer and making adjustments thereafter.

After some talk about quality standards and bonuses the conversation turned to the draft. With only about six weeks to go until the formal end of the draft, Chief of Naval Operations Admiral Zumwalt asked, "Is it too late to reconsider asking for standby authority?" Admiral Thomas H. Moorer, chairman of the Joint Chiefs of Staff, seconded Zumwalt's query. He added that he knew "Mr. Hebert and Mr. Stennis would support this position [seeking extension of induction authority]." But General Creighton W. Abrams, chief of staff of the Army, disagreed. "Many people in the Army, officers and senior NCO's think [the AVF] . . . is a bunch of crap," Abrams said. Asking for an extension would be misinterpreted as lack of support for the concept. Clements told the Joint Chiefs, "it would be a mistake to extend the draft." He considered peacetime selective service as a "crutch" that led to inefficient management of manpower resources. Congress and the people would restore induction authority if it were really necessary in the future, he assured the military chiefs, but for the present, the subject was closed.[20]

The last-minute talk about extending the draft by members of the Joint Chiefs of Staff infuriated Kelley. On his last day in office he vented his feelings to Clements. The mission to move the armed forces from draft dependency to an all-volunteer basis had been accomplished, he said. "All that remains is to determine how well the All-Volunteer Force will function—not whether it can be achieved, because that has been determined already," Kelley said. In a reference to the recent meeting with the Joint Chiefs of Staff, he expressed distress "that a few members of the Defense team are talking and acting as though the decision to end the draft is yet to be made." Kelley also took a parting shot at the Army. He told Clements the Army's recruiting standards were "unrealistically high" and recommended termination of the $2,500 bonus test for volunteers for combat skills. "I believe the Army can meet its requirements without the bonus," he said, and ending it would force that service to lower standards.[21]

Kelley's frustration with the Joint Chiefs of Staff following the exchange of 14 May 1973 was understandable; singling out the Army by attacking the combat arms bonus and Army quality standards was not. Abrams had supported his view that asking for a last-minute extension of induction authority would be counterproductive. Although he opposed the Army's high enlistment standards, other factors contributed to Kelley's particular distress with the Army. In fact, Kelley had come to believe that, in spite of Abrams' expressions to the contrary, the Army was leading an effort to reopen the decision to end the draft.

Charges of Sabotage

Between January and June 1973 the Army initiated several management and organizational actions that adversely affected the momentum of the effort to achieve the all-volunteer goal by the end of fiscal year 1973. Additionally, in April 1973 the Army Audit Agency completed an examination of the recruiting effort and issued a report that raised questions about the overall management of the effort in addition to documenting significant recruiter malpractice. Taken together with the establishment of higher enlistment standards, these events convinced some observers that the Army had embarked on a program aimed at subverting the Modern Volunteer Army Program, thereby forcing a return to the draft.

On 11 January 1973, the Department of the Army announced that the headquarters of the United States Army Recruiting Command, then at Fort Monroe, Virginia, would be relocated to Fort Sheridan, Illinois. Relocation of USAREC headquarters was but one part of a major reorganization of the Army aimed primarily at creating functionally oriented organizations that provided clearer lines of command and control between Army headquarters and its field agencies. Additionally, the reorganization, dubbed Operation STEADFAST, sought to achieve greater control over resources in a period of declining budgets. The reorganization abolished the Continental Army Command, reduced headquarters elements in the United States, and created two functionally oriented commands, the Forces Command (FORSCOM) and the Training and Doctrine Command (TRADOC). FORSCOM took up residence at Fort McPherson, Georgia. TRADOC took over Fort Monroe and, because of a shortage of facilities, displaced USAREC. Fourth Army headquarters, abolished by the reduction of intermediate staffs, vacated Fort Sheridan. Because the Army wanted to maintain a presence near Chicago, the decision was made to move USAREC to that location.[22]

STEADFAST had nothing to do with recruiting. Planning for the reorganization occurred months before the order to execute the move was issued, and little consideration was given to the impact it would have on USAREC operations. In fact, the impact proved to be considerable. USAREC accomplished its relocation to Fort Sheridan in three phases beginning in April and ending in July 1973. The physical move itself was accomplished efficiently, but due to the disruption of the Recruiting Command's automated data processing system (ADP) and the loss of nearly half of the military and two-thirds of the civilian personnel assigned to the headquarters, recruiting operations suffered during a period when the Army was already experiencing difficulty in meeting its quotas. USAREC headquarters moved its two computers separately. Each was out of service three weeks. Thus for six weeks the command operated with only 50 percent of its ADP capacity. Furthermore, only 20 percent of the ADP personnel chose to move to Illinois; most of the civilians found comparable jobs in Virginia. USAREC overcame the problem by augmenting the staff at Fort Sheridan with uniformed ADP specialists on a temporary basis until new civilians could be hired, trained, and integrated into the operation. The Data Control Branch, responsible for quality control and distribution, was severely affected. Many of its positions remained vacant for over ninety days.[23]

During the same period that USAREC headquarters moved to Fort Sheridan, the recruiting field force labored to meet its accession quota under the higher quality standards imposed on 1 February. But the strength of the field recruiting force declined from its authorized level of 4,725 by 425 recruiters. USAREC permitted the drop in the number of personnel assigned to recruiting duty following a report by the Army Audit Agency that criticized several aspects of the Recruiting Command's operations. The audit had found that only three-quarters of the Army's recruiters actually served in "production" assignments and that the Army's original decision in 1970 to double the force "appeared to be based on a management decision to mount a major effort to ensure that a volunteer Army was achieved" and did not reflect a careful analysis of recruiting markets. The audit found too many recruiters in some areas and not enough in others and recommended a thorough study to determine the optimum size and distribution of the force. Since the audit report indicated a conviction that the recruiting force was too large, USAREC allowed the number of recruiters to decline through attrition while it conducted the study. In the end the Optimum Recruiter Force Size Study, released in July 1973, recommended a modest reduction in the authorized strength of the "on-production" recruiter force from 4,725 to 4,508.[24]

The Army Audit Agency also uncovered evidence of extensive recruiter malpractice. For example, recruiters in two districts set up unauthorized preenlistment training centers where applicants received instruction and coaching designed to help them increase their scores on intelligence tests. Between November 1971 and June 1972, when the audit was conducted, 14,690 volunteers attended preenlistment training in the two districts. The Audit Agency estimated that the unauthorized programs diverted $410,000 in resources from the recruiting effort. Despite the elaborate and expensive scheme, only 15 percent of the unauthorized candidates were able to enlist. Another example of recruiting malpractice involved shipping applicants to another armed forces examining and entrance station (AFEES) after they had failed to qualify for enlistment at the first. A limited survey uncovered 222 cases in which volunteers found to be unqualified for enlistment at one AFEES were shipped to a second. Of the 222 applicants who were reexamined, 109 were enlisted, 25 with known disqualifications. "Duplicate examinations lowered the quality of Army enlistments and consumed resources," the report concluded. Shipping applicants to a second AFEES and housing and feeding them during the reexamination process cost the Army an additional $42.32 per prevolunteer in FY 72 according to the Audit Agency. More troublesome, however, was the fact that the revelation had come at a time when the Army was trying to improve overall quality.[25]

USAREC reacted swiftly to the allegations of recruiter malpractice. Maj. Gen. John Q. Henion, commanding general of the Recruiting Command, asked the U.S. Army Criminal Investigation Command (CID) to investigate the allegations. The CID conducted incognito inspections of recruiting offices and performed background checks on a sample of recruiters' records. Its investigators reported to Henion that "recruiter malpractices were widespread throughout the command and that a large number of recruiters had a background of serious offenses of a felony nature." The general responded by establishing a Special Actions Division in his headquarters to deal with malpractice. He asked CID to conduct a 100 percent check of his recruiters' backgrounds, and he centralized investigation of all allegations of malpractice. The records check of 6,257 personnel revealed 416 recruiters with serious incidents in their past; 58 were subsequently transferred to other duties. The Special Actions Division also investigated 1,402 allegations of malpractice by the end of June 1973. One thousand were unsubstantiated. Of the remainder, 140 revealed clear malpractice, and the individuals involved were turned over to the Judge Advocate General for prosecution.

The Recruiting Command could not isolate the cause for the sudden spate of malpractice incidents but concluded that a combination of factors contributed to the problem. The paramount condition leading to the rash of malpractice reports in 1972 and 1973 appeared to be pressure on the recruiter to meet qualitative and quantitative goals in a period when the entire recruiting business was in a rapid state of flux. Experienced recruiters accustomed to depending on large numbers of draft-motivated volunteers faced a bewildering array of changes including new enlistment options and qualitative standards. "Frequent policy changes to enlistment criteria have created confusion, impacted on recruiter morale and initiative, and, in some instances, placed some recruiters in a position of being unable to accomplish their assigned objectives," concluded one report by the Special Actions Division. Furthermore, the rapid expansion of the recruiting force "may have lowered the expertise and experience level of the recruiters which may be conducive to the commission of errors that may appear to be willful violations and/or misrepresentations."

Whatever the cause, the combination of allegation, investigation, relief, and, in a minority of instances, prosecution of recruiters for malpractice had a chilling effect on the Recruiting Command. Recruiters remembered men coming into their office with short hair and wearing Army-issue shoes asking to enlist and telling them of all sorts of disqualifying problems. "They would be [CID] posing as civilians," one recruiting sergeant recalled, "and they would try to enlist and they'd have something in their background that, if you enlisted them, it was fraud." Recruiters suspected of malpractice were relieved from duty while the allegations were investigated. Although the vast majority of recruiters relieved were cleared of charges and returned to duty, during the period of their relief their fellow recruiters had to carry the burden of making production quotas while shorthanded. In a few cases entire stations were relieved pending investigation of alleged malpractice. "They came in on Monday and I was the only recruiter left in the station," another remembered. "That's how I became a station commander, because the only other guy in the station was the commander and he was relieved for malpractice," a master sergeant recalled of his first tour of duty as a recruiter. Another former recruiter remembered having to make the entire quota of a two-man station by himself during the month following the relief of the station commander. "I had a good friend that was up the highway about ten miles.... I wrote eight contracts and he wrote eight. My objective was 16, his objective was four. I was 50 percent and he was 200 percent. I was an asshole and he was a hero with DRC [District Recruiting Command]."[26]

While the Recruiting Command struggled to meet its goals under the more stringent quality standards of February 1973, it was thus also attempting to clear its reputation and move to Fort Sheridan with the least disruption of its field operations. Meanwhile, another decision was made by the Department of the Army that cast doubt on its true level of commitment toward the volunteer force concept. In April Lt. Gen. Bernard Rogers, deputy chief of staff for personnel, proposed to disestablish the remaining vestige of the Modern Volunteer Army Program and drop the term from the Army's lexicon. DCSPER, which had taken over proponency of the MVA Program from SAMVA in July 1972, reasoned that, since the Department of Defense had directed the services to integrate Project Volunteer fund items into their budgets completely beginning with their 1975 requests, the maintenance of a separate office to monitor Project Volunteer actions was no longer necessary. Furthermore, since the chief of staff of the Army had directed the discontinuance of special commander's progress reports on Modern Volunteer Army actions, "the term MVA has served its purpose."

Proponents of the volunteer force concept within the Department of Defense objected. General Montague noted that the Army currently could not meet its manpower requirements and suggested that announcement of a further decentralization of the management of the programs designed to end reliance on the draft coupled with dropping the term Modern Volunteer Army might prove counterproductive. He feared that relegation of the soldier-oriented programs to "routine status" risked making them "susceptible to cuts during upcoming budget sessions." Gus Lee, director for procurement policy in Kelley's office, agreed. "The announcement of the termination of the MVA program and the discontinuance of the term MVA might be subject to misinterpretation and could suggest that aggressive actions to sustain the volunteer force are no longer necessary."[27]

Despite Montague's and Lee's objections, General Rogers went ahead with the plan, and General Abrams approved the action on 8 June 1973. Abrams too worried that the decentralization of the remaining Modern Volunteer Army Program management actions and discontinuance of the term MVA might be misconstrued as official withdrawal of support for the concept. He thus directed that phaseout be done in a "low-key" fashion. The Army made no public announcement; major commanders learned of the decision quietly through a *Weekly Summary* article. Consistent with Abrams' concern, the article emphasized that "normalization of the MVA Program must not be construed as a lessening of interest in those things which composed the essential philosophy of the program—deep and personal concern for the soldier, increased professionalism, enhanced morale and esprit, improved Army life and seeking out and obtaining the best men and women possible to fill the Army's ranks." Commanders were enjoined to perpetuate and strengthen "these positive elements of the MVA [which] are now a part of the body of the Army."[28]

None of the policy changes or actions initiated in early 1973 with respect to the qualitative standards of recruits, location of USAREC headquarters, or the complete integration of volunteer Army programs into the Army staff system was intended to subvert the objective of attaining the zero-draft goal. Taken in conjunction with several months of poor recruiting results it is easy to see why outside observers might conclude that some sort of conspiracy existed to sabotage the all-volunteer force.

One such observer was Stephen Herbits. By 1973 Herbits had devoted virtually his entire adult life to the cause of achieving an all-volunteer force. Through his service on the Gates Commission and as an assistant to Senator Stafford he had come to know the issues and personalities involved in achieving the AVF intimately. He had strong opinions on the subject, including a conviction that the armed services, if left to their own devices, preferred the open-ended supply of men offered by selective service. He believed that they would revert to the draft unless forced to stay the course toward the AVF. In May 1973 Herbits joined Roger Kelley's staff essentially as an understudy to General Montague, the special assistant for the all-volunteer force. By that time it was known that Kelley would be leaving at the end of May. Montague too was scheduled for a new assignment later in the summer. Kelley and Montague wanted to have a strong-willed supporter of the AVF with contacts on Capitol Hill in place before they departed.

Herbits arrived in the Department of Defense when a large turnover in leadership was under way. Secretary of Defense Richardson left abruptly at the end of April 1973 when President Nixon named him attorney general. Nixon nominated James R. Schlesinger to succeed Richardson on 10 May, but Schlesinger was not confirmed until July. At the Army level, Secretary of the Army Robert Froehlke left office in May and was succeeded by Howard H. Callaway later the same month. Assistant Secretary of the Army for Manpower Hadlai Hull became assistant secretary of the Army for financial management at the end of March. He was replaced by Karl Wallis, former special assistant to Melvin R. Laird. Thus Herbits arrived in a period when something of a leadership vacuum existed in the Army and the Defense Department, particularly in the manpower area. As he surveyed the Army's recent policy changes and looked at the downward trend in recruiting, he perceived a hidden agenda.

The Army, Herbits concluded, was returning to the "old ways" and by neglecting or subtly withdrawing support for its Modern Volunteer Army Program was permitting the AVF to fail. Herbits presented his case in a series of memos to Lt. Gen. Robert Taber, the principal deputy assistant secretary of defense who took over the Manpower and Reserve Affairs Office after Kelley's departure. Herbits argued that the Army should be directed to roll back its quality standards and that in the future any service changes to qualitative enlistment standards should be cleared by the assistant secretary of defense for manpower in advance. He considered the Army's action to reduce recruiting strength "just another self-inflicted wound when the patient is already bleeding heavily," and suggested that Taber place blame for recruiting shortfalls on Army policies when asked about the problem in upcoming Senate hearings.

Herbits also considered Army leadership personally at fault. The new secretary of the Army, Howard Callaway, initially supported the higher enlistment standards that he inherited from his predecessor. In a letter to William

Clements, Callaway challenged Roger Kelley's assertion that the all-volunteer force was an accomplished fact. "The mission will be accomplished," Callaway said, "but it still requires attention and work." He disagreed with Kelley that standards were too high. High standards were necessary to assure critics of the AVF that the volunteer system would work without jeopardizing security. "I do not intend to be the man who accepts a below-standards force as an answer to providing the numbers needed for a 13-division Army," Callaway declared. Herbits saw Callaway's insistence on high standards differently. The standards were too high, he reiterated in a memo to Taber, and by insisting on the 70 percent high school diploma graduate standard the Army created the impression that anything less constituted an admission that the volunteer principle was incapable of providing quality and quantity.

Herbits chronicled other actions by Callaway and Army Chief of Staff General Creighton Abrams that have, "perhaps unintentionally, transmitted signals that the all-volunteer force is neither important nor desirable." Callaway had terminated the "Today's Army Wants To Join You" advertising theme, and Abrams had told an Associated Press reporter that he was unprepared to predict the outcome of the volunteer effort. An article critical of the AVF had appeared in the *Weekly Summary*. Herbits also noted that the Recruiting Command's use of CID investigators to root out malpractice "has panicked recruiters." Furthermore, he reported that no USAREC majors or lieutenant colonels had been picked for promotion or attendance at a senior service college by recent selection boards. The result was a systematic emasculation of the Recruiting Command. If these were deliberate acts they constituted insubordination, Herbits contended; if they were acts of omission—if no one in the Army's leadership had thought through the consequences of the combined policies in terms of their impact on recruiting—they indicated stupidity. In either case the Army's policies had to change.[29]

Mounting criticism of the Army's manpower program within the Defense Department coincided with expressions of concern in the press and Congress. A spate of news articles that appeared in prominent publications in May and June 1973 questioned the prospects for the AVF in the last weeks before induction authority expired. All pointed to the Army's inability to achieve its required number of recruits and suggested that either quality standards would have to come down or the draft might have to be revived. The *Wall Street Journal* reported that the Nixon administration, "beset by inflation and Watergate," was proclaiming that the AVF was a success, but cautioned that "the self-congratulations may be a bit premature." The *Wall Street Journal* and the *Washington Post* both reported that unnamed Pentagon officials suspected the Army of setting standards that could not be met. The *Post* quoted Roger Kelley, who said darkly that "foes of the all-volunteer concept 'can demonstrate the need for a draft by letting failure occur.'"[30]

Expressions of concern came from both houses of Congress. The Senate Armed Services Committee began hearings on personnel authorizations for the coming year on 11 June 1973. From the outset its members displayed concern over the rising cost of military manpower and the ability of the services to achieve the all-volunteer goal. The senators based their concern on the findings of a report prepared for the Armed Services Committee by Martin Binkin and John D. Johnston of the Brookings Institution entitled "All-Volunteer Armed Forces: Progress, Problems, and Prospects." The authors had concluded that the services' ability to end reliance on the draft ahead of schedule in January 1973 "was due principally to large reductions in military manpower, on the one hand, and the ability to attract sufficient volunteers as a result of increased financial incentives and recruiting efforts, on the other." In the future, Binkin and Johnston predicted that "to maintain an all-volunteer armed force of 2.23 million active personnel under current policies will require that one out of every three (33 percent) qualified and available men will have to volunteer for active military service before reaching age 23." Although they considered the transition to the AVF generally successful and concluded that an adequate supply of volunteers existed for most military jobs, Binkin and Johnston expressed concern over the supply of volunteers for "critical skills" such as hazardous or unattractive military specialities and positions requiring higher than average intelligence. In addition, the Brookings authors worried that not enough volunteers would come forward to fill the reserve components or provide the services with the necessary numbers of health professionals. They expressed concern that the bonuses offered for combat skills and those proposed in the still-pending Uniformed Services Special Pay Act might not be the best answer to ending these shortages.[31]

During the hearings the senators referred often to the Brookings report either directly or indirectly. General Taber, the main witness for the Department of Defense, took numerous questions on the high costs, the use of bonuses to attract volunteers to critical skills positions, and the overall quality of enlistees. Taber adhered to the administration's position that "the ability of the Armed Forces to maintain a peacetime military force on a voluntary basis has, in most respects, been demonstrated." He acknowledged that shortages existed in some areas but asserted that prompt passage of the Uniformed Services Special Pay Act would alleviate remaining problems. Taber neatly sidestepped questions about alternatives to the AVF. When, for example, Senator Strom Thurmond of South Carolina, the ranking minority member of the committee, asked if retaining induction authority and drafting men for military service would be a less expensive alternative, Taber replied that the decision to end the draft had already been made. He further observed that when all the "hidden costs" of conscription were taken into account, the draft was no less expensive than an all-volunteer force.

The Army witness, Lt. Gen. Bernard Rogers, deputy chief of staff for personnel, also came under close scrutiny. Rogers defended the Army's high recruiting standards but admitted that because of them the Army had not achieved its quantitative goals since January. Does that mean we are headed back to the draft? asked Senator Barry Goldwater of Arizona. Rogers replied that he did not know and hastened to add that the Army was in an "uncharted area." That response prompted Senator Nunn to ask what constituted the lowest strength at which the Army could operate given existing missions. Rogers replied that if Army strength were reduced to 750,000 "something would have to give." He said approximately 170,000 recruits were needed to maintain a strength of 792,000, the force necessary to man the Army's thirteen active divisions at full strength. If the Army received only 100,000 volunteers, it would "experience a trained strength shortfall of 50,000 in FY 74." Would the Army reduce quality standards to assure quantity? asked Nunn in a written follow-up question. "The Army does not foresee any future points in time when it will drop quality as a criterion and go to quantity," was the reply. Rogers came away from the hearings convinced that the Senate Armed Services Committee was considering a further reduction in the Army's strength due to the service's apparent inability to achieve its stated qualitative manpower goals and its apparent unwillingness to reduce quantitative standards.[32]

By the end of June 1973 concern over the Army's inability to maintain its strength in a truly all-volunteer environment reached a critical stage. Within the Department of Defense Herbits was accusing the Army of sabotaging the AVF. Outside, the press and Congress were asking embarrassing questions, and because of the leadership transition going on at the top of the Defense Department the questions were going unanswered.

At this juncture William Clements, acting secretary of defense, took charge of the situation. He took his advice from General Montague through General Taber. Montague, who shared Herbits' zealous support for the all-volunteer force, did not accept Herbits' thesis that some in the Army were actively engaged in acts of sabotage. Nevertheless he informed Taber that, "I am not able to find any key service managers or manpower elements which exhibit a positive, action-oriented approach to solving manpower problems associated with the all-volunteer force." He agreed that action was necessary and pressed Taber to urge Clements to exert "stronger more centralized control over the use of military manpower during the transition to the all-volunteer force." Clements agreed. He scheduled a meeting of the Volunteer Task Force for 2 July, the first working day after the expiration of induction authority. He also called a meeting with Secretary of the Army Callaway, General Abrams, and their manpower assistants. Clements was prepared to direct the Army to relax its qualitative standards in order to achieve the quantity of recruits required to maintain enlisted strength at authorized levels.[33]

Induction authority under the 1971 Selective Service Act expired at midnight on 30 June 1973, the last day of fiscal year 1973. The Army ended the period almost 14,000 men understrength. The Recruiting Command had achieved only 87.1 percent of its objective for non–prior-service enlistments. By June the problems facing the volunteer Army, well known for months within military circles, had become common knowledge. The *New York Times* summed them up well in a front page story on 1 July, the first day of the draft-free era: "Lag in a Volunteer Force Spurs New Talk of New Draft." The article observed, "Not since 1940 and the passage of the pre–World War II conscription act has the United States gone longer than a year without draft call-up authority." The dismal showing of the Army, which the *Times* called the "most critical" of the services in terms of its need for volunteers, in the six months "trial" without inductions prompted many military men, "a majority of whom appear to favor draftees as soldiers," and key members of Congress to disclose the "belief that some form of draft may soon have to be reinstated—some said within a year." The *Times* summarized the findings of the GAO and Brookings Institution reports, repeated Roger Kelley's comments about sabotage, and reviewed the difficulties experienced by the Recruiting Command including the investigations of recruiting malpractice. The report also quoted an active duty Army general, Maj. Gen. Harley Moore, Jr., the commanding general of Fort Gordon, Georgia, who called the all-volunteer force an "'optimistic mistake,'" an opinion which Moore claimed was shared by many officers. General Westmoreland, retired for a year, agreed, according to the report. The "Army Chief of Staff who presided over the President's phase-out of the draft" called the decision to end the draft "one of 'political appeal' but one that made him 'not confident' that military manpower requirements could be met," a quote based on a written reply from Westmoreland to the newspaper. Although the article also quoted such supporters of the all-volunteer force as Roger Kelley and former Secretaries of Defense Laird and Richardson, it did not quote any current members of the Departments of Defense or Army in support of the effort. The overall tone of the piece was distinctly negative. The *Times* message was that the draft had ended, but the volunteer force was not working. It offered no solutions to the problem.[34]

The *New York Times* article incensed Herbits and steeled his resolve to achieve centralized control over the all-volunteer force effort. On the morning of 2 July, prior to the meeting between Clements and the services on the AVF issues, Herbits fired off yet another strong memo to Taber. The *Times* article reinforced "my point that it is Service leadership that is responsible for this bad and misleading press" on the failure of the AVF, he told Taber. Herbits blamed the Army for most of the "bad press." He demanded that General Moore be relieved, that Clements or the secretary of defense tell General Abrams "that he must begin to promote the AVF with complete and ruthless leadership," and that the Army be required to prepare a public relations program to sell the volunteer concept internally and an action plan to make the volunteer Army work by 20 July.[35] The next move was up to the Army.

Notes

[1] *DAHSUM*, 1973, pp. 61, 142–45, 149–50; 1974, pp. 110–18.

[2] Memo, Hull for Kelley, 20 Oct 72, sub: Revised FY 74 Project Volunteer Priorities, OSA file 202.10, RG 335, WNRC; OSA Program/Budget Decision Memorandum, 5 Dec 72, sub: All-Volunteer Force Expansion and New Initiatives Proposals for FY 1974, OSD file 340, RG 330, WNRC.

[3] OSD Program/Budget Decision Memorandum, 5 Dec 72, sub: All Volunteer Force Expansion and New Initiatives Proposals for FY 1974, OSD file 340, RG 330, WNRC.

[4] *New York Times*, 28 Jan 73.

[5] Memo, Resor for Hull, (n.d.) sub: Recruiting and Reenlistments—Use of Draft the Last Half of FY 73, OSA file 202.10, RG 335, WNRC.

[6] Annual Historical Report, USAREC Directorate of Recruiting Operations, 1 July 1972–30 June 1973, USAREC Archives (hereafter cited as USAREC AHR).

[7] USAREC AHR.

[8] Ibid.

[9] Intervs, author with Clayton Gompf, 14 Jun 83, and with Paul Phillips, 23 Sep 83.

[10] Memo, Montague for Kelley, 30 Jan 73, sub: Quality Issues, Herbits Papers; Lee and Parker, *Ending the Draft*, pp. 377–78.

[11] Phillips Interv and Interv, author with Roger Kelley, 19 Oct 83; Lee and Parker, *Ending the Draft*, pp. 382–86; Memos, Montague for Kelley, 21 and 22 Feb 73, sub: Expanded Test of the Enlistment Bonus Under the Combat Arms Definition, and 6 Apr 73, sub: Lack of Army Preparation to Use Expanded Enlistment Bonus, Herbits Papers; Annual Historical Summary, DA, ODCSPER, 1 Jul 72–30 Jun 73, pp. 8–12; USAREC AHR.

[12] U.S. Congress, Senate, Committee on Armed Services, *Hearings, Nominations of Elliot L. Richardson and William P. Clements*, 93d Cong., 1st sess., 1973, pp. 11–12, 154–56.

[13] Excerpts from a speech by Senator Nunn before the Georgia General Assembly, 5 Mar 73, reprinted in U.S. Congress, Senate, *Congressional Record*, 93d Cong., 1st sess., 1973, March 22, 1973, pp. 9244–45.

[14] U.S. Congress, Senate, Committee on Armed Services, *Hearings, Fiscal Year 1974 Authorization for Military Procurement, Research and Development, Construction Authorization for the SAFEGUARD ABM, and Active Duty and Selective Reserve Strengths*, 93d Cong., 1st sess., 1973, pp. 18–21, 155–58 (hereafter cited as FY 74 Authorization, Senate).

[15] Memo, Montague for Kelley, 3 Apr 73, sub: Material for Congressional Meetings, Herbits Papers.

[16] General Accounting Office, *Problems in Meeting Military Manpower Needs in the All-Volunteer Force* (Washington, D.C.: Comptroller General of the United States, 1973).

[17] Ibid., pp. 9, 17.

[18] U.S. Congress, House, Committee on Armed Services, Subcommittee no. 2, *Hearings, Cost Escalation in Defense Procurement Contracts and Military Posture*, 93d Cong., 1st sess., 1973, pp. 1791–92, 1821–24.

[19] Memo, Montague for Kelley, 7 May 73, sub: Meeting with Deputy Secretary of Defense, Herbits Papers.

[20] Memo, Montague for Kelley, 14 May 73, sub: First Meeting of DOD Task Force on the All-Volunteer Force, Herbits Papers.

[21] Memo, Kelley for Clements, 31 May 73, sub: The All-Volunteer Force, OSA file 201.10, RG 335, WNRC.

[22] Maj James Q. Bowden, "The Army Reorganization of 1973," unpublished research paper, USMC Command and Staff College (April 1985).

[23] USAREC Fact Sheet, 26 Jan 73, sub: USAREC Relocation Plan (OPLAN HORACE GREELEY); USAREC Directorate of Recruiting Operations, Annual Historical Report, 1 July 72–30 June 73, both in USAREC Archives.

[24] U.S. Army Audit Agency Report of Audit, "Recruiting the All-Volunteer Army," Audit Report: SO 73–49, 13 Apr 73, pp. 11, 15–16; HQ, USAREC, "Optimum Recruiter Force Study," 1 Jul 73, both in USAREC Archives.

[25] Army Audit Agency Report 5073–49, pp. 4, 39–42.

[26] Ltr, CG, USAREC to Commanders Recruiting Districts, 21 Mar 73, sub: Investigation and Disposition of Allegations of Recruiters Crimes; Ltr, CG, USAREC to ADCSPER, 30 Apr 73, sub: Recruiters With Criminal Records; USAREC Special Actions Division Fact Sheet, 24 Jul 73, sub: Summary of Investigations/Inquiries of Recruiting/Processing Irregularities and Malpractices Conducted by USAREC Elements; attachments to USAREC AHR, 1 July 1972–30 June 1973; Intervs, author with four recruiters of the transition period, 20 Oct 83.

[27] Draft DCSPER Summary Sheet, n.d., sub: Concluding Phases of the Modern Volunteer Army, n.d. w/attached Memo, Montague for Lt Col Wright, 17 Apr 73, sub: Army Paper: Concluding Phases of the Modern Volunteer Army, Herbits Papers; Memo, Lee for Chief, Volunteer Army Office, DCSPER, 19 Apr 73, sub: Concluding Phases of the Modern Volunteer Army, 19 Apr 73, Background Material.

[28] DCSPER Fact Sheet, 31 May 73, sub: DPPB Long Range Objective No. 14, Title: Concluding Phases of the Modern Volunteer Army (MVA) Program; DCSPER Summary Sheet, 5 May 73, sub: Concluding Phases of the Modern Volunteer Army, w/CSA approval dated 8 Jun 73, Background Material; "Decentralization of the Modern Volunteer Army," *Weekly Summary* 23, no. 23 (13 June 1973); 16–17.

[29] Memos, Herbits through Montague for Lt Gen Taber, 5 Jun 73, sub: Prior Clearance for Mental Standards Changes, and 7 Jun 73, sub: Shortage in Army Recruiters, both in Herbits Papers; Ltr, Callaway to Clements, 8 Jun 73, sub: The All-Volunteer Force, OSA file 202.10, RG 335, WNRC; Memo, Herbits for Taber, 21 Jun 73, sub: Current Army Approach to the All-Volunteer Force, Herbits Papers; Interv, author with Herbits, 3 Nov 83.

[30] "Foes of All-Volunteer Army Hit," *Washington Post*, 4 Jun 73; "Goodbye Draft: Will the Volunteer Army Work?" *Wall Street Journal*, 28 Jun 73. See also "Signs That The Volunteer Army May Come Up Short," *U.S. News & World Report*, 28 May 1973, p. 54.

[31] Martin Binkin and John D. Johnston, "All-Volunteer Armed Forces: Progress, Problems, and Prospects," Report prepared by the Senate Armed Services Committee, published as a Committee Print, 1 Jun 73, pp. 1, 27–36, 40–44.

[32] U.S. Congress, Senate, Committee on Armed Services, *Hearings on Fiscal Year 1974 Authorization for Military Procurement, Research and Development, Construction Authorization for the SAFEGUARD ABM, and Active Duty and Selected Reserve Strengths*, 93d Cong., 1st sess., 1973, pp. 5204, 5230, 5232, 5235–36, 5278, 5244, 5256–58, 5266–67. Rogers expressed his opinion that the SASC was

considering a cut in Army strength to Gus Lee following the hearings. See Lee and Parker, *Ending the Draft*, p. 388.

[33] Memo, Montague for Taber, 29 Jun 73, sub: Quality Criteria for Enlistment; Information Memo for Deputy Sec Def, no author or date, sub: Agenda Item on the All-Volunteer Force for the 2 July Armed Forces Policy Council (attributed to Montague, c. 30 Jun 73), Herbits Papers.

[34] "Lag in a Volunteer Force Spurs Talk of New Draft," *New York Times*, 1 Jul 73.

[35] Memo, Herbits for Taber, 2 Jul 73, no subject, Herbits Papers.

Senator Sam Nunn (D-Ga.). As a freshman senator and new member of the Armed Services Committee in 1973, Nunn took a special interest in initiatives affecting the all-volunteer force (Office of U.S. Senator Sam Nunn); below, *in August 1972, Secretary of Defense Melvin R. Laird briefs the media at the Pentagon about progress toward ending the draft and implementing the all-volunteer force* (NARA).

Senator John C. Stennis (D-Miss.), chairman of the Senate Armed Services Committee, meets with noncommissioned officers at Fort Lewis, Washington, to solicit their views about the MVA Program (NARA); below, *Assistant Secretary of Defense Roger T. Kelley discusses MVA Program initiatives with soldiers at Fort Carson, Colorado* (NARA).

Brig. Gen. Paul D. Phillips (U.S. Army, Ret.), Assistant Secretary of the Army (Manpower and Reserve Affairs) from 1971 to 1978 (MHI); below, *in February 1973, a drill sergeant at Fort Polk identifies a target for Pvt. Dwight Stone, the last man to be drafted into the U.S. Army* (NARA).

Two recently hired civilians replace military KPs in a dining facility at Fort Polk, Louisiana, in February 1973. This major part of the MVA Program was nearly terminated by Congress, which questioned both the $100 million cost and the appearance that the Army was making life too soft for recruits (NARA).

Secretary of the Army Howard H. Callaway prepares his lunch at a Fort Carson dining facility during a tour of the installation in August 1974 (NARA); below, Callaway talks with WAC trainees at Fort McClellan, Alabama, in November 1973. Increasing the number of women in the Army helped ease some of the demands on recruitment objectives for critical skill and combat arms positions (NARA).

CHAPTER XIV

Making It Work
The New Army, 1973

William Clements appeared before the Armed Forces Policy Council on Monday, 2 July 1973, and after reviewing the recruiting results for the previous few months told the members, who included the secretaries and chiefs of the several services, that "My job and that of everyone in the Department is to make the volunteer force work and work well. It's clear from the figures we have just reviewed that we aren't doing well enough." Clements added that he detected an air of negativism in statements to the press and Congress on the subject and a lack of "strong, positive action to avoid problems or overcome them if they occur." He singled out the Army for examples: General Abrams had told a member of the press he was not prepared to predict the outcome of the AVF; the Army had raised its qualitative standards despite indications that they could not be achieved; the Army had also allowed the strength of its field recruiting force to drop below authorized levels. "I want more and timely action to meet the President's All-Volunteer Force objective," Clements said. He announced that he was extending the $2,500 enlistment bonus for combat skills "pending further evaluation" and encouraged the services to experiment and be innovative. "Most of all," Clements concluded, "we all have to take a positive attitude that the volunteer force is both desirable and completely feasible."[1]

Pressure from the Department of Defense and congressional criticism were not enough to spur a reinvigorated Army effort to make the all-volunteer force work. Secretary of the Army Howard Callaway proved to be the moving force behind the ultimate successful accomplishment of the transition. Callaway was not new to the Army. He had graduated from West Point in 1949 and served as an infantry platoon leader in Korea. Returning to private life in 1952, he then became active in business and politics in his native Georgia. In his home state he served one term in Congress from 1965 to 1966 and was an unsuccessful candidate for governor in 1966. In 1968 he managed Richard Nixon's presidential campaign in the South, and in 1970 Stanley Resor named Callaway a civilian aide to the secretary of the Army for the Third Army Area. During his confirmation hearings Callaway acknowledged that he preferred the draft because he believed everyone should serve in some capacity. But he also acknowledged the reality that the draft was ending. "So as I see the job of the Army," he went on, "it is to make the volunteer Army work." He promised to establish a partnership between the Army and Congress to achieve that end.[2]

During his first month in office Callaway maintained a low profile while he reacquainted himself with the Army. Initially he defended the controversial policies that were the focus of congressional and press criticism of the Army's volunteer force effort. But by the end of June 1973 Callaway concluded that the policies governing recruit quality had to change. He did not want the Department of Defense dictating change, and he shared General Rogers' assessment that continued recruiting shortfalls might lead Congress to cut the service's overall strength. He instructed the Army's leadership to forget speculation about a return to the draft. Congress would not approve a revival of peacetime conscription and the public would not stand for it. We have two choices, he said, "a good volunteer army or a bad volunteer army." In order to retain the initiative the Army had to devise a plan to make the volunteer force concept work before Congress or the Defense Department dictated the terms. Above all, the program had to avoid the appearance of reducing qualitative standards to achieve numbers.[3]

Clements had scheduled a meeting with Callaway and Chief of Staff Abrams for Friday, 6 July. Army manpower managers speculated that the deputy secretary of defense would direct them to roll back qualitative enlistment standards. Callaway preempted Clements. At the meeting he briefed Clements on a plan, prepared by General Rogers' office, to reduce first-time enlistment standards without lowering the overall quality of the Army. Callaway gained approval of his scheme and embarked on a comprehensive program to sell his new approach to skeptics in Congress. At the same time he launched a personal campaign to shore up support for the volunteer Army from key groups within and outside of the service. Callaway's program worked. Although new enlistments continued to lag behind requirements for several more months, criticism of the Army's effort to achieve the AVF began to abate. By the end of 1973 trends in enlistments improved, and on the first anniversary of Laird's announcement ending draft calls Callaway reported that the transition was a success. By the end of fiscal year 1974, a full year after the expiration of induction authority, most knowledgeable observers concluded that the all-volunteer force was indeed working. Although some problem areas remained, talk of returning to the draft had ended.

The Issue of Standards

Since February 1973 spokesmen for the Army had defended the 70 percent high school diploma graduate goal with such vigor that they created the impression that any reversal of that policy would constitute admission that the Army could not succeed at meeting its manpower requirements in the all-volunteer environment. The Army's dilemma in July was to find a way to lower standards gracefully without giving the impression that it had given up on the AVF. The solution, worked out by General Rogers' staff, involved a new approach to enlisted manpower management. Traditionally the Army recruited or inducted enough men and women to replace losses annually. Once enlisted, a soldier was expected to serve a full tour. Early discharge for unsuitability or poor performance was unlikely. The plan developed by the Office of the Deputy Chief of Staff for Personnel required a radical shift from the traditional way of thinking.

Rogers' staff proposed to continue to seek approximately ninety thousand high school graduates a year to meet high skill requirements. But they also wanted to admit more enlistees who were not high school graduates into the Army. Since four out of five enlistees who were not high school graduates became successful soldiers, the limitation on the number of dropouts accepted for enlistment meant that recruiters were forced to pass up good potential soldiers. Henceforth the Army would permit recruiters to enlist those who were otherwise qualified but were not high school graduates in sufficient numbers to meet the Army's quantitative needs provided the total proportion did not exceed 50 percent.

To assure that the quality of trained soldiers remained acceptable, Rogers' staff proposed a new initiative called the Trainee Discharge Program (TDP). The recruiter could only estimate a volunteer's qualitative potential for service based on tests and educational level. The recruit's performance in basic and advanced training offered a far better measure of potential. Why not increase the number of men and women enlisted and discharge those who proved to be unsuitable for service during training? "This action is long overdue," argued an unidentified action officer. Under the existing system misfits normally did not become identified until they reached a unit. Identifying individuals who could not or would not become soldiers during initial training reduced the chance that units would receive troublemakers. Furthermore, discharging recruits from training could be accomplished without prejudice to the individual or the Army. The individual could receive an honorable discharge and if separated within 179 days of enlistment would not be eligible for costly Veterans Administration benefits.

One catch in the proposal was that the Army would have to over-recruit to compensate for higher losses generated by the program. Manpower analysts on Rogers' staff estimated that recruiters would have to enlist approximately eleven thousand additional volunteers to offset losses from the Trainee Discharge Program if the program began in October. The Army estimated it needed 169,000 first-time volunteers in fiscal year 1974. If the TDP were approved it would need 180,000. In the fiscal year just ended recruiters had brought in 162,371. Callaway approved the concept on 5 July contingent on Clements' concurrence. Clements liked the idea; in a masterful understatement he termed it "timely." Callaway directed the Army staff to flesh out the proposal and prepare a plan for informing key members of Congress and the press of the new program.[4]

Elements of Callaway's staff and its Army counterparts, notably the Office of the Deputy Chief of Staff for Personnel and the chiefs of legislative liaison and public affairs, completed the proposals for Callaway by 18 July. General Abrams approved the programs on 23 July, and Callaway received the package on the 24th. He immediately approved the basic plan, which proposed increasing the number of enlistees who were not high school graduates in the Army and discharging recruits who did not measure up to Army standards before their 179th day of service, but stipulated that a system be devised to "track" volunteers in order that those who performed poorly could be identified with the recruiter who enlisted them. He also directed that the Recruiting Command's policies and practices be reviewed, that the field recruiting force be brought up to strength, that efforts be directed toward the enlistment of junior and community college graduates, and that steps to create an "elite recruiting command" be identified. Callaway approved the congressional and public information plans and immediately plunged into the effort to convince both constituencies that the Army was serious about making the all-volunteer force work.[5]

Callaway explained the Army's new program to key members of Congress and their staffs on 24 and 25 July 1973. He announced the revised enlistment standards and new discharge program on 27 July. The announcement did not end criticism of the Army's effort to achieve the goals of the all-volunteer force. Indeed, press reports about the recruiting effort and articles and editorials critical of the AVF in general and the Army in particular continued through the summer and into autumn. The revised enlistment standards and new discharge program did not become effective until 1 September. The review of recruiting policies and practices and the increase in the strength of the field recruiting force, which began concurrently, took time also. Reinvigoration of the Recruiting Command took until November to complete, and new recruiters required up to six months to become fully effective in the field. To ease the burden on recruiters, USAREC pared the number of enlistment options from 40 to 27. In October the chief of staff approved yet another expansion of the Women's Army Corps, to 50,000 by the end of fiscal year 1974, and an increase in the recruiting goal for women in the fiscal year from 12,000 to 14,100.[6]

Recruiters in the field needed time to assimilate all the revised enlistment standards, the higher quotas for women, and the changes in the enlistment options available to volunteers. Between the announcement of the first of the changes and the end of the calendar year recruiting continued to lag behind requirements. In July 1973 the Army had achieved only 76 percent of its recruiting objective while the Air Force had enlisted 101 percent of its goal. The Navy had missed its objective by only 3 percent and the Marine Corps had come up 8 percent short. From August to October the Army missed its recruiting goals by 19, 16, and 12 percent, respectively.[7] In the face of such gloomy news Callaway had his work cut out for him.

Selling the All-Volunteer Army

On 28 August 1973, the day the Army announced its revised enlistment standards and early discharge program, the press reported that the Senate Armed Services Committee had voted unanimously to cut troop strength 7 percent in the coming fiscal year in order to reduce personnel costs. Army strength would be cut 9 percent to 732,400.[8] Following five months of poor recruiting and given the tone of the authorization hearings just concluded, the Army should not have been surprised by the committee's action. Efforts began at once to restore the cuts. The thrust of Callaway's actions on behalf of Army strength was to convince congressmen, skeptics in the press, and the general public that the Army could meet its recruiting goals in an all-volunteer environment. He addressed critics and supporters alike, challenging the former and encouraging the latter. He quickly became the Army's best salesman for the AVF.

One of Callaway's first steps to sell the volunteer Army began as a fence-mending exercise. Congressman Charles Bennett of Florida, who was not among those briefed on the Army's new enlistment and discharge programs, learned of them through the press on the same day as the Senate Armed Services Committee decision became known. He construed the proposed reduction and new standards as an admission that the all-volunteer force was a failure. Bennett, who a week earlier had cosigned a letter to all members of Congress urging support for the AVF through passage of the Uniformed Services Special Pay Act, fired off a letter to the secretary of defense complaining that the reduction of Army standards damaged his credibility. "I would appreciate it very much," he wrote, "if you would let me know if the voluntary services program is succeeding and whether standards are, in fact, having to be dropped to achieve it."

General Taber replied for the secretary of defense with a general explanation of the Army's recruiting situation and a vague summary of the new enlistment standards and discharge program. Callaway, who received a copy of Taber's reply to Bennett, took the additional step of sending an explanation of his own. He explained more clearly than did Taber that the Army was not reducing the number of high school graduates it sought but simply increasing the number of dropouts it permitted recruiters to enlist. The Training Discharge Program was a check-and-balance to assure quality control. He expressed guarded optimism that the new system would work, apologized "for any actions taken by me as a challenge to your credibility," and solicited Bennett's continued support. Callaway's reply, not Taber's, drew a favorable response from Bennett. "You can count on my continued efforts in your corner," Bennett promised.[9]

About the same time Callaway received an offer from Congressman William L. Dickinson of Alabama to make a speech on the House floor favorable to the volunteer Army effort if Callaway's office would provide some material. Callaway had his staff prepare a one-minute speech for Dickinson, which the congressman eventually used on 15 October. In his remarks Dickinson told his colleagues in the House that their continued expressions of doubt about the AVF had "done a great deal to hurt the all-volunteer concept" and created one of the "biggest problems" for Secretary Callaway in making it work. Dickinson urged his fellow representatives to "get behind our Secretary of the Army and see if we can make the all-volunteer concept work."[10]

The positive results of Callaway's efforts toward Bennett and Dickinson led to the development of a program specifically designed to improve congressional support for the volunteer Army. Callaway addressed a letter to every member of Congress explaining the thrust of the Army's efforts to make the AVF work, offering to visit the congressmen in their offices to elaborate on the effort, and soliciting support. Thereafter Callaway and other key Army civilian and military leaders began a series of visits with key members of Congress and congressional caucuses. With Callaway's approval the Legislative Liaison Office arranged for congressmen to visit military installations in their districts or major Army training centers where local commanders briefed them on the all-volunteer Army program and extolled its virtues.

By December the program was well under way. Members of the Army staff gave nineteen briefings to members of Congress and participated in several radio or television taping sessions with congressmen for rebroadcast in their home districts. One briefing proved to be highly successful. Maj. Gen. DeWitt Smith, the assistant deputy chief of staff for personnel, met with Senator Daniel Inouye of Hawaii, a decorated combat veteran of World War II and avowed skeptic of the volunteer concept. During the briefing, which developed into a philosophical discussion between the senator and the general, Inouye remarked that he feared a volunteer force might turn into another "French Foreign Legion" the kind that "turned" on President DeGaulle over his policies toward Algeria. Following the discussion he told Smith that he was "reassured" and would support the volunteer Army. Encounters such as the Smith-Inouye meeting encouraged Callaway. He participated in many of the taping sessions himself, and he directed the chief of information to expand the program.[11]

Callaway's efforts to cultivate goodwill for the volunteer Army bore early fruit in September when Senator John C. Stennis, the venerable chairman of the Senate Armed Services Committee, spoke from the floor of the Senate on behalf of the AVF. Opening the annual debate on the defense authorization bill, Stennis declared that "Congress is certainly obligated to see that the plan is given a fair trial and not dropped, at least until it has been given an exhaustive trial." Stennis added that Congress should not consider reviving conscription for at least two years. He had spent most of the Labor Day recess touring military bases and reported that despite his frequent expressions of doubt over the appropriateness or feasibility of the all-volunteer concept, "as of now I can see there is a chance that it can be made to work." He singled out the success of the 9th Infantry Division at Fort Lewis, Washington, a unit-of-choice organization activated in May 1972 which, with a force of its own recruiters, successfully enlisted all of its soldiers. Based on his observations Senator Stennis concluded that "it will be a severe but not impossible problem for all the four services to fill their ranks with volunteers if the necessary quality is maintained." He predicted that the Army would continue to have the greatest difficulty and said he was willing to spend the money necessary to preserve quality even if strength had to be reduced. Whether strength remained the same or was reduced to preserve quality was up to the services and their military and civilian leaders, Stennis continued.[12] The message was similar to the one Callaway was spreading, and the secretary of the Army quickly thanked Stennis for his expression of support.

Cultivating support in the hallways and cloakrooms of Capitol Hill represented only part of Callaway's personal effort to boost the fortunes of the all-volunteer Army. Like most secretaries of the Army Callaway spent a large part of his life speaking to civic and business forums, addressing veterans organizations, and touring Army installations. He made his search for support for the all-volunteer Army a central element in the speeches he made. His message remained identical to the one he had first articulated in his confirmation hearings: like it or not, the draft is not going to be restored. We must make the volunteer Army work. Carping does not help.

Again his efforts proved fruitful. A member of the Atomic Energy Commission who heard Callaway address the subject of the volunteer force wrote to tell him that while he remained convinced that ending the draft was "not in the best interests of the country," he agreed with Callaway that "short of imminent hostilities there is virtually no likelihood of the reinstatement of a draft to UMT." After hearing Callaway address the subject in those terms, the writer concluded, "Once that point is recognized, the obvious next step is—How do we provide for the safety of our country within the existing ground rules?"[13]

In addition to boosting the AVF at speaking engagements, Callaway employed a direct-mail campaign to solicit support from business leaders and prominent Americans who had served in the Army. In September he cohosted a luncheon for high-level business leaders at the Pentagon with Deputy Secretary of Defense Clements where Callaway, as the principal speaker, made his standard speech on the volunteer force. The following month he sent each of the attendees a follow-up letter with a copy of his annual address to the Association of the U.S. Army meeting attached. The letter and the enclosed speech reemphasized his conviction that

> our immediate challenge is to—
> —Convince everyone that there is no alternative to a successful volunteer Army.
> —Assure the potential enlistee that service to the country is a meaningful part of his or her life—that Army service is a step forward—not an interruption.
> —Give all men and women who serve in the volunteer Army a standard of living comparable to that available in the civilian community.

Callaway concluded the letter by urging the addressee to "discuss the contents of this message in the business community" to help him achieve the goals outlined.[14]

Another campaign to enlist support from prominent Americans who had served in the Army originated in the Office of the Chief of Public Affairs. Callaway quickly endorsed the plan to send letters to sports figures and entertainers inviting them to Washington for a briefing and assisting them in the preparation and local distribution of testimonial statements on behalf of the

Army. He signed and sent off the first group of ten letters in January. Of the ten addressed, mainly professional football players and popular singers, only one, Elvis Presley, replied, and he declined. Undaunted, Callaway dispatched five additional letters in April. The second effort elicited no responses and the program died. It was the only element of Callaway's effort to cultivate positive public support for the volunteer Army that proved to be unsuccessful.[15]

Callaway also directed his attention at improving (from the Army's perspective) the news media's coverage of the all-volunteer Army. The succession of poor recruiting months beginning in February 1973 and continuing through the summer, combined with negative comments by outgoing Department of Defense personnel concerning alleged "sabotage" of the AVF, contributed to reports and editorials critical of the Army's management of the AVF and suggestive that a renewal of the draft would soon be necessary. Initially Callaway moved carefully with the media. He invited journalists and editors to Washington for briefings on the volunteer Army and efforts under way to make it work and asked them for a fair hearing. When a favorable article or supportive editorial came to his attention, Callaway quickly dispatched a letter of appreciation to the editor. For example, when the *Atlanta Journal* ran an editorial on the Army's efforts to achieve the goals of the AVF and concluded "under its present leadership the Army is headed in that direction," Callaway sent a private letter of thanks to the *Journal* for giving the Army a "fair shake."[16]

More frequently, at first, Callaway received copies of unfavorable articles or critical editorials from members of Congress or volunteer Army supporters with requests for an explanation or rebuttal. Thus when Congressman Frank Horton of New York, who styled himself "one of the earliest and strongest supporters of the All-Volunteer Force," sent Callaway a clipping of a critical piece by columnist George Will, the Army secretary responded with a detailed three-page letter addressing Will's charges point for point. Will, who was also a member of Senator Allott's staff, which supported the AVF, had criticized the Army's management of the volunteer force in terms that strongly resembled the charges Stephen Herbits had made earlier in 1973. Will claimed that no shortage of volunteers existed; the real problem was the Army's insistence on standards that were too high. He suggested that Army complaints about insufficient numbers or low-quality recruits were aimed either at stampeding Congress into restoring the draft or diverting budgetary resources from the other services to the Army. Callaway assured Horton that neither he nor any other responsible Army official was out to sabotage the volunteer force. He described the new standards and discharge program and pointed out that it was complicated and needed time to work. "We are guardedly optimistic that this system...will positively assist in achieving our procurement objectives," Callaway concluded, adding that he had "little patience with any hand wringer" who condemned a program before it had time to work.[17]

The Army secretary avoided direct confrontations with the press over interpretations of the Army's personnel problems in the fall of 1973. When particular papers continued to emphasize the negative aspects of the Army's recruiting effort despite Callaway's efforts to garner some journalistic support, he complained to the assistant secretary of defense for public affairs. The Army, Callaway said, was making an honest effort to rectify its recruiting problems. His attempts to gain public support from business leaders seemed to be paying off. "What we have not been able to overcome is the negative twist encountered so frequently in media reports." He asked for assistance.[18]

Callaway's memo was an expression of frustration. The independent-minded members of the fourth estate continued to vex the Army as long as it continued to fall short of its recruiting goals.

Callaway devoted at least as much energy to selling the volunteer force internally to the Army as he did trying to convince members of Congress, business and civic leaders, and the press that the Army was sincere in its efforts to achieve the AVF. His message to the Army was the same: the draft would not be revived; the alternative to a successful all-volunteer Army was failure. Working closely with General Abrams he carried that message to the Army in a number of ways. On 5 October Abrams held a one-day conference at the Pentagon with senior commanders and staff officers from Europe, the United States, and the Army staff. He told them that recruiting was the Army's number one priority and asked them to get involved in stimulating renewed vigor into the all-volunteer Army effort in the field. The following week Callaway dispatched letters to every active duty general officer in the Army. In the letter Callaway repeated again the message that "any thoughts of reviving the draft in today's climate are unrealistic." He told the generals that recruiting was everyone's job. "To obtain an all-volunteer force requires that all of us actively help create and maintain, to the maximum feasible extent, a climate conducive to attracting the required number and quality of men and women." He enjoined them to address the issue formally and informally with troops and in speaking engagements, "particularly those to the civilian audiences whose support is essential." Finally, the secretary of the Army asked for thoughts and ideas," whether your comments take the form of fresh ideas, complaints, or philosophy," on how to make the volunteer Army work. Following his speech to the annual meeting of the Association of the U.S. Army on 15 October, in which Callaway again stressed his determination to make the AVF work, the secretary of the Army sent similar letters to 187 Army National Guard generals, 300 U.S. Army Reserve generals, some 1,800 retired generals, and the directors of about 200 veterans organizations.[19]

The letters to general officers generated an impressive response. Many of the Army's generals took Callaway at his word and responded with "fresh ideas, complaints, or philosophy." Maj. Gen. Frederick Kroesen, commander of the 82d Airborne Division, wrote to say that he was not concerned with the Army's failure to meet its objectives for 1973. "Given the anti-military mood of the press, the academicians, and the population in general, and given the growing pains any new program encounters, I think we should have expected a shortfall." Kroesen's real concern, however, dealt with his perception that "we are not matching our recruiting effort with a program aimed at what is in fact the most precious asset of the volunteer Army, the men who are already in it." He complained that large numbers of officers and noncommissioned officers from his division had recently been involuntarily and abruptly reassigned to recruiting duty. The moves hurt individual and unit morale. Kroesen also observed that with the demise of special funding for volunteer Army initiatives improvements in barracks and facilities had to be stretched out or terminated for lack of money. Three battalions of his division continued to live in World War II temporary barracks, "and will remain in these facilities at least through 1980." He concluded that in the field "there is a general feeling that we are reacting too strongly and too rapidly to the requirement to increase the number of new recruits, that we are doing so at the expense of long term benefit for soldiers we already have."

Kroesen's points mirrored the responses of many other general officers. All charged that in its rush to achieve the all-volunteer goal, the Army had short-changed the soldier by promising more than it could or was prepared to deliver. As another officer put it, "All too often we make promises with respect to assignments, schooling, benefits (commissaries, PX's, quarters, retirement, space-A travel, medical and dental care, etc.) only to break them at some point in time during the individual's service." The same officer told Callaway that, "It's time to drop the slogan 'The Army Wants To Join You' and approach it more from the standpoint of presenting a clear and accurate picture of what life in the Army is really like."

Altogether Callaway received sixty-four personal replies from active duty generals. His staff reduced the generals' suggestions to four categories: increased job satisfaction, better personnel management and leadership, improved living and working conditions, and improvement in the Army's public image. Most of the ideas had been considered in one form or another during the experimentation phase of the transition. The real significance of the responses is their indication that the Army's uniformed leaders understood Callaway's message and took it seriously.

Not all agreed with the volunteer concept. Maj. Gen. George S. Patton, Jr., sent Callaway a ten-page letter which, though it contained some specific suggestions for improving training and urged better housing in remote areas, focused mainly on Patton's philosophical objections to ending the draft. Patton, like his father, was an avid student of history. He told Callaway he could not find a single example in the past "where hired soldiery was not symbolic of fading power." Military service represented a "sacred obligation." Under the all-volunteer concept he feared that the Army would return to the kind of force described in James Jones' novel *From Here to Eternity*, an army that drew many of its enlistees from "a rather low class group with a large complement of dregs, drunks and never do wells." He also worried that the officer and noncommissioned officer corps would "turn inward" and that society would lose interest in military affairs. The result could be "decreases in civilian control." Above all, Patton doubted the ability of the Army to sustain the pay scales necessary to attract the quality of enlisted personnel and officers necessary to maintain the active force. "I sense excessive emphasis on buying us," he observed. "I deeply believe that we cannot pay a man enough to make him willing to die for us.... There must be something more." [20]

Callaway's personal staff read all of the replies and highlighted the recommendations. Callaway read the responses as well and dictated personal responses to those he considered particularly thoughtful or useful. When he received an unsolicited response from a master sergeant who had seen one of the general officer letters, Callaway directed that a new letter be developed and sent to sergeants major throughout the Army to involve them in the effort to make the AVF work.[21]

Callaway's programs to sell the all-volunteer Army inside and outside of the Army did not solve the recruiting situation. What the barrage of letters and speeches did accomplish was to convince members of Congress, business leaders interested in and concerned about defense issues, military leaders, and veterans that the secretary of the Army was serious about making the AVF work in the Army. Callaway's activism also helped defuse the adversarial relationship that had developed between the Army and the Office of the Assistant Secretary of Defense for Manpower and Reserve Affairs over the issue of quality versus quantity in the first half of 1973.

The Issue of Race

The future racial balance of the MVA was a matter of deep concern to many of the Army's leaders. Although the sensitive subject was rarely if ever raised in formal deliberations, it nevertheless played a part in the Army's approach to the transition.[22] The Gates Commission had concluded that the transition to an all-volunteer force was not likely to change the racial composition of the armed forces. Army leaders, including Secretary Callaway, were more concerned, and the Army secretariat prepared quarterly reports on both black enlistments and the racial composition of the Army's various components. Socioeconomic factors further complicated the ethnic picture of the changing force. The better qualified blacks, those with high school diplomas or in Mental Categories (MC) I–III, tended to enlist in the Air Force and Navy, perceiving greater career opportunities there. In contrast, the Army began receiving an increasing percentage of MC IV black enlistments until it reached about three times their proportional representation in the nation at large. Given the relative proportion of black and white reenlistment rates—which at one time was 1.7 black to 1.0 white—such trends could at the very least cause critics of the AVF to claim it a failure.

The secretary and his primary assistants had more immediate concerns. Some believed the Army might reach a "tipping point" in its racial balance when whites would increasingly avoid enlisting or reenlisting in the service for ethnic reasons. Such a scenario might lead to a predominantly black enlisted force led by a predominantly white officer corps—or a predominantly black Regular Army beside a predominantly white reserve force, Air Force, and

Navy. A less extreme case was a future Army in which many of the small combat units were almost entirely black (a situation that later did occur in a few infantry units), resulting in a de facto return of the old, segregated Army. Other questions concerned how such an Army would fare in combat, with blacks suffering losses out of all proportion to their number in the U.S. population, or the use of such troops to suppress race riots and similar civil disturbances. A final problem was the higher cost of training an Army that depended increasingly on lower mental category soldiers, whatever their ethnic origins, who also had a high turnover rate. Undoubtedly the civil unrest taking place in the United States during the 1960s encouraged such fears, but they also reflected a genuine concern that the new Army might not have the flexibility to handle its diverse security responsibilities irrespective of the war in Vietnam.

Concern over racial balance thus played a part in orienting the Army's revamped recruiting and retention program. Some recruiting offices were moved out of the ghettos and into the suburbs, recruiting goals for MC I through III–As, the top half of the mental categories, were raised, as were those for high school graduates, while MC IV accessions were limited, recruiter credit for MC IV–C eliminated, and the Trainee Discharge Program (TDP) established to identify the least capable recruits rapidly. Although the Recruiting Command never discouraged black applicants, it did emphasize to recruiters "the necessity to make whites aware of the many advantages available to them in the Army."[23] Such practices did not, however, discourage blacks from joining the Army in even greater numbers. Apparently the Army was still perceived as an institution offering greater opportunities for advancement than comparable civilian organizations. Nevertheless, because of the Army's emphasis on recruiting high-quality soldiers—a premise of the MVF from its inception—the Recruiting Command walked a fine line to prevent the specter of acute racial imbalance from becoming a reality.

Notes

[1] Talking Paper, n.d., sub: Insuring the Success of the All-Volunteer Force, attached to Memo for Deputy Secretary of Defense, n.d., sub: Agenda Item on the All-Volunteer Force for the July 2 Armed Forces Policy Council; Memo, Lt Gen Taber for Assistant Secretaries of the Military Departments (M&RA), 2 Jul 73, sub: Continuation of the Enlistment Bonuses for Infantry, Armor and Artillery Skills, all in Herbits Papers.

[2] U.S. Congress, Senate, Committee on Armed Services, *Hearings on the Nomination of Howard H. Callaway of Georgia to be Secretary of the Army*, 93d Cong., 1st sess., 8 May 1973, pp. 1–2, 21–24.

[3] Interv, author with Howard H. Callaway, 23 Sep 83.

[4] Memo, Executive to the Secretary of the Army for Chief of Legislative Liaison, 9 Jul 73, sub: Quality/Quantity; Memo, Clements for Callaway, 11 Jul 73; DCSPER Summary Sheet w/attachments, 18 Jul 73, sub: Sustaining the Volunteer Army, OSA file 202.10, RG 335, WNRC.

[5] Callaway's stipulations on approving the program to "Sustain the Volunteer Army" are noted on the approval sheet of DCSPER Summary Sheet, sub: Sustaining the Volunteer Army, 18 Jul 73. The stipulations are recorded by Callaway's military assistant Lt. Col. Charles Dyke and dated 26 July. Callaway's order to immediately man the field recruiting force at full strength and his desire to create an elite recruiting force are recorded in Memo, ASA(M&RA) for DCSPER, 31 Jul 73, sub: Strength of Recruiting Force, and in a note by Colonel Dyke on Memo, Acting DCSPER for SA, 17 Aug 73, sub: Sustainment of the Volunteer Army, 17 Aug 73, all in OSA file 202.10, RG 335, WNRC.

[6] Annual Historical Summary, ODCSPER, 1 July 1973 to 30 June 1974, pp. 51–55, 66–67.

[7] The Department of Defense made monthly reports to the press on recruiting progress. See *New York Times*, 9 Aug 73, 12 Sep 73, 14 Oct 73, and 18 Nov 73.

[8] *New York Times*, 28 Jul 73.

[9] Ltr, Bennett to Secretary of Defense, 28 Jul 73; Reply by Taber, 13 Aug 73; Reply by Callaway, 20 Aug 73; Reply by Bennett, 6 Sep 73, all in OSA file 202.10, RG 335, WNRC.

[10] Memo, Callaway for Chief of Legislative Liaison, 11 Sep 73; Memo, CWD for Callaway w/attached draft speech, 19 Sep 73; Ltr, Dickinson to Callaway, 25 Sep 73, all in OSA file 202.10, RG 335, WNRC; U.S. Congress, House, *Congressional Record*, 93d Cong., 1st sess., 1973, p. 34140.

[11] Memo, Chief of Legislative Liaison for SA, 21 Sep 73, sub: Plan for Increasing Congressional Support of the Volunteer Army; Memo, Chief of Legislative Liaison for SA, 14 Dec 73, sub: Volunteer Army Briefings/Tapings (Thru 17 Dec 73); Memo, Chief of Public Information for SA, 19 Dec 73, sub: Participation of Army Personnel in Radio/Television Tape Interviews and Discussions with Members of Congress, all in OSA file 202.10, RG 335, WNRC; Annual Report of Major Activities, 1 July 1973–30 June 1974, Office of Chief of Information, DA, 10 Feb 75.

[12] News Release, Senator John C. Stennis, 24 Sep 73, in OSA file 202.10, RG 335, WNRC.

[13] Ltr, Edwin G. Triner to Callaway, 12 Sep 73, OSA file 202.10, RG 335, WNRC.

[14] DCSPER Information Paper, 18 Oct 73, sub: Letters by the Secretary of the Army Soliciting Support for the Volunteer Army; Ltr, Callaway to H. Ross Perot,

17 Oct 73, OSA file 202.10, RG 335, WNRC. Similar letters were mailed to twenty-two other business leaders including the chairmen of the boards of Exxon, General Dynamics Corporation, and the Morgan Guarantee Trust and the presidents of RCA, McGraw Hill, and several newspaper chains.

[15] Memo, Chief of Public Information for SA, 7 Dec 73, sub: Support for the Volunteer Army; Memo, Chief of Public Information for SA, 17 Jan 74, same subject; Ltr, Callaway to Elvis Presley, 31 Jan 74 (similar letters were sent to five professional athletes, three entertainers, and a manufacturer of sporting goods); Ltr, Tom Diskin (for Elvis Presley) to Callaway, 19 Feb 74; Memo, Chief of Public Information for SA, 13 Apr 74, sub: Prominent Veterans Mailing Program; Ltr, Callaway to Donald O'Connor (similar letters were sent to three television news personalities and a professional football player); all in OSA file 202.10, RG 335, WNRC.

[16] "The Volunteer Army," *The Atlanta Journal*, 29 Oct 73, p. 18; Ltr, Callaway to Editor, *The Atlanta Journal*, 1 Nov 73, copies in OSA file 202.10, RG 335, WNRC.

[17] Ltr, Horton to Callaway, 2 Oct 73 w/copy of "The Army's 'Problem,'" by George Will, *Washington Post*, 28 Sep 73; Ltr, Callaway to Horton, 1 Nov 73, all in OSA file 202.10, RG 335, WNRC.

[18] Memo, Callaway for ASD(PA), 19 Nov 73, sub: Press Accounts of DOD Volunteer Force, OSA file 202.10, RG 335, WNRC.

[19] Memo, Callaway for Clements, 10 Oct 73, sub: Army Recruitment; Ltr, Callaway to Maj Gen George Putnam, 11 Oct 73; DCSPER Information Paper, 18 Oct 73, sub: Letters by the Secretary of the Army Soliciting Support for the Volunteer Army, all in OSA file 202.10, RG 335, WNRC.

[20] Memo, Deputy DCSPER for Callaway, 14 Dec 73, sub: Letters from General Officers Concerning the Volunteer Army; Ltr, Maj Gen Kroesen to Callaway, 26 Oct 73; Ltr, Col(P) Symmes to Callaway, 19 Nov 73; Ltr, Maj Gen Patton to Callaway, 13 Dec 73, all in OSA file 202.10, RG 335, WNRC.

[21] Ltr, M Sgt Hawley to Callaway, 14 Nov 73; Ltr, Callaway to Sgt Maj Van Autreve, 21 Dec 73; MFR, SPADA, 21 Dec 73, sub: Volunteer Army, all in OSA file 202.10, RG 335, WNRC.

[22] Internal DA and Army staff documents examined by the author, in fact, never even address the subject. The following discussion is based on the comments of General (Ret.) Bruce Palmer, Jr., the Army's vice chief of staff, 1968–72, and Brig. Gen. (Ret.) Paul D. Phillips, the former deputy assistant secretary of the Army for manpower and reserve affairs, on the draft manuscript.

[23] Comments of General Phillips.

CHAPTER XV

Success at Last

In August 1973 another charger entered the lists for the AFV, William K. Brehm, the new assistant secretary of defense for manpower. Brehm, who had been the Army's first assistant secretary for manpower from 1968 to 1970, had participated in the early plans and decisions that culminated in the creation of SAMVA and the development of the Modern Volunteer Army Program. He was no stranger to the issues and problems the Army faced and was understanding of and sympathetic to Callaway's plight. Over the next twelve months he would do much to ease the strained relations between the Army and OSD on manpower issues. Increasingly the Army and Defense Department would work together for the necessary congressional support to achieve the AVF goal.

Cooperation and Dissent

Brehm set the tone which would govern his relations with the Army during his confirmation hearings on 2 August 1973. While he agreed with the senators of the Armed Services Committee who questioned him that the high cost of personnel was a matter of concern and promised to work to make the best use of people for the amount spent, he refused to be led into critical statements on specific programs, such as enlistment bonuses, which the Army supported and required. Brehm also avoided commenting about remarks made by Senators Sam Nunn and Stuart Symington critical of the Army's new enlistment standards. He did promise, however, to advise Congress if, after careful observation, he concluded that the all-volunteer force could not be made to work.[1]

Continuation of the enlistment bonus was of special concern to the Army. By 1973 the Army, which initially had favored proficiency pay over enlistment bonuses, supported preserving the bonuses. Clayton Gompf, the Army's deputy assistant secretary for military personnel policy, considered the bonus "the solution of the volunteer force." In the summer of 1973 the Army was offering enlistment bonuses of $2,500 to high school graduates in the upper three mental categories who enlisted in the combat arms for four years. The Army wanted to expand bonus authority in order to attract volunteers to other combat-related skills that remained difficult to fill, such as military police. From May to July 1973 the Army, with Defense Department approval, tested the effectiveness of the bonus for that purpose, with encouraging results. However, the test ended when Senator Harry Byrd of Virginia, chairman of the General Legislation Subcommittee of the Senate Armed Services Committee, objected that the extension of the bonus to critical skills exceeded the intent of Congress. Although Congress extended the existing bonus legislation in July 1973, it clarified the language of the law by specifying that bonuses were to be used only to attract enlistments for armor, artillery, and infantry skills. In response the Army redoubled its efforts to obtain congressional action on the Uniformed Services Pay Act.[2]

Army and Defense Department manpower analysts differed over the bonus. Clay Gompf and Paul Phillips wanted an expansion of bonus authority in terms of both the amount that could be offered and the skills for which it could be paid. Defense Department policy analysts in the Office of the Assistant Secretary of Defense for Manpower wanted to reduce the amount offered and make the bonus available to those who were not high school graduates. Armed with data which showed that bonuses did less to induce men to volunteer than they did to channel men already inclined to enlist into those skills for which the bonuses were offered, the Defense Department analysts proposed reducing bonus payments to $1,500 and offering them regardless of graduation from high school. They reasoned that since the volunteers were already committed to service, lowering the size of the bonus would not affect overall enlistment and that $1,500 would be sufficient to channel volunteers to the critical skills. This represented another expression of the market approach to procurement. The Army objected that lowering the bonus and offering it to high school dropouts would increase the flow of lower quality volunteers into the critical skills for which the bonus was offered. Brehm arrived in the middle of the debate, and both sides expected a favorable decision.

Brehm's solution was to sustain the Army's position temporarily and to press Congress for a speedy resolution of the impasse over the bonus portion of the Uniformed Services Special Pay Act. Specifically, he asked Deputy Secretary of Defense Clements to request that the Senate Armed Services Committee take up the bonus issue separately. Clements complied with Brehm's request. In November, following passage of the fiscal year 1975 defense authorization bill, Stennis' committee moved to settle the bonus question. The Senate Armed Services Committee recommended that bonuses of up to $3,000 be offered to four-year volunteers who enlisted to serve in any critical skill in any service. The Senate approved the proposal on 20 December 1973.

House action on the measure came the following spring. Neither the House Armed Services Committee nor the full House posed objections to the bonus provisions of the Senate bill. Most action dealt with an amendment to the Senate bill authorizing women to attend the service academies. Hebert's committee reported a bill without the amendment. House floor debate focused on the women's issue rather than the bonus; passage occurred on 18 March 1974. The final bill provided flexibility for setting bonus amounts and the skills for which they could be paid. It also went beyond recruiting and created a flexible reenlistment bonus providing up to $15,000 over the course of a full career to servicemen who remained in critical skill areas (the maximum amount was limited to skills associated with the nuclear power field).[3]

The Army prepared the implementation plan for the new bonus scheme. Under the plan $1,500 or $2,500 was offered for volunteers who enlisted for four years in thirty-two critical skill areas. The amount of the bonus depended on the degree of difficulty experienced in filling the position vacancies and the level of education or mental aptitude required for the skill. As success was met in filling requirements for certain skills they would be removed from the list. Conversely, if shortages developed in areas not covered by the flexible bonus program those skills could be added to the list of positions qualifying for the bonus.[4]

Brehm also supported Army efforts to increase benefits for enlisted recruiters as part of Callaway's program to develop an elite recruiting force. Brehm endorsed Callaway's requests for increases in special duty pay for recruiters and in cost ceilings on leased housing. Recruiters did not receive an expense account per se, but a special duty pay was designed to offset out-of-pocket expenses associated with recruiting. With Brehm's support the Defense Department authorized the increase. Thereafter recruiters received an extra $50 per month for the first six months of an assignment, $100 a month during the next twelve months, and $150 monthly as long as they remained on recruiting duty beyond eighteen months. However, congressional action was necessary to raise limitations on leased housing costs, and Congress refused to support the proposed increase.[5]

Another area in which Brehm provided support to the Army was in his opposition to the continued effort by members of his staff to centralize control over the services' management of their recruiting programs. In October, for example, Callaway approved a request by Phillips and the deputy chief of staff for personnel to remove recruiter credit for Mental Category IV enlistments, those volunteers who scored in the lowest acceptable test range. The Army would still accept volunteers from that group, but, in order to encourage recruiters to concentrate their efforts on better qualified prospects, they would not receive credit for enlisting them. Callaway approved the change over the objections of Maj. Gen. John Henion, the commander of the Recruiting Command. Henion argued that the change would hurt recruiter morale. "We have repeatedly assured the field recruiting force that it could expect stable quality criteria for some time," Henion wrote. "A change at this time would definitely hurt my credibility and that of other Army leaders." He urged no change in standards at the present time and ninety-day notice to the field of any future changes. The DCSPER overruled Henion, and Callaway approved the change "in order to raise slightly the quality of our FY 74 accessions."

Stephen Herbits, who continued to serve as the special assistant for the all-volunteer force in Brehm's office, obtained a copy of Henion's memo (probably from his predecessor, General Montague, who was now Henion's deputy) and drew on it to urge Brehm to overrule the Army. In a strong memo to Brehm, Herbits charged the Army with duplicity. The Defense Department "has just given the Army on the one hand $150 special pay for recruiters," and the Army has responded by delivering "a morale defeater of the largest proportion," Herbits wrote. He termed the action "destructive management" and recommended that Brehm ask the secretary of defense to reverse the Army's position, direct the Army to make no further changes in enlistment criteria until it met its objectives for three successive months, and require submission for clearance of future proposed changes in criteria.[6]

Brehm declined to follow Herbits' approach. Instead, he wrote a polite note to Callaway proposing that they meet on a biweekly basis "to review the results of the Army's new initiatives and its progress toward the AVF in general." He made no mention of the recent decision on recruiter credit for Category IV C enlistees. The meetings began on 14 November, but neither Callaway nor Brehm kept notes of their substance. Brehm preferred to avoid direct confrontations on such issues.[7] Besides, he had a more effective device for putting indirect pressure to bear on the Army.

By October the monthly release of recruiting results had become a regular media event in the Pentagon. Brehm or his deputy presided at a news conference, provided the Pentagon press corps with detailed statistics on the results of the previous month, and answered questions. As long as the Army continued to fall short of its objectives Callaway could expect to experience the glare of public attention. If he and the uniformed leaders of the Army insisted on maintaining high standards in the face of personnel shortages, eventually they would be forced to account for themselves before the skeptical armed services committees of Congress. Brehm believed that Callaway would either succeed in making the volunteer Army work or, as he himself had promised in his confirmation hearings, admit that standards or strength would have to come down to achieve the AVF goal.[8]

Congress did not wait for proof that the all-volunteer force could work before reducing strength and establishing qualitative standards. As previously noted, the Senate Armed Services Committee recommended a massive reduction in active duty strength in August 1973. The committee's proposal aimed at reducing the headquarters and support troop level by approximately 156,000, a 7 percent cut, with attendant savings of $1.6 billion in annual personnel costs. The Army's share of such a strength cut amounted to 71,400, a reduction from 803,800 to 732,400.

When the measure went to the floor of the Senate the reduction in strength became entangled in efforts by Senator Mike Mansfield to reduce overseas forces. On 26 September the Senate approved an amendment by Mansfield to the defense authorization bill to reduce land-based forces overseas by 40 percent over a three-year period. Although administration officials and their supporters in the Senate had expected the move, they were surprised by the timing of Mansfield's amendment. As a result, opponents of the amendment failed to marshal all of their supporters to the floor of the Senate in time to kill it. Later in the day, after what one observer called "one of the most intensive administration lobbying efforts of the 93d Congress," which included a visit to Capitol Hill by the secretary of defense and, reportedly, overseas phone calls from the NATO commander to several senators, the Senate reversed itself and rejected the proposal by a vote of 51 to 44. However, in a compromise measure approved two days later the senators agreed to return home 110,000 troops stationed overseas. The Nixon administration opposed both the strength reduction and the redeployment of overseas troops, but on 1 October the Senate approved the package by a final vote of 91 to 7.[9]

Earlier, the House Armed Services Committee had recommended a 43,000-man reduction of the armed forces out of a similar concern for the growing size of personnel costs. On the floor the reduction was trimmed to approximately 13,000, of which 12,179 would come from the Army. The House bill contained no provision for redeployment of troops from overseas. The overseas troop reduction, which the administration continued to oppose, was deleted by the House-Senate conference established to resolve differences between the bills. The conferees also agreed to a strength reduction of 43,000, not surprisingly the original figure recommended by Hebert's committee. The final defense authorization bill for fiscal year 1974 thus required the Army to slim down to a strength of 781,000 by the end of June 1974, a reduction of 22,888 personnel.[10]

The Army accomplished the congressionally mandated reduction in strength with considerably less trauma than it experienced with a similar, albeit larger, reduction two years earlier. Because of recruiting shortfalls the Army was already approximately 3 percent understrength when the legislation passed. The reduction thus eased the burden on recruiters. Additional reductions were achieved by involuntarily separating approximately 4,900 reserve officers on active duty and releasing lower quality, retirement-eligible enlisted men. Indeed, at the insistence of the Office of the Assistant Secretary of the Army for Manpower, most of the reduction was accomplished qualitatively rather than through reduced accessions. Thus, in the final analysis, the reduction in strength during fiscal year 1974 worked to the advantage of those working to improve the quality of the Army and to realize the all-volunteer force.[11]

Congress also imposed qualitative enlistment standards on the armed forces in 1973. The action originated in the Defense Subcommittee of the House Appropriations Committee, chaired by George H. Mahon of Texas. Mahon, who also chaired the full committee, shared the skeptical views of many of his colleagues on the Hill concerning the all-volunteer force but, like Senator Stennis, he believed the AVF deserved the chance to prove itself. His committee devoted a substantial portion of its hearings and subsequent report on defense appropriations for fiscal year 1974 to the problems and prospects for the volunteer force. Mahon's committee worried about the rising cost of personnel in the draft-free environment and the growth in size and expense of the services' recruiting efforts. Nevertheless, it recommended that the services receive virtually everything they asked for to sustain their recruiting efforts in FY 1974, "in order not to be accused of in any way sabotaging or hindering the all-volunteer force efforts."

Mahon also worried that the services might lower quality in order to achieve their required strength levels. In its report the committee singled out the Army's reduction in standards, announced in July. The new Trainee Discharge Program, announced at the same time as a means to eliminate marginal soldiers before they joined units, was not evaluated by the committee. Mahon expressed the hope that the AVF would work, but he believed that the services should make more of an effort to screen out nonproductive personnel before they enlisted. Having been criticized for setting standards too high, the Army now faced the prospect of having Congress place floors on recruiting standards. Mahon's committee proposed to establish limits on the proportion of non–high school graduates and Mental Category IV personnel the services could enlist in order to "provide a positive incentive to prevent further deterioration in the overall quality of our armed forces." The limits set were 45 and 18 percent, respectively. Committee staff members worked out the limits informally with Army representatives. The Defense Department opposed the measure. Deputy Secretary of Defense Clements argued that the limitation would "assure that the Army and Marine Corps fail to enlist sufficient numbers of non–prior-service males to meet recruiting objectives, and therefore end-strengths for fiscal year 1974." [12]

The Joint Chiefs of Staff (JCS) expressed indignation over the limitations on qualitative enlistment standards proposed by the House Appropriations Committee as well as another recommendation reducing funds aimed at upgrading the services' reenlistment and career counseling programs. Chief of Naval Operations Admiral Elmo R. Zumwalt told Secretary of Defense Schlesinger that the chiefs "are becoming increasingly concerned over the inconsistent congressional actions which have approved the All-Volunteer Force concept by allowing the military induction authority to expire but, in the same time frame, have curtailed needed executive authority to recruit, train, and retain the qualified personnel needed to man such a force." He proposed to send a strongly worded letter to the appropriate congressional leaders warning that "The effort to achieve an All-Volunteer Force is doomed to failure in the absence of clear congressional backing expressed not only in military legislation but also in other legislative activities."

Brehm's office scotched the JCS proposal. Donald Scrull, acting deputy assistant secretary of defense for manpower requirements and analysis, told Brehm that Zumwalt's letter would do more harm than good. Scrull feared that a letter such as the chief of naval operations proposed might be perceived as a threat designed to "coerce Congress to support all of our funding requests," and as such might backfire. The Defense Department preferred to work behind the scenes. The Senate Appropriations Committee responded favorably to Clements' more temperate approach and removed the restrictive language on quality from its version of the bill. Nevertheless, the offensive section limiting the proportion of high school dropouts and Mental Category IV personnel in the services survived the Senate-House conference on the measure and became law on 20 December 1973.[13]

Supporters of the all-volunteer force on Capitol Hill and in the Department of Defense saw dark motivations behind the legislative limitation on enlistment standards. "We always saw ourselves as fighting a two front war," recalled Andrew Effron, Congressman William Steiger's staff assistant for volunteer force issues. "On the one hand, we faced opposition on the Hill from people like Hebert and Stennis, who opposed the AVF as a matter of principle." Effron's associate, Stephen Herbits, believed that the Senate's failure to oppose more strenuously the limitations imposed on recruiting standards resulted from its realization that failure by the services to fill their ranks under the terms of the limitations would result in a de facto reduction in strength. Thus the senators, whose 156,000-man reduction had been thwarted by the House, found a "back door method for obtaining what they could not obtain through the regular authorization process." Herbits and Effron continued to see opposition to the AVF from within the services as well. To Herbits, the Army's behind-the-scenes role in establishing the limitations imposed by the House Appropriations Committee was but another example of deliberate sabotage. Effron was more inclined to see service opposition as bureaucratic inertia.[14]

Turning the Corner

By the end of 1973, when the appropriations bill which included the limitations on high school dropouts and Mental Category IV enlistments passed, the Army's efforts to halt the slide in recruiting began to pay off. The Army recruited 15,660 men and women in November, 660 more than its objective for the month. For the first time since February the Army exceeded its goal. The Defense Department's Public Affairs Office rushed the good news to the Pentagon press corps ahead of the scheduled monthly manpower briefing, and on 17 December Brehm announced the results formally. He reported that in addition to achieving 104 percent of its overall objective the Army recruited 101 percent of its non–prior-service male objective and 114 percent of its non–prior-service female objective in November. In terms of qualitative results the Recruiting Command enlisted 12,050 volunteers who scored in the average or above average mental groups (84 percent of the total). Brehm acknowledged that the Army was below its target for high school graduates; only 43 percent of the November volunteers had the desired diploma. Although the Army was running at approximately 52 percent high school graduates for the year, Brehm admitted that the figure could drop below 50 percent if the November trend continued. On the other hand, the assistant secretary added, the Army's new Trainee Discharge Program showed promising results for the first two months of operation.[15]

The reversal of recruiting trends in November, which officials in the Recruiting Command and analysts in the Office of the Assistant Secretary of the Army for Manpower assured was not an aberration, prompted Callaway to go on the offensive. He directed his staff to begin working on a report to be titled "The Volunteer Army: One Year Later." Callaway intended to release the report, which would show the progress made in achieving the all-volunteer Army since the end of draft calls, through congressional and media outlets.[16]

Clay Gompf and Paul Phillips prepared the document, and Callaway reviewed the entire draft before approving it. The report highlighted the progress made toward achieving true all-volunteer status since the last draftees entered the Army in December 1972. It noted that the Army had achieved 84.2 percent of its enlisted accession requirement in calendar year 1973 and, while "anything less than 100% is unacceptable," labeled trends since midyear "encouraging." Progress had also been achieved in the area of quality enlistments. The Army had obtained 50 percent of its male volunteers from the "above average" mental groups since the end of inductions, representing an improvement over previous years. But, the report acknowledged, the "minimum essential quality required by the Army in order to assure skill trainability is 61% above average recruits."

Throughout, the "One Year Later" report blended success with an acknowledgment of shortcomings tempered with the promise of further progress. To assure that progress, the report solicited the support of the American people. "Many of the volunteer Army's problems are national problems and should be viewed as such," it observed. As long as segments of the society considered service in the Army as "suckers'" work it would be unable to attract the quantity or quality it needed. The Army had proved what it could do in a year. It had learned what had to be done to accomplish the mission of obtaining the all-volunteer force. "We need understanding and support" to finish the job, the report concluded.

Callaway used the report as the basis for his testimony to Congress at the beginning of the fiscal year 1975 authorization cycle. Every member of Congress received a copy. Once again he blanketed the public and private sectors with mass mailings. This time, however, the activist secretary of the Army was on the offensive. He did not ask for ideas or help to make the volunteer Army work. "The volunteer Army is a reality," he asserted. "It is no longer just a concept. It is here now, on the ground, ready to fight if need be, stronger than when the draft ended." By implication, he invited continued support for a successful venture.[17]

Not everyone agreed that the Army had done enough to make the volunteer force a success. On 11 February 1974, *Newsweek* published a column by Milton Friedman that resurrected charges that the Army's failure to achieve its enlistment accession goals for 1973 had resulted from "either gross incompetence or deliberate sabotage." The culprits were Army officers abetted by retired officers serving in civilian positions in the Pentagon. Friedman repeated charges made by Stephen Herbits the previous summer that the Army permitted the strength of its field recruiting force to decline and changed enlistment standards so frequently that field recruiters could not keep up with them. The results of these actions were to demoralize the remaining recruiters in the field. Friedman further charged that the Army juggled recruiting results by adding one month's shortfall to the next month's quota in a manner designed to magnify the gap between accessions and requirements and thus give the impression that the recruiting failure was greater than it actually was. Finally, Friedman reported, Army promotion and selection boards discriminated against officers on recruiting duty. The Nobel laureate, who had served on the Gates Commission, claimed to have researched the facts of the performance of the volunteer Army "deeply." Both the tone and specifics of Friedman's charges suggest that his information came from his former colleague on the commission, Stephen Herbits, who continued to question the sincerity of the Army's all-volunteer effort.[18]

Friedman sent an advance draft of the article to Secretary of Defense Schlesinger, who asked Brehm to look into the charges. Brehm's staff assured him that Friedman's information had bases in fact but that his interpretation of those facts was erroneous. Brehm replied directly to Friedman, with whom he had worked as an Army liaison to the Gates Commission. "I know the Army well enough to be certain that they are committed to [the all-volunteer force]," Brehm assured Friedman. He pointed out that in the previous four months the Army had achieved 95 percent of its recruiting goals and in January 1974 had recruited over 19,000 volunteers, "quite possibly the largest monthly total of true volunteers in history." Brehm concluded that "the Army has received more abuse than it really deserves" in its effort to make the AVF work, and he added that he had yet to see a bureaucracy that "reacted perfectly to a major new challenge."[19]

Friedman's allegations attracted some attention. James Lehrer repeated the reports on promotion board discrimination and recruiting force being understrength in a Public Broadcasting System special on the first year of the draft-free Army and asked rhetorically, "Is this consistent with an army hierarchy totally committed to trying to make this difficult transition really work?"[20] Friedman's charges also came up during the opening round of hearings on the FY 1975 defense authorization bill by the House Armed Services Committee. Frank Slatinshek, the chief counsel of the committee, asked Callaway to respond to the points raised in Friedman's column. Callaway replied in detail. He presented data which demonstrated that each charge was based on outdated facts or on a biased interpretation of those facts. Callaway termed Friedman's charge that the Army's recruiting shortfalls resulted from incompetence or sabotage by middle level officers or retired officers working for the Army "not only a harsh judgment but an irresponsible one based largely on presumptuous statements." Expressions of doubt about the appropriateness of the all-volunteer force concept by serving or retired officers, or, for that matter, by elected officials, did not amount to sabotage. "These people have staked their reputations and positions on the proposition that the Volunteer Army will be a success," he continued. "They know that the only alternative is failure, not the draft."[21]

The subject of Army reluctance to vigorously adopt the all-volunteer force concept came up again in the House Appropriations Committee's hearings on the FY 1975 budget. Congressman John Flynt of Georgia quoted retired Lt. Gen. George Forsythe, who had said in a recent interview that although the Army had conducted experiments aimed at achieving the all-volunteer goal as early as 1970, "it is just in the last year that the Army itself has come around to accepting the Volunteer Army concept. Many people in the Army just thought it would go away." Flynt asked the Army witness to comment. Lt. Gen. Bernard Rogers, the deputy chief of staff for personnel, responded that there were those in the Army who did not agree with the volunteer concept, just as there were members of Congress, including members present, who believed that all citizens owed service to the country. But that did not mean the Army opposed the volunteer force goal. "I don't need to tell you, Mr. Chairman, we are moving in an uncharted area," Rogers said, "and George Forsythe was out there in the vanguard." Since the early days when Forsythe led the Army's experimental effort, "we have learned to do our business better in our recruiting." Rogers pointed to the Trainee Discharge Program as another example of how the Army had learned better "to get the quality we want." He concluded by repeating Callaway's message that the Army knew Congress would not vote to restore induction authority in peacetime and therefore was committed to making the AVF work "despite the psychological approach of some people."[22]

Because of the Army's "qualified success," in Callaway's words, in achieving the goals of the volunteer force during calendar year 1973, Congress seemed more willing to accept the Army's version of its commitment to the AVF than that of critics like Friedman. During the congressional hearings on defense authorizations and appropriations conducted in the early months of 1974, members of Congress known for their skepticism about the Army's ability to achieve its quantitative and qualitative goals continued to probe witnesses for signs of failure. The answers they received were positive and uniformly supportive of the volunteer principle. For example, when asked about the quality of the volunteers the Army was receiving, General Rogers expressed the opinion that soldiers in the volunteer Army were as good as those who came in under the draft. When Derek Vander Schaff, a staff assistant to the House Appropriations Committee, suggested that Rogers' reply was political and based on what his superiors wanted him to say, the general bristled. "Those of us who have been in this business for 30 years can judge the quality of individuals," Rogers retorted. "I have no reason to speak from the political side on this one," he continued, "but I have every reason to be concerned because this is my business, about the quality of the man we are getting in the Army." He acknowledged that without the draft the Army found few college and graduate students in the enlisted ranks, but he also expressed confidence that the Training Command, aided by the authority to screen out poor performers, would provide the units with "the kind of person you would like to receive if you were a unit commander." For that reason Rogers opposed extension of the limitations on recruit quality imposed by the committee a year earlier. "Let the Army establish its own quality standards and then recruit to those standards," he urged.[23]

So confident was the Army that it could meet its manpower needs under the all-volunteer system that it asked for an increase in strength of 3,000 in fiscal year 1975 for the purpose of activating an additional combat brigade. The addition of the brigade would raise the Army's number of active divisions to 13 1/3. General Abrams also announced that through management decisions aimed at reducing the size of headquarters troops, civilianization, and the transfer of some support units to the reserve components he hoped to be able to further increase the number of active combat divisions without increasing active duty strength.[24]

Congress approved the requested strength increase, in no small measure because the Army had demonstrated that it could make the all-volunteer force work. Through the early months of 1974 Army recruiters had continued to achieve better than 90 percent of their monthly quotas. Because the reduction in end strength ordered by Congress effectively wiped out the shortfall in accession requirements that built up during the first six months of fiscal year 1974, the Army was only 1 percent below authorized strength in May when the House Armed Services Committee made its recommendations on the strength increase. "It now seems apparent that this increase in combat forces is feasible and will be a reality," Hebert's committee reported. At the same time, the committee restated its reservations of the previous year that the all-volunteer force could in fact meet its needs in terms of both quantity and quality in the long run. The provision authorizing an increase in strength by 3,000 men encountered no opposition in either body of Congress and was approved along with the final bill on the last day of fiscal year 1974.[25]

Results

As if to give the lie to continuing expressions of doubt about their ability, Army recruiters achieved 104 percent of their objectives in May 1974 by enlisting 14,820 men and women. Of that number 13,000 were first-time volunteers, 82 percent scored in the average or above average mental groups, and 54 percent possessed high school diplomas. The following month, the last of the fiscal year, Army recruiters broke their previous best record for a single month by enlisting 27,900, 123 percent of their goal. Of the 25,940 non–prior-service volunteers in June, 82 percent scored in the Mental Category I–III range and 67 percent were high school graduates.[26]

Callaway positively glowed. On 1 July he met reporters at the Pentagon and declared the volunteer Army a success. The Army had ended fiscal year 1974 with slightly more than 783,000 men and women on active duty, approximately 1,400 more than its authorized end strength. It achieved that strength by enlisting nearly 200,000 volunteers and reenlisting some 58,000 soldiers. "It's a successful volunteer Army and I'm extremely proud to be a part of it," he said. "It's a success by every indicator; our quality is good and within all established standards our combat readiness is up." Callaway thanked Congress and the American people for their positive support and made special note of the efforts of the Recruiting Command "that made this possible."

Following his statement Callaway took questions from the press. The questions dealt with the quality, cost, and racial mix of the volunteer Army. Callaway told the reporters that Army quality was better than a year ago. He asserted that, based on the proportion of high school graduates and average and above average recruits entering the service, the Army "will make or continue to make regardless of the law, the restrictions placed by the House Appropriations Committee of 55 percent high school graduates and no more than 18 percent Mental Category IV." Furthermore, through innovations such as the Trainee Discharge Program, through which the Army was releasing an average of 1,600 unsuitable recruits a month, unit quality would improve as well. Callaway admitted that personnel costs were high in the Army. He surprised reporters by saying that manpower in the Army, which he described as the "most labor intensive" of the services, accounted for 70 percent of the Army's budget if one included everything that was personnel related including retirement. But he refused to attribute the high cost of military manpower to the all-volunteer force. He reminded the Pentagon press corps that Congress had agreed to pay service men and women at levels comparable to civilian wages before the end of the draft. Pay comparability, not the AVF, constituted the largest single factor in the increase in military personnel expenses.

Callaway took umbrage with questions on the racial balance of the Army. He admitted that a higher percentage of blacks entered the Army in fiscal year 1974 than in earlier years when the draft was in effect. During the draft the proportion of blacks inducted and serving in the Army roughly approximated their representation in the society, about 13 percent. The figure rose in the transition to the AVF, and in fiscal year 1974 blacks constituted 27 percent of Army enlistees and overall made up about 21 percent of the Army. Callaway said the trend did not concern him. To him the large number of blacks and other minorities entering the Army "indicates a positive perception on the part of blacks in America that they do have a good opportunity in the Army and I can promise you they do." The Army would not set quotas limiting racial content. "That would be totally contrary to everything we believe in," he declared. But the secretary of the Army did hint that in the coming year recruiters would expand their efforts to areas previously less well covered, such as wealthier suburban regions, and he agreed that "to the extent we keep our Army relatively based upon the same composition as the country as a whole, I think that's good."

Callaway admitted that the Army had not solved all of its manpower problems. "Doctors and dentists and professional people are a tough problem," he said. No one was being drafted, and the Army anticipated shortages, particularly in the area of health professionals "because the pay we can offer is not anywhere close to what the average [medical] doctor can make." The Army and the other services continued to work with Congress on this unfinished business. However, he remained positive and optimistic, reiterating his assertion that the Army was "far more ready than when the draft ended." He attributed the Army's improved readiness to three factors. First, the high personnel turbulence engendered by Vietnam had ended. Second, there was high morale in the Army, a product of the fact that "people coming into the Army are there because they want to be in the Army." Finally, he credited the Army's leadership both for making the all-volunteer Army work and for sustaining morale.[27]

Later that day Callaway expressed his personal gratitude to the Army's leaders in the form of a letter to each general officer. "A good deal of the volunteer Army's success thus far can be attributed to the enthusiastic efforts of friends like you," he wrote. "With your encouragement and support, the Army will continue to reach its goals." But he cautioned against overconfidence. More volunteers were needed in the coming year than the one just ended. Furthermore, although the qualitative limitations established by Congress for the fiscal year just ended had been achieved, the Army needed to move more vigorously in search of higher quality volunteers in the future. He enjoined them to keep up the pressure.[28]

Callaway's announcement and the Army's success passed largely unnoticed and unheralded. The *New York Times*, which a year earlier announced the beginning of the induction-free era on the front page with the doleful headline "Lag in Volunteers Spurs Talk of New Draft" dutifully reported the success of fiscal year 1974 in a brief factual story on page 23. Congressman Dan Daniel of Virginia, a member of the House Armed Services Committee, announced the results to the House on 30 July without analysis and to no comment.[29] The apparent success of the volunteer Army was not newsworthy in the summer of 1974 as Richard Nixon, whose administration had ended the draft, was fighting a losing battle for his political life. One of the few who noticed the success of the AVF that summer also noted the Nixon connection. Columnist George Will, who himself had a hand in ushering in the all-volunteer force while a member of Senator Allott's staff, observed, "As the rafters crash down around him let us pause to praise one of Mr. Nixon's finest achievements, the all-volunteer armed force." Will went on to recount the persistent criticisms of the Army and its efforts to achieve the zero-draft goal. To the critics he held up "the facts," as outlined by Callaway, whom he quoted. The volunteer Army was a success, Will concluded, and in the atmosphere of the day it "stands out as the rarest kind of government achievement."[30]

Notes

[1] U.S. Congress, Senate, Committee on Armed Services, *Hearings on the Nomination of William Keith Brehm To Be Assistant Secretary of Defense*, 93d Cong., 1st sess., August 2, 1973, pp. 5–14.

[2] Lee and Parker, *Ending the Draft*, pp. 340–42. Lee quotes Gompf from a 1976 interview, see fn. 2, p. 341.

[3] Memo, ASA(M&RA) for ASD(M&RA), 10 Aug 73, sub: Assessment of Combat Arms Bonus; Memo, Gus Lee for Deputy Secretary of Defense, 17 Aug 73, sub: Ground Combat Enlistment Bonus; Memo, Herbits for Lt Gen Taber, 20 Aug 73, sub: Draft Memo to DEPSECDEF on Army's Combat Bonus Request, OSD 340, RG 330, WNRC; *Congressional Quarterly Almanac* 30, 1974, pp. 606–08; Lee and Parker, *Ending the Draft*, pp. 343–44. The Enlistment Bonus Revision Act (P.L. 93–277) became law in May 1974 and went into effect 1 June.

[4] DCSPER Information Paper, 25 Sep 73, sub: USSPA Enlistment Bonus for Critical Skills; Memo, ASA(M&RA) for SA w/attachment, 9 May 74, sub: Volunteer Army Actions as of 8 May 74, item 7, Enlisted Personnel Bonus Revision Act, all in OSA file 202.10, RG 335, WNRC; Annual Historical Summary, ODCSPER, 1 Jul 73–30 Jun 74, p. 23.

[5] Ltr, Callaway to SecDef, 24 Sep 73, sub: Enhancement of Army Recruiting Duty, OSD file 340, RG 330, WNRC; USAREC Chart, n.d. (c. Oct 73), sub: Events Affecting Recruiting Success, provided by HQ, USAREC; Memo, ASA(M&RA) to SA, 3 Dec 73, sub: Volunteer Army Actions, and 9 May 74, same sub, all in OSA file 202.10, RG 335, WNRC.

[6] Memo, Callaway for Deputy Secretary of Defense, 10 Oct 73, sub: Army Recruitment, OSA file 340, RG 330, WNRC; Memo, Maj Gen Henion for Maj Gen Smith, n.d., sub: Elimination of Category IV B and C Males; Memo, Herbits for Brehm, 16 Oct 73, sub: Army's Elimination of Category IV C's, all in Herbits Papers.

[7] Memo, Brehm for Callaway, 25 Oct 73, OSA file 202.10, RG 335, WNRC.

[8] Brehm Interv.

[9] *New York Times*, 28 Jul 73; U.S. Congress, Senate, Armed Services Committee, *Report of Defense Department Authorizations for FY 74*, (93d Cong., 1st sess., Rpt 93–385, 1973, pp. 131, 147; *Congressional Quarterly Almanac* 29, 1973, pp. 9, 10–15. Mansfield's earlier efforts to reduce overseas troop strength had also ended in defeat. In 1971 he failed to attach an amendment to the selective service extension bill which would have cut strength in Europe by 50 percent; later in 1971 he failed again in an attempt to amend the FY 72 appropriations bill in a similar fashion.

[10] U.S. Congress, House, Armed Service Committee, *Report on Defense Department Authorizations for Fiscal Year 1974*, 93d Cong., 1st sess., Rpt 93–383, 1973, pp. 72–73; *Congressional Quarterly Almanac* 29, 1973, pp. 888–89, 902–03.

[11] *DAHSUM*, 1974, pp. 50, 54. Memo, ASA(M&RA) for SGS, 25 Sep 73, sub: Strength Reduction Planning, OSA file 202.10, RG 335, WNRC.

[12] U.S. Congress, House, Committee on Appropriations, *Department of Defense Appropriations for Fiscal Year 1974*, 93d Cong., 1st sess., Rpt 93–662, 1973, pp. 19–21, 29–36; Paper, n.d. or author (attributed to Herbits), sub: History of Section 718, OSD file 340, RG 330, WNRC; Lee and Parker, *Ending the Draft*, pp. 389–90.

[13] Memo, Zumwalt for SecDef, 8 Dec 73, sub: All-Volunteer Force; Memo, Scrull for Brehm, 21 Dec 73, sub: Proposed JCS Letter on All-Volunteer Force, both in OSD file 340, RG 330, WNRC; *Congressional Quarterly Almanac* 29, 1973, pp. 172–77.

[14] History of Section 718; Effron Interv.

[15] ASD(PA) Memo for Correspondents, 4 Dec 73; ASD(PA) News Release, 17 Dec 73, sub: Recruiting Results for November; Transcript of Briefing by ASD(M&RA) Brehm, 17 Dec 73, all in OSD file 340, RG 330, WNRC.

[16] Memo, Lt Col Dyke for Executive, OCLL, 19 Nov 73, sub: Provision of Material in Support of the Volunteer Army to Congressmen for Inclusion in News letters; Memo, Col Sullivan to Lt Col Dyke, 4 Dec 73, same subject; Memo, Lt Col Dyke for Col Crowe, 10 Dec 73, sub: Volunteer Army Report, One Year Later, all in OSA file 202.10, RG 335, WNRC.

[17] The Volunteer Army—One Year Later, n.d.; Ltr, Callaway to the President, 14 Feb 74, both in OSA file 202.10, RG 335, WNRC.

[18] Milton Friedman, "Volunteer Armed Force: Failure or Victim?" *Newsweek* 83, no. 6 (11 February 1974): 82.

[19] Ltr, Friedman to SecDef, 28 Jan 74; Draft Memo for Brehm, no author or subject, 14 Feb 74; Ltr, Brehm to Friedman, 19 Feb 74, all in OSD file 340, RG 330, WNRC.

[20] "Uncle Sam Requests the Pleasure Of...," Transcript of National Public Affairs Center for Television program aired 18 March 1974 and provided by Lt. Gen. George Forsythe.

[21] U.S. Congress, House, Armed Services Committee, *Hearings on Defense Department Authorizations for FY 75*, 93d Cong., 2d sess., February 14, 1974, pp. 359–65.

[22] U.S. Congress, House, Appropriations Committee, *Hearings on Department of Defense Appropriations for 1975*, 93d Cong., 2d sess., April 22, 1974, p. 966.

[23] Ibid., pp. 958–65.

[24] Written Statement of General Creighton W. Abrams, Chief of Staff, U.S. Army, presented to Committee on Armed Services, House of Representatives, 14 Feb 74, in U.S. Congress, House, Armed Services Committee *Hearings on U.S. Military Posture and Department of Defense Authorization for FY 75*, pp. 277–79.

[25] U.S. Congress, House, Rpt 93–1035, 93d Cong., 2d sess., 1974, pp. 64–65; *Congressional Quarterly Almanac* 30 (1974): 575, 577, 584–86.

[26] OASD(PA) News Releases, 11 Jun 74 and 18 Jul 74, both in OSD file 340, RG 330, WNRC.

[27] OASD(PA) News Release w/transcript of News Briefing with Callaway, 1 Jul 74, OSD file 340, RG 330, WNRC.

[28] Ltr, Callaway to Maj Gen John A. Wickham, Jr., 1 Jul 74, OSD file 340, RG 330, WNRC. Identical letters were sent to all active duty general officers.

[29] *New York Times*, 2 Jul 74; U.S. Congress, House, *Congressional Record*, 93d Cong., 2d sess., 30 July 1974, pp. 25685–86.

[30] George F. Will, "All-Volunteer Armed Force: The Rarest Kind of Achievement," *Los Angeles Times*, 7 Aug 74, copy of clipping found in OSD file 340, RG 330, WNRC, with comment by Brehm to Clements, "This represents the best kind of cooperation from the press."

Chapter XVI

Unfinished Business
The Medical Professionals

By the end of June 1974 the Army had demonstrated its ability to maintain its active enlisted force at authorized strength with acceptable quality and without the pressure of induction authority. The major innovations designed to attract volunteers to the Army and increase retention were in place and functioning. But not all aspects of the transition to the volunteer force had been completed by mid-1974. Two specific problem areas remained, procurement and retention of medical professionals and recruiting for the reserve components. Both areas had been identified as potential trouble-spots by the PROVIDE study group and the Project Volunteer report. The Gates Commission also considered the subjects. The Defense Department sponsored legislation to ease the projected "doctor shortage" as early as 1972, but, for a variety of reasons, Congress did not complete actions on the proposal until May 1974.

Likewise, expected shortages in the reserve components continued to receive little tangible attention by 1974. In both instances delays resulted from funding limitations and political and bureaucratic disagreements over the size of the requirements and timing of the anticipated shortage. Because all parties involved in the transition to the AVF agreed that a shortage in medical professionals would develop rapidly upon expiration of induction authority that subject received more prompt attention than did the reserve components. Anticipated reserve manning problems received little more than lip service in the early days of the transition and only piecemeal attention thereafter.

Medical Personnel

Despite evidence that as many as half of the junior officers (lieutenants and captains) on active duty at the peak of the Vietnam conflict considered themselves draft-motivated volunteers and that enrollment in Reserve Officer Training Corps (ROTC) programs would decline after the end of inductions, the PROVIDE study group anticipated no significant problems in the general area of officer procurement in an all-volunteer environment. The Gates Commission also expressed confidence that the end of the draft would not significantly affect officer procurement. It did recommend increasing the number of full scholarships available to ROTC cadets "as a way of attracting applicants not likely to enter the program without them—especially those whose skills or aptitudes are in short supply in the military." The commission also believed that higher entry pay, proposed for officers as well as enlisted personnel, would prove sufficient to offset the loss of draft pressure. The Department of Defense Project Volunteer committee concurred with the view that officer procurement would "be somewhat easier than recruiting the enlisted force," and included a request to increase ROTC scholarships and subsistence payments to both scholarship and non-scholarship ROTC cadets as part of the first Project Volunteer budget. Congress approved both requests.[1]

The Army's experience with officer procurement during the transition generally ratified the optimism of the early studies. Enrollment in ROTC programs, which constituted the Army's largest source of new officers, declined initially after the end of induction authority but turned upward in 1974. The decline did not adversely affect Army officer procurement because the simultaneous reduction in the strength of the Army following the end of operations in Vietnam necessitated not only a cut in overall officer strength but a decrease in the number of new officers commissioned. Indeed, the requirement to reduce the number of officers on active duty to authorized levels dictated that the Army commission fewer new lieutenants than actually needed in fiscal years 1973, 1974, and 1975 at the same time as it involuntarily released 4,900 reserve component captains and majors from active duty. The Army initially planned to commission slightly more than 13,000 officers in 1973. Pressures to reduce commissioned strength reduced that figure by some 1,200 in 1973 and an additional 2,400 the following year. In 1975 the Army commissioned only 9,224 officers, the lowest number since the end of World War II. Thus, at no time during the transition to the AVF did the supply of officers become a problem.[2]

If the Army encountered few if any problems acquiring the majority of the officers it needed during the transition from the draft to the all-volunteer force, the same cannot be said for that group of officers who made up the service's corps of medical specialists, particularly medical doctors and dentists. All three studies of the feasibility of an all-volunteer force agreed that the services would experience difficulty attracting enough medical professionals to provide health care even to the smaller post-Vietnam forces that were anticipated. The PROVIDE study group stated bluntly, "Without the draft, the Army could not meet its manpower requirements for physicians and dentists." The Gates Commission agreed. The commission found that between 1966 and 1970, 60 percent of all medical school graduates entered the Army forces. "All but a handful enter because of the threat of being drafted." Subsequent studies by the assistant secretary of defense for health and environment revealed that only one-sixth of serving physicians could be considered true volunteers. Another sixth entered the services out of obligations for government-supported education or training programs. The remaining two-thirds of the armed forces' medical doctors came into the respective services through direct induction or under the provisions of the draft-deferred "Berry Plan" which permitted selected doctors to postpone obligated service until the end of specialty training. Since draftees and Berry Plan doctors served only two years, the services lost approximately one-third of their physicians annually.[3]

At the beginning of the transition to the all-volunteer force, the commissioned strength of the Army Medical Department, which included medical, dental, and veterinary doctors, nurses, and medical specialist and service officers, stood at just under 20,000, approximately 6,000 of whom were medical doctors. The overall strength of the Medical Department and the number of physicians could be expected to decline with the rest of the Army as it phased out of Vietnam. Indeed, by the end of June 1974 the authorized strength dropped to 16,122 and 4,302, respectively.[4] However, the anticipated decline in requirements promised little respite for the Army, for even as the number of active duty personnel declined, demographic projections indicated that the number of active duty family members, retirees, and their family members eligible for health care in Army facilities would grow. Furthermore, the United States was experiencing an overall shortage of health care personnel which would make competition for the services of physicians and other medical professionals keen. Without the draft to assure a steady supply of physicians, the Army and other services needed new ways to attract such personnel.[5]

The PROVIDE Group, the Gates Commission, and the Project Volunteer committee all recommended the development of new incentives to attract physicians and dentists into the armed forces. The Army study group also urged the establishment of a national medical school similar to the military academies to prepare career-minded individuals for service as military doctors. The Gates Commission and the Project Volunteer Committee expressed interest in the concept of a uniformed service academy of health sciences but recommended further study. The Defense Department did not include the proposal in its first Project Volunteer budget request. The services and the Department of Defense considered the scholarship concept crucial because scholarships, once authorized, could be offered immediately to students at all levels of medical training and would stimulate a more immediate flow of physicians into the military.[6]

The idea of a national academy for medical doctors had existed since 1947, but little had even been accomplished. However, F. Edward Hebert, the autocratic chairman of the House Armed Services Committee, personally supported the concept and insisted that it be included in a legislative package with the scholarships. The Uniformed Services Health Professions Revitalization Act of 1972, passed in September of that year, thus included provision for such an institution, although funding still depended on congressional largess at some later date.

Under the scholarship program developed by Congress, students received full tuition and fees plus a monthly allowance of $400. The Army received 1,850 of the 5,000 scholarships created and began awarding them in January 1973. By June 1974 the Army had 1,346 students participating in the program, and that summer 532 scholarship recipients graduated and entered the Army Medical Department. The Berry Plan continued to provide the largest number of medical professionals to the Army through fiscal year 1976. However, by the following year the supply of medical trainees deferred from induction prior to the expiration of the draft but still obligated to serve was exhausted. Long-term shortages of general practitioners and some specialists were expected until graduates of the Uniformed Services University of Health Sciences became available in 1981.[7]

Health Care

Simultaneously while the services sought ways to attract volunteer medical personnel, they developed means to stretch their existing resources further. The Gates Commission had recommended the civilianization of some medical activities to reduce the work load of military physicians. The services and Department of Defense opposed this idea vigorously. The Army argued that civilianization of military hospitals would "eliminate an essential resource for the training of medical officers, dental officers, military nurses, MSC officers and enlisted medical personnel in one of the necessary elements of operational military medicine—namely, patient care." The Army also doubted that civilianized military hospitals in remote areas could attract the right mix of specialists. To convert only those hospitals located at desirable military installations to civilian operations, on the other hand, would mean relegating the remaining military-staffed facilities to the less appealing locations with obvious results to the retention of the career personnel assigned there.[8]

The Defense Department's alternative to the civilianization of military health care was to seek ways to maximize the efficiency of its existing force of medical professionals by substituting physician assistants and nurse extenders for doctors, relieving doctors from management and clerical responsibilities, and replacing the services' aging health facilities with modern efficient plants. The Project Volunteer committee also proposed reducing the patient load of military physicians by encouraging family members of active duty personnel to seek health care from civilian sources through liberalized procedures authorizing such alternative care. Families qualifying for health care in civilian facilities were reimbursed for the costs of care received under the Civilian Health and Medical Program of the Uniformed Services (CHAMPUS). But the rising cost of health care in the United States, a regular feature of the economic inflation in the 1970s, frustrated the services' effort to give families a choice between civilian and military health care. Congress, concerned about the increased costs of the CHAMPUS program, tightened restrictions on eligibility for civilian health care and limited or terminated payments for certain treatments previously authorized by the program. The action effectively forced more people into the military health care facilities.[9]

Improving physician efficiency by providing modern medical facilities promised to be a major undertaking for all the services. Each developed a massive five-year plan to modernize their health care plants, which the Department of Defense endorsed promptly. But the construction and renovation necessary to complete such an undertaking could not be completed in time to relieve physician shortages expected in the immediate transition years. The surgeon general of the Army estimated that the Army Medical Department required approximately $170 million per year for its program. To cope with short-term deficits, the Army accelerated plans to replace doctors with physician assistants and nurse extenders. The Army adopted both of these programs from the civilian medical community which already was experiencing a doctor shortage. The former involved offering specialized training to senior enlisted medical corpsmen after which they would perform paraprofessional duties previously restricted to physicians. All the services developed physician assistant programs.

The Army's program involved twelve months of classroom and bedside instruction followed by six months of supervised clinical training. Its physician assistants were commissioned as warrant officers and were to be used to replace doctors in maneuver battalions and troop clinics. The Army led the other services in expanding the duties of its professional nurses by embarking on nurse practitioner programs in the OB-Gyn, pediatric medicine, anesthetist, ambulatory care, intensive care, public health, and psychiatric and mental health fields.[10]

Replacing physicians with nurse practitioners or clinicians made good sense on two counts. First, the expansion of nursing practice in the Army brought the professional activities of the Army Nurse Corps more in line with trends in the larger medical community. Second, and of more immediate importance given the situation facing the service, the Nurse Corps was one of the few areas relatively untouched by the end of the draft in terms of its effect on supply of qualified personnel. Indeed the Army Nurse Corps filled its annual requirements throughout the period despite the curtailment of two of its more attractive incentive programs and an increase in entry standards. The Army Student Nurse Program and Walter Reed Army Institute of Nursing were terminated in 1975 and 1976, respectively, for budgetary reasons; the last graduates from those programs entered the Army in 1977 and 1978. Although gradually the ANC began to receive many of its accessions through ROTC, which opened to women in 1974, most Army nurses received their commissions by direct appointment. In 1976 the Army required all applicants for ANC active duty to possess a baccalaureate degree in nursing. Yet, despite the rising standards, the ANC continued to met its accession quotas without undue difficulty.[11]

The long-range programs to increase physician efficiency and stretch the supply of doctors with extenders could only slightly ameliorate the overall shortage of medical doctors in the immediate years of the transition to the all-volunteer force. Too few serving doctors expressed a willingness to stay on beyond their initial service obligation. The major obstacle to physician retention according to all studies that examined the issue was the significant difference between the pay received by medical officers and their civilian counterparts. The Gates Commission, for example, found the gap between the pay of civilian and military physicians so great that it doubted anything short of "substantial" changes in the "pecuniary rewards" offered to military doctors would suffice to increase voluntary retention. Military doctors with more than eight years' service already received continuation pay, and doctors who served beyond the two-year obligation, mostly draftees and Berry Plan physicians, received $150 per month more. The Gates Commission proposed to increase the schedule of physicians' pay beginning in the third year of service annually until the eighth year when it would reach $1,050 a month.[12]

The Department of Defense incorporated the concept of special pay for doctors into its legislative proposal, entitled the Uniformed Services Special Pay Act, which Senator Gordon L. Allott of Colorado introduced in March 1972. The measure also contained provisions for enlistment and reenlistment bonuses that proved controversial with members of Congress. The bill languished for over a year and congressional inaction on the subject contributed to complaints, such as those of the Joint Chiefs of Staff cited earlier, that the legislative branch was urging the services to achieve an all-volunteer force without giving them the wherewithal to accomplish the mission. Secretary of the Army Callaway made early action on the Uniformed Services Special Pay Act one of his top priorities when he spoke with congressmen during the difficult recruiting period between June and October 1973. In November 1973 the Defense Department asked Senator Stennis to separate the troublesome enlistment and reenlistment bonus provisions from the doctors' pay portion of the bill and conduct separate hearings on each. Stennis agreed, and the legislative logjam was broken. The subsequent Uniformed Services Variable Incentive Pay Act for Physicians cleared Congress in May 1974.

With the enactment of that law the final hurdle to providing sufficient military doctors for the all-volunteer force was cleared, and Department of Defense spokesmen expressed guarded optimism that a shortage of doctors would be avoided. Nevertheless, the Army continued to experience a deficit. The same budgetary and personnel constraints that led to the curtailment of the Army Student Nurse Program led to the discontinuation of all active duty medical training programs in fiscal year 1975. Thereafter a major source of military doctors became direct appointments. Although the Army had many volunteers for its uniformed medical officer positions, too often the volunteers were foreign medical graduates who failed to meet the Army's standards. Despite a reduction in the authorized strengths of its Medical and Dental Corps the Army continued to experience shortages of doctors and dentists throughout the 1970s.[13] The problem was not really close to being resolved until the establishment of the Uniformed Services University of Health Sciences.

Notes

[1] PROVIDE, Vol II, pp. 5-4–5-8; Gates Commission Report, pp. 67–78; Report of Project Volunteer Committee, op. cit., p. 6; Lee and Parker, *Ending the Draft*, pp. 344–48.

[2] Annual Historical Summaries of the ODCSPER for FY 73, 74, 75, pp. 33– 41, 14–17, 6–9 respectively. For a summary of officer procurement in the other services during the transition, see Lee and Parker, *Ending the Draft*, pp. 348–50.

[3] PROVIDE, Vol. II, p. 13-6; Gates Report, pp. 85, 88; Office of the Assistant Secretary of Defense (Health and Environment), Health Personnel All- Volunteer Task Force Report, Phase I (1 Apr 73), p. 8.

[4] Annual Report of the Surgeon General, U.S. Army, Fiscal Years 1971 and 1974, pp. 70 and 19 respectively. Hereafter TSG, FY 71.

[5] The PROVIDE Study Group estimated that, given the growth of the U.S. population, the estimated number of physicians graduated from the nation's medical and osteopathic schools would be insufficient to maintain the existing ratio of 149 physicians to 100,000 population. A similar decline in the ratio of dentists-to-population also appeared certain. See PROVIDE, Vol. II, pp. 13-1 to 13-2.

[6] PROVIDE, Vol. II, pp. 13–19 to 13–20; Gates Report, p. 91; Project Volunteer Report, p. 19; Lee and Parker, *Ending the Draft*, pp. 330–32.

[7] Lee and Parker, op. cit.; TSG FY 74, pp. 20–27, and FY 75, pp. 15-22.

[8] Gates Report, pp. 89–90; ODCSPER Analysis of the Gates Commission Report, op. cit., p. 8-2.

[9] Project Volunteer Report, p. 20; TSG, FY 75, pp. 10–12.

[10] TSG, FY 73, pp. 84–85; Capt. Gary A. Guimond, USAF, "That More May Be Healed," *The Retired Officer*, 28, no. 4 (April 1972): 30–33; Health Personnel All-Volunteer Task Force Report, Phase I, op. cit., pp. 159–71.

[11] See Mary E. V. Frank, and Robert V. Piemonte, "The Army Nurse Corps: A Decade of Change, 1974–1984," *American Journal of Nursing* 85, no. 8 (September 1985): 985–88.

[12] Gates Report, pp. 91–93.

[13] DCSPER Information Paper for the SA, sub: Uniformed Services Special Pay Act (USSPA), 25 Sep 73; Memo, ASA(M&RA) for SA, 3 Dec 73, sub: Volunteer Army Actions, OSA file 202.10, RG 335; TSG, FY 72, p. 143; *DAHSUM*, FY 74, pp. 55–56; FY 75, p. 42; FY 77, pp. 48–50; FY 79, pp. 59–61; Lee and Parker, *Ending the Draft*, pp. 334–36.

CHAPTER XVII

Unfinished Business
The Reserve Components

The reserve components of the Army, comprising the United States Army Reserve and the Army National Guard, consisted of approximately 550,000 men on paid drill status in organized units in 1969. These units constituted the "Selected Reserve" that was designed to supplement the active forces of the Army as needed in an emergency. Reservists and guardsmen not in units or on paid drill status but subject to recall by Congress to serve as individual replacements made up the "Ready Reserve." The Army called its Ready Reserves the Individual Ready Reserve (IRR).

During the draft years most inductees spent two years on active duty and the balance of their six-year military service obligation in the Army Reserve or National Guard. Volunteers who spent less than six years on active duty also completed the balance of their total enlistment agreement in one of the reserve components. Men who did not serve in a reserve unit were assigned to the IRR (the National Guard equivalent of the IRR was the Inactive National Guard or ING). They did not drill or receive reserve pay, but they were subject to recall in a national emergency and, on paper, constituted a formidable pool of pretrained replacements. Furthermore, because the Vietnam era draft resulted in a high annual turnover of enlisted men and because many of those leaving the Army with a reserve obligation did not drill in Army Reserve or National Guard units, the size of the IRR swelled to 1.6 million by mid-1973. For this reason the IRR received virtually no attention during the debate over ending the draft or in the immediate years following the end of inductions. Indeed, it was not until the late 1970s that the size of the IRR came to the attention of defense policymakers. The little attention, discussion, and resulting programs affecting the reserve components that did occur during the transition to the all-volunteer force focused on the selected reserves.[1]

Policy and Planning

Although the Army and the Department of Defense recognized that the reserve components comprised an important link in the national security chain, they relegated them to a low priority status largely because of budgetary constraints. Policy analysts concluded that the potential problems affecting manpower in the reserves would lag behind those expected in the active force. Policymakers thus deferred dealing with the reserves and concentrated on making the volunteer concept work in the active Army, hoping that they would have time to return to the reserves later. Congress sustained this approach despite the fact that the reserve components employed influential lobby organizations in the states and on Capitol Hill and had powerful allies on the key congressional committees.

With some relatively minor exceptions, President Lyndon Johnson had not called the reserves to active duty during the Vietnam War, believing such a move would destroy his social programs and ultimately widen the conflict.[2] But the decision to forgo large-scale use of the reserve components in Vietnam meant an expansion of the active Army and diversion of equipment intended for Reserve and National Guard units to the active component. At the same time, once the decision had been made not to mobilize but to use the draft to expand the Army, large numbers of draft-eligible men began volunteering for the Guard and Reserve. Service in the reserve components resulted in exemption from the draft. As a result, the reserve components began to resemble a large holding force whose precise military value was extremely problematic. As early as 1966 the Department of Defense estimated that 71 percent of the volunteers for the selected reserves were draft motivated; in 1968 Army National Guard units reported waiting lists totaling 100,000; and in 1970 the National Guard Association reported that the proportion of draft-motivated volunteers in some units had reached 90 percent.[3]

By the end of the Vietnam War the reserve components were, in the words of one historian, in a state of "disrepair and disarray." Units had been stripped of equipment needed for the war, and the reservists and guardsmen themselves were frequently viewed as draft evaders.[4] The reserve components faced an uncertain future in the post-Vietnam period. Their roles needed clarification, their units needed modern equipment, and, faced with an end to conscription, they had to look for new sources of manpower. Opinions varied on precisely how the end of the war and the end of the draft would affect Reserve and National Guard enlistments and how best to provide for a smooth transition to the all-volunteer system.

The Army's Project PROVIDE study group predicted that the end of the draft would affect the quality and quantity of reserve components enlistments differently than those of the active Army. In the absence of a draft the length of the average active duty enlistment would increase, while the average length of reserve enlistments would decline. In the draft era conscripts served for two years on active duty and completed the remainder of their six-year military service obligation in the Ready Reserve. Reserve component volunteers normally served six months on active duty for training followed by five-and-a-half years in the selected reserves. The PROVIDE study group speculated that the length of an initial enlistment in the selected reserve probably would have to be reduced to three years. Thus, while the end of conscription would reduce enlisted personnel turbulence in the active Army, it would increase the problem in the reserve components. Butler's study group also calculated that in the absence of draft pressure the strength of the reserve components would drop "60 percent by 1975 unless enlistment is stimulated through increased Reserve incentives and benefits." Such measures might include offering tuition assistance to reservists enrolled in accredited schools, enlistment and reenlistment bonuses, extension of commissary and exchange privileges, housing allowances, servicemen's life insurance, and other benefits to reservists during drill periods and a reduction in the eligibility age for retirement benefits from 60 to 50.[5]

The reserve components detailed two full-time representatives to the PROVIDE study group. Study group working papers and documents from the National Guard Bureau and Office of the Chief of Army Reserve suggest that some early disagreement occurred over reserve obligations and recruiting options under consideration. One proposal considered by the PROVIDE group involved eliminating any reserve obligation for active duty volunteers. The study group reasoned that the presence of an obligation to serve even in the Individual Ready Reserve following active duty service might serve to deter youths from volunteering in a zero-draft environment. The chief of the National Guard Bureau objected to the proposal to eliminate the reserve service obligation for volunteers specifically because such a move would "quickly eliminate mobilization fillers from the Individual Ready Reserve." The chief of the Army Reserve agreed that without the draft or a residual reserve service obligation for active duty volunteers the IRR would be diminished to a career base of approximately 20,000 officers and 2,000 enlisted men. The proposal was dropped. PROVIDE study group members also worried that more active recruiting by the reserve components in an all-volunteer environment would cut into the active Army's recruiting market. Reserve component studies assured the active duty recruiters that U.S. Army Reserve and Army National Guard recruiters posed no such threat.[6]

The Gates Commission also examined the reserve components in an all-volunteer environment, but found less cause for concern. The commission asserted that 110,000 paid drill spaces could be safely eliminated from the selected reserves, thereby substantially reducing the recruiting requirement for the Army Reserve and National Guard. The reduction was warranted on two grounds, according to the commission. First, the Vietnam experience proved that neither the government nor the public supported large reserve call-ups for ambiguous purposes. Second, fewer reservists would be needed to back up the smaller active military establishment contemplated after the end of involvement in Vietnam. Given such a reduced requirement, the commission proceeded to assert that its proposed pay increase for the active forces, which automatically applied to reservists in paid drill status, would be sufficient to attract enough volunteers to the reserve components. The commission also proposed a 6 percent increase in drill pay for reservists serving beyond six years to stimulate reenlistments. As the transition to an all-volunteer reserve force proceeded, the presence of true volunteers in the reserve ranks combined with the incentive of higher drill pay would be sufficient to increase the reenlistment rate by 80 percent.

The commission also addressed fears that the pool of civilians anxious to enlist in reserve units would dry up following the end of the draft. Reports that volunteerism for the reserves was largely draft-motivated were exaggerated, the commission reported. It presented data showing that draft motivation was highest among volunteers with college educations. High school graduates, dropouts, and youths eighteen years old or younger were not as highly motivated to enlist by the draft as were older, more educated reserve enlistees. Furthermore, the commission stated, the reserves had become accustomed to an "educationally rich force" that was an unnecessary luxury. "If recruitment is focused on a younger, less well-educated group, the flow of volunteers will be substantially larger than is implied by the draft motivation of the present force."[7] The commission did not address the IRR.

The Army challenged the Gates Commission's assumptions, assertions, and recommendations regarding the reserve components on virtually every point. The Office of the Deputy Chief of Staff for Personnel prepared a detailed analysis of the commission report. The analysis, which General Kerwin made required reading for all of his subordinates, challenged the assumption that the selected reserve could be cut by 110,000 drill spaces. The Army would need more, not fewer, reserve units in the peacetime environment as the active force shrank. That the commission failed even to address the Individual Ready Reserve especially vexed the Army analysts, although as the transition proceeded they paid scant attention to the subject themselves. Both the DCSPER review and Secretary of the Army Resor considered that the omission indicated a fundamental lack of understanding of the relationship of the reserves to the active forces. Finally, both the Army staff analysts and Resor's manpower experts questioned the commission's assumptions that increases in pay alone would assure sufficient reserve volunteers in the absence of draft pressure. The study prepared by Kerwin's staff doubted the optimistic predictions made by the commission concerning reserve non–prior-service volunteers, the ability of the Army Reserve and National Guard to recruit active service separatees, and the prediction that reenlistments in the reserves would increase following the transition to a purely volunteer system. The Army staff analysis reasserted the need for a package to build and maintain an effective reserve force in an all-volunteer environment.[8]

The Department of Defense concurred in the Army's assessment of the Gates Commission report on the prospects of the reserve components in a zero-draft situation. In his comments on the report to President Nixon, Secretary of Defense Laird singled out the commission's exclusive reliance on pay increases to maintain reserve component "strength and readiness." Laird echoed the view that the reserves would take on greater importance in peacetime following the end of the draft. Assistant Secretary of Defense Roger Kelley's Project Volunteer committee drew up the final Defense Department recommendations on the subject, which Laird endorsed. The Project Volunteer report included proposals gleaned from the PROVIDE study including a reduction of reserve retirement eligibility to age 50, extension of medical care and servicemen's group life insurance to reservists on active duty for periods less than thirty days' duration, expanded educational and training programs, and, perhaps most significant, consideration of some form of a reserve draft in the event that other measures failed to maintain an adequate reserve component for the respective services.[9]

Resources

Although the Army and the Defense Department agreed that the reserve components faced potentially serious problems in making the transition to an all-volunteer environment, neither provided much in the way of resources to meet those problems. Early in the planning stage of the first Project Volunteer budget for fiscal year 1972, Secretary Kelley included $40 million for unspecified Guard and Reserve incentives. Money for reserve component volunteer force initiatives quickly vanished as the size of the total authorization for Project Volunteer was cut in the Nixon administration's effort to reduce overall expenditures. Although the Army continued to worry about the strength and readiness of its reserve components, it did little else in terms of providing money for reserve recruiting or incentives. Sometime between April, when the Army and Defense Department formalized their critiques of the shortcomings of the Gates Commission recommendations on the reserves, and June 1970 the Army concluded that the reserve components would have to take a back seat to the active forces during the initial stages of the transition.

Evidence of this change is found in the chief of staff's response to a report on the Gates recommendations pertaining to the reserve components prepared at his request by an ad hoc committee of the Army Reserve Forces Policy Committee, an advisory body composed of Army Reserve and National Guard general officers. The committee report repeated the by then familiar list of shortcomings contained in the Gates report but concluded "that the concept of an All-Volunteer Army Reserve Force is feasible if sufficient time, money and other assets are made available." It recommended that the reserve components receive the "same realistic incentives" envisioned for the active force and a "fair and realistic share of the manpower and money involved" in recruiting an all-volunteer Army, and that the effort begin "without delay." Westmoreland considered the report unsatisfactory. He forwarded it to the secretary of the Army with the comment that the committee failed to address the "real problems of severe fiscal constraints" facing the Army. Clearly a decision had been made not to provide the reserve components with monetary resources to begin efforts to achieve the all-volunteer goal.[10]

Without any money to offer the reserve components, the Army fell back on urging the Reserve and National Guard to implement no-cost initiatives identified by the PROVIDE study in their units. Early in October 1970 Maj. Michael Urette from the All-Volunteer Army Division of the Office of the Deputy Chief of Staff for Personnel briefed the Army Reserve Forces Policy Committee on the progress the Army staff was making toward achieving the

AVF goal. He reminded the committee of the reduction in funds that limited the scope of the Army's efforts and proceeded to tell the Army Reserve and National Guard representatives that his office had identified nearly two hundred "improvement actions" that could be implemented by both reserve and active component units to enhance service attractiveness and recruiting with existing resources. Urette added that the Army planned to implement the actions as soon as they were staffed in order to keep ahead of "political pressures" that demanded an all-volunteer Army. He added, "if we don't take actions to meet this goal, we can foresee another Gates Commission which will direct the actions we will have to take." He added that the services were under great pressure to try everything to make the volunteer force work at little or no cost before going to Congress and asking for more money.[11]

Within days of Major Urette's briefing to the representatives of the reserve components, the orderly process he described was replaced as General Westmoreland appointed General Forsythe SAMVA and committed the Army to achieving the zero-draft goal on a priority basis. In his speech to the Association of the U.S. Army on 13 October 1970, Westmoreland acknowledged the critical role the reserve components played in the "One Army" concept and would play in the volunteer era the Army was entering. The reserve components would take on increased importance as the size of the active Army decreased, the chief of staff asserted. "We know that many in Army reserve components are motivated to enlist as an alternative to being inducted," he said. Thus a major problem facing the Army in the transition would be "to increase the number of volunteers in the Army Reserve and National Guard at the same time we increase volunteers in the Active Army." To do so required imagination and effort on the Army's part to make service in the active and reserve components attractive and to acquire money and popular support from Congress and the American people for that purpose.[12] But shortly thereafter the Army was reeling under the changes wrought by the "High Impact Actions" announced on 2 November and discussing further changes promised by Forsythe's SAMVA operation. Almost all of the initial effort and money thus went to the active Army, and the reserve components continued to receive a low priority.

Forsythe's SAMVA staff identified enlistments for the active Army's combat arms elements as the crucial testing ground for the all-volunteer force and developed the experimental phase of the Modern Volunteer Army Program accordingly. In December 1970, less than two months after Forsythe took over as the project manager for the volunteer Army, Lt. Col. Jack Butler briefed the Army Reserve Forces Policy Committee on the new scheme and how it would affect the reserve components. Butler summarized the Modern Volunteer Army Program and Project VOLAR, which were still in the drafting stage, and explained how each aimed at increasing enlistments and retention primarily in the combat arms. He spoke of plans to increase the recruiting force and experiment with paid radio and television recruit advertising, of proficiency pay for the combat arms and an end to KP, of privacy in the barracks and changes in basic training. After about twenty minutes Butler paused. "By this time, Gentlemen, you have noticed we have not mentioned the Reserves," he said. He acknowledged that the reserve components faced serious problems, but "bluntly speaking," asserted that "there is not enough money to do everything, so in ordering our priorities we have placed primary emphasis on the active army."

Butler explained that the decision not to provide MVF funds for the reserve components beyond a small amount for increased advertising in fiscal year 1972 was based on analysis that the end of the draft would affect the active Army sooner than the reserve components. The Office of Reserve Components, headed by Lt. Gen. William R. Peers, was working closely with SAMVA and had developed a three-phase program to increase recruiting and retention in the reserves beginning in July 1971. Key to this effort were the no-cost initiatives to attract active force separatees to enlist in Army Reserve or National Guard units and to encourage quality reservists to reenlist. Butler emphasized the experimental nature of Peers' program. "We want to avoid crashing into programs which later prove to be not only costly but non-productive," he said. "Since we have some time before a critical state in the reserve components is reached, we are moving with deliberate speed."[13]

The Army Reserve and National Guard generals who made up the committee gave Butler mixed reviews. Most soberly agreed that the combat arms of the active force faced serious and immediate manning problems, but they questioned his assertion that the reserve components' personnel shortages would not begin at the same time and need funding too. Maj. Gen. Leonard Holland, adjutant general of the Rhode Island National Guard, accused the active force of speaking "with forked tongue here." Everybody paid lip service to the One-Army concept, but when it came to handing out money the active component always came first.

Maj. Gen. Stuart Menist, commander of the 91st Division (Training) of the Army Reserve and chairman of the committee, recalled the committee's report of 25 May to Westmoreland commenting on the recommendations of the Gates Commission. Menist wanted to know the fate of that portion of the report to the chief of staff containing the committee's recommendations for initiatives considered necessary to achieve an all-volunteer Army reserve component and the recommendation that they be instituted at once. He accused the Army staff of ignoring the committee. Menist also demanded that Butler explain his remark that funding for reserve programs could be delayed because the impact of the end of the draft would not hit them as soon as the active force.

Butler replied that the reserve components themselves had challenged the PROVIDE group's figures that 80 to 90 percent of drill-pay status reservists were draft motivated. He cited the National Guard's own analysis that projected a retention of 66 percent despite a decline in enlistments. Faced with conflicting figures, Butler said, SAMVA decided to embark on a no-cost program for the reserves until the true magnitude of the problem became clearer. He told Menist that he was well aware of the committee's recommendations. "We would love to go with these programs now, if only in the test phase," but there just was not enough money to go around. At the moment the secretary of the Army considered the active Army a higher priority than the reserve components.

Maj. Gen. Donnelly Bolton, the representative of the deputy chief of staff for operations and plans, tried to come to Butler's rescue. The problem, Bolton said, had to do with allocating resources; the issue was not reserve components versus active force. "If we had the Surgeon General and the Signal Officer and the Ordnance people sitting around here, and they see all this dough going to the combat arms, they are asking the same question as you are." Perhaps so, replied Maj. Gen. Horace B. Hanson, Jr., commander of the 87th Maneuver Area Command of the Army Reserve, but announcing that the reserve components were receiving a lower priority and virtually no money to achieve the all-volunteer force would not sit well with the voting rank and file of the Guard and Reserve. "If you go away from the One-Army concept and you let this impact hit your communities, which will reflect back on your congressmen, you are in serious trouble," he told Butler. Menist agreed. He asked Butler to go back to General Forsythe and explain the committee's concern and furthermore promised to discuss the matter with the secretary of the Army himself.[14]

Butler did convey the committee's attitude to General Forsythe, and at the next meeting, in February 1971, Col. Robert M. Montague, Jr., Forsythe's deputy, appeared to mend fences. Montague told the committee that he would like to be able to report that because of Butler's exchange with them in December 1970 Forsythe had reviewed the Modern Volunteer Army Program and found funds for reserve component initiatives. Unfortunately, Montague continued, he could not say that. All the money for the fiscal year 1971 phase of the MVA Program was coming "out of the Army's hide." Fiscal year 1972 would be equally austere; the reserve components could expect approximately $1 million for advertising out of the $727 million budget for the entire Army. Montague hastened to add that most of that amount, approximately $500 million, would be absorbed by pay raises for the Guard and Reserve as well as for the active Army. He offered some hope for money in fiscal year 1973. The budget for that year "is still wide open," he said, and hinted that the request would include funds for reserve components enlistment and reenlistment bonuses.[15]

A month later SAMVA circulated its draft Master Program for the Modern Volunteer Army. On the subject of the reserve components, the master program asserted adherence to the One-Army concept. Many of the initiatives outlined for testing in the active forces would have application in the reserves, but the initial effort would concentrate on determining what worked to increase enlistments and retention in the former. Once the impact of the end of the draft reached the reserves, "it will be necessary to provide additional incentives and benefits to assure adequate accessions for the reserve components." But, according to the master plan, "the impact will not be felt until a zero-draft posture is achieved." Thus no money would be provided for the reserve components in FY 1971 and only the previously mentioned $1 million for advertising would be allocated in FY 1972. The statements represented formal admission that the reserve components had been relegated to a second-class status in the effort to achieve an all-volunteer Army.[16]

When Roger Kelley presented the administration's initial package for the transition to the all-volunteer force to Congress in February 1971, he reflected the Army and other services' position that actions and expenditures on behalf of the reserve components could wait. He assured the Senate Armed Services Committee that the Guard and Reserve would meet their manpower requirements in FY 1972 and promised to return with legislative proposals when they were needed. Despite expressions of concern by the official organs of the reserve components and the presence of congressmen sympathetic to Guard and Reserve issues on the key committees of both houses, Congress went along with the administration.[17]

Reserve Recruiting

Optimistic predictions that the reserve components would not feel the effects of declining draft pressure quickly proved incorrect during fiscal year 1972. Waiting lines of youths anxious to join the Guard and Reserve dwindled with the inauguration of the lottery draft and the reduction of inductions that accompanied the withdrawal from Vietnam and reduction of the active forces. Paid drill strength of Army Reserve units fell nearly 24,000 in two years beginning in July 1971. Enlisted losses exceeded gains by over 17,000 in the Army National Guard in fiscal year 1972 when 5,572 fewer men enlisted directly from civilian life compared to fiscal year 1971. The chief of the National Guard Bureau reported that waiting lists for Army National Guard units "became virtually nonexistent" during the last quarter of fiscal year 1972.[18]

Prior to the advent of the all-volunteer force, responsibility for recruiting and retention in the Guard and Reserve had rested with the individual unit commander. The key offices that directed reserve component affairs, the Office of the Chief of Army Reserve and the National Guard Bureau, established standards and issued guidance, but paid little attention to personnel matters given the buyer's market all units enjoyed. The Personnel Division of the Office of the Chief of the Army Reserve did not even have a recruiting and retention branch until 1972. Although both reserve component offices quickly established programs to affiliate their recruiters with USAREC and sought guidance and assistance from the Army's professional recruiters, neither established organizations analogous to the active Army's Recruiting Command.

The reserve components recruiting program for the volunteer era evolved over approximately a two-year period. The process was heavily influenced by the tradition of decentralization and lack of monetary resources available to Reserve and Guard recruiters. Each component designated one officer and two noncommissioned officers in each unit responsible for recruiting. These individuals received extra drill periods for that purpose and worked closely with local active Army recruiters. The Army National Guard developed a nonresident correspondence course on recruiting and retention, and by the end of June 1972 more than 3,000 guardsmen had enrolled in the program. The Army Reserve followed suit. Completion of the nonresident course led to attendance at a one-week course for reserve component recruiters conducted by the Adjutant General's School at Fort Benjamin Harrison, Indiana. Eventually over 7,000 reservists and guardsmen passed through the course. Both components created positions for full-time civilian recruiting and retention technicians. In May 1972 a committee representing the National Guard, the Army Reserve, the U.S. Army Recruiting Command, the chief of the Office of Reserve Components, the Office of the Deputy Chief of Staff for Personnel, and the Continental Army Command established formal guidelines for coordinating reserve component recruiting efforts.[19]

Following the active Army's lead the Guard quickly expanded enlistment opportunities for women and began actively to seek minority volunteers. The Army National Guard identified one-quarter of its authorized strength positions as available for women. In the first full year of recruiting non–prior-service women the Guard exceeded its modest goal of 400 by 118 volunteers. The Army Reserve also recognized the benefits of substituting women for men. In 1972 the Army Reserve carried only 483 women on the rolls of its units; two years later the figure jumped to nearly 7,000.[20] Both components also began to seek volunteers from minority groups. During the Vietnam War, when the Guard and Reserve enjoyed long waiting lines of high school graduates and college men, minorities found entry into the reserve components difficult. The impression that racial discrimination persisted in the reserves discouraged qualified blacks from enlisting and reinforced the de facto segregation of the reserve components. In the late 1960s the Guard and Reserve came under internal pressure from the Department of Defense to actively seek minority enlistments in an effort to reduce racial tensions in the country.[21]

Westmoreland and Resor spoke on the issue of race relations in the Army on numerous occasions. Resor made it the basis of his address to the annual meeting of the Association of the U.S. Army in October 1970. In December of that year he made what was perhaps the most direct charge to the reserve components on the subject when he met with the Army Reserve Forces Policy Committee and told it bluntly, "Participation of minority groups in the reserve components has ... been disappointing." He randomly listed some figures. The Alabama National Guard, 15,000 strong, contained but 21 blacks. Army Reserve units in New York, where blacks constituted 9.3 percent of the population, included only 1.9 percent blacks in their ranks. "I think it is time for us to use our best imagination to see if we can't do something to improve the situation," he concluded.[22]

Under pressure to increase their minority content and faced with a rapidly declining supply of draft-motivated volunteers of any race, the reserve components finally launched recruiting drives aimed at achieving representation in their units proportionate to the population of the community. In fiscal year 1973 the number of blacks in Army Reserve units jumped from approximately 7,000 to over 13,000. In the National Guard, black representation rose from 1.2 to 5.45 percent of assigned strength between the beginning of fiscal year 1972 and the end of fiscal year 1974.[23] As with the active force's opening its ranks to women, the reserve components' recruitment of women and minorities was driven by necessity, not altruism.

Increased non–prior-service enlistments in the Guard and Reserve by women and minorities in the transition years proved insufficient to offset the decline in draft-motivated enlistments by white males who had been the primary source of volunteers in the past. Deprived of sufficient funds to attack the problem with bonuses and other incentives, the Army turned to administrative solutions for the reserve components. Army studies of the reenlistment intentions of active duty soldiers revealed that personnel who had not indicated an inclination to reenlist within 100 days of their impending separation were unlikely to do so. They might, however, consider joining a reserve component unit rather than finishing their military service obligation in a nonpaying standby status in the IRR.

In August 1971 the Army thus began a test of the reserve components Active Army In-Service Recruiting Program at Fort Lewis, Washington, and Fort Knox, Kentucky. Army Reserve and National Guard counselors were assigned to each post where they discussed the options and benefits of service in drill-pay status units of the selected reserve with soldiers about to separate from active duty. The Army offered a sixty-day early separation to active duty soldiers who agreed to a one-year enlistment in the Guard or Reserve. The test proved extremely successful. In the first four months the reserve components counselors at Lewis and Knox secured 700 enlistments for National Guard units alone.

In January 1972 the Army expanded the In-Service Recruiting Program to all posts in the United States and Hawaii and Germany. Active duty soldiers were offered early releases of up to 179 days to join reserve units. By the end of March 25,000 men took advantage of the offer. The response proved so great that units in Europe suffered severe personnel shortages. The Army suspended the option for European-based soldiers and continued it in the United States but cut the early release provision back to sixty days. By the end of fiscal year 1972, 55,675 prior-service men had joined the reserve components under these provisions. The National Guard achieved 271 percent of its objectives under this program; the Army Reserve 203 percent of its goal. Nevertheless, both components ended the year understrength. The Guard finished the fiscal year at 96.9 percent of its authorized paid drill strength, and the Army Reserve finished at 90.5 percent.[24]

In a further effort to make up the shortages in Guard and Reserve strength, the Army began to press the Department of Defense to seek legislation authorizing incentives aimed at stimulating enlistments and encouraging reenlistments in the selected reserves. In March 1972 the Defense Department included requests for enlistment and reenlistment bonus authority for the reserve components as part of the Uniformed Services Special Pay Act. As previously noted, the bill languished in Congress until late 1973. In December 1973 Assistant Secretary of Defense for Manpower William K. Brehm withdrew the request for reserve bonuses from the final version of the bill. Brehm claimed that the manpower needs of the reserve components were uncertain. Furthermore, Congress remained divided over portions of the package, and the Department of Defense and the services wanted quick action on special pay for physicians. Once again the reserve components were relegated to a lower priority. When induction authority expired the reserve components remained without any significant incentive program.[25]

Still lacking tangible incentives to offer volunteers or encourage reenlistments in its reserve components, the Army focused its attention on enlarging and refining the In-Service Recruiting Program and developing new recruiting initiatives. In 1973, for example, National Guard and Army Reserve recruiting personnel were assigned to the Army's sixty-four main recruiting stations. These reserve recruiters contacted individuals who declined to enlist in the active Army in an effort to interest them in volunteering for a reserve component unit. In the first three months of the program they secured over 1,400 enlistments. Both the Guard and the Reserve also began experimenting with new enlistment options. Under one option, known as "3X3" and available only to high school graduates who scored in the upper three mental categories, prospective volunteers could choose to join a selected reserve unit for three years and revert to nonpay standby status for the remainder of their reserve contract period rather than commit themselves to six full years of paid drill status. A variation of this option was a "4X2" enlistment which involved four years of service in a unit followed by two in the IRR.[26]

At the same time the two reserve components of the Army placed command emphasis on recruiting and retention in an attempt to dramatize the importance of the issue and pressure unit commanders into spending more time on personnel procurement. In March 1973 the Director of the Army National Guard, Maj. Gen. LaVern Weber, told state adjutants general to meet their authorized strength or risk losing units. The National Guard Bureau already had asked six states to give up units to other states which had a proven record of exceeding strength requirements. In November Weber addressed a National Guard recruiting conference where he told recruiters not to count on incentives and exhorted them "to overcome the lack of incentives and concentrate on recruiting non-prior service Guardsmen." At the same conference the Adjutant General of Indiana, Brig. Gen. Alfred Ahern, told recruiters the secret of his state's success at exceeding its goal for the year by 1,250. Indiana had conducted a statewide campaign during the year in which successful unit commanders, not just units, were identified. Furthermore, Ahern said, he put out the word that unit commanders who met their recruiting goals got to keep their jobs. In February 1974 *The National Guardsman*, the official publication of the National Guard Association, began a monthly feature entitled "Recruiting Newsmakers" that recognized the accomplishments of Guard recruiters. Weber also launched an award program, "The Chief's 50," which recognized the top recruiter in each state. The National Guard recruiters who enlisted the most volunteers in a year from their states won a trip to Washington where they and their spouses were feted by Weber and the National Guard Association for a week.[27]

Both the National Guard and Army Reserve succeeded in maintaining their authorized strength through June 1974. In fact, boosted by major recruiting drives in the first months of the year, the Guard ended the period 8 percent over authorized strength and the Reserve 2 percent overstrength. Thus when he declared, "The volunteer Army is a success by every indicator," at his press conference on 1 July 1974, Secretary of the Army Callaway had no qualms about including the reserve components in his assessment.[28]

Indeed, the reserve components' non–prior-service recruiting efforts that year proved so successful that they also began to stress quality over quantity. At a semiannual recruiting conference held in March 1974 at New Orleans, representatives from both the Guard and the Reserve heard Army Guard Director General Weber express the Defense Department's official praise for their success to date. Weber went on to stress the need for greater attention to the quality of non–prior-service and in-service transfer recruits. Another spokesman told the recruiters, "The brush fire is over. We got the numbers needed, now we must regroup and seek quality." [29]

The reserve components achieved their goals in the first year without induction authority by successfully tapping previously unmined sources of recruits, specifically women, blacks, and active duty separatees. Volunteers from these new sources made up for the loss of draft-motivated volunteers. But several problems remained to confront the reserve components that Callaway avoided mentioning. The strength of the Individual Ready Reserve already had begun a sharp decline, and beginning in 1975, reserve component manpower analysts predicted, retention would plunge as the enlistment terms of Vietnam-era volunteers began to expire. The declining quality of new entrants threatened to complicate the latter problem further.

The combined strength of the IRR and its National Guard counterpart, the ING, peaked in 1973 at 1.6 million and plunged steadily through the 1970s. At the end of 1974 the Army reported the enlisted strength of the IRR at 463,762; a year later the figure was only 303,172. Three factors contributed to the decline. First, Vietnam-era draftees assigned to the IRR upon release from active duty were completing their military service obligation and dropping out. Second, because the active Army itself was getting smaller and enlistments in the active force were increasing in length, fewer soldiers passed from the all-volunteer Army to the Standby Reserve. Finally, the very success of the reserve component In-Service Recruiting Program, which encouraged active duty separatees to join selected reserve units, reduced the number of men passing into the IRR. To deal with the problem the Department of Defense proposed legislation extending the military service obligation of new volunteers to age twenty-eight, effectively lengthening their obligation from six to an average of nine years. Defense manpower analysts predicted that expanding the period of obligated reserve service would eliminate the IRR shortage by 1982.[30]

In 1974 the strength of the IRR and its ability to effectively contribute to the mobilization requirements of the total force remained very much an unaddressed academic problem. Despite official exhortations to achieve quality and quantity in reserve component recruitment, the prospects that the strength of the selected reserves could be maintained even without qualitative constraints also appeared to be an open question in mid-1974. Indeed, even as he urged reserve component recruiters to begin stressing quality in his New Orleans address of March 1974, General Weber warned them that they would soon face a "mass exodus" of draft-motivated volunteers. Weber had identified only half of the problem. The other half had to do with the quality of those reservists leaving units compared to that of those entering from the draft-free environment. During the years when reserve component units enjoyed waiting lists no one involved in Guard or Reserve recruiting had given the subject much thought. Regulations required units to take high school graduates ahead of nongraduates. The National Guard, for example, enlisted only 7 percent non–high school graduates in 1970. As a result of the former policy, the proportion of Mental Category IV recruits in the selected reserve units also was low during the draft years. But as waiting lists declined recruiters became less choosy. By 1974 the non–high school graduates constituted more than half of the Guard's recruits. *Table 5* graphically demonstrates the trend.

Table 5—ARMY NATIONAL GUARD NON–PRIOR-SERVICE ACCESSIONS

Fiscal Year	Category IV		Non–High School Graduates	
	Number	Percent	Number	Percent
1970	5,367	5	7,201	7
1971	3,199	6	2,021	4
1972	4,436	9	8,473	18
1973	4,471	16	9,294	34
1974	8,075	29	16,027	57

Source: Verbatim Transcript of Army Reserve Forces Policy Committee meeting of 12 September 1974, p. 136.

If, as predicted, Vietnam era reservists left the selected reserves without reenlisting and continued to be replaced by large numbers of volunteers lacking high school diplomas and scoring in the lowest acceptable mental category, the overall quality of the Guard and Reserve would erode in a matter of three to four years. But in 1974 personnel analysts in the Office of the Deputy Chief of Staff for Personnel had only identified the problem, and no real consensus on its extent had emerged. Indeed, according to Defense Department analysts, "the RC still have an excellent quality base in the overall enlisted grade struc-

THE RESERVE COMPONENTS

ture." Indeed, compared to the active Army, the reserves appeared better off in 1974. Only 11 percent of reserve component enlisted men lacked high school diplomas, compared to 27 percent in the active force. But Congress did not constrain reserve recruiters in 1974 as it did USAREC recruiters, and that year only 50 percent of those who joined the Guard and Reserve units combined were high school graduates, whereas Army recruiters accepted only 44 percent dropouts. Unlike the active Army Recruiting Command, the reserve components lacked an overall master quality plan for the future. No one knew what the qualitative requirements of the Guard and Reserve really were. Some analysts speculated that reserve units could get along with lower quality because reservists were assigned their jobs early and worked in familiar environments throughout their enlistment. Others speculated that the reserve components required a higher quality base because of infrequent and shorter training periods.[31] If the latter case proved true, the Army Reserve and National Guard possessed few tools to attract and retain quality in 1974.

By May 1974 only one substantive recommendation by the PROVIDE committee and successor studies on incentive needs for reserve component recruiting had been approved by Congress. Reserve recruiters lacked the ability to offer enlistment bonuses to prospective volunteers, and unit commanders could not entice skilled reservists to reenlist with reenlistment bonuses. The reserve components of the all-volunteer Army thus faced an uncertain future in 1974.[32]

Notes

[1] G. V. (Sonny) Montgomery, "Individual Ready Reserve: The Potential for Improvement," in *The Anthropo Factor in Warfare: Conscripts, Volunteers and Reservists* (Washington, D.C.: National Defense University Press, 1988), pp. 379–94.

[2] John D. Stuckey and Joseph H. Pistorius, "Mobilization for the Vietnam War: A Political and Military Catastrophe," *Parameters* 15, no. 1 (Spring 1985): 26–38. Johnson explains his decision in his memoirs; see Lyndon Johnson, *The Vantage Point: Perspectives of the Presidency, 1963–1969* (New York: Holt, Rinehart & Winston, 1971), pp. 145–53.

[3] Westmoreland, *Report of the Chief of Staff*, pp. 36–37; Lawrence M. Baskir and William A. Strauss, *Chance and Circumstances: The Draft, the War and the Vietnam Generation* (New York: Vintage Books, 1978), pp. 50–51.

[4] Richard B. Crossland and James T. Currie, *Twice the Soldier: A History of the United States Army Reserve, 1908–1983* (Washington, D.C.: Chief of Army Reserve, 1984), pp. 211–12.

[5] PROVIDE, 2, chap. 12, pp. 1–5, 7–14.

[6] CORC Memo, 15 May 69, sub: Information for PROVIDE Study Group, and CAR Memo, 22 May 69, sub: Input to Interim PROVIDE Report, Background Material.

[7] Gates Report, pp. 98–101, 106–09, 111–15.

[8] Ltr, Resor to Gates, 10 Jan 70, OSA file 202.10, RG 335, WNRC; ODCSPER Analysis of the Gates Commission Report, 3 Feb 70, file 327.02, All-Volunteer Army, HRC, CMH.

[9] Memo, Laird for Nixon, 11 Mar 70, sub: Future of the Draft, OSD file 340, RG 330, WNRC; Project Volunteer Report, draft of 29 Apr 70, OSD file 350, RG 330, WNRC.

[10] When, how, and who made the decision not to fund reserve component initiatives to achieve an AVF remains unclear. Money for reserve component initiatives disappeared from the first Project Volunteer budget so quickly that specific programs and funding levels were never clearly identified. Lee and Parker attribute this to "inter-service competition for funds for the Active Forces...." See *Ending the Draft*, p. 306. The Army Reserve Forces Policy Committee submitted its report to Westmoreland on 25 May 1970, and he passed it to Resor on 12 June with the comment that it was unrealistic. See Memo, Chairman ARFPC thru CofSA for SA, 25 May 70, sub: The Report of the President's Commission on an All-Volunteer Armed Force, w/3 Incl, and Memo, CofSA for SA, 12 Jun 70, sub: Army Reserve Forces Policy Committee Report, CMH Files.

[11] Verbatim Transcript of Army Reserve Forces Policy Committee meeting, 2 Oct 70, pp. 147–73, ARFPC file, RG 319, WNRC.

[12] Address by Westmoreland to AUSA Conference, 13 Oct 70, Speech files, Westmoreland Papers, HRC, CMH.

[13] Verbatim transcript of Army Reserve Forces Policy Committee meeting, 20 Dec 70, pp. 33–52, ARFPC file, RG 319, WNRC.

[14] Ibid., pp. 55–78.

[15] Summary of Minutes of the Meeting of the Army Reserve Forces Policy Committee, 18 Feb 71, pp. 3–6, ARFPC files, RG 319, WNRC.

THE RESERVE COMPONENTS

[16] Master Program for the Modern Volunteer Army, 1 Mar 71, pp. G–1 to G–3, 3–A–5 to 3–A–6.

[17] For Kelley's testimony see Lee and Parker, *Ending the Draft*, pp. 307–10. A good example of the reserve components' reaction to the Gates Report and the administration's approach to funding the early stages of the transition is found in "The Zero Draft and the National Guard," *The National Guardsman* 25 (March 1971): 2–12.

[18] Baskir and Strauss, *Chance and Circumstances*, p. 51; Crossland and Currie, *Twice the Soldier*, p. 231; *Annual Reports, Chief of National Guard Bureau*, FY 1971, pp. 77; FY 1972, pp. 29, 72 (hereafter cited as CNGB).

[19] Annual Historical Summary, Office of the Chief, Army Reserve, FY 1972, p. 9; Annual Historical Summary, Office of Reserve Components, FY 1972, pp. 32–33; DA Circular 135–49, 12 Oct 72.

[20] CNGB, FY 1973, p. 29; Crossland and Currie, *Twice the Soldier*, pp. 242–44.

[21] Summary of Minutes of the Army Reserve Forces Policy Committee meetings of 28 Feb 69, p. 12, and 8 May 70, p. 16, Army Reserve Forces Policy Committee files, RG 319, WNRC.

[22] Verbatim transcript of meeting of 20 Dec 70, pp. 100–105, Army Reserve Forces Policy Committee files, RG 319, WNRC.

[23] Crossland and Currie, *Twice the Soldier*, p. 244; CNGB, FY 1972, p. 30, FY 1974, p. 134.

[24] Verbatim transcript, Army Reserve Forces Policy Committee meeting of 9 and 10 September 1971, pp. 132–37; Summary of meeting of 9–10 December 1971, pp. 11–12, ARFPC files, RG 319, WNRC; *DAHSUM*, FY 1972, pp. 107–09.

[25] For details on the Defense Department's handling of proposals for reserve component incentives see Lee and Parker, *Ending the Draft*, pp. 310–16.

[26] *DAHSUM*, FY 1973, pp. 95–96; FY 1974, pp. 72–73.

[27] Brian McKiernan, "The Commander's Got To Push It!" *The National Guardsman* 38, no. 1 (January 1974): 24–27; "A Hard Fact!" *The National Guardsman* 37, no. 5 (May 1973): 16–19. Note: The monthly feature "Recruiting Newsmakers" made its debut in *The National Guardsman* as part of the McKiernan article. It became a regular feature the following month.

[28] OASD (PA) News Release, 1 Jul 74, OSD file 340, RG 330, WNRC.

[29] "Quality, Not Numbers," *The National Guardsman* 38, no. 6 (June 1974): 30–33.

[30] *DAHSUM*, FY 1972, p. 109; FY 1974, p. 73; FY 1975, p. 59; *Defense Manpower: The Keystone of National Security*, Report to the President and Congress (Washington, D.C.: Defense Manpower Commission, 1976), pp. 128–29, 421–23. Note: The Defense Manpower Commission, an independent study group created by an act of Congress in November 1973, examined all aspects of the military manpower issue for approximately 18 months before submitting its report. Findings and recommendations of the commission are summarized in Chapter X.

[31] Verbatim transcript of briefing by Maj Jack Stevens, ODCSPER, Recruiting, to Army Reserve Forces Policy Committee, 12 Sep 74, ARFPC files, RG 319, WNRC.

[32] Congress approved full-time Servicemen's Group Life Insurance for guardsmen and reservists on paid-drill status in May 1974 and increased the value of the low-cost coverage to $20,000. Crossland and Currie, *Twice the Soldier*, p. 236.

CHAPTER XVIII

The Transition in Perspective

The active Army's transition from the draft to the all-volunteer force ended in 1974. For the Army the two key steps in making the transition occurred well before the actual goal was achieved. Both involved changing the way the Army and its members thought about an all-volunteer force. The first step occurred in 1968–69 during the study phase of the transition when the Army staff and senior leadership concluded that an all-volunteer Army was within the realm of probability and could be militarily effective if properly supported. The second, more difficult step occurred during the experimental phase from October 1970 to June 1972, when attitudes toward volunteerism and soldiers as individuals began to change. After 1974 issues arising over the all-volunteer force became a matter of working through problems and crises growing out of the unintended consequences of policy changes concerning the balance between manpower requirements and resources for the procurement, retention, and management of military personnel.

Overview

The Army's transition from the draft to the AVF occurred in three phases that took place within the larger context of America's withdrawal from Vietnam. Prompted by the frustrating course of the conflict in Vietnam, many Americans reexamined the assumptions of the Cold War policy of containment that evolved in the years after World War II. The Nixon administration made ending direct involvement in Vietnam its highest foreign policy priority. Accomplishing that goal depended in part on renewed relations with China and detente with the Soviet Union. The attempt to identify common interests between the United States and its adversaries and the desire to reduce direct support to allies led in turn to a policy, known as the Nixon Doctrine, that returned the burden of defense to local forces. Vietnamization represented the first manifestation of the Nixon Doctrine. Reduction of overseas commitments held the promise of a reduction in defense spending at home. Indeed, in his major campaign speech on the volunteer Army concept, in October 1968, Nixon observed that reductions in the size of the post-Vietnam force would help offset the costs associated with ending the draft.[1]

The decision to end the Cold War draft and reduce force structure at the end of the Vietnam War and the beginning of a period of reduced tensions with longstanding adversaries resembled earlier American demobilizations. But for the

Army the potential end of the draft posed problems. Unlike earlier postwar demobilizations, the manpower reductions occurred concurrently with the disengagement from Vietnam. Because it had borne the brunt of the fighting and suffered the highest casualties of the Vietnam War, the Army was, in the public's mind, the least popular of the armed forces. Given these conditions few Army leaders believed a volunteer concept would work even at reduced force levels. Most agreed with the manpower studies of the mid-1960s that without the draft not enough men would volunteer.

The Army remained officially silent on the subject of a volunteer force through the mid- and late 1960s as public and legislative sentiment for draft reform and then outright abolition of conscription grew. But behind the scenes the Army undertook an examination of the feasibility of a post-Vietnam volunteer force. The creation of the Career Force Study Group in September 1968 and its successor, Project PROVIDE, early in 1969 marked the beginning of the Army's transition to the AVF. General Westmoreland's decision to order the original study as well as the more detailed follow-on investigation was not unusual or uncharacteristic of his or the Army's approach to problem solving. About the same time Westmoreland commissioned other study groups to examine the Army's leadership training and practices, equipment and weapons requirements, and organization. All of these study groups recommended some changes in the Army programs that fell under their scrutiny, and many of the recommendations eventually resulted in action. In that sense the decision to study the volunteer force concept simply reflected good organizational management on the Army's part.

Nevertheless, the Career Force Study Group's preliminary findings, issued before the creation of the President's Commission on an All-Volunteer Armed Force, and the recommendations of the Project PROVIDE Study Group, which went to the chief of staff of the Army before the Gates Commission rendered its report, were significant. Although the study groups registered concern that attempting to recruit strictly on a voluntary basis would be risky, they concluded that the venture was feasible within certain force levels provided sufficient monetary resources were assured. That Westmoreland and his key lieutenants on the Army staff approved those recommendations, again ahead of the publication of the Gates Commission report, was also significant. The PROVIDE recommendations constituted more than a contingency plan. When he approved them, Westmoreland authorized the implementation of certain low- or no-cost initiatives designed to improve service attractiveness to begin immediately. But the real significance of the early approval of the PROVIDE recommendations lies not merely in the approval but in the logic behind that approval. The Army's two top uniformed leaders, Westmoreland and Palmer, understood that the draft probably would be ended during the Nixon administration whether they liked it or not. Although Westmoreland never reconciled himself to terminating induction authority, to oppose the inevitable clearly was not in the Army's interest. The PROVIDE study had confirmed what many Army leaders knew intuitively: because of its prominent role in the Vietnam conflict the Army was held in very low public esteem. To oppose what appeared to be the will of the people would be unwise.

But Westmoreland and Palmer accepted the logic of the PROVIDE recommendations for positive reasons too. As Westmoreland later wrote, "The war was having a disastrous effect on the active Army as a whole and to a lesser degree on the reserve components." Drug abuse, racial tension, dissent, and corrupt behavior by officers and noncommissioned officers created an atmosphere that undermined the professional ethos of the institution. Westmoreland and other senior officers saw in the volunteer force the opportunity to regain control of the Army. In order for the Army to shape the direction of the transition, it had to take the lead. Thus, Westmoreland was prepared to accept the volunteer concept; and in the detailed recommendations of the PROVIDE report he had a blueprint ready when the Nixon administration decided to move. The PROVIDE study group became an implementation task group within the Army staff, and, because it was well organized and had thought through the problems and issues that the Army would face in ending the draft in advance of the other services, it proved to be a major influence on the direction that the Department of Defense manpower planners took when they developed the Project Volunteer Program in 1970. Again, because it was well organized and better prepared to address volunteer force issues, the Army proved adept at arguing for and receiving the largest share of the first Project Volunteer budget request. Seen in this context, Westmoreland's decision to support the all-volunteer force concept and proceed with the implementation schedule of the PROVIDE report in advance of an administration timetable was logical. Indeed, the Army's acceptance of the AVF represents an excellent case study in institutional self-preservation.

Phase one of the Army's transition to the all-volunteer force took place quietly and behind the scenes. Phase two began dramatically in October 1970 when General Westmoreland publicly declared his support for ending the draft and appointed a special assistant to oversee the program. Until April of that year the planning and the decisions on implementation and the timetable of the PROVIDE plan occurred within the military side of the Department of the Army. As the administration's intentions with regard to the recommendations of the Gates Commission became clear, the civilian leaders of the Army quickly entered the planning process. By midyear it became clear that the administration intended to end reliance on conscription simultaneously with the withdrawal of active Army units from Vietnam. This decision upset the deliberate pace of change envisioned in the PROVIDE recommendations, which were based on the assumption that transition would follow the end of the war. Furthermore, the Army's leaders had assumed that the administration would preserve the machinery of conscription to include retaining induction authority. This was not the case. Faced with the impending loss of induction authority and the knowledge that the Army had only two years to make the transition to draft-free personnel procurement, the senior military and civilian leaders decided to accelerate the pace of their activities.

Recognition that innovations necessary to foster conditions conducive to stimulating more voluntary enlistments and increasing reenlistments cut across command and staff lines. The heightened sense of urgency created by the compressed timetable for achieving an all-volunteer force spurred the Department of the Army leadership to action. The immediate result was the creation of the Special Assistant for the Modern Volunteer Army (SAMVA). Westmoreland and Secretary of the Army Resor gave the SAMVA, Lt. Gen. George I. Forsythe, broad authority, and Forsythe's office quickly became the focal point of efforts to change the Army.

Forsythe's operation produced a period of frenetic activity in the Army. Westmoreland lent command support to Forsythe by approving and announcing in December a series of policy changes designed to eliminate irritants of Army life without affecting professionalism or unit readiness. Forsythe launched an experimental program, Project VOLAR, aimed at identifying and refining measures that would increase enlistments and reenlistments in the combat arms. Simultaneously, Forsythe's office developed a master plan for achieving the Modern Volunteer Army. Meanwhile, Westmoreland ordered the rapid expansion of the U.S. Army Recruiting Command which, in coordination with SAMVA, began experimenting with new techniques and enlistment options designed to attract volunteers.

The VOLAR experiments and some of the recruiting innovations initially created unintended confusion and controversy in and out of the Army. Prior to the publication of the Gates Report, few in the Army outside of those on the Army staff dealing with the issue gave the volunteer force concept much thought. Until Westmoreland's speech in October, most soldiers assumed that the transition to a volunteer force would occur in the distant future if at all. The suddenness of the announcement and the rapidity of the changes that followed provoked an outpouring of comment within the Army; much of it was uninformed and negative. Furthermore, VOLAR and the Modern Volunteer Army Program promised much but delivered little initially because in the rush to get started SAMVA announced its ideas and intentions before funding was available.

The advertising experiment provoked further controversy. The use of paid radio and television recruiting commercials angered conservatives in Congress who believed broadcasters should air the ads as a public service. The message "Today's Army Wants To Join You" also proved controversial. Although advertiser surveys showed the campaign to be highly effective with the target audiences, most Army observers disliked the slogan and never accepted it. The news media dwelled on the more sensational aspects of the Army's attempts to eliminate irritants of service life, such as beer in the barracks, "rap sessions" between soldiers and their commanders, psychedelic barracks, and greater off-duty freedom for junior enlisted service members. As a result many career soldiers and friends of the Army in retiree and veterans associations as well as members of the key congressional committees whose support the Army needed to authorize and fund the transition questioned Forsythe's efforts.

THE TRANSITION IN PERSPECTIVE

Such observers perceived VOLAR and the Modern Volunteer Army Program as pandering to the youth culture.

Forsythe, Westmoreland, and other defenders of the Army's approach to achieving the all-volunteer goal toured the country speaking to military and civic groups to explain their programs. Gradually the furor subsided. Commanders found that greater freedom did not lead to undiscipline. Furthermore, through the VOLAR experiments Forsythe's people developed data on innovations that contributed to higher retention. New recruiting options and higher pay helped attract more volunteers. By the end of 1971 Forsythe was confident that his operation had identified the right mix of incentives and initiatives that, if properly supported, could assure an all-volunteer Army. By integrating volunteer Army programs with the base line of the so-called Soldier-Oriented Budget he assured that funding for those programs survived much of the budget cutting that occurred in the cost-conscious Nixon administration.

The experimentation phase ended in June 1972 when Forsythe's operation was disbanded and management of the transition was restored to regular command and staff channels. Despite the confusion generated by the sudden creation of SAMVA, Forsythe and the people associated with his effort performed a crucial service. In a narrow sense they conceived and directed the test-bed for the volunteer Army. On a higher level they helped educate the Army on the need to respect young soldiers as individuals and treat them as entry-level members of the profession of arms. Sadly, some career soldiers never understood the larger purpose of SAMVA. Years later they would continue to castigate VOLAR and the initial confusion that accompanied it.

The final phase of the Army's transition to the all-volunteer force began in July 1972, the start of the last full year of induction authority. By that date those Army civilian and military leaders charged with achieving the zero-draft goal expressed cautious optimism that they had the right mix of recruiting and reenlistment incentives and policies and programs to attract and retain the requisite number of men and women. Two years later, after the Army completed a full fiscal year without draftees, Secretary of the Army Howard Callaway declared the effort a success and the transition complete. In the process, however, the Army rode a roller coaster as it worked out the details of its volunteer force program.

At the beginning of the final phase of the transition the Modern Volunteer Army Program lacked sufficient command support. Westmoreland and Forsythe had retired and the SAMVA office was disestablished. The Army staff took over the implementation of the SAMVA's program along functional lines. The chief of staff of the Army designate, General Creighton Abrams, was not confirmed until October 1972, and General Bruce Palmer, Jr., the acting chief of staff, who had preferred a less flamboyant approach to ending the draft from the start, did not accord the program the degree of attention it had received earlier. Problems soon developed.

Quantity vs. Quality

According to Brig. Gen. (Ret.) Paul D. Phillips, the former deputy assistant secretary of the Army for manpower and reserve affairs under Brehm, the issue of quality was the most critical factor in the transition.[2] Phillips saw a wide disparity in the philosophy of OSD and that of the Army in the application of resources for obtaining the Modern Volunteer Army. Defense Department officials viewed cost as the most critical factor and tended to creep up on the problem, applying a few resources here and there and being absolutely sure of the results before continuing further. An analogy here might be made, Phillips suggested, to the way OSD controlled the war in Vietnam. The Army, on the other hand, recognizing the huge problems it faced, wanted to be bold in the application of resources, to start big, scaling down later if necessary but believing that an early success in recruiting and retention was a key to a successful transition.

From the Army's point of view its initial recruiting problems were formidable and in the United States unprecedented. About 75 percent of its personnel needs had been satisfied by the draft and draft-induced enlistments; furthermore, these acquisitions had always been of higher quality than the true volunteers in terms of educational background and mental category. Thus to increase the number and the quality of the true volunteers—those considering making the service their career—the Army needed an edge, or at least equality, in the marketplace in order to compete not only with the civilian economic community but also with the other services. Proficiency pay, bonuses, career options, shorter service terms, more rapid promotions, pay increases, and improvements in service life were thus all part of a total package that also included advertising and a revised sales force. The recruiting force had to be reoriented to a higher quality market in the high schools and suburbs and away from the pool halls, back alleys, and jails. However, many of these initiatives were expensive and growing more costly every day as the inflation of the late 1960s and early 1970s steadily eroded the purchasing power of each defense dollar.

Not surprisingly, Phillips recounted that Army leaders were extremely frustrated by the OSD approach toward MVA funding issues. The attitude of DOD officials such as Herbits toward the use of bonuses—even after congressional approval—the advertising tests, reprogramming of funds, and recruiter relief, and the lack of cooperation sometimes exhibited by the other services, threatened to dissipate the head of steam that Forsythe and his successors were trying to create. Thus while some OSD officials charged that the Army was either uninterested in making the AVF work or actually out to sabotage it, some Army leaders believed OSD to be the culprit.

Regarding the economic issues, the Army's best defense lay in its data showing that it was cost-effective to "buy" quality. Low mental category and high school dropout loss rates over an extended period simply made them less economical than higher quality recruits despite the bonus and other "up front" costs needed to attract better candidates. Such Army spokesmen as

Phillips also argued that "quality begets quality" and that "quality people are willing to join and to stay in a quality organization and will refuse to stay (reenlist) in a rag tag organization." Similarly, Phillips noted, "recruiters recruit people like themselves," and thus the effort within the Army to improve the quality of USAREC personnel was also vital.

TABLE 6—PERCENT EXPECTED ARMY ATTRITION DURING FIRST 36 MONTHS OF SERVICE BY QUALITY AND SEX

Quality Group	Male	Female
HSDG[1]		
MC I–IIIA	22	42
MC IIIB	25	45
MC IV	26	48
Non–HSDG		
MC I–IIIA	39	[2] n/a
MC IIIB	42	[2] n/a
MC IV	([3])	[2] n/a

[1] High school diploma graduate.

[2] Females not taken in these categories until after 1980.

[3] Males not taken in this category over long enough time to determine loss rates. It would be greater than 42 percent.

NOTE: This chart made in 1980. After MC IV men were taken in non–NHSDG and women were taken also as non–NHSDG, the average rate for non–NHSDG jumped to 50 percent.

Finally, General Phillips, writing in retrospect, believed that the Army's goal of 70 percent high school graduates (or above) in the force was a modest objective, one that reflected the educational level of the Army in the last years of the draft. (*See Table 7.*)

According to Phillips, if the Army had set its goals too low and "made the numbers," not only would we have had a poorer Army, but it would have been accused by opponents of the AVF of lowering standards to create the appearance of success. But if the Army had set its goals too high, it might have failed to make the numbers, thereby running the risk of a cut during the following year in end strength. However, a "failure" of this nature would also have assured an adequate and more flexible application of resources in the future, and "with adequate resources, we could buy quality." Thus Phillips and others could point out that over the long run the attention given to quality did not necessarily result in a smaller force and that the average of 80–90 percent high school graduates in the Army of 1990 was a direct result of the policies set within the secretary of the Army's office during the transition.

TABLE 7—EDUCATIONAL LEVEL OF ARMY DURING LAST YEARS OF THE DRAFT

Year	Percent in MC I–IIIA	Percent of High School Diploma Grads
1967	53.4	73.6
1968	52.8	68.3
1969	53.4	68.3
1970	53.2	69.3
1971	53.9	66.1
1972	56.4	[1] 60.6
1973	55.9	[2] 60.9
1974	48.1	46.7
1975	52.7	54.3
1976	50.5	55.6
1977	40.4	56.2
1978	43.4	70.1
1979	37.0	56.0

[1] An atypical year. The last full year of the draft but one in which the Army was cut 50,000 man-years effective in the middle of the year, causing drastic reductions in planned draft calls which may explain the drop in HSDG. During this year the Army was also on a policy that precluded drafting more in any month than had been drafted in any of the months before. This artificiality was supposed to ease the way into the no-draft era and appeal to the politicians. In fact, all it did was to assure that units were not kept up to strength.

[2] The transition year in which draftees came in only during the first six months, again in decreasing numbers each month.

NOTE: Figures supplied by General Phillips.

In the spring of 1973, however, none of the long-term results were yet apparent. With the Defense Department's announcement that no further draft calls would be made, the Army immediately began to experience difficulty enlisting volunteers in the numbers needed. The shortfall was obviously the unintended consequence of a conscious effort by Army manpower specialists to increase the quality of recruits. The relocation of USAREC headquarters from Fort Monroe, Virginia, to Fort Sheridan, Illinois, during the same period complicated matters. Starting in October 1972 Phillips and Gompf began to tinker with enlistment criteria and recruiter objectives and credits to encourage the field recruiting force to seek out more qualified volunteers. The recruiters responded accordingly. But in their effort to enlist more high school graduates, the Army fell short of the overall quantitative objective for fiscal year 1972.

Yet, as in the case of the "seventy percent high school diploma graduate decision," the Army policymakers knew the risk they were taking. Manpower analysts at the Department of Defense level had cautioned against the move. But, as in the Army's decision to press on with its paid radio and television recruiting experiment in early 1970 against the wishes of the other services and

DOD, the decision to exercise its prerogative and change enlistment goals in February 1972 revealed a streak of stubborn independence. Army manpower analysts and managers resented attempts by the Office of the Assistant Secretary of Defense for Manpower to review, approve, or overrule their decisions. When recruiters proved unable to meet their quantitative goals under the higher qualitative guidelines, the policymakers resisted pressures to revise their decision until a face-saving solution could be devised. Bureaucratic inertia had its counterpart in bureaucratic momentum.

The decision to relocate USAREC headquarters was taken without adequate consideration of the potential consequences such a move could have on recruiting operations. The disruption of the Recruiting Command's fledgling computer system and loss of the many civilian employees, who chose not to make the move, complicated an already difficult situation and added to the impression that some in the Army were out to sabotage the all-volunteer force effort. When induction authority expired on 30 June 1973, the Army's ability to achieve and maintain an all-volunteer status was thus still very much in doubt. Many key congressional figures and opinion leaders in the media were predicting failure and openly talking of the need to restore the draft. Despite the recruiting successes in the decades that followed, a subject beyond the scope of this study, the value of the recruiting policies adopted by the Army during the transition remained difficult to judge.

Leadership

Secretary of the Army Callaway refused to concede failure or to permit the Department of Defense to dictate manpower policy to the Army. Under his regime the transition to the all-volunteer force again assumed a high priority status. Callaway, by making the success of the effort a matter of personal interest, by lobbying Congress for needed support, and by seeking advice and support from soldiers and civilians alike, focused attention on the problems yet to be solved and created an attitude conducive to success. Certainly others share credit for reversing the fortunes of the all-volunteer Army between July 1973 and June 1974. General Rogers' contribution as deputy chief of staff for personnel proved crucial. Under his leadership, close working relationships were forged between the Army secretariat and staff. William Brehm's role as assistant secretary of defense for manpower proved equally important. Brehm refused to be stampeded by conspiratorial views of sabotage and gave the Army time and room enough to work out solutions to its problems.

But Callaway clearly led the effort. Callaway's leading role in the final phase of the Army's transition from the draft to the all-volunteer force points up the important role played by individual leaders in the effort. The successful transition was not simply the result of forces set in motion proceeding to an inevitable conclusion. People made a difference in its course and outcome. If Callaway deserves credit for his part in successfully completing the transition, Westmoreland certainly should be recognized for taking the lead in starting it.

Although he never wanted to end the draft per se, Westmoreland saw the need to study the problems associated with ending the Army's dependence on inductees and the importance of being ready with a program should the contingency arise. When it became obvious that the Nixon administration would proceed to end the draft, Westmoreland again took the lead and by his positive public support for Forsythe and his Modern Volunteer Army Program helped to allay some of the early confusion and opposition to the effort.

Forsythe himself made a difference. He saw in the requirement to achieve a volunteer Army the opportunity to reform the Army. He thus pulled into his organization a number of like-minded young officers who then had the opportunity to try out some of their ideas and those of numerous soldiers who responded to Forsythe's call for suggestions. Forsythe's efforts did not result in a wholesale reformation of the Army, but they did contribute to an outpouring of discussion about leadership roles and organizational, personnel, and training policies and practices in the Army at a time when professional spirits were at a low ebb.

Others played a less public role. Lt. Col. Jack Butler, the original action officer given the requirement to prepare the first study on the feasibility of ending the draft in September 1968, shaped the final outcome profoundly. His assumptions, tentative findings, and initial recommendations led to the establishment of Project PROVIDE, which in turn shaped the Army's response to the Gates Commission report and contributed to the ultimate Department of Defense transition plan. Butler also supplied vital continuity between the Volunteer Army Division and SAMVA when Westmoreland decided to accelerate the Army's transition effort in the autumn of 1970.

Several individuals in the Office of the Assistant Secretary of the Army for Manpower also made a difference. William K. Brehm, the first person to head that office, vigorously defended the Army's interests in the early struggle to achieve policy consensus and funds for the experimental phase of the transition. Brehm also brought especially talented people into his office, including John Kester, Clayton Gompf, and Paul Phillips, who continued to play important roles long after he departed.

These key Army managers were of course aided by a variety of management tools developed and gradually perfected by their staffs. Well before the Vietnam withdrawal, Brehm's office, for example, employed first crude and later very sophisticated manpower computer models that permitted decision makers to examine myriad manpower programs varying such things as dollars, manyears, end strengths, the sizes of draft calls by month, the quality of accessions, sex and age of accessions, the size of the training base, training base loads, and many others. Such data were used to develop the budget, to support the budget request, and to manage the resultant manpower authorizations. Of the other computer models, none was more needed and useful than the REQUEST system, an airline-like reservation system used to keep track of the many options available to potential recruits and the spaces available in the training base. It also permitted the Army staff to keep track on a daily basis, if necessary, of how recruiting was progressing by quantity, quality, race, age, and sex.

In addition to computer programs, OASA(M&RA) and the ODCSPER developed a set of about ten management charts specifically for the transition, tracking loss rates over time by race, sex, educational attainment, and mental category. From such data Army leaders were able to determine the desirability of quality from a cost-effectiveness standpoint and to shore up their arguments to OSD and to the Congress for financial resources.

The Larger Perspective

All of the above notwithstanding, the Army would not have ended its reliance on the draft on its own accord. Pressure to end conscription came from the society and had its origins both in the historic American antimilitary tradition and its aversion to compulsion and in the contemporary reaction to the Vietnam War. Classical conservatives and antiwar liberals joined in an unusual coalition in Congress to undermine support for selective service extension. Richard Nixon embraced the issue in his 1968 campaign for the presidency and, after satisfying himself that ending the draft indeed was feasible, made it a policy goal of his first administration. Without those kinds of outside pressures the Army, like any large organization, would have continued with the status quo of the draft.

Just as outside pressures forced the Army to consider ending its dependency on inductees, so too did outside organizations shape the course of the Army's transition to the all-volunteer force. Again, people made a difference. Nixon himself acknowledged the significant role played by Martin Anderson in bringing and keeping the idea before him. Congressional staff aides such as Stephen Herbits and Andrew Effron played similar roles in the offices of Congressman, later Senator, Stafford and Congressman Steiger, respectively. Herbits became something of a self-appointed watchdog of the services' efforts to end reliance on conscription. As one of the early advocates of ending the draft, he was never satisfied with the extent or pace of change and on several occasions accused the Army of attempting to undermine the transition. Although several of the Army's leaders expressed their philosophical preference for continuing the draft, no conspiracy to sabotage the transition existed. The disagreements between critics of the Army's efforts and those charged with accomplishing the task were over the means rather than the ends.

If ardent supporters of the all-volunteer force outside the Army complained of foot dragging and obstructionism, so did people within the Army. Forsythe and Brehm constantly complained to the secretary of the Army and chief of staff that the Department of Defense did not give them enough money or policy support to begin the early experiments necessary to launch the volunteer Army effort. The role of Roger Kelley in shaping the overall Defense Department effort to end the draft cannot be overlooked; Kelley sought to create a consensus among the services and to forge a uniform policy to guide their transition. The Army never completely accepted Kelley's outlook, yet the ensuing disagreements forced Army leaders to sharpen their own proposals.

Neither did Army leaders accept congressional limitations on their efforts. F. Edward Hebert's refusal to permit a continuation of radio and television recruiting advertisements is a case in point. Recruiting and manpower policy planners requested funds for paid broadcast media ads year after year during the transition only to be told that Hebert would not budge on the subject. Likewise, Brehm and Forsythe expressed their frustration at Kelley's and congressional opposition to their idea for proficiency pay for the combat arms. Later Callaway considered congressional slowness to approve additional recruiting and retention bonuses to have been a major obstacle in his path.

Other administration and congressional actions hampered the Army's efforts to accomplish the mission of ending its reliance on the draft according to the timetable those branches of the government had established. The Nixon administration cut the Department of Defense Project Volunteer and the Army's budget requests for funds to support the transition routinely as part of its larger effort to reduce government spending. Congress caused a major setback to Forsythe's experimentation program in 1971–72 and to the Recruiting Command's fledgling program to attract more volunteers in the same time frame when it ordered the 50,000-man reduction in strength of the active Army midway through fiscal year 1972. Congress also made it difficult for the Army to meet its quantitative manpower requirements when it imposed restrictions on the number of Mental Category IV and non–high school graduates that could enlist in 1973. Only the last example had anything directly to do with the transition to the volunteer force. The other instances point out how easily programs can be frustrated by apparently unrelated policies.

When Secretary of the Army Callaway proclaimed the volunteer Army a success on 1 July 1974, he effectively ended the transition from the draft to the AVF. The Army's success in meeting its manpower requirements within congressional guidelines muted the critics of the previous winter. But observers in and out of the government continued to view the all-volunteer force very much as an experiment. Congress, at Senator Nunn's initiative, established a special Defense Manpower Commission to "conduct a comprehensive study and investigation of the overall manpower requirements of the Department of Defense on both a short-term and long-term basis," in order to determine the best ways to meet those requirements.[3] Earlier, Senator Stennis, who remained a firm skeptic on the chances for success of the all-volunteer force, urged his colleagues to give the experiment a "fair trial." The transition was over; the trial could begin.

Between 1974 and 1983 the all-volunteer Army would travel a somewhat rocky road in terms of its ability to attract and retain its authorized numbers and quality. The reactions of the interested public, media, and Congress rose and fell with the success and failure of the effort. The early success of the Army in maintaining strength at an acceptable qualitative mix muted critics of the AVF in 1974. By 1975 trends began to change. As recruiting again became difficult in the latter half of the decade and the Army failed to retain expected numbers of volunteers and career enlisted personnel despite the many initia-

THE TRANSITION IN PERSPECTIVE

tives taken during the transition years, many began to question the efficacy of the concept once again. By 1979 the AVF reached a crisis point. Thereafter, the situation changed. A combination of internal and external forces combined to reverse the negative trends, and by 1982 the Army, as well as the other services, was setting and breaking recruiting and reenlistment records almost on a monthly basis.

For a variety of reasons the Army's reserve components also fared well once funds and attention had been focused on their particular problems. Again, the story of the post-1974 Army is beyond the scope of this book.

Clearly, however, it was their volunteer "Total Army" that was ultimately tested in the Caribbean and Central American crises and in the sands of Southwest Asia. The results showed that this new force could meet the demands of limited conventional war and of an increasingly complex military technology while fulfilling the nation's security responsibilities which appeared to be diminishing only gradually in size and scope.

Notes

[1] Paul Y. Hammond, *Cold War and Detente: The American Foreign Policy Process Since 1945* (New York: Harcourt, Brace, Jovanovich, Inc., 1975), pp. 255–83, 286–87; Richard M. Nixon, "The All-Volunteer Armed Forces," an address given over the CBS Radio Network, Thursday, October 17, 1968, in John W. Chambers, ed., *Draftees or Volunteers: A Documentary History of the Debate Over Military Conscription in the United States, 1787–1973* (New York: Garland Publishing, Inc., 1975), pp. 572–78.

[2] The following discussion is based on the comments of General Phillips on the draft manuscript.

[3] Sec. 702, Title VII, P.L. 93–155 (26 Nov 73), reprinted in App. B–1, *Report of the Defense Manpower Commission,* p. 478.

Bibliographical Note

As is appropriate for an official history, the principal documentary sources for this analysis of the Army's response to and role in the end of the draft in the United States are the records of the several Army and Department of Defense offices involved most directly with the decisions and events themselves. The most complete collection is that of the Office of the Secretary of Defense (OSD), File 350, Record Group 330, which is maintained at the Washington National Records Center, Suitland, Maryland. This collection contains the working files of the Office of the Assistant Secretary of Defense for Manpower, Reserve Affairs, and Logistics. In addition to the records of the Defense Department on the subject, the file contains copies of many Army documents on the transition to the all-volunteer force.

No similar single body of records exists at the Army level. The records of the Office of the Secretary of the Army (OSA) are uneven, reflecting the level of interest successive incumbents devoted to the subject. The records reflect greater interest in the subject prior to the creation of the Office of the Special Assistant for the Modern Volunteer Army and following its dissolution. These files are maintained at the Washington National Records Center under File 202.10, Record Group 335.

Coherent Army staff files are nonexistent. At each stage of the Army's progress from the initial decision to study the feasibility of ending the Army's reliance on conscription in 1968 through the formal announcement of the end of the transition in 1974 official Army staff files on the subject were transferred from one proponent to another. The records on many specific actions ended up in a variety of Army staff files. The most important set of Army records on the subject, those of the Special Assistant for the Modern Volunteer Army (SAMVA), were broken up in 1972. The most complete collection of relevant Army files that survives is in a group of records assembled in the early 1970s by the authors of two Department of the Army monographs on the Modern Volunteer Army. These records, entitled "Background Material Collected by the Center of Military History in preparation of the Modern Volunteer Army Monograph Series," are contained in Record Group 319 and are also maintained by the Washington National Records Center. They contain many SAMVA records as well as records of the "Career Force Study" and "Project Volunteer in Defense of the Nation (PROVIDE)," which predated creation of the SAMVA office, and end with the disestablishment of SAMVA in 1972.

An additional incomplete set of documents pertaining to the Army's role in the transition is maintained by the Center of Military History in its Historical Records Collection. The combination of these four collections makes it possible for the researcher to piece together a fairly complete paper trail of decisions and actions from the beginning of the Army's internal debate on ending draft dependency through mid-1974 when Secretary of the Army Howard "Bo" Callaway declared the transition successfully ended.

At the "operational level" of the transition the "Background Materials" collected for the Modern Volunteer Army Monographs remain the best source except for decisions and actions pertaining to the U.S. Army Recruiting Command (USAREC). No formal historical records collection exists for this command. A collection of documents was maintained in the post museum at Fort Sheridan, Illinois, at the time this study was prepared. These files were not well maintained and were euphemistically called the "USAREC Archives" by the post historian. Few members of the USAREC staff knew of their existence. They nevertheless represent the best available glimpse into the official mind of the recruiting service of the period.

Unofficial Records

In addition to the records maintained by official sources, I consulted records preserved in unofficial repositories. One such set represents the working papers of Stephen Herbits, one of the congressional staff authors of the House Wednesday Group's book, *How To End the Draft*, published in 1967. Herbits later served as a member of the Gates Commission, returned to Capitol Hill as a staff assistant to Congressman Robert Stafford, and eventually joined the staff of the Assistant Secretary of Defense for Manpower, Reserve Affairs, and Logistics as a special assistant. Herbits left government service in 1974 and donated his papers to the Hoover Institution Library at Stanford University. Herbits' papers, along with his occasional writing and commentary on the progress of the all-volunteer force following his return to private life, present a decidedly different perspective on the Army's commitment to and role in the transition.

An additional unofficial source of records made available to the author was the personal papers of John Kester. Kester served as an assistant secretary of the Army for manpower under William Brehm during the early stages of the transition. He played a key role in the recruiting experiments of 1971, especially the paid radio and television recruiting advertising experiment. His small collection of memorandums and notes covering his tenure on the secretary of the Army's staff combined with his personal recollections of the period helped clarify both the decision-making process and the atmosphere of the time.

Published Works

Published works on the Army's role in the transition from the draft to the all-volunteer force are few in number. Most secondary sources on the end of the draft focus on the national debate and consider the Army's role in the process only tangentially. Some of the more important sources consulted and used in this study are listed below; others are referenced in the text. In addition to secondary sources on the end of the draft, other studies of the Army as an institution in the turbulent years in which the draft was ending are listed below:

Baskir, Lawrence M., and Strauss, William A. *Chance and Circumstance: The Draft, the War, and the Vietnam Generation.* New York: Vintage, 1978.

Bowman, William; Little, Roger; and Sicilia, G. Thomas, eds. *The All-Volunteer Force After a Decade: Retrospect and Prospect.* Washington, D.C.: Pergamon-Brassey's, 1986.

Bradford, Zeb B., Jr., and Brown, Frederic J. *The United States Army in Transition.* Beverly Hills, Calif.: Sage Publications, 1973.

Chambers, John W., II. *Draftees or Volunteers: A Documentary History of the Debate Over Military Conscription in the United States, 1787–1973.* New York: Garland, 1975.

Crossland, Richard B., and Currie, James T. *Twice the Soldier: A History of the United States Army Reserve, 1908–1983.* Washington, D.C.: Chief of Army Reserve, 1984.

Flynn, George Q. *Lewis B. Hershey, Mr. Selective Service.* Chapel Hill, N.C.: University of North Carolina Press, 1985.

Gerhardt, James M. *The Draft and Public Policy: Issues in Military Manpower Procurement, 1945–1970.* Columbus: Ohio State University Press, 1971.

Johnson, Hayes, and Wilson, George C. *Army in Anguish: The Washington Post National Report.* New York: Pocket Books, 1972.

Korb, Lawrence J. *The Joint Chiefs of Staff: The First Twenty-Five Years.* Bloomington: Indiana University Press, 1976.

Latham, Willard. *The Modern Volunteer Army Program: The Benning Experiment, 1970–1972.* Washington, D.C.: Department of the Army, 1974.

Lee, Gus C., and Parker, Geoffrey Y. *Ending the Draft: The Story of the All Volunteer Force.* Alexandria, Va.: Human Resources Research Organization, April 1977.

Moore, Harold G., and Tuten, Jeff M. *Building a Volunteer Army: The Fort Ord Experiment.* Washington, D.C.: Department of the Army, 1975.

Morden, Bettie J. *The Women's Army Corps, 1945–1978.* Washington, D.C.: U.S. Army Center of Military History, 1990.

Tarr, Curtis W. *By the Numbers: The Reform of the Selective Service System, 1970–1972.* Washington, D.C.: National Defense University Press, 1981.

Taylor, William J., Jr.; Olson, Eric T.; and Schrader, Richard A., eds. *Defense Manpower Planning: Issues for the 1980s.* New York: Pergamon Press, 1981.

Westmoreland, William C. *Report of the Chief of Staff of the United States Army, 1 July 1968 to 30 June 1972.* Washington, D.C.: Department of the Army, 1977.

Periodicals

In addition to major daily newspapers and weekly news magazines that followed the end of the draft, two journals and one weekly newspaper provide special insight into the Army's transition from the draft to the all-volunteer force. The *Army Times*, a weekly newspaper which covers official and unofficial happenings in and about the Army in particular and national security in general, provides a useful view of the Army in the period under consideration in this volume. The *Army Times* frequently "scooped" the major news media on issues concerning the draft and, through its "Letters to the Editor" section, provided active and retired servicemen with a vehicle to express their opinions on many aspects of the transition as it occurred. *Army*, the monthly journal of the Association of the U.S. Army (AUSA) offers a similar, though somewhat more official, perspective on the period. As the "professional association" of the Army and its unofficial lobby, the AUSA with *Army* provided a vehicle for the Army's leaders to "state their case" on the VOLAR and MVA experiments and for officers in the field to react to those statements indirectly and without prejudice. The *Recruiting and Career Counseling Journal*, the official publication of the U.S. Army Recruiting Command (USAREC), is a different kind of source. It provided recruiters in the field with current information on changes in policy, quotas, and success stories. As an official publication it tended to put a positive spin on everything and must be treated accordingly, but it is a useful guide to the recruiter's world for the period.

Two very useful sources on the role and activities of Congress on the end of the draft in particular and military affairs in general are *CQ*, the weekly publication of Congressional Quarterly, Inc., and *The Congressional Quarterly Almanac*, Congressional Quarterly, Inc.'s annual summary of major legislation and treatment of issues by the Congress. The former provides weekly summaries of hearings and committee and floor actions by both the House and the Senate; the latter summarizes major congressional debates, such as that on the end of the draft, and the annual activities of both bodies on defense authorization and appropriation bills.

Oral History

As I conducted my research on the Army's role in and experience with ending reliance on the draft it became apparent that many gaps existed in the official record. As noted above, the physical record is uneven. Furthermore, obvious differences of opinion existed at different levels over motives, bases for decisions, and the results of many actions and initiatives. Because most of the principal decision makers were still alive and willing to talk freely, I determined early on in my research to supplement the official record with oral histories.

The U.S. Army Military History Institute, Carlisle Barracks, Pennsylvania, is home to the Army's "Senior Officer Oral History Program." The program, established in 1970, utilizes U.S. Army War College students to conduct interviews of retired Army leaders. The collection currently contains over 200 interviews. Two which proved especially useful in the early stages of my research were oral histories of General (Ret.) Bruce Palmer, Jr., vice chief of staff of the

Army during the transition to the all-volunteer force, and Lt. Gen. George I. Forsythe, Jr., the Special Assistant for the Modern Volunteer Army (SAMVA).

The Senior Officer Oral History Interviews referenced above were conducted in the mid-1970s and covered far more than the end of the draft. My more focused research soon led me to Palmer and Forsythe, who consented to personal interviews. They in turn led me to others, and the interviews grew into a major project in which I interviewed over twenty subjects. In all but one or two cases (when I experienced equipment failure and resorted to taking notes), I recorded the interview. The Center of Military History professionally transcribed the interviews, and they were reviewed and authenticated by the subjects. Both the tapes and transcripts and my working notes are now on file at the Military History Institute. Key subjects interviewed, and the positions they held relevant to this topic, included:

Martin Anderson, Assistant to President Nixon, 1969–1973.

William K. Brehm, Assistant Secretary of the Army (Manpower & Reserve Affairs), 1968–69, and Assistant Secretary of Defense (Manpower, Reserve Affairs, & Logistics), 1973–74.

Col. (Ret.) Jack R. Butler, Project Officer, Career Force Study, 1968, and Project Director, Project PROVIDE, 1969–70.

Howard H. Callaway, Secretary of the Army, 1973–75.

Lt. Gen. (Ret.) George I. Forsythe, Jr., Special Assistant for the Modern Volunteer Army, 1970–72.

Col. (Ret.) Clayton Gompf, Deputy Assistant Secretary of the Army (Manpower), 1970–84.

Stephen Herbits, Member, President's Commission for an All-Volunteer Force, 1969–70, and Special Assistant to the Secretary of Defense (Manpower, Reserve Affairs, & Logistics), 1973–74.

Roger T. Kelley, Assistant Secretary of Defense (Manpower, Reserve Affairs, & Logistics), 1969–73.

General (Ret.) Walter T. Kerwin, Jr., Deputy Chief of Staff of the Army for Personnel, 1969–73.

Melvin R. Laird, Secretary of Defense, 1969–73.

Brig. Gen. (Ret.) Robert M. Montague, Jr., Deputy Special Assistant to the Secretary of the Army for the Modern Volunteer Army, 1970–72, and Special Assistant to the Assistant Secretary of Defense (Manpower, Reserve Affairs, & Logistics), 1972–73.

General (Ret.) Bruce C. Palmer, Jr., Vice Chief of Staff of the Army, 1968–73.

Brig. Gen. (Ret.) Paul D. Phillips, Deputy Assistant Secretary of the Army (Manpower & Reserve Affairs), 1970–78.

Stanley R. Resor, Secretary of the Army, 1965–71.

General (Ret.) William C. Westmoreland, Chief of Staff of the Army, 1968–72.

Index

Abrams, General Creighton W., 179n12, 204–05, 209, 211, 213, 214, 225, 227–28, 233, 248–49, 285
Active duty, *vs.* reserve, 31–32, 268
Adamson, Brig. Gen. J. B., 49, 50
African Americans
   Army Reserve enlistment of, 272
   enlistment of, 6, 183–84, 235–36
Ahern, Brig. Gen. Alfred, 274–75, 276
Air Force, debate over AVF budget, 56–57
Alcohol
   abuse, 25
   control of, 71
All-Volunteer Armed Force. *See also* Career Force Study; Modern Volunteer Army; VOLAR; Westmoreland, General William C.
   annual cost estimate of, 23
   AVF budget, 54–60
   combat *vs.* noncombat positions, 37
   Commission on, 13. *See also* Gates Commission
   composition of Commission on, 29–30
   evaluation of studies on, 33–34
   manpower and budget requirements, 35–36
   means and ends, 34–37
   Presidential Commission on an, 33–34, 40
   proficiency pay, 68–69
   quality *vs.* quantity of, 157–60, 183, 185–88
   recruiting medical personnel for, 256
   recruiting system for, 63–64
   testing implementation of, 67–69
   transition's phases to, 22
   zero-draft alternative to, 26
All-Volunteer Army Division, establishment of, 50
Allott, Gordon L., 260
Anderson, Martin, l5n20, 19–20, 29, 38, 40, 43, 291
Antidraft movement, Vietnam era, 11–12
Army
   approaches to draft reduction, 32
   AVF budget issues, 50–51, 54–60
   budget 1974, 197–99
   budget and Modern Volunteer Army expenses, 153–55
   changes in civilian leadership, 149–50
   dependency on draftees, 31
   establishment of All-Volunteer Army division, 50–52
   evaluation of all-volunteer Army studies, 38–42

Army—Continued
   High Impact Actions Toward Achieving a Modern Volunteer Army, 70–74
   life-style improvement and innovations, 88–90, 108–09, 112, 197–98
   manpower and social problems in the, 24–25
   marketing AVF to the, 233–35
   marketing of the Modern Volunteer Army, 111, 122
   paid advertisement for recruiting, 140–44
   pro-pay scheme, 135–37
   public image of, 22, 32
   recruiting system, 63–64
   recruiting *vs.* Navy, Marine Corps, and Air Force, 120–24
   reduction in personnel, 228–29
   reforms experiments, 82. *See also* Fort Benning; Fort Carson; Fort Ord
   reorganization, 206
   Selective Service Extension and Military Pay Act and RIF, 165–67
   transition from draft to AVF, 281
   vs. DOD on qualitative enlistment, 187–88
Army 75 Personnel Concept Study, 189
Army Medical Department, 257
   special pay for doctors, 260. *See also* Uniformed Services Special Pay Act
   specialized training programs, 259
Army Nurse Corps, 259
Assistant Secretary of Defense. *See* Kelley, Roger
AVF. *See* All-Volunteer Armed Force
Ayer & Son, N. W., 140–42, 143, 144, 146

Bailey, Brig. Gen. Mildred, 193–94
Battelle study. *See* Army 75 Personnel Concept Study
Beal, Thaddeus R., 55–56, 90, 145
Belieu, Kenneth E., 154
Bennet, Col. John B., 30
Bennett, Charles, 229–30
Berry Plan, for medical personnel, 256–57
Beuke, Col. Henry, 120–21
Binder, L. James, 102
Binkin, Martin, 211–12
Blandford, John, 136–37
Bolton, Maj. Gen. Donnelly, 270
Braswell, Edward, 138

Brehm, William K., 24, 30–31, 32, 34, 37, 40, 50, 135–36, 149–50, 245, 247, 273–74, 289, 290, 292
   AVF and budget problems, 51, 53–54
   enlistment bonus issue, 239, 240–41
   marketing of the Modern Volunteer Army, 122
   recruiting program issue, 241–42, 244
Brinker, Maj. Gen. Walter E., 31
Burns, Arthur, 19
Butler, Col. Jack R., 17–18, 19, 21–22, 24, 26, 34, 43, 50, 53, 54, 64, 68, 116, 290. *See also* Career Force Study; PROVIDE
   reserve components to AVF, 268–70
   WAC and, 189–91

Callaway, Howard "Bo," 237*n*5, 292
   AVF enlistment success, 249–50
   lobbying effort on behalf of AVF, 228–35, 247–48, 289–90
   recruiting program issue, 241, 242
   revised enlistment standards and TDP, 210–11, 213, 227–28
   transition to AVF, 225–26, 245, 246, 249–51, 260, 275, 285
Calley, Lt. William, 155–56
Cambodia, 43
Career Force Study, 17–19
Career Force Study Group, 282. *See also* PROVIDE
CHAMPUS. *See* Civilian Health and Medical Program of the Uniformed Services (CHAMPUS)
Chief of Staff, U.S. Army. *See* Abrams, General Creighton W.; Marshall, General George C.; Scott, Maj. Gen. Hugh L.; Westmoreland, General William C.
Civilian Health and Medical Program of the Uniformed Services (CHAMPUS), 258
Civilianization, 108
   Congress and KP, 167–69
   medical activities, 258
Clements, William P., 202, 203–05, 210–11, 213, 214, 225, 226, 227, 231, 240, 243–44
Commutation fee, 5–6
Congress
   approval of extension of induction authority, 59–60
   authorization of and appropriation for zero-draft, 43
   civilianization of KP and, 167–69
   compulsory peacetime military service and, 7
   criticism of Army's manpower program, 211–12
   draft extension and, 160–61
   end of draft hampered by, 292
   enlistment bonus issue, 170–71, 240
   lobbying for support of AVF by, 230–31

Congress—Continued
   marketing of the Modern Volunteer Army to, 111
   postwar draft and, 9
   quality standards and, 203, 243–45
   reduction in Army strength, 242–43
   Republic dual military system and role of, 4–5
Connor, Lt. Gen. Albert O., 22, 30–31, 107. *See also* PROVIDE
Conscription, 6–7, 17
Continental Army Command
   abolition of, 206
   Women's Army Corps and, 191–92
Continental Line, 4
Crowder, Maj. Gen. E. H., conscription legislation drafted by, 7, 135

Daniel, Dan, 168–69, 251
Davidson, Maj. Gen. Phillip B., 85
Davison, General Michael S., 106–07, 108
Defense Department
   budget for AVF, 47–49
   position on draftees' assignment to Vietnam, 182
   zero-draft progress report, 182–85
Defense Program Review Committee, 61*n*5
Deferment, 9–11
DePuy, Lt. Gen. William, 49
Dickinson, William L., support for AVF, 229, 230
Dominick, Peter, 60
Draft. *See also* Selective Service Act
   end of, 181
   historical perspective, 4–5
   lottery, 12
   Nixon's position on, 19–20
   nuclear force and, 9
   role of World War I, 6–7
   social implications of abandonment of, 18–19
   Vietnam War, 11
Drug abuse, 25
Dyke, Lt. Col. Charles, 237*n*5

Eaker, Lt. Gen. Ira C. (USAF, Ret.), 75
Education
   level of, 288
   mental test scores and, 183, 185
   qualitative enlistment standards, 186–88, 200, 227
Effron, Andrew, 66, 168, 244–45, 291
Eisenhower, Dwight D., 9
Enlistment, 31. *See also* Recruiting
   bonus *vs.* proficiency pay, 69, 122, 135
   bonuses, 170–71, 183, 201, 225, 239–41
   mental test scores, 183, 185
   pro-pay *vs.* proficiency pay, 138–39
   race issue and, 235–36

INDEX

Enlistment—Continued
   retention, 107–08, 285
   soldier profile and, 105–06
   TDP and revised standards, 227–28
   women, 188–89, 272
Enrollment Act, 5–6
Experimental Modern Volunteer Army Training Program, 85. *See also* Fort Ord
Ewing, William, 143

Fisher, O. C., 203
Fitt, Alfred B., 20
Flanagan, Peter, 41
Flynt, John J., 167, 247–48
Forsythe, Lt. Gen. George I., 60, 69, 73, 116, 141, 149, 155–57, 159–60, 170, 171–72, 174–75, 197, 247–48, 268–69, 284–85, 286, 289–90, 292. *See also* All-Volunteer Armed Force
   appointment to project manager of AVF, 53–54
   criticism from the public and media, 74–78
   experiments with Army reforms, 82, 85–87, 89–90
   proficiency pay issue and, 135–36, 137–38, 139–40, 145–46
   recruiting experiments and, 122, 123–24, 128, 129, 132*n*23
   retirement of, 177–78
   revision and budget of Modern Volunteer Army Program, 150–51, 152–53, 154
   special assistant for Modern Volunteer Army (SAMVA), 63, 66–67, 68, 71–72, 111–12
Fort Benning, 82–83, 89, 174–75
   Benning Plan Study Group, 83–84
   media reaction to experiments at, 102
Fort Bragg, 87, 175
Fort Carson, 65, 82, 84, 89, 110; media reaction to experiments at, 101–02
Fort Ord, 82, 84–86, 103
Fredericks, Capt. Grant L., 109–10, 178
Friedman, Milton, 20, 29–30, 38, 246–47, 248
Froehlke, Robert F., 66, 111–12, 149–50, 159, 168, 170, 171–72, 176–77, 193–94, 198–99, 210
   paid advertising and, 145
   revision and budget of Modern Volunteer Army Program, 151, 153, 154
   WAC increase, 192

Gates, Thomas S., 13, 29, 33–34, 37, 38
Gates Commission, 13, 15*n*20, 17, 21, 29–30, 40–41. *See also* PROVIDE
   draft findings, 35–38
   evaluation of All-Volunteer Armed Force, 33
   members, 45*n*1
   military women and, 191

Gates Commission—Continued
   PROVIDE rebuttal to findings of, 37–38
   racial composition of AVF, 183
   reserve components and AVF, 265–66
   significance in draft ending, 43
Goldwater, Barry, 10, 160–61, 212–13
Gompf, Clayton, 66, 149–50, 178, 186, 199–200, 239, 240, 246, 288, 290
Gruenther, General Alfred, 29
Gurney, Chan, postwar draft bill and, 9

Haines, General Ralph E., Jr., 77, 106, 108, 110, 112, 172
Hanson, Maj. Gen. Horace B., Jr., 270
Harrington, Michael, 139
Hatfield, Mark, 12, 160–61
Hebert, F. Edward, 48, 101, 160, 257
   paid advertising and, 144, 145–46, 167, 176, 292
   proficiency pay and, 136–37, 138, 140
Henion, Maj. Gen. John Q., 129, 207, 241–42
Herbits, Stephen, 29–30, 34, 38, 66, 232, 291
   AVF failure and, 210–11, 213–14
   KP work and, 168
   recruiting program issue, 241–42, 244–45, 246–47
Hershey, General Lewis, 8, 10, 11, 20–21
Hittle, James, 141
Holland, Maj. Gen. Leonard, 269
Horton, Frank, 232
Hougen, Col. John, 127
Hughes, Col. David, 65
Hull, Hadlai A., 144, 145, 149–50, 152–53, 159, 166–67, 170, 171, 201, 210
Humphrey, Hubert, 12

Individual Ready Reserve (IRR), 263
Inouye, Daniel, 230

Jacobson, Raymond, 90
Johnson, Lyndon B., 264
   commitment of American men to Vietnam, 10–11
   Project 100,000, 158
   Selective Service Act extension, 12
Johnston, John D., 211–12

Kean, Col. John, 129
Kelley, Roger T., 21, 30, 32, 33, 34–35, 38, 39, 40, 42, 43, 49, 55, 57, 118–20, 132*n*23, 159, 176–77, 178, 191, 193, 195*n*12, 210–11, 213–14, 291. *See also* Project Volunteer
   AVF final assessment by, 203–04, 205
   enlistment bonuses and, 170–71
   enlistment standards and, 185–86, 187–88, 199–201, 203

Kelley, Roger T.—Continued
　Modern Volunteer Army Program budget and, 153, 154, 197–99
　proficiency pay and paid advertising, 121, 122, 136–37, 144, 292
Kennedy, Edward M., 160–61
Kerwin, Lt. Gen. Walter T. "Dutch," 30–31, 34, 47, 49, 51, 53–54, 73, 119, 132n23, 145, 152–53, 170, 175, 266
Kester, John, 45n10, 122, 136–37, 138, 140–41, 143–44, 149–50, 178, 290
Kissinger, Henry, 41, 58
Komer, Robert, 64, 65–66
Kroesen, Maj. Gen. Frederick, 233–34

Laird, Melvin R., 20, 30, 33–34, 50, 54, 119, 136–37, 154, 155, 181, 182–84, 198–99, 201, 202, 213–14
　bonus vs. proficiency pay, 69, 122, 170
　debate over AVF budget, 57–59
　paid advertising and, 143, 145
　position on Gates Commission findings, 40–42
　reserve component to AVF, 266–67
　views on Westmoreland, 61n7
Lee, Gus, 35, 66, 121, 209, 216n32
Lehrer, James, 247
Lewis, Capt. John, 127
Lincoln, Abraham, 5

McGlothlin, Brig. Gen. William, 121
McGovern, George, 184–85
McNamara, Robert S., 48
　Defense Manpower Study under, 10
　education and medical standards for induction, 158
Mahon, George H., 168, 243–44
Major Construction, Army (MCA), 89
Mansfield, Mike, 242–43
Marshall, Burke, 12
Marshall, General George C., draft and, 7–8
Mauldin, Bill, 101
Meckling, Dean William, 30, 38
Menist, Maj. Gen. Stuart, 269–70
Meyer, Brig. Gen. Edward C., 175
Military institutions, influences on staffing, 3–4
Military occupational specialties. See MOS
Militia Act, 5
Militia system, historical background, 4
Modern Volunteer Army
　High Impact Actions Toward Achieving a, 70–74
　Master Program for the, 74, 79n9, 111, 270
　media criticism of High Impact Actions Toward Achieving a, 74–78
　special assistant for the. See SAMVA

Modern Volunteer Army Program
　advertising campaign controversy, 121–23, 284
　American Legion and, 76–77
　budget issues, 82, 118, 152–55, 173
　Congress and KP civilianization, 167–69
　critique of, 77–78
　effect of Army RIF on, 166
　end of experimentation phase, 171
　launch of, 67–69
　pro-pay vs. proficiency pay, 135–39
　professionalism over Army life, 110–12
　review and evaluation of, 156–57, 172–74
　revision of purpose and goals, 150–51
　WAC increase as part of, 191
Montague, Brig. Gen. Robert M., Jr., 72, 155, 167–68, 170, 174, 178, 241–42
　appointment as SAMVA, 64
　as chairman of Central All-Volunteer Task Force, 193, 200, 201, 203, 209, 210, 213
　innovative techniques, 65–66, 68
Moore, Maj. Gen. Harley, 213–14
Moorer, Admiral Thomas H., 204–05
Morden, Col. Bettie, 196n20
MOS, 18, 85–86
　bonuses for, 201
　WAC and, 193
MVA. See Modern Volunteer Army
MVAP. See Modern Volunteer Army Program

National Guard, 6, 7
National Guard, Army, recruiting and retention, 272
Navy, debate over AVF budget, 56–57
Nixon, Richard M., 12, 13, 20, 21, 40, 48, 59, 140, 149, 161, 176–77, 210, 251, 266–67, 291
　move toward zero-draft, 42–44, 46n21
　Nixon Doctrine, 281
　reelection bid and end of draft, 181–83, 184–85
Norstad, General Lauris, 29
Nuclear force, Eisenhower administration and, 9
Nunn, Sam, 202, 212–13, 239, 292

Odeen, Philip, 57–58
Oi, Walter, 30
Operation STEADFAST, 206

Packard, David
　AVF budget review, 58–59, 154
　proficiency pay and, 123
Palmer, General Bruce, Jr., 25, 26, 51, 67, 72–73, 74, 102, 113, 141–42, 150, 151, 152, 155, 171–72, 176–77, 179n12, 282–83, 285
Pastore, John O., 169
Patton, Maj. Gen. George S., Jr., 234–35

INDEX

Pay and benefits, career soldiers, 32
Peers, Lt. Gen. William R., 269
Phillips, Brig. Gen. (Ret.) Paul D., 149–50, 178, 192, 240, 241, 246, 288, 290
    overall review and evaluation of MVA Program, 172–74, 286–87
    qualitative enlistment standards, 186, 187–88, 199–200, 201
Pike, Otis, 139
Pirnie, Alexander, 166–67
Preparedness Movement, 6–7
President, U.S. *See* Johnson, Lyndon B.; Lincoln, Abraham; Nixon, Richard M.; Roosevelt, Franklin D.; Wilson, Woodrow
Program Evaluation Group, 30, 38
Project 100,000, 158–59, 186
Project Volunteer, 32, 34, 39
    aims and composition of, 30–31
    AVF budget, 48–49
    health care and, 258
    MVA Program budget, 153
Project Volunteer in Defense of the Nation. *See* PROVIDE
PROVIDE, 21–24, 28n14, 29, 71
    abolition of Task Group, 50
    beginning of the Army's transition to AVF, 282–83
    evidence of social upheaval in the Army, 25
    Project VOLAR and, 81–82
    recruiting budget, 32
    reserve components, 265
    Task Group, 47
    USAREC and, 116–17
    WAC and, 189–90
Proxmire, William, 169

Quaal, Ward, 143

Recruiting. *See also* Project 100,000; USAREC
    advertisement and, 117–18, 120–21, 172
    decrease in, 199–200
    incentive for reserve, 274–75
    incentives and techniques, 120–22, 285
    medical and professional personnel, 250
    medical and professional personnel for AVF, 256–57
    qualitative enlistment standards, 186–88, 200–201, 211, 226–27
    racial balance and, 236, 250
    release of monthly results, 242, 245
Reduction in Force (RIF), 165–67, 179n1
Regan, Ted, 141–42
Registration, as a civic duty, 7

Regular Army, 7; military system of the Republic and, 4–5
Reserve. *See also* National Guard; Reserve Officer Training Corps (ROTC)
    AVF and recruiting for, 255
    duration of duty, 264–65
    educational level of, 36
    In-Service Recruiting Program, 273–74
    life insurance, 279n32
    minority participation, 272–73
    no-cost initiatives for recruiting and retention of, 269
    quality and military value of, 264
    Ready. *See* Individual Ready Reserve (IRR)
    resources for AVF, 267–71, 278n10
    Selected *vs.* Ready, 263
    vs. active Army, 31–32
Reserve Officer Training Corps (ROTC), 255–56
Resor, Stanley R., 37–38, 51, 66, 89, 90, 135, 136–38, 143, 149–50, 266, 272, 284
    presentation of AVF budget, 53–55
    proficiency pay authorized by, 122
Rhodes, John, 168–69
Richardson, Elliot, 202, 204, 210, 213–14
Rogers, Lt. Gen. Bernard, 212–13, 216n32, 226–27, 289
    Army's commitment to AVF, 247–48
    disestablishment of Modern Volunteer Army Program, 208–09
    innovative approaches to problem solving, 64–65, 70, 82
Rome, Arnold & Company, 142
Roosevelt, Franklin D., 7–8
ROTC. *See* Reserve Officer Training Corps (ROTC)
Roth, William, 143
Rumsfeld, Donald, 12
Rush, Kenneth, 198

SAMVA, 54, 63–64. *See also* Forsythe, Lt. Gen. George I.
    creation of, 284–85
    defense of paid advertising campaign by, 145
    evaluation of VOLAR Project by, 104–06
    no-cost program for AVF reserve, 269–70
    phasing out of, 152, 155, 171, 179n12
    Soldier-Oriented Budget, 152–55
Schlesinger, James R., 137, 210, 244, 247
Schulcz, Capt. Arthur, 127
Schultz, George P., 137
Scott, Maj. Gen. Hugh L., conscription and, 6
Scrull, Donald, 244
Sears, Brig. Gen. Leslie R., 167–68

Secretary of Defense, U.S. *See* Laird, Melvin R.; McNamara, Robert S.; Richardson, Elliot; Schlesinger, James R.
Secretary of the Army, U.S. *See* Callaway, Howard "Bo"; Froehlke, Robert F.; Resor, Stanley R.
Secretary of War, U.S. *See* Stimson, Henry L.
Selective Service Act, 7–8, 12, 42
Selective Service Extension and Military Pay Act, 107, 149; discharge and, 165
Selective Service System, 9–10, 20–21, 41
Sheridan, Edward, 89
Shillito, Barry, 89
Siegle, Lt. Col. John, 102–03
Sikes, Robert L., 168–69
Slatinshek, Frank, 136–37, 138, 247
Smith, Maj. Gen. DeWitt, 129, 230
Special Assistant to the Modern Volunteer Army. *See* Forsythe, Lt. Gen. George I.; SAMVA
Special Pay Act, 170
Stafford, Robert T., 66, 111, 168, 169, 291
Steele, Col. William B., 83
Steiger, William, 66, 168–69, 291
Stennis, John C., 48, 60, 160, 202, 243; support for AVF, 230–31, 260, 292
Stevenson, Adlai, 10
Stimson, Henry L., 7–8
Symington, Stuart, 239

Taber, Lt. Gen. Robert, 210–11, 212, 213, 214, 229
Talbot, Maj. Gen. Orwin C., 83–84
TDP. *See* Trainee Discharge Program
Thurmond, Strom, 212
Trainee Discharge Program, 227, 229, 244, 250
Training, universal military, 8–9
Trigg, Brig. Gen. Thomas K., 107
Truman, Harry, 8–9, 44
Tucker, Gardiner, 137

Uniformed Services Special Pay Act, 260, 273–74
Urette, Maj. Michael, 267–68
U.S. Army, Europe. *See* USAREUR
U.S. Army Recruiting Command. *See* USAREC
USAREC, 115–16
  adjustment in manpower and techniques, 126–28
  advertising campaign, 124, 141
  malpractice, 207–08
  move to Fort Sheridan, 206–07, 288–89
  recruiting experiments, 124–25
  reserve recruiting, 271, 276–77
  revised enlistment standards and TDP, 228
  Selection Center Experiment, 128–30
  zero-draft and enlistment, 116–19
USAREUR, 87–88, 90–91. *See also* Davison, General Michael S.

Van Deerlin, Lionel, 143–44
Vander Schaff, Derek, 248
Vavra, Harry, 193
Vietnam War, 11–13
  draftees' assignment restriction, 181–82
  end of draft and, 41
  recruiting during, 126
  tours of duty limitation, 31
  VOLAR and, 87
VOLAR, 68. *See also* All-Volunteer Armed Force
  advertising campaign and, 141
  Army reform experiments and, 81–82
  discontinuation of term, 172
  evaluation of Project, 104–06
  launching of Project, 284
  leadership and supervision under, 103–04
  living space and food service under, 87–91, 101–03
Volunteerism, 3. *See also* Militia Act
  PROVIDE and, 22
  vs. conscription, 6, 11

WAC. *See* Women's Army Corps
Waldeck, Lt. Col. James, 174–76
Wallis, Karl, 210
Washington, General George, 4
Weber, Maj. Gen. LaVern, 274–75
Wednesday Group, 12
Westmoreland, General William C., 21–24, 25, 26, 34, 43, 66, 67, 116, 149, 151, 155, 170, 171–72, 179n12, 213–14, 272, 282–83, 284. *See also* PROVIDE
  commitment to AVF, 49–53, 61n7, 268, 285, 289–90
  implementation of High Impact Actions Toward Achieving a Modern Volunteer Army, 70–74. *See also* PROVIDE
  proficiency pay and paid advertising and, 123–24, 135–36, 138–39, 141–42
  study on all-volunteer Army, 17, 19
  support for the Modern Volunteer Army Program, 69, 175–77
Will, George, 232, 251
Wilson, Woodrow, 6
Wollstadt, Paul, 33–34, 38–39, 140–41, 143–44
Women's Army Corps, 18, 22, 188–93, 195n17; funding for expansion of, 192
Wool, Harold, 30
World War I, conscription and, 6–7
World War II, draft during, 8
Wyman, Louis C., 111, 168–69

Zais, Lt. Gen. Melvin, 107
Zero-draft goal, 26, 40, 182–84
Zumwalt, Admiral Elmo R., 51, 204–05, 244

www.ingramcontent.com/pod-product-compliance
Lightning Source LLC
Chambersburg PA
CBHW060230240426
43671CB00016B/2901